Classics in California Anthropology II

WILLIAM DUNCAN STRONG

(Photo courtesy Lowie Museum)

Aboriginal Society
in
Southern California

By William Duncan Strong

Foreword by Ralph Beals
Introduction by Lowell John Bean

1987

Malki Museum Press

Morongo Indian Reservation

Banning, California

ISBN-0-939046-00-8

Reprinted from the University of California Publications in American Archaelogy and Ethnology, Vol. 26, 1929, by permission of the Regents of the University of California

Classics in California Anthropology

This book is the second in Malki Museum Press' series of classics in California anthropology. The first publication in the series was David Prescott Barrows' The Ethno-botany of the Coahuilla Indians of Southern California (Malki Museum Press, 1967).

Printed in the United States of America
Rubidoux Printing Company, Riverside California

FOREWORD

William Duncan Strong was a complex and rewarding person to know, both professionally and personally. Born in Portland, Oregon, in 1899, Strong's first university studies were in zoology. His shift to anthropology occurred after he met A. L. Kroeber, who became his principal teacher, mentor, and friend. Although Strong's main concern became man and his works, he never lost his earlier interest in nature, and long before ecology became a popular word he was deeply interested in the relations between man and his environment.

Strong and I first met as students at Berkeley around 1924. The circle of anthropologists at that time was small, and we participated in the same discussion groups, moved in much the same social circles, and came to share some of the same lifelong friends. After he obtained his doctorate in 1926, he returned often to Berkeley and we also met at meetings. In 1942-1943, we were both at the Smithsonian Institution in Washington and had close professional and personal contacts. In later years, despite our residence on opposite sides of the continent, I saw a good deal of him in New York and California as well as at meetings. The longer I knew him, the better I liked him. Indeed, my first impression as a young man was of a very self-confident, even dogmatic, aggressive, masculine outdoorsman. Only with time did I discover that he was a gentle, sensitive, unpretentious, and even rather shy person. He enjoyed life, and he lived it with a good deal of zest. But he also loved all living things, including people. He had a deep hatred of war, cruelty, and injustice, and a contempt for the stupidities of bureaucracy. Indeed, his considerable success as an administrator when this role was forced upon him rested upon his ability to ignore or cut through bureaucratic irrelevancies.

In World War I, Strong crossed the Atlantic 30 times on convoy duty as a seaman in the United States Navy, although he did not set foot on European soil until 1960. His dislike of war did not stem primarily from this experience, however, but from his sensitivity to the suffering and death war caused. World War II was a difficult time for him. He had been revolted by Nazi atrocities and participated in war activities, but his principal satisfaction was the part he played in developing a series of survival manuals for the armed forces. He could not rejoice in victory but only mourn the casualties.

Similarly, Strong's love of nature was that of the student and observer rather than of the hunter. Everywhere he went he made extensive notes on the flora and fauna, even keeping a listing of the birds he saw from his Riverside Drive apartment in New York. On a long weekend in Palo Alto in the summer of 1955, we spent much of our time outdoors, and our conversation was frequently interrupted by his delight as he identified a new bird or plant.

Even in his archaeology, Strong never forgot that the remains he excavated and studied were the products of people seeking to meet the problems of living. His work in archaeology was excellent, whether in the Plains, Honduras, or Peru, but its originality owes much to his interest in ethnology and history. This is particularly evident in his early book, *An Introduction to Nebraska Archaeology*, and he is the principal developer of the direct historical approach to archaeological problems. His involvement in archaeology was in part a product of the kinds of jobs and research opportunities available to him in the 1930's and later. In his personal reminiscences, his experiences in Southern California and among the Naskapi of Labrador recurred frequently, and he once remarked to me that he wished he could finish with "these damned Peruvian potsherds" and complete his ethnography of the Naskapi.

In his ethnographic work, Strong preferred to live with the people he studied and to participate as fully as possible in their daily life. This sometimes led him into dangerous and even foolhardy behavior. In Labrador, he horrified his Naskapi companions by attempting to take the trail breaker position in soft snow in front of a sled team, although he had but barely learned to run on snowshoes. Had he fallen, the savage Naskapi sled dogs would have attacked him and almost certainly injured him seriously before they could be driven off. The sled train was thrown into confusion and delay while his companions removed him from his dangerous position. On another occasion in southern California, after observing his friends in a bull-dogging exhibition, he entered into the competition despite lack of experience. An element of bragadoccio no doubt entered into accounts of such instances, but Strong usually told them as examples of the worry and trouble he caused his companions through his stupidity and inexperience.

A foreword such as this is not the place for a complete review of Strong's contribution to anthropology but something must be said about *Aboriginal Society in Southern California* and his related paper, *An Analysis of Southwestern Society*. Together they illustrate Strong's liking for a mass of data, his ability to blend field work and documentary study, and his competence in organizing large masses of data into a regional analysis that illuminates the various social units within an area, characteristics equally evident in his major archaeological publications. He wanted to know not only what people did but why. Without rejecting the emerging functionalism, then still somewhat of a novel approach, he criticized its denial of history. Rather, as he himself wrote, "either one of these approaches is even meaningless without the other." *Aboriginal Society in Southern California* is one of the earliest and one of the best efforts by a United States anthropologist to combine structural-functional analysis with historical data and interpretation. The work represents the most extensive and intensive field study of the Shoshonean-speakers of southern California undertaken up to the mid-1920's. It is the first to bring out in such detail the close interrelation between the organization and functioning of those societies and the ceremonial and ritual practices and religious ideologies. Strong was the last field worker to be able to talk with people who had lived in the various societies before the many changes and adaptations necessary to survive the massive impact of United States culture. His work is thus a major source of data on the past and, even though details may be modified, his analysis and reconstruction present the nearest thing to an accurate single account of aboriginal society in southern California we are likely to have.

In terms of modern anthropology, *Aboriginal Society in Southern California* is of course dated. Most young anthropologists today would focus on the condition of the contemporary Indians, the pressures of the modern industrial society of the area, and the ways in which the modern Indian has adapted to this society. Strong would approve of such studies as being more meaningful to the welfare of the people involved. But he would add, I am sure, that if one wishes to know how and why they survived and retained their identity, it is necessary to look behind the present. Certainly anyone who wishes to understand how it once was, or to understand the basis of the strength of character and intellect that made survival possible, must find *Aboriginal Society in Southern California* an indispensable source.

—Ralph L. Beals

INTRODUCTION

Several generations of anthropological researchers have drawn upon William Duncan Strong's *Aboriginal Society in Southern California*
as the most valuable and richly suggestive reference work on native
cultures of the region. Almost singlehandedly, Strong brought an ethnographic perspective into sharp focus and posed problems which have
absorbed and will continue to absorb scholars for years to come. Any
adequate discussion of his contributions—including newer findings
which reinforce or conflict with his data—would require a discussion
almost as long as his monograph. For that reason, I will attempt to
confine my remarks to specific points which may assist the contemporary reader.

Strong's ethnographic collections are especially remarkable when
one considers that in a span of less than a year in the field he was
able to observe so much, record so much detail with such precision,
and arrive at a synthesis of materials over a broad range of the cultural
spectrum with such perception and exactitude that no scholar since
has significantly challenged his findings. The data base which Strong
established can be used by ethnographers, and archaelogists from many
theoretical points of view. Where new interpretations have been made
since 1929, they usually can be found suggested first by Strong or allowed for by his careful management of data relative to conclusions.

Prior to Strong's monograph, several talented scholars and students
carried out investigations among each of the groups which he under-
took to understand. In the late 1890's, David Prescott Barrows collected
data on plants uses, material culture, and settlement patterns of the
Cahuilla. Soon afterward, A. L. Kroeber began collecting a large number of artifacts in southern California and accumulating some ethnographic data on southern California Indian groups, particularly the
Cahuilla and Luiseño, which he later published. Three other resource-
ful ethnographers also began investigations in southern California in
the first decade of the twentieth century. Constance Goddard DuBois,
a sensitive field worker with considerable literary ability, worked ex-
tensively among the Diegueño and Luiseño, concentrating primarily
on religion and folklore. A storekeeper at Rincon, Philip S. Sparkman,
painstakingly collected information on the culture of the Luiseño
and some data in linguistics, folklore, and ethnobotany, which Kroeber
encouraged him to publish. In addition, T. T. Waterman published
several brief papers on the Diegueño and one of the first scholarly
treatments of creation stories in southern California.

Almost a decade passed after these initial studies before anthropologists again turned their attention toward southern California.

Meanwhile, a large body of literature was developing on northern and central California as a result of fieldwork by Kroeber, Edward W. Gifford, Roland Dixon, S. A. Barrett, and others. Then between 1916 and 1922, Gifford refocused interest on southern California, publishing a number of papers on social organization, kinship, lineage systems, and clans and moieties—all reflecting scientific advancements in the discipline of anthropology and its emerging preoccupations. In 1920, Lucile Hooper published the first general survey of Cahuilla culture, although its cursoriness became evident when Strong brought out his monograph. Edward H. Davis examined funeral practices of the Luiseño and Diegueño in two papers. Finally, Ruth Benedict spent a summer at Morongo Indian Reservation, Banning, working among the Serrano. Out of her fieldwork came two papers, one on folklore and the other on social and cultural material. Unfortunately, some of her data proved unreliable and later was effectively challenged by Strong.

The publications of these seven researchers and scattered minor contributions by others, mostly popular writers or amateurs, comprised the principal sources of ethnographic knowledge of southern California prior to Strong. In general, most of these works were narrow in scope, reflecting the specialized interests or limited training of their researchers, and the fact that few of them spent any significant time among the people whom they studied. Among such pioneer studies, Barrows' *The Ethno-Botany of the Coahuilla Indians* (University of Chicago Press, 1900) is a classic—the first professional ethnobotany and ethnography of a single California Indian group. Despite a lack of formal training, DuBois' literary approach and overwhelming personal concern for the welfare of southern California Indian people made it possible for her to collect highly esoteric materials in ritual and philosophy. Her monograph *The Religion of the Luiseño Indians of Southern California* (Berkeley, 1908) was the longest treatment on any subject of the period (186 pages), a rich source of ideas for many areas that Strong would explore in greater depth. Gifford's salient contributions on kinship and social organization—particularly his recognition of the nature of dichotomous social organization and the lineage and moiety principles as basic building blocks for social and political units in southern California—provided Strong with a conceptual model from which to expand his own inquiry.

Drawing upon such earlier studies, Strong set forth to assemble an ethnography that would encompass the Shoshonean-speaking people of southern California. In addition to ethnographic material, he reviewed a vast array of published and unpublished material from historical sources, archaelogy, and linguistics, defining problem areas to investigate in the field. The monograph that followed his research is an impressive blending of historicism and functionalism—since he sought to comprehend the historical roots from which southern California cultural patterns derived as they related to environmental factors.

Strong's great achievement was to succeed in presenting an unusually complete ethnographic account from the perspective of both past and present. An indefatigible worker, he acquired the confidence of many of the most learned men in southern California's Indian communities. They trusted Strong and they assisted him in collecting an immense amount of data that made it possible to describe conditions as they existed in social, economic, political, and ceremonial life in 1925. Then, working through the memories of older people, Strong proceeded to attempt a reconstruction of the patterns of change in these institutions back to the 1850's. His astonishing insight into these processes remains a marvel to all contemporary scholars working in the region.

Strong's innovative approach and his keen appreciation of the subtleties of southern California social organization led to his providing part of the foundation for seminal contributions published several years later by Julian Steward, which pioneered the development of cultural ecology as a research concern of anthropology—a major turning point in anthropological theory. His recognition that southern California cultural patterns could not be neatly correlated with ethnic boundaries—that a flow of cultural elements occurred between various cultures—pointed the way for future studies in the dynamics of diffusion. Even today, many of the clues Strong offers for research in this area have not been capitalized upon sufficiently, although the significence of intercultural relationships, are increasingly recognized in such recent literature as Raymond White's *Luiseño Social Organization* (1963) and the author's own *Mukat's People* (University of California Press, 1972)

Again and again, Strong observes that one cannot understand the nature of any one Indian group in the 1920's, nor for that matter many decades earlier, without being aware of a totality of cultural interrelationships from the Gabrielino and Chumash along the western shores of the Pacific Ocean to the Diegueño farther south and the interior peoples along the Colorado River. For Strong (p. 145): "The entire culture of the southern California Indian, like that of all such closely related groups may well be regarded as a liquid medium that flowed more or less evenly from group to group, thinning out more and more the farther each cultural influence extended from its source . . . " Again, analyzing gift exchange among the southern groups and those of the San Gorgonio Pass area, he suggested (p. 263) that it was "almost certain that in aboriginal times the western half of southern California was practically one ceremonial unit".

Barrows in 1900 had predicted the dissolution of southern California Indian culture within a decade. In contrast, Strong recognized that an ancient residue of tradition was constantly being modified by new ideas spreading from one cultural group to another, even as he was working in the field. Thus, he pinpointed the flexible and adaptive syndrome characteristic of southern California which revivifies the past in new forms from generation to generation. Curiously, despite his perspicuity, Strong in his time also chose to believe as Barrows had that the "next decade will see the end of nearly all native institutions in the area".

Yet thirty-five years after publication of his monograph, cultural persistence continues to be exhibited by southern California Indian groups in many ways. There are native speakers and young people learning their own language; funeral rituals still are maintained; secular games, songs, and dances are regularly performed; some families continue to practice exogamy; native foods are often eaten and well-remembered; medical knowledge from the past is still utilized, if often surreptitiously; and, finally, traditional leadership roles, while sometimes taking on new patterns, exert themselves in recognizeable ways in contemporary political situations. Although rapid changes are taking place among southern California Indian people, it would be injudicious of any ethnographer to suggest that the end of native culture is even remotely near.

Strong writes with clarity and scarcely requires any explication, although it is worth calling attention to some of his more important concepts and briefly noting recent contributions which may illuminate his research. In addition, it seems proper here to call attention to some of the contributions modern scholars are making or have made to our knowledge of southern California native culture, and to indicate major sources of archival and artifactual materials for the region.

Tribal Territories—In the light of present knowledge, Strong was astonishingly successful in assigning territorial areas for each of the Shoshonean groups. His discussion of the location of the Serrano corrected erroneous conclusions made by Ruth Benedict and is indicative of his analytical ability and the quality of his data. In one area, he was less sure of his data and properly left questions of aboriginal occupancy unanswered. The San Jacinto region has been assigned at various times to both the Luiseño and Serrano, and occasionally the Cahuilla. In recent years, Raymond White and the author have advanced the argument that the Cahuilla occupied this territory. The ecological situation lends probability to Cahuilla occupancy, which is also supported by oral literature of the Cahuilla, the consistent recollections of elderly Cahuilla who name village sites and landmarks for the area, and unpublished data collected by C. Hart Merriam.

The Moiety System—Two points are worth presenting concerning Strong's discussion of moiety systems in southern California. First, Strong speculated as to whether the moiety system principles were in operation among the Luiseño as well as the Cahuilla and Serrano. Subsequent field work by Raymond White, presented in his monograph on Luiseño social organization, has suggested that this was indeed the case and moieties were not only instruments of marriage regulation, but also important axis for political and economic cooperation. According to White, moiety reciprocation constituted a major basis of economic activity within the Indian *rancherias,* and a high frequency of celebrations and ceremonies probably tended to level and equalize the consumption of foodstuffs throughout the Luiseño population. The same holds true for the Cahuilla. In my recent book *Mukat's People,* considerable attention is given to marriage regulating and ritual reciprocity aspects of the moiety system as principal adaptations for controlling the distribution of surplus goods, particularly foods. A second point raised by Strong concerns the degree to which moiety principals actually regulated marriage. He was inclined to feel such rules were weakly enforced by the Cahuilla. My own fieldwork over ten years indicates that the moiety principle was probably taken with great seriousness and was a major factor in determining marriage choice. Present-day Cahuilla report that it sometimes arises as a problem in spouse selection even today.

The Lineage Principle—Although Gifford first clearly recognized the significance of the lineage principle in southern California social organization, Strong demonstrated its importance by a rigorous analysis of how it functioned, providing firm proof that lineage was the basic organizational and economic unit for the people studied. While his research did not include the Yuman-speaking Diegueño, subsequent fieldwork by Fred Hicks and Katherine Luomala has demonstrated that the principle applied to this group also. The Diegueño are remarkably different, however, since a degree of flexibility occurs in their organizational framework which cannot be found among the Shoshonean-speakers. The reasons for this remain to be analyzed. Strong also observed peculiar variations in the management of Serrano political and ritual affairs as compared with their close kin, the Luiseño and Cahuilla. Although White and the author have examined some causative elements in Luiseño and Cahuilla social organization, no one has yet attacked the problems of why variations in social structure occur in southern California and whether such differences are historical, cultural, or ecological peculiarities.

The nature of the lineage principle among the Gabrielino is still unclear, but it appears that it also was the main articulating principle for their social organization. The data may never be at hand for a complete understanding of how these complex people managed their society, since their culture was essentially extinguished during the mission and early American periods. The Kitanemuk, another group about which little has been published, do lend themselves to some future analysis. Field notes left on the Kitanemuk by the late John P. Harrington are quite extensive and are currently being studied by Thomas Blackburn and the author.

Recent scholarship has viewed the lineage system in southern California as an instrument of ecology rather than a product of history. This point of view was most clearly developed by Julian H. Steward in his *Theory of Culture Change* (University of Illinois Press, 1955). Raymond White, Fred Hicks, and the author have further refined this concept in studies on southern California native culture. Unfortunately, since Steward presented his methodology, there has been an implicit assumption on the part of many researchers that historical elements are unimportant in understanding causal factors in social structure.

An argument can be made that the types of social organization found in southern California are initially explainable as corporate groups (patrilineally organized), which are found frequently around the world wherever certain ecological conditions occur. Strong is well aware of the historical dimension, however, and would have viewed such an argument as naively simplistic. Repeatedly, he discusses southwestern influences, offering hints of the harvest awaiting researchers who will explore the relationships of southern California culture to southwestern cultural traditions. Needless to say, the impact of southwestern influence on southern California is still scarcely appreciated, and because of deemphasis on diffusionist studies in recent years represents an almost totally neglected field of study.

Less than a score of papers, most of them not specifically directed toward the problem, sum up our current knowledge of southwestern influences in California. The bulk of this material was summarized by Jessie D. Jennings (ed.) in *The American Southwest: A Problem in Cultural Isolation* (Mem. Soc. Amer. Archaeol. No. 11, 1956). The meagerness of available material is illustrated by the fact that one of the most significant contributions on the subject is a paper of less than four pages by Robert F. Heizer, demonstrating that historical sources can shed light on trade between southwestern peoples and southern California groups. L. L. Sample followed Heizer's cue with a longer paper on trade and trails in aboriginal California, but the ethnohistorical approach offers far more possibilities than have been exploited as yet. Jay Ruby in an unpublished dissertation presented convincing archaeological evidence from the historical record of a long, continuous contact with southwestern cultures. Harry W. Lawton (unpublished), while analyzing myths of southwestern and California peoples, has noted an unusual number of congruent elements, especially those correlating with agricultural complexes. His study led to a collaboration with the author in investigating the possibility of aboriginal agriculture among the Cahuilla, Kamia, and Diegueño. Our research has suggested the probability of a Colorado Desert agricultural complex, which employed distinctly southwestern agricultural techniques. Philip J. Wilkie is studying cultivated plant remains from various sites on the Colorado Desert. Some of these are typical of crop varieties grown along the Colorado River, although it is not established yet whether the archaeological materials are from the aboriginal or post-contact period.

Full Development of the Clan—The lineage-clan system in California probably reached its fullest development among southern California Shoshonean groups, organized as they were into autonomous political-economic land-holding units with exogamous moieties regulating marriage and ritual obligations. The use of fictive kin concepts extended kin relationships far beyond the patrilineage itself to the sib and moiety level. These groups employed symbolic representations, such as the ceremonial bundle and moiety designations, around which members could rally support above the patrilineage level. These symbolic representations served as rallying points for various groups both in the aboriginal and post-contact period. The fact that the moiety system recognized all members as distant kin strengthens the argument for full clan development.

Walter Goldschmidt in a 1948 article, "Social Organization in Native California and the Origin of the Clan" (*Amer. Anthrop.*, Vol. 50, pp. 444-456), suggested that development of fictive kinship groups and symbolic representations are indicative of full clan development. Goldschmidt argued that the necessary criteria for full clan development were not present in native California. If full clan development had occurred, he suggested that it would have served as an instrument for political expansion. The author's own research indicates that all of Goldschmidt's criteria for full clan development were present in southern California. The rigid, segmentary lineage typical of the Shoshoneans in southern California had greater organizational potential than the flexible sib organization of the Yuman-speaking Diegueño.

Very likely the intrusion of the Shoshonean-speaking groups into southern California was due to their successful development of the clan system as an instrument for expansion. In fact, it appears possible that such Yuman-speaking groups as the Diegueño may have adopted the lineage-sib system as a defense strategy in response to their Shoshonean neighbors.

Leadership Roles—Strong emphasized the ritual responsibilities of leadership roles, but more recent scholarship has indicated that such roles were equally important in southern California in serving political, judicial, economic, and legislative ends. A group of elite families existed throughout southern California that maintained political power through the control of ceremonial privileges and firm patrilineal inheritance rules over many generations. Leadership families tended to intermarry, and had relatively greater wealth and social position with attendant privileges than other people. They dressed differently and more elaborately, expected deferential behavior from others, and carefully guarded their ranked positions. Children from these families were trained in esoteric knowledge, subjected to more intensive socialization procedures, and expected to behave in a manner consistent with the prestige of their heritage. As White noted in his monograph on Luiseño social organization, techniques of political strategy and administration involved the ways in which knowledge and privilege were controlled and dispersed. The principal factors of power lay in the control and management of sacred ritual paraphernalia and traditional knowledge. Even today such factors are of significance in the exercise of leadership roles in the modern reservation system. George Phillips has recently completed a book-length study of Indian resistance leaders of historic times, particularly Antonio Garra and Juan Antonio, which should add significantly to our knowledge of southern California Indian leadership.

World View and Values—The great body of oral literature assembled by Strong has provided a foundation for continuing study of world view and value systems among southern California groups. In 1963, White in his monograph on Luiseño social organization presented a detailed analysis of the Luiseño theory of knowledge which goes far toward explaining the cosmological concepts and value system of this group. He pointed out that their cosmology reflected philosophical adaptations to environmental conditions and traced the incorporation of traditional ideologies into new institutions. In a somewhat similar manner, the author in *Mukat's People* drew attention to the ecologically adaptive factors of normative and existential postulates among the Cahuilla, demonstrating that a rather precise set of assumptions were developed in relation to the environment. Studies presently being conducted suggest that traditional ideologies continue to be operative also among the Cahuilla. An interesting field for study would be the Serrano, who lived under slightly different ecological conditions, and the Diegueño, who lived in an environment similar to the Cahuilla, but whose cultural background was different. A comparison of value systems and ideologies of the various southern California groups might establish whether minor ecological variations are reflected in philosophical systems, social organization, and ritual. Certainly, although similar philosophical concepts and psychological traits developed throughout all of the lineage-based groups of southern California, each group maintained very distinctive differences, which could well be indicative of ecological variations rather than earlier cultural influences.

Shoshonean Scholarship After Strong—Most new material published on Shoshonean-speaking groups of southern California since Strong's monograph will be found cited in a publication which the author collaborated on with Harry W. Lawton, A *Bibliography of the Cahuilla Indians of California* (Malki Museum Press, 1967). It therefore seems necessary to discuss only a few of the more significant works in the field and mention some of the workers presently engaged in Shoshonean scholarship in southern California.

When Strong began his fieldwork little material was available on the Gabrielino. Most interpretations of Gabrielino culture have derived from Hugo Reid's *The Indians of Los Angeles County*, first published in the *Los Angeles Star* in 1852. Reid's material, collected with the help of his Indian wife in the 1840's, seemed for a time atypical and peculiar to students of California Indian culture. Now, seen in the perspective of later work on neighboring people, his material appears quite consistent with our general knowledge of the region, testifying to Reid's keen appreciation of the ethnographic situation he observed. Our information base on the Gabrielino, however, still remains far more limited than for other groups.

The most recent study of the Gabrielino is Bernice Johnston's *California's Gabrielino Indians* (Southwest Museum, 1962), which made use of some of J. P. Harrington's field notes as well as his annotations relating to this group from Father Geronimo Boscana's *Chinigchinich* (Fine Arts Press, 1933). Robert F. Heizer has also added to our knowledge of this group by editing and annotating a recent reprint of Reid's work, *The Indians of Los Angeles County: Hugo Reid's Letters of* 1852 (Southwest Museum, 1968). Unpublished linguistic and ethnographic data collected by the late John P. Harrington and more extensive analysis of Spanish and Mexican archival resources will hopefully extend our understanding of the Gabrielino and their undoubtedly generative role in the cultural development of native southern California. One fertile source of investigation is the San Gabriel Mission records, which are currently being studied by William Mason for data on intermarriage and population movement. Archaeological investigations can also be expected to increase our knowledge of the Gabrielino. In this area, the University of California Archaelogical Survey has become a major center for Gabrielino research. Among scholars who have worked on the Gabrielino in recent years are Clement Meighan, Charles Rozaire, Thomas Blackburn, Jack Forbes, and Chester King.

Very little research has been published on the Cupeño since Strong. Strong relied heavily on unpublished field notes of E. W. Gifford and P.-L. Faye in his analysis of Cupeño culture. His treatment of this group provides one of the most thorough examinations of resource ownership, tribal amalgamation, and population resettlement in California literature. Strong found that the original Cupeño group, whom Kroeber classified as a separate tribe, were similar to the Cahuilla in cultural background. Subsequent linguistic studies by William Bright and Jane Hill have confirmed that the Cupeño language is more closely related to Cahuilla than any other Shoshonean language. The author on the basis of oral traditions has suggested in his book *Mukat's People* that the original Cupeño group, the Kupakiktum, was a Cahuilla sib which amalgamated in recent times with Luiseño and Diegueño groups. Florence Shipek (unpublished) has also suggested that the Cupeño were an intrusive conquering group who displaced Yuman-speaking people in the area. A major contribution to Cupeño studies can be anticipated with the publication of linguistic materials and oral literature collected several years ago by Jane Hill, who also plans to publish the notes gathered by P.-L. Faye in working among these people nearly forty years ago. An Indian group, the Cupeño Cultural Center, is planning to assemble and preserve materials on their culture. In addition, two other linguists, Roderick Jacobs and Hansjakob Seiler are preparing Cupeño material for publication. Jacobs is the first fieldworker to study in depth all of the language groups of southern California, and his comparative studies are eagerly awaited.

The most detailed ethnographic treatment of the Luiseño since Strong, as noted earlier, is Raymond White's monograph *Luiseño Social Organization* (Berkeley, 1963). Significant information on this group, particularly relating to ritual and settlement patterns, may be found in the annotations which John P. Harrington supplied for Boscana's *Chinigchinich* (Fine Arts Press, 1933). A useful basic work in linguistics is Villiana Hyde's grammar, *An Introduction to the Luiseño Language* (Malki Museum Press, 1971), which was edited by Jacobs. Another important linguistic contribution is William Bright's *A Luiseño Dictionary* (University of California Press, 1968).

The first detailed ethnographic analysis of the Cahuilla since Strong is the author's *Mukat's People,* which examines the relationship of the physical environment to Cahuilla institutions. In addition, the author has recently published in collaboration with Katherine Siva Saubel an extensive ethnobotany of the Cahuilla, *Temalpakh: Cahuilla Indian Knowledge and Usage of Plants* (Malki Museum Press, 1972). An important recent work in the area of Cahuilla linguistics and folklore is Hansjakob Seiler's *Cahuilla Texts with an Introduction* (Indian University Publications, 1970). A projected dictionary and grammar of the Cahuilla and future comparative work on Cahuilla dialects by Seiler should prove impressive contributions to the literature. Some data on Cahuilla alliances with Yuman-speaking groups and Cahuilla resistance against the European conquerors in the historic period may be found in Jack Forbes' *Warriors of the Colorado* (University of Oklahoma Press, 1965).

A work of major importance on the Cahuilla, long ignored by most scholars, is Francisco Patencio's *Stories and Legends of the Palm Springs Indians* (Times-Mirror, 1943). In this moving and personal document, Patencio, who was born in 1856, recorded the oral history of his people and presented many autobiographical recollections. Unfortunately, the materials were recorded by an amateur, Margaret Boynton, who must also be credited with inspiring Patencio to write his book, and edited by a printer who often took his own liberties with the text. Patencio's book has recently been reprinted by Palm Springs Desert Museum, and is deserving of a greater audience than it originally received.

Research on the Serrano since Strong has been a virtually neglected field. Some excellent data on a Serrano group, the Kitanemuk, may be found in C. Hart Mirriam's *Studies of California Indians* (University of California Press, 1962). A non-professional's work, G. Hazen Shinn's *Shoshonean Days* (Arthur H. Clarke Company, 1941), also contains fragments of ethnographic material on the Serrano of the San Gorgonio Pass from 1885-1889.

A Shoshonean group not dealt with by Strong is the Chemehuevi, who have also been greatly neglected in ethnographic research. A. L. Kroeber spent a brief period with the Chemehuevi and much of our knowledge of this group is summed up in a chapter of his *Handbook of the California Indians* (Washington, 1925). The most significant published contributions since Kroeber have been those of Isabel Kelly, who is best known for her studies of Southern Paiute shamanism. Some data on this group may also be found in Julian H. Steward's *Basin-*

Plateau Aboriginal Sociopolitical Groups (Washington, 1938). Historical material on the Chemehuevi of the Twenty-Nine Palms Region is presented in Lulu O'Neal's A *Peculiar Piece of the Desert* (Westernlore Press, 1957) and Harry Lawton's documentary non-fiction novel *Willie Boy* (Paisano Press, 1960). John P. Harrington collected ethnographic data on the Chemehuevi, assisted by Carobeth Laird, who was married to Harrington for a number of years. For a period of almost half a century, Carobeth Laird has continued to pursue the research she began under Harrington and continued with her Chemehuevi husband, George Laird. Her book-length study, *The Chemehuevi*, scheduled for publication next year, promises to be a major ethnographic addition to California literature. Her daughter, Georgia Culp Laird, is also making many contributions to our knowledge of the Chemehuevi as editor of the magazine, *The Chemehuevi Newsletter*, which regularly includes a significant amount of cultural and historical material.

Archival and Other Resources—Far more literature exists on southern California Indian culture in archival sources than has been published. The largest, most valuable collection is probably that of John P. Harrington, housed in the Anthropological Archives of the Smithsonian Institution, Washington, D. C., which is finally being catalogued by Jane Marsh. Harrington collected data for over thirty years on the Luiseño, Kitanemuk, Gabrielino, Cahuilla, Chumash, Serrano, Cupeño, Chemehuevi, and Diegueño peoples. His material on the Luiseño is immense in quantity and superb in quality. His Cahuilla material, some of which has been copied and made available through the Smithsonian for use of scholars at Malki Museum, Banning, are not as extensive, but have proven valuable in several studies. The Cupeño and Diegueño material contains some unique data. The Kitanemuk, Serrano, and Chemehuevi data is extensive and rich, a virtually untapped research source. The Gabrielino materials are limited mostly to linguistic notes. The Chumash collection is currently being studied by Thomas Blackburn, and is so abundant that it will fill in many critical gaps in our knowledge of these people. A large amount of other Harrington material is also temporarily housed at the Department of Linguistics, University of California, Berkeley.

Another very important collection of southern California Indian material may be found in the Anthropological Archives of the Bancroft Library, University of California, Berkeley. Here are kept the field notes of David Prescott Barrows on the Cahuilla, P.-L. Faye's data on the Cupeño, Sparkman's notes on the Luiseño, Waterman's papers on the Diegueño, Serrano material (mostly on basketry) collected by Bert Giroux, and the field notes of A. L. Kroeber and E.

W. Gifford, who collected among most southern California groups. The papers of C. Hart Mirriam are on file at the Archaeological Research Facility, University of California, Berkeley.

The Southwest Museum in Los Angeles houses some field notes of J. P. Harrington, Constance Goddard DuBois, and Edward Davis, and the papers of George Wharton James, J. Smeaton Chase, and Charles Francis Saunders. They also have a collection of southern California Indian photographs equalled only by collections at the Lowie Museum, University of California, Berkeley, and the Museum of the American Indian (Heye Foundation), New York City. The latter institution also owns a large collection of field notes of DuBois and Davis.

The largest historical collection is at the Bancroft Library, and consists of primary source documents from the Spanish, Mexican, and early American periods. The Santa Barbara Mission archives are a source for material on baptisms, marriage, and village sites. Several significant historical collections may be found at The Huntington Library, San Marino. Among these are George W. Beattie's historical notes on southern California Indians, the William Weinland papers on missionary activities on southern California Indian reservations from 1891 to 1930, the Cave Couts collection on San Diego County, and Grace Nicholson's collection of photographs and sketches of Indians and her large amount of data on basketry. Other important historical materials, including the Anthony Coronel papers and the Thomas Workman collection, may be found at Los Angeles County Museum.

Recordings of southern California music are housed at several institutions. The largest collections are in the Anthropological Archives at the Smithsonian Institution (Luiseño), The Folkmusic Archives of the University of Indiana (Luiseño), the Southwest Museum (Cahuilla and Luiseño), and Lowie Museum (Cahuilla, Luiseño, Serrano, and Diegueño). Some recordings are also housed at the Museum of Man, San Diego. The most valuable and extensive collections of music still lie in private collections owned by southern California Indian families. In fact, inexpensive tape recorders have ensured the preservation of much southern California music that would otherwise have been lost, mostly by the Indian people themselves.

Artifact collections from southern California are found in numerous museum collections. The most extensive and best collections are in the east. The Museum of the American Indian in New York has an outstanding collection, much of it acquired by Edward Davis and mostly Diegueño, although the Cahuilla, Luiseño, and other groups are well represented. The Smithsonian Institution possesses an outstanding collection, some materials of which were collected as early as 1870 by Edward Palmer and in 1890 by Horatio N. Rust, an Indian agent. The American Museum of Natural History has a small, but impressive collection. The Lowie Museum in Berkeley has the largest collection in California of Cahuilla, Luiseño, and Diegueño artifacts, much of it collected early in the century by Kroeber, Sparkman, and Waterman.

The Southwest Museum of Los Angeles has an extensive collection, and possesses the advantage of having most of its artifacts on display. The San Diego Museum of Man and Los Angeles County Museum also exhibit large collections. Smaller but very good collections may be found at Malki Museum on the Morongo Reservation, Banning, Riverside Municipal Museum, the San Bernardino County Museum, the San Jacinto Museum, and the Santa Ysabel Mission Museum. Palm Springs Desert Museum has an interesting collection of Cahuilla materials, but little of it is currently on public display. A number of museums in Europe in Copenhagen, Berlin, Rome, Paris, and London also have southern California Indian materials.

Perhaps the major problem confronting scholars working on southern California Indian materials is the fact that they are so scattered and so inaccessible, resulting in the squandering of vast sums of research money in traveling expenses. The most critical research need is for some means of coordination—either through an agency or agreements between institutions—that will make materials more readily available. Too many institutions conceive of their role as simply preservation, and the lifetime efforts of many dedicated scholars repose in dust-covered boxes becoming more yellow and brittle every year.

—LOWELL JOHN BEAN

University of California Publications in

AMERICAN ARCHAEOLOGY
AND ETHNOLOGY

VOLUME XXVI

1929

EDITORS

A. L. KROEBER
R. H. LOWIE

ABORIGINAL SOCIETY IN SOUTHERN CALIFORNIA

BY

WILLIAM DUNCAN STRONG

UNIVERSITY OF CALIFORNIA PRESS
BERKELEY, CALIFORNIA
1929

University of California Publications in American Archaeology
and Ethnology

Volume 26, x + 349 pp., + index, 7 maps

Issued May 28, 1929

University of California Press
Berkeley, California

———

Cambridge University Press
London, England

CONTENTS

MAPS

ABORIGINAL SOCIETY IN SOUTHERN CALIFORNIA

BY

WILLIAM DUNCAN STRONG

INTRODUCTION

The following pages represent the partial gleaning of a field whose full harvest might only have been gathered a century and a half ago. The forced segregation of the Indian into the missions of southern California inaugurated a process destined to wipe out nearly all trace of aboriginal Californian culture in the region of its highest development. Although a large part of the native population has perished before the swift march of western civilization, in the barren desert and mountain regions of southern California a considerable number still survive. Of these the younger and more progressive have in large part taken over the ways of the white man and are today a very influential element in the community. But it is from the people of an older generation whose eyes look backward to a remote but familiar past, not forward into an alien future, that these somewhat fragmentary notes have been obtained.

The coastal peoples of southern California disappeared soon after the advent of the missions, and the meager historical accounts of the early Spanish explorers and missionaries constitute the only written records concerning them. Comparative work in archaeology indicates that these coastal groups, notably the Chumash of the Santa Barbara region, were the most advanced peoples in southern California. This is certainly true as concerns the arts of life which are represented in the archæological findings, and comparative ethnographic studies indicate that here was also the center of social and religious influence. The native groups just bordering this coastal strip have likewise lost all but traces of their old culture, but concerning them we have the more adequate accounts of Boscana and Hugo Reid, and in addition the later studies of Sparkman, Du Bois, Kroeber, Waterman, Gifford, and others. The more easterly groups of the San Jacinto, Santa Rosa, and San Bernardino mountains, as well as those of the northern Colorado desert, have received comparatively little attention from the ethnologist. These people retained their old culture much later than did the people of the coast, and for this, and other reasons to be dealt with later, they offer the best opportunity for any research to determine the general pattern of aboriginal society in southern California. With this end in view the writer spent six months during the winter of 1924–25 among the Serrano, Cahuilla, Cupeño, and Luiseño on their various reservations and rancherias in Riverside and San Diego counties, gathering material relating to their territorial, political, and ceremonial organization. The present paper is based on these studies, with the addition of such comparable material as will show the relationship of the special groups studied to the general pattern of native society over southern California.

The field work was carried out under a research grant to the Department of Anthropology of the University of California, and the author was materially aided by Dr. A. L. Kroeber and Mr. E. W. Gifford. To these well-known authorities on California ethnology I am greatly indebted; to the former for his guidance and encouragement in a new field, and to the latter for the use of his detailed censuses and other notes relating to the Cupeño which have been included in the present account. In the field, Dr. J. R. Wilson and his family, of Hemet, California, were extremely helpful, both in making contacts with the people with whom it was essential to work, and in other ways too numerous to mention. The troubled nature of southern California Indian politics made Dr. Wilson's assistance invaluable in convincing the various factions of the non-partisan nature of my work. To the many informants who have contributed the greater part of the material presented in the following pages I am profoundly grateful. Wherever possible the sources of this information have been acknowledged as presented.

Whenever, as in the present case, the ethnologist follows some time after the effacing hand of civilization has done its work, he must perforce assume the rôle of social paleontologist. Little but the bones or framework of social institutions survive when the whole social organism has ceased to function. Yet it is from these remains that he must assiduously reconstruct the image of that which formerly existed. To understand the complete interrelationship of all phases of native life from this framework is often impossible. The functioning of a group day by day, the whole round of daily occurrences, and the relations which exist with all near-by groups, are essential to any clear understanding of the dynamics of social organization.

But if one can be content with reconstructing the mold within which these forces were once active much may be done, so long as members of the groups survive who remember the old forms that once regulated their lives. From such informants not only the *mores* of the group may be obtained, but also adequate objective data to determine the degree of efficacy and control which the various rules and beliefs formerly exerted. In this manner a reasonably accurate picture of the social machinery may be obtained, but it is a still and not a moving picture. One can say with a fair degree of accuracy how things were but much more rarely why they were that way. This is obviously true of nearly all natural phenomena, but in human society it is sometimes possible to explain a given custom if one knows the main contributing factors. Other customs can only be explained historically, for they have been adopted from outside sources. The fabric of society is largely made up of the interplay of these functional or internal traits and of diffused or acquired customs. A complete study of the social and ceremonial organization of a given group has of necessity these two aspects, first the integration and development of the group within itself, and secondly the relation of the group to external agencies of cultural diffusion. These constitute the warp and woof of any society or culture and on their correct analysis depends an understanding of either phenomenon.

The influence of diffusion and its probable effect on early social patterns in southern California has been dealt with in a previous paper,[1] the present study being primarily concerned with the problem of the development and integration of that society *in situ*. It is here especially that the student regrets the somewhat fossilized nature of much of the material at hand, but when one considers the vast changes that have occurred in southern California during the last three-quarters of a century the marvel is not the paucity but the amount and comparatively living quality of the data still to be secured. The next decade will see the end of nearly all native institutions in the area, but in the interval a great deal may yet be learned concerning the culture of the surviving groups.

---

[1] William Duncan Strong, An Analysis of Southwestern Society, Am. Anthr., n.s., 29:1–61, 1927.

Approximate Phonetic Values of Letters Used

a; as in English father

ā; as in English hat

e; as in English met

ē; as in English fate

i; as in English pin

ī; as in English pique

o; as in English not

ō; as in English note

u; as in English put

ū; as in English rule

aī; as y in English thy

au; as ow in English cow

c; as sh in English shout

ñ; as ng in English sang

tc; as ch in English change

x; like Spanish jota

z; as s in English gods

'; glottal stop

Other consonants given same value as in English.

I. THE SERRANO

The appellation of Serrano includes four main groups in southern California: the Kitanemuk of upper Tejon and Poso creeks, the extinct Vanyume of Mohave river, the extinct Alliklik who lived near the Chumash on the upper Santa Clara drainage, and the Serrano proper of the southern San Bernardino mountains. The present account deals solely with the latter group, who are today greatly reduced in numbers.[2] The term *Serrano* is unfortunate, since any hill-dwelling group of whatever ethnic affiliation answers to such a term.

The Serrano,[3] as well as the Kitanemuk, Vanyume, and Alliklik languages, are all of the southern California branch of the Shoshonean stock. The dialect of the Serrano is markedly different from that of their southern neighbors, the Pass Cahuilla, but the culture of the two groups is very similar. The Serrano were taken into the missions and after the secularization the people seem to have been so reduced in numbers that only a few resumed anything approaching their old mode of life. The main group that did so seem to have been the Māroña clan or band who lived on Mission creek, and it is by the term Morongo thus derived, that the Serrano are usually known at present. The tribal designation of Cow-ang-a-chem given the dialectic group by Barrows has not since been verified;[4] the term tahtam merely signifies "people," and the term kaiviatim is merely a native translation of the Spanish "Serrano."[5] In a recent study Benedict used a group term tamakuvayam for certain Pass clans,[6] but this is a Serrano version of temamkamwitcem, a term applied by the Desert Cahuilla to all groups north of Twenty Nine Palms.[7] The neighboring Cahuilla use the term ismailem to designate the Serrano-speaking groups,[8] and

2 The Federal Census for 1910 reports 119 Serrano, 89 of whom were of full blood.

3 As used in the present paper this term applies only to the Serrano proper.

4 Ethno-Botany of the Coahuilla Indians (University of Chicago Press, 1900), 19.

5 Kroeber, Handbook of the Indians of California, Bur. Am. Ethn., Bull. 78: 617, 1925.

6 A Brief Sketch of Serrano Culture, Am. Anthr., n.s., 26:368–369, 1924.

7 Boas states that the Cupeño (Agua Caliente) applied the term tamankamyam to the Serrano. Proc. Am. Assoc. Adv. Sci., 44:261, 1895. Both these terms are translated "northerners."

8 Benedict, *op. cit.*, 368.

this seems to be as near a Serrano group name as can be obtained. Considering that general linguistic similarity was the only bond between most of the groups lumped under one name in southern California, it is not surprising that tribal names are not recognized where no tribal unity ever seems to have existed.

The central home of the Serrano was the San Bernardino mountains; to the east their range met that of the Chemehuevi; to the north the Kitanemuk and more alien Kawaiisu; on the west were groups of the Gabrielino; and to the south in the San Gorgonio pass were clans of the Pass Cahuilla. Such was their general position but the exact boundaries of their range have been subject to considerable dispute, especially in regard to their western and southern extension. In approaching this problem one important fact must be borne in mind, namely, that the Serrano do not seem to have ever been a tribe in the sense in which that term is generally used. Like their neighbors, the political unit of the Serrano was the localized lineage which was nearly always autonomous. The entire dialectic group was therefore never politically united, nor do there seem to have been even large portions of it amalgamated. The small local groups occupied definite favorable territories but rarely extended their boundaries very far from the clan locale. The problem of distribution is therefore largely one of locating the individual groups, not the plotting out of tribal domains. The limits of the territory occupied by any dialectic or linguistic unit can be determined only by the spread of the independent constituent groups. This statement is applicable to Serrano, all three Cahuilla divisions, Cupeño, Luiseño, and Diegueño; only when the Yuman tribes of the Colorado are encountered may one speak of tribal territories in the technical sense.

One complicating factor in regard to the original ownership of the San Bernardino, Redlands, and Riverside districts may be eliminated at the start. This is the occupancy of the area by the Cahuilla discussed by a number of writers.[9] Kroeber's suggestion that the

---

[9] Möllhausen, Wanderungen durch die Prairien und Wüsten des Westlichen Nordamerika, 1860, p. 439, mentions three or four families of Kawia Indians in a state of peonage on an estate some miles west of the mouth of the Cajon Pass in 1854. Whipple, Pac. R. R. Rept. III, pt. 1, p. 134, III, p. 34, recorded Cahuilla vocabularies at Cucamonga ranch from a Cahuilla chief who had been baptized at San Luis Rey. The vocabulary published by Father Juan Caballeria from ''Guachama'' near San Bernardino is also Cahuilla: History of the San Bernardino Valley, 39–53 (no date, no place). Gatschet, in the Magazine of American History for 1877, places the Cahuilla ''in and around San Bernardino valley.'' Barrows, *op. cit.*, 32, mentions the Cahuilla in the San Timoteo canyon. These references are given by Kroeber, present series 4:131–135, 1907 (cited hereafter as Shoshonean).

Cahuilla were brought to the San Bernardino mission as a guard is correct.[10]   Mountain Cahuilla informants, one of whom (Alec Arguello) had lived in the San Timoteo pass, stated that five Mountain Cahuilla clans under the leadership of Juan Antonio, a well-known captain, were brought to the district in about the year 1846. They settled first at the village of pulatana near Jurupa (Riverside), and later moved to sahatapa in the San Timoteo canyon near El Casco. They remained there until some time in the decade between 1850 and 1860 when the group was nearly exterminated by a smallpox epidemic. This event is mentioned by Barrows,[11] but his statement that the epidemic occurred in the "forties" (1840–50) does not agree with statements of the Cahuilla who actually lived in the San Timoteo canyon.   The statement of the latter placing the event in the next decade (1850–1860) is likewise in accord with the historical evidence.

Map. 1. Serrano Territory. Squares indicate Wildcat, circles Coyote
Moiety Clans.

This question is dealt with more fully in the present paper when the Mountain Cahuilla are discussed. We can therefore regard this occurrence of Cahuilla in the San Bernardino region as an historic intrusion, and eliminate them from the problem of original ownership in the territory under discussion.

Kroeber states that the San Bernardino valley, including the Redlands, San Bernardino, and Colton districts,[12] was formerly occupied by the Serrano. In a later publication, however, he states of the Serrano that "they probably owned a stretch of fertile lowland south of the Sierra Madre, from about Cucamonga east above Mentone and halfway up San Timoteo canyon. This tract took in the San Bernardino valley and probably just failed of reaching Riverside; but it

[10] Shoshonean, 133, 1907.   [11] *Op. cit.*, 32.   [12] Shoshonean, 132.

has also been assigned to the Gabrielino, which would be a more natural division of topography, since it would leave the Serrano pure mountaineers.''[13]

On the basis of information received from Serrano, Palm Springs Cahuilla, and Mountain Cahuilla (who had lived in San Timoteo canyon), I have come to the opinion suggested in the last sentence quoted. All informants questioned, and they were all old people, agreed on the fact that the sites of San Bernardino, Redlands, and Crafton had originally been occupied by people who spoke the San Gabriel language. The original owners had been succeeded by the Mountain Cahuilla who were brought down to the San Bernardino mission about 1846, while the Serrano, or ismailem, as the Cahuilla term them, had originally occupied the foothills of the San Bernardino range bordering the San Bernardino valley. The Serrano, however, had always occupied the Yucaipe valley just southeast of Crafton. The Gabrielino group at Crafton was called tekenetpauitcem in the Cahuilla language, the Gabrielino group at Redlands was called in the same language watcicpakiktum, but the name given the Gabrielino group at San Bernardino was not remembered. The four main informants whose independent statements concurred on these points were Rosa Morongo, a Pass Cahuilla woman married among the Serrano; Jesusa Manuel, a Mountain Cahuilla woman married among the Serrano; Alec Arguello, a Mountain Cahuilla man who formerly lived in San Timoteo canyon; and Alejo Potencio, old clan leader of the Palm Springs Cahuilla. Both of the men had seen and talked with Gabrielino who had formerly lived at the sites in question, while the two women had received their information from their older relatives. There is no reason to doubt the sincerity or honesty of these four informants, and the exact concurrence of each in regard to the language of the ''Kisiannos,'' as the Gabrielino were called, is strong evidence in favor of original Gabrielino occupation.[14]

One important piece of evidence disputes this conclusion and that is the statement of Hugo Reid who formerly lived at San Gabriel where he had married a Gabrielino woman. He says, ''Jurupa, San Bernardino, etc., belonged to another distinct tribe possessing a language not at all understood by the above Lodges; and, although reduced by the Spanish missionaries to the same religion and labor,

---

[13] Handbook, 615–616.

[14] Benjamin Morongo, an old Serrano questioned by Gifford, likewise stated that the valley including the San Manuel reservation site, was formerly occupied by Gabrielino. Gifford, Clans and Moieties in Southern California, present series, 14:179–180, 1918 (cited hereafter as S. Cal.).

they never mixed their blood, they being considered much inferior, and called *Serranos* or *Mountaineers*. They look upon them to this day, with great disdain.''[15] This is a positive statement by a man in a position to know, and it cannot be disregarded. It is possible that the ''Serrano'' referred to are another small linguistic group, intermediate between the Serrano proper and the Gabrielino, but this is mere conjecture. Some of Reid's statements in the light of recent investigation, as well as such contemporary accounts as that of Boscana,[16] seem too general and somewhat exaggerated. It is possible that he was misinformed or made the statement without sufficient evidence, but to assume this on even the best native information at a so much later date would be rash. One can only bear in mind the fact that natives whose memories go back into the time when Reid was writing concur in the opposite opinion. There, until further evidence comes to hand, the matter must rest.

An equally disputed question concerns linguistic (or as the term has been loosely used, ''tribal'') affiliations of the groups originally occupying the San Gorgonio pass. In this regard Kroeber makes the following statement:

It has been stated that the Indians of the Morongo reservation near Banning are mixed Serranos and Cahuillas. This is literally true. Nevertheless the number of true Serranos on this reservation is small. The Indians are predominatingly Cahuilla, and both tribes state that the pass in the vicinity of the reservation was always Cahuilla territory. These Banning Cahuilla however answer indiscriminately to the name of Serrano or Cahuilla, and seem to apply either name to themselves.[17]

This last statement lies at the basis of the entire dispute, for neither the term Cahuilla nor Serrano seems to have the slightest significance to either group who have been so designated. The first name only calls to their mind the Cahuilla reservation in the San Jacinto mountains, the latter any persons who dwell on or near mountains. Therefore to ask such a native whether he was a Cahuilla or a Serrano would be like asking a northern Scot whether he were a Scotchman or a Highlander: the answer might be interesting but inconclusive. There is only one way to approach the problem and that is by finding out the native dialect of each local group, for the Serrano and Cahuilla dialects are markedly different and a few test words give more positive evidence than any number of general questions. This seems simple, but as one might expect that a group name would be known

---

[15] The Indians of Los Angeles County, Los Angeles Star, 1852, Letter No. 1.

[16] Chinigchinich, *in* Life in California, by Alfred Robinson (ed. 1; New York, 1846), 227–341.

[17] Ethnography of the Cahuilla Indians, present series, 8:35, 1908.

to the people thus designated much grief may be experienced before it becomes obvious that the case is far otherwise.

That the Pass division of the Cahuilla occupied the San Gorgonio pass has been generally accepted, but in a recent work Kroeber changed his opinion giving the region in question to the Serrano.[18] This was done in accord with the findings of Benedict who worked on the Morongo reservation near Banning in 1922, making a study of Serrano culture.[19] This general region, due to the breaking down of the culture, the assembling of all dialectic groups on one reservation, and the lack of any tribal unity, is the most complex in southern California. Benedict's main informant, Mrs. Rosa Morongo, was really a Pass Cahuilla by birth and a Serrano by marriage and ceremonial affiliation. Instead of being born at Akavat, north of Beaumont (in Serrano territory),[20] she was born at pīhatapa, in the Banning Water canyon which was called malkī, the general Cahuilla name for the Banning district. Her father was clan leader of the pisatañavitcem clan (Pass Cahuilla) and her mother was of the kauisikiktum clan (Palm Springs Cahuilla). Before the present author met Mrs. Morongo he was told this by Francisco Nombre and Alejo Potencio (clan leaders respectively of the Desert and Palm Springs Cahuilla). Mrs. Morongo confirmed these statements on being asked, without reference being made to the previous information received. She married Captain John Morongo, a well-known leader of the māriña Serrano clan, and on his death assumed the ceremonial leadership of that clan's rather broken-down organization. As the result of her early marriage into a Serrano group she speaks that language as freely as her own.[21] Hence the majority of the Pass clan names recorded by Benedict are Serrano translations of Cahuilla names. As Mrs. Morongo seems better qualified to speak of Serrano culture in general than any of the few real Serranos on the reservation, the present author has little to add to much of Benedict's account, but it is unfortunate that the informant's bilingual talents should have led to such a mix-up in regard to former territorial ownership in the Pass.

[18] Handbook, 693, n. 1.

[19] A Brief Sketch of Serrano Culture, Am. Anthr., n.s., 26:366–392, 1924.

[20] Benedict, *op. cit.*, 366.

[21] Mrs. Morongo stated that her own language was īvīatim (Cahuilla) and her acquired language ismaīlem (Serrano). A comparison of the two as spoken by her convinced me that such was the case. To further verify the matter, several months after leaving the reservation, I sent a request to the Reverend Mr. Wineland, of Banning, for test vocabularies in her father's, her own, and her daughter's languages. The first two lists are pure Cahuilla, the third Serrano. Data in regard to her personal history, kindly secured by Mr. Wineland at this time, corroborate the statements made above.

SERRANO CLANS

At the present day it is probably impossible to secure a complete list of Serrano clans and clan territories, for actual knowledge of the old conditions has almost disappeared. The following list combines the information received from Mrs. Rosa Morongo, Mrs. Jesusa Manuel, and Mrs. Miguel Savatco, for no one informant could give a complete list. The present clan list (table 1) agrees closely with that published by Gifford,[22] and less closely with the clan list of Benedict.[23] The reason for this latter discrepancy has already been mentioned. It is quite possible that certain of the clans in the two former lists not recorded here were omitted by my informants, and for that reason I have compared all three lists in the following summary.

TABLE 1

SERRANO CLANS

G[24]	B[25]	S[26]	Clan	Territory	Moiety	Group
2	12	1	mōhīatniyum......	northwest of The Pipes...................	W	A
1	11	2	māriña.................	yumisēvul, Mission creek................	C	A
4	13	3	aturavīatum........	The Pipes (10 mi. NW of yumisēvul)	C	A
9	15	4	pervetum.............	Santa Anar., vicinity Big Bear lake		
8	(15)	5	yūhavetum (pine trees)................	from Highlands NE through Bear valley......................	C C	A A
11	......	6	tamīanūtcem.......	Twenty Nine Palms...................	W	B
......	14	7	mamaītum............	Twenty Nine Palms...................	C	B
6	......	8	mavīatem............	Vicinity of Victorville, N of San Bernardinos...................	C	C
7		9	amūtcakaīem.......	Base of San Bernardinos, S of Victorville.....................	(?)	C
......		10	apīhavatum..........	About Arrowhead Peak and Springs	C	C
5	......	11	kaīwīem................	N slope San Bernardinos, around Lake Arrowhead.....................	C	C
......	1	12	wa'atcem	S slope San Bernardinos between Santa Ana and Mill creeks...........	C	(?)
......	3	13	yūcaīpaīem..........	Yucaipe valley.....................	C	(?)

---

22 Present series, 14:179–180, 1918.   23 Am. Anthr., n.s., 26:368–369, 1924.

24 Gifford, *ibid.*; in addition, this list includes Serrano clans 3, 10, 12, 13, and 14 which were unknown to my informants.

25 Benedict, *ibid.*; in addition, this list includes Serrano clan 2, unknown to my informants; clan 4 is a Serrano translation of tepamōkikitum, Mt. Cahuilla clan, no. 1; clan 5 is a Serrano translation of pisatañavitcem, Pass Cah. clan, no. 9; clan 6 same as clan 5; clan 7 is a Serrano translation of malkī, Cahuilla name for Banning district; clan 8 is a Serrano translation of wakiñakiktum, Pass Cah. clan, no. 6; clan 9 is a Serrano translation of paluknavitcem, Pass Cah. clan, no. 8; clan 10 is a Serrano translation of wanikiktum, Pass Cah. clan, no. 5; clan 16 is the term translated as "money" applied to the females of the yūhavetum clan; clan 17 is a Serrano translation of haviñakiktum, Pass Cah. clan, no. 4; clan 18 is a Serrano translation of tetcanaakitum, Pass Cah, clan, no. 7; clan 19 is a Serrano translation of wakiñakiktum, Pass Cah. clan, no. 6.

26 Strong.

CLAN GROUPINGS

The seeming complexity of Serrano ceremonial organization is in all probability largely due to the fragmentary nature of our knowledge. As a functioning organization Serrano society for the most part disappeared several generations ago and as a result such gleanings as may now be obtained are often contradictory. The fact that the ceremonial life of their southern neighbors persisted up to the present generation enables us to gain an idea of the general nature of Serrano clan organization, but as the Serrano seem to have possessed certain unique characteristics, the analogy is but a sad substitute at best. Before considering the detailed organization of the clans in so far as they are remembered, and the unique developments they represent, it will be well to consider the larger Serrano interclan groupings.

In late historic times the māriña clan of the coyote moiety, formerly located at yumisēvul or Mission creek, seems to have held a dominant position among both the neighboring Serrano and the Pass Cahuilla clans. Equally important because of special duties it performed was the mōhīatniyim clan of the wildcat moiety, living northwest of The Pipes at mukunpat. The former clan possessed the ceremonial chief or kīka and the dance house, the latter clan the ceremonial assistant or paha and thè fetish bundle containing the sacred feathers. Thus the māriña chief always called the ceremony but the mohīatniyum paha and his clansmen officiated as well. Since these two groups commonly intermarried and were of opposite moieties, their reciprocal relationship is obvious.

Another clan of the coyote moiety, the aturavīatum clan, was also reciprocally allied with the mōhīatniyum clan in the same manner. The aturavīatum had a chief, a dance house, and a sacred bundle or fetish.[27] The māriña and the aturavīatum clans were responsible on alternate years for the annual mourning or image-burning ceremony, and the mōhīatniyum clan, which had no ceremony of its own, shared in both. This triangular linkage formed the central organization of the eastern Serrano clans but it was further complicated. The aturavīatum clan each year held the mourning ceremony for the pervetum and yūhavetum clans of the coyote moiety (see map 1). The last two clans are said to have possessed a clan chief, dance house, and fetish bundle, and the reasons for this involved relationship are not clear. The last two clans may have been branches of the atura-

---

[27] According to Miguel Savatco, the present kīka of the clan.

vīatum clan whose ceremonial affiliation still persisted after their separation, but there is no evidence to prove or disprove this. Similarly, the māriña clan always invited the mamaītum clan of the coyote moiety, located at Twenty Nine Palms, to all ceremonies; and also six of the neighboring Pass Cahuilla clans (nos. 4–9, p. 91). These clans in turn invited the māriña clan to their ceremonies, and an exchange of shell money was carried on between all the groups at the time of the ceremony itself, and on the occurrence of a death in any one of the clans, when all the others sent a certain amount of shell money to the clan leader of the deceased. Since no Serrano informants were very clear in regard to this exchange, it is discussed in more detail later when the Pass Cahuilla are considered.

This ceremonial exchange, and probably participation in each other's ceremonials, extended to the tekenetpauitcem Gabrielino clan at Crafton,[28] the watcicpakiktum Gabrielino clan at Redlands,[28] and to the havaīkiktum and one other Luiseño "party" at Saboba. The degree to which these distant clans participated in each other's ceremonies is not clear, but two Serrano informants[29] agreed that the mōhīatniyum paha always carried these beads to the other groups for both the māriña and aturavīatum clans. It is of interest that both these informants claimed that the "old" Saboba language was nearly the same as ismaīlem, i.e., Serrano, but had changed considerably in the last fifty years.

A second ceremonial grouping formerly existed at Twenty Nine Palms, where the mamaītum clan of the coyote moiety possessed the clan chief and dance house, while the tamīanutcem clan of the wildcat moiety possessed the paha and the fetish bundle. These two clans commonly intermarried and acted together in all ceremonial matters. Both clans are now extinct.

Of the third ceremonial grouping almost nothing is known. This probably included the mavīatem, amūtcakaīem, apīhavatum, and kaīwīem clans which were located in the northern San Bernardino mountains. Probably these groups are all extinct, but Serrano informants at the San Manuel reservation claimed that one or two survivors of these groups still lived near Victorville. If this is true it may still be possible to obtain some information in regard to them. Serrano informants say that these clans were all ceremonially united,

---

[28] Both these clan names were given by Mrs. Rosa Morongo in the Cahuilla dialect. Whether the people there were actually Gabrielino or spoke a differentiated Serrano dialect is not clear. This has been previously discussed, see p. 8.

[29] Mrs. Rosa Morongo and Mrs. Miguel Savatco.

but they remember them only in the vaguest way. Three of the clans are said to have belonged to the coyote moiety, but the moiety affiliation of the amūtcakaīem clan is not remembered. Possibly these groups were allied with Vanyume or Kitanemuk groups, but nothing definite is known in this regard.

The two southwestern Serrano clans, waatcem and yūcaīpaīem, near the Santa Ana river and Yucaipe valley, respectively, are also of unknown ceremonial affiliation. It seems probable that they were formerly linked with the valley Gabrielino groups[30] who were their nearest neighbors, but here again the hand of time has obscured the record. Both groups are now extinct.

All bonds between the groups so far discussed were of a purely ceremonial nature, and there appears to have been no sort of tribal or political union between them. The two clans of the wildcat moiety (nos. 1 and 6), as they appear to have had no hereditary clan leaders, were probably somewhat under the control of the reciprocally related coyote moiety clans (nos. 2 and 7), but even this relationship was in the main ceremonial. It is therefore erroneous to speak of such a mythical thing as a Serrano "tribe," for none such existed within historic times, and there is no reason to believe that it ever did. Nearly all the westerly Serrano clans were likewise united ceremonially with clans speaking alien dialects, and these in turn were autonomous political units, not tribal segments.

The ceremonial linkage between all Serrano clans is graphically shown in the diagram (table 2), where the squares represent clans of the coyote moiety and the circles clans of the wildcat moiety. It is undoubtedly significant that the two eastern ceremonial groups each revolve around one of the two wildcat clans; perhaps the same was true of the four northwestern clans if clan 9 was of the wildcat moiety. Certainly the reciprocal ceremonial relations between intermarrying clans played a large part in determining the linkage of the clans. This question involves the degree to which moiety exogamy prevailed among these groups, a point which will be discussed shortly.

About forty years ago the kauisiktum Pass Cahuilla clan at Palm Springs was first included in the Serrano-Pass Cahuilla ceremonial exchange, most of the former clans having already dropped their ceremonial activities. At present two Serrano clans, the mārriña or Morongo and the aturaviatum on the Morongo reservation near

---

[30] The present author assumes that these San Bernardino valley groups were originally of Gabrielino speech affiliation, but as has been previously stated the question is a disputed one.

Banning, continue their ceremonies in conjunction with the wanikiktum Pass Cahuilla clan located on the same reservation, and the
kauisiktum Pass Cahuilla clan at Palm Springs. Each clan performs
its annual mourning ceremony once every two years, to which the
other three are invited. Since the mohīatniyum clan is extinct, at
least as a ceremonial unit, each of the Serrano clans is now an independent organization possessing its own ritualistic paraphernalia
and ceremonial leader. These four clans, two Serrano and two
Pass Cahuilla, at the present day represent the last active religious
organizations of either group.

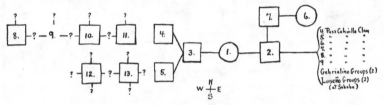

Table 2. Ceremonial Linkage of Clans.

CLAN ORGANIZATION

The basis of the Serrano clan seems to have been the male lineage,
whose ceremonial significance was augmented by the psychic importance attached to the lineage leader, the sacred ceremonial house, and
the sacred bundle. Since this priest, house, and fetish complex entered
so powerfully into the consciousness of the members of the lineage,
superseding the basic ties of kinship with those of a religious and
ceremonial nature, the grouping may well be called a clan. This clan
included, therefore, all the males and descendants of males in the
group, and the wives of these males as well. As previously indicated
the Serrano clans were unique in sharing the priest, house, and fetish
complex with other clans of the opposite moiety. A Serrano woman
always retained her own lineage name, but on her marriage was incorporated into the clan of her husband; and in so far as a woman entered
into the ceremonial life of the Serrano in former times, she in large
part gave up the ceremonial ties that were hers by birth and assumed
those possessed by her husband. This transfer of women, from ceremonial affiliation with one clan to another on marriage, seems to have
been characteristic of all the southern California groups save the
Yuman peoples of the Colorado river, where the clan name was carried
by the women of the clan although passed down in the male line.

GENEALOGY 1

Máriña Clan[31]

Rafael Morongo
+ *palaknavitcem* (PC)
Jolianna Morongo*
+ Will Pablo (*wanikiktum*) (PC)
Nancy Morongo*
+ *móhíatniyum*

John Morongo
+ *kavalim* (Cup.)
Annie Morongo
+ *kavalim* (Laws) (Cup.)
Sarah Morongo
+ —— Martin (?)

Joaquina Morongo*
+ *awilem* (DC)
Magdalena Morongo*
+ *awilem* (DC)

Tom Morongo
+ *móhíatniyum*

Francisco Morongo
+ *wavaaikiktum* (DC)

2. Captain John Morongo
3. + *Rosa pisatañavitcem* (PC)
(informant)

Tom Morongo
+ *kawisiktum* (PC)

Jose Morongo
+ *móhíatniyum*

Manuela Morongo*
+ Valentine *móhíatniyum* (paha)

Jose Antonio Morongo
+ *móhíatniyum*
Benjamin Morongo[32]
+ *móhíatniyum*

1. Capitan Sia (Morongo)
+ *kawicpavimčavitcem* (DC)

pilóta (?) (Morongo)
+ *haviñakiktum* (PC)

[31] * indicates that couple moved away to home of man. Numerals refer to succession of clan leadership.
[32] This man was not mentioned by the informant, but I have put him in the genealogy at this place because of Gifford's statement (*op. cit.*, 182) that he was the uncle of Thomas Morongo.

In spite of the transfer of ceremonial affiliation from one clan to another, the women of the Serrano and kindred southern California groups always retained their hereditary lineage names and at times participated in the ceremonies of their natal groups. As postmarital residence was predominatingly patrilocal, the degree to which a woman might associate with her hereditary clansfolk largely depended on the distance between her father's and her husband's villages.

A genealogy (genealogy 1) of the most important Serrano clan of historic times was obtained from Mrs. Rosa Morongo, whose husband, Captain John Morongo, was a member of the māriña Serrano clan. This genealogy (p. 16) refers to the time of the informant's marriage, some fifty-odd years ago, and is said to include all the māriña people who were then alive. It is clearly that of one direct male lineage, whose common male ancestor was apparently only two generations removed. If there were other collateral lines they were unknown to the informant.[33] All but the younger members of this clan are dead, and they were too young at the time the group moved from Mission creek to the Morongo reservation to remember any details of the old life. Hence Mrs. Morongo, in spite of being a Cahuilla by birth, appears to be the best informant on the Serrano obtainable.

Formerly the māriña clan always had a male kīka or clan leader; the office in theory passing from the incumbent to his oldest son. Often the oldest son was passed over in favor of a better adapted younger son, as was the case when Captain John succeeded Capitan Sia. On the death of Captain John Morongo his wife succeeded to the ceremonial leadership of the clan, but this decided break with custom seems to have been due largely to disintegration in modern times. Her son, John Morongo, a very able man of middle age who would be the correct kīka, makes no claim to the office as he has no active interest in the old customs. Mrs. Morongo stated that even under the old rules a woman might succeed to the clan leadership, but this seems dubious.[34] It was further stated that a woman could never hold the office of paha. In their old territory the māriña, as well as the other clans, owned various food-gathering areas in the vicinity of their clan locales to which they made trips as the different native crops became ready for gathering. The māriña, aturavīatum, and mohīatnīyum clans usually went on hunting and food-gathering

---

[33] It should be noted that Benjamin Morongo, mentioned as an informant by Gifford, *op. cit.*, 180, was not included by Mrs. Morongo in this genealogy. Since Benjamin died only recently the omission shows the genealogy to be incomplete.

[34] Gifford also states that in rare cases a woman might become kīka, *op. cit.*, 181.

expeditions together, under the leadership of the māriña clan's kīka.[35] This grouping of the clans may have been a late manifestation only, but data in this regard are scant.

Almost equal to the kīka in authority and influence was the paha. Of the three clans just mentioned only the mohīatnīyum clan had a paha, and he had charge of the sacred matting, muurtc, and the sacred feathers, vumtc, of both his own and the māriña clan. The aturavīatum kīka is said to possess a sacred bundle (muurtc) of cactus fiber, but does not have any sacred feathers at present. Likewise the mamaītum clan had the kīka, but a clan of the opposite moiety had the sacred bundle. This was the tamīanūtcem clan that also had the paha who officiated at the ceremonies of both clans. The pervetum and yūhavetum clans are said to have each had a kīka, dance house, sacred bundle, and paha, but as both came to the aturavīatum clan to hold their mourning ceremonies their complete ceremonial independence appears rather dubious.

Each Serrano clan seems to have centered its ceremonial life around a sacred bundle, but the custom of having this bundle in the possession of a clan of the opposite moiety is unique in the area. The two cases that are reasonably clear, i.e., the relationship of clan 2 to clan 1, and of clan 7 to clan 6,[36] indicate that the clan of the coyote moiety had the kīka in each case, while the sacred bundle was owned and handled in all ceremonies by the paha of the wildcat moiety clan. There was, therefore, reciprocity between intermarrying groups, and a further relationship involving the possession of the important sacred bundle. Unfortunately the data so far obtained in this regard are incomplete and it is impossible to ascertain the exact nature of this relationship. The paha, besides having charge of all ceremonial impedimenta,[37] notified the people when ceremonies were due, carried the shell money between groups, and attended to the division of shell money and food at all ceremonies. The office was passed from father to son in the same male lineage.

Another hereditary office was that of tcaka, or singer. So far as can be ascertained, this office is only reported for the māriña clan, but it seems probable that the office is identical with that of hauinik among the Cahuilla, and that there was at least one such person in each ceremonial group. This man knew all the myths of

---

[35] Compare Benedict, *op. cit.*, 391–392, and Gifford, *op. cit.*, 182.

[36] See Serrano clan list, p. 11.

[37] Gifford, *op. cit.*, 182, also records this custom.

the creation and all the clan songs. Mrs. Morongo said that this duty was often performed by the kīka, in which case there was no tcaka.

A general consideration of the Serrano clans indicates clearly that all the groups so designated were not equivalent. Those to the west, in regard to which we have only hearsay evidence, seem to have been made up of male lineages possessing the complete priest, house, and sacred bundle complex; whereas the eastern clans were interrelated in a seemingly complex manner, wherein a clan of one moiety possessed the priest leader and the ceremonial house, and a clan of the opposite moiety possessed the ceremonial assistant and the sacred bundle. This state of affairs, as will be demonstrated, is not in accord with that prevailing among any of the Cahuilla, Cupeño, or Luiseño groups. Among all of these groups indications of moiety reciprocity are encountered, but among none of them is the priest, house, and sacred bundle complex divided between the two moieties. This anomalous condition occurring among the Serrano may be due to a number of causes. First, it may represent a broken-down system of once independent clans, similar to the religious "parties" of the Luiseño; but the fact that the condition was the one formerly prevailing and that it is now superseded by a new individual clan grouping militates against this view. Secondly, it may be a further extension of the moiety idea wherein the partial moiety reciprocity of the more southerly groups is further accentuated by an actual division of the all-important priest, house, and fetish concept. Thus the clan of the opposite moiety with whom intermarriage is most common becomes an integral part of the ceremonial unit, and the cooperation of both groups becomes necessary for any ritualistic activity. This seems the most probable explanation of the phenomenon under discussion, but the evidence on which this conclusion is based is so fragmentary that it may be regarded as only tentative.

Another unique characteristic of the Serrano clan is the tendency to designate the men and the women of certain clans by different names. This has previously been noted by Gifford,[38] and a similar case was recorded in the present investigation. According to Mrs. Jesusa Manuel, a Mountain Cahuilla woman who had married a yūhavetum man, the men of the latter clan were called by that name, which means "pine trees,"[39] while the women of the clan were collectively designated as kotcavīem or "money." This latter name included females who had married into as well as those born in the

---

[38] *Op. cit.*, 180.   [39] Cf. Gifford, *op. cit.*, 179.

clan. The term might refer to the marriage price of women, but there seems to be a deeper significance to the custom. According to Benjamin Morongo, women of the māriña clan were called malena, while the men were called morongo; and mōhīatniyum men were called nudi, and women yetcaiwa.[40] Mrs. Miguel Savatco said that men of the aturavīatum clan were called aturavat, and the women atūatc. Comparable customs are found among the Desert Cahuilla,[41] and while the custom at present seems vague and rather meaningless, it may represent Yuman influence, as Gifford[42] has suggested. When more is known of the Chemehuevi and Kitanemuk the place of this nominal sex dichotomy within the clan may become clearer. There seem to be no traces of it among the western Cahuilla, the Cupeño, or the Luiseño.

THE SACRED BUNDLE

The great importance of the sacred bundle concept in southern California was first clearly indicated by Benedict.[43] Today each of the active Serrano clans has a mat which they call muurtc, made from cactus fiber, and in this wrapping they keep their ceremonial equipment. The bundle is in the possession of the clan leaders, Mrs. Rosa Morongo, ceremonial leader of the māriña clan, and Miguel Savatco, of the aturavīatum clan. Formerly at their old territory on Mission creek, the māriña bundle was kept by the mōhīatniyum paha and a string of eagle and other bird feathers was wrapped in it. These sacred feathers were called vumtc.[44] At present, according to members of the clans in question, neither of the bundles contains sacred feathers. The mamaītum and tamīanūtcem clans likewise shared such a bundle, which was kept by the latter clan. This bundle was made of tule matting and was called muurtc. It did not contain any sacred feathers.

The Serrano differ from their southern neighbors in that the paha rather than the kīka was custodian of the bundle and between ceremonies carefully hid it away, either in the dance house, or in a secret cave in the mountains.[43] The details concerning the care of these sacred objects are scant, but they were obviously regarded with great veneration and were carefully preserved. The sacred feathers (vumtc) were far more important than the feather bands made of flicker and other woodpecker feathers worn by the dancers. The bands are called wīwut, and are similar to those employed throughout almost

[40] Gifford, op. cit., 180.   [42] Cf. Gifford, op. cit., 181.   [44] Benedict, op. cit., 391.
[41] Present paper, p. 68.   [43] Op. cit., 375, 389.

the entire Californian area. Both types of feather ornaments were wrapped in the muurtc, along with rattles, head plumes, ceremonial wands, and the strings of shell money. The māriña clan differed from the other Serrano clans in that they hung up their sacred feathers and exposed the ceremonial wrapping from Wednesday night until Saturday during the week-long mourning ceremony. All the other clans kept theirs hidden.

The ceremonial employment of the sacred bundle and its contents is well described by Benedict:

The first great event of the week [during the mourning ceremony] is the all-night ceremony on Wednesday when the feathers are brought to the ceremonial house. These are the most sacred possessions of the Serrano, and are kept during the year under the care of the paha in a secret cave in the mountains. The ceremony on Wednesday night begins with a great supper. After supper they sing, led by the ceremonial singer, the tcaka, an hereditary officer, a Maringa, until at the direction of the paha all lights are extinguished, and the assembled people wait in silence till the feathers are brought. They first know that the feathers have come when they hear the paha praying in a peculiar voice in the darkness. The words are indistinguishable, but what he says concerns the beginning of things. This lasts about an hour. Then the fires are relighted and the feathers are hung around the room. In old times the paha and other dancers danced with the feathers at this time, but the last man who could dance this dance died twenty-five years ago. Besides, the feathers are falling to pieces now, and require very careful handling.[45]

The ceremonial importance of the clan leader, or kīka, among the Serrano is not clear, largely because their organization has been so badly broken down. At present this official presides at all ceremonies and is caretaker of the sacred bundle and paraphernalia, but the word-of-mouth accounts of former times assign this last duty to the paha. Apparently the latter official played a much larger part in social and ceremonial life among the Serrano than among the Cahuilla, Cupeño, or Luiseño where he is entirely subordinate to the clan priest or leader. The duties of the kīka seem to have been of an advisory nature; he set the time for ceremonies, "called them" as the Serrano say, and told the people when to go on their various food-gathering expeditions.[46] Formerly the kīka lived in the kitcateratc,[47] as was the case among most of the Cahuilla, Cupeño, and Luiseño groups. Whether he derived magical power and authority from the sacred bundle, as was the case among the Cahuilla and their neighbors, is also uncertain. Benedict states that the paha prayed over the sacred bundle during the mourning ceremony.

[45] *Op. cit.*, 375.

[46] According to Benedict, *op. cit.*, 392, he distributed all material so gathered to all the clan through the paha.

[47] Benedict, *op. cit.*, 379.

According to legend the first tule ceremonial house was made by Pakrokitat, and every chief has had one since that time.[48] Naming ceremonies, mourning ceremonies, and the curing of the sick were all done in this ceremonial house or kitcateratc, "big house." Here, in the case of the māriña clan, the sacred feathers were hung up during the latter half of the mourning ceremony. During this ceremony the paha swings a bullroarer and any person who looks to see where the noise comes from is tied up in the kitcateratc with the sacred feathers until his family pay to have him released.[49] When a deer was killed there was an all night ceremony in the "big house," and in the morning the carcass was cut up and divided.[50] Before a man became a full-fledged shaman it was essential that he dance before the assembled clan in the ceremonial house.[51] All these ceremonial functions involving the "big house" demonstrate its importance among the Serrano and, as later consideration of the groups to the south will show, its deep ceremonial significance is widespread in southern California.

THE MOIETY

In spite of Benedict's recent statement to the contrary,[52] the Serrano must definitely be included among the dichotomous groups of southern California. Furthermore the system of endogamous groupings among the Pass Cahuilla and Serrano which the same author outlines is not borne out either by the actual cases of marriage recorded, or by data secured from informants among the groups in question. These assumed endogamous groupings, in connection with a far too wide extension of the linguistic designation Serrano, seem to have obscured the problem of the moiety.[53]

The so-called "endogamous" groupings are merely clan groupings of a purely territorial nature, and the fact that such near-by groups often intermarried is to be expected. Propinquity as a force in mating naturally exerts a strong influence on all peoples. Two genealogies of clans included in Benedict's Serrano classification show that no such rule was enforced, and no informants questioned by the present author had ever heard of such a rule. The māriña genealogy (genealogy 1) gives eighteen cases of marriage for a typical Serrano

---

[48] Gifford, *op. cit.*, 181.

[49] Benedict, *op. cit.*, 376.

[50] *Ibid.*, 379.

[51] *Ibid.*, 384.

[52] *Op. cit.*, 371.

[53] As has been previously demonstrated, Benedict has grouped Serrano, Gabrielino, and Pass Cahuilla groups all under the term Serrano.

clan.[54] This shows six marriages with the mohīatniyum clan in accord
with moiety exogamy, and eleven with outside clans not included in
Benedict's endogamous grouping.[55] According to Benedict[55] the pisatañavitcem clan[56] was in the first endogamous grouping mentioned.
Of twelve cases of marriage recorded for this clan (genealogy 7) only
two are with clans included in the assumed endogamous grouping,
five are with clans in the second so-called endogamous grouping
(ismailem, i.e., Serrano), and five are with Pass Cahuilla clans, the
majority of which are included in the third assumed endogamous clan
group. Obviously there is here no objective basis for predicating any
such endogamous groupings.[57]

On the other hand each clan group of the Serrano, as was the case
with the Cahuilla and Cupeño, possessed in addition to its individual
name the appellation of either coyote or wildcat. The Serrano term
for a wildcat group is tuktum, and for a coyote group wahīyam. As
Benedict says, "It is undoubtedly significant that no hesitation was
shown in assigning to any group its animal designation. Even where
the proper marriage affiliation had been forgotten, the fact that they
were 'coyote' or 'wildcat' was unclouded."[58] According to all Serrano
informants questioned it was regarded as unethical for two wildcat
groups, or two coyote groups, to intermarry, but they all said that
the old rule had had little importance, in late years, especially. All
informants emphatically denied that there were any other rules limit-
ing the choice of mates, and I feel certain that the group limitations
of marriage given by Benedict never existed save as those of contiguous
clan groups that on account of propinquity commonly tended to
intermarry.

In the region of the San Gorgonio pass there was a great disproportion of coyote clans as compared with wildcat clans, and this
undoubtedly had an effect in the breaking down of moiety exogamy.
It is significant, however, that in the māriña genealogy the six cases
of intermarriage with other Serrano clans are all according to the
rule of moiety exogamy; while of the eleven cases of marriage with
Cahuilla clans, only one case accords with the rule. Our data are

---

[54] One case of marriage is with a man of unknown clan affiliation.

[55] *Op. cit.*, 370.

[56] *Op. cit.*, 369, given as Pihatüpayam. See present paper, p. 111, for Pass
Cahuilla marriages.

[57] Most of these marriages occurred from twenty to sixty years ago. Among
the Cahuilla and Cupeño such genealogies demonstrate the efficacy of moiety
exogamy, and these Serrano cases should likewise show the influence of marriage
rules.

[58] *Op. cit.*, 370.

too limited to assert positively that the practice of moiety exogamy
was in the ascendant among the Serrano clans, but there is no doubt
that they recognized such a rule even though they did not live up to it.
According to an informant of one of the northern Serrano clans,
which are predominatingly of the coyote moiety, the rule was known
but was not obeyed. For example, the pervetum and the yūhavetum
clans commonly intermarried, but they were always called wahīmaīam,
"coyotes not knowing each other," by other clans. This had a derog-
atory implication, and demonstrates the fact that the rule was known
although circumstances had made it impracticable of application.

Not only did the Serrano recognize the moiety as a factor in limit-
ing marriage, they also carried out the practice of moiety reciprocity
in ceremonial activities to a more complete degree than any of their
southern neighbors. This has been previously discussed in relation
to the Serrano clans, especially in regard to the position of the ceremonial assistant or paha, and the sacred bundle or muurtc. The
evidence shows that the mārиña and the mōhīatniyum clans frequently
intermarried. They likewise shared in all ceremonial activities and
in many utilitarian pursuits. The sacred bundle of the two clans was
formerly kept by the mohīatniyum paha, while the mārиña clan
possessed the clan leader, kīka, and the ceremonial house. In much
the same way the aturavīatum clan of the coyote moiety was ceremonially connected with the mohīatniyum wildcat clan, forming a
triple ceremonial union with a clan of the opposite moiety as the
common link. At Twenty Nine Palms there was an identical union
between two intermarrying clans of the opposite moiety. Strong
traces of moiety reciprocity occurred among the various Cahuilla,
Cupeño, and Luiseño groups, but the Serrano system shows more
dependence of the clans of one moiety upon the clans of the other
than occurred elsewhere in southern California.

The principle of the moiety obviously entered very deeply into the
life of these groups, as was also the case in south central California,
but the particular names by which the divisions are designated seem
almost fortuitous. It is therefore necessary to divorce the totemic
concept from that of dichotomy per se, and to consider each separately
in order to understand their nature and relationship. This phase of
the problem calls for later consideration but should be noted here in
order that both the apparently superficial discrepancies and the deeper
similarities of dichotomy in southern California be properly evaluated.
Today the ideas connected with the moiety among the Serrano are

vague;[59] but when they are considered in relation to the culturally allied Cahuilla and Cupeño, their significance becomes manifest.

The Serrano moieties are also associated with other animals than the two name-giving species. With the coyote are associated the buzzard (widikut) and the wolf (wanats); and with the wildcat are the mountain lion (tukutcu) and the crow (gatcawa).[60] The animals associated with each moiety are said to be related to one another.[60] The members of each moiety call their various totemic animals by the term for great-grandparent. According to native theory these animals were assigned to their respective moieties by the creator Pakrokitat.[61] In all probability there was once a much more complete division of the animal kingdom between the two, but if so it has been forgotten. Wildcat people were reputed to be slow and lazy, and coyote people swift in movement.[62] There was no prohibition in regard to killing or eating the totem animal,[62] at least within the memories of present informants. Formerly there was much joking between people of opposite moieties, and there were several songs of this nature. This joking seems to have entered into more serious ceremonies, for it is said that the kīka of a coyote clan would often ridicule the paha of the associated wildcat clan. Mrs. Miguel Savatco stated that many years ago all Serrano men applied face paints in a striped design, while all Serrano women used face paints in a dotted design. This custom suggests the nominal sex dichotomy previously mentioned for the Serrano, and has some similarity to the two types of design used by Cupeño girls after their adolescence ceremony.[63]

THE JOKING RELATIONSHIP

According to Benedict the Serrano family

. . . . along with its remoter connections, is bisected into joking and respect relatives. All relatives of one's own direct line, and their siblings of the same sex, belong to the category to which respect is due; all siblings of opposite sex (mother's brother, father's sister, grandmother's brother, etc.) to the joking category. Their children have status of their parents. Thus cross-cousins to the third and fourth generations are joking relatives; parallel cousins, respect relatives. This holds reciprocally also, so that a man never jokes with his brother's children, nor a woman with her sister's. At marriage the husband and wife assume each other's joking categories. In the small communities that were the rule among the Serrano, then, from the point of view of any single individual this differentiation of status practically bisected the entire community.[64]

---

[59] Benedict, *op. cit.*, 371.   [60] Gifford, *op. cit.*, 178.   [61] Gifford, *op. cit.*, 178.
[62] *Ibid.* Cf. Benedict, *op. cit.*, 371.
[63] Girls of the coyote moiety employed a striped design, those of the wildcat moiety a dotted design.
[64] *Op. cit.*, 372.

Benedict believes that this distinction between siblings of identical and of opposite sex in the direct ancestral line, with its associated respect or joking implication, is the determining factor in the Serrano relationship classification. Thus cross-relatives of different moiety affiliations, such as the wife's mother's brother, the wife's father's sister, the grandmother's brother, and the grandfather's sister are all designated by one term, as opposed to the classification of parallel or respect relatives.[65] Since this classification may cut directly across the hypothetical moiety alignment of relatives, it seems to support Benedict's contention that the Serrano had no true moiety division.[66]

This would indeed be important evidence in support of the latter view were the Californian groups possessing moieties characterized by any "conventional scheme of unilateral descent such as is found among tribes that are organized into exogamic moieties."[67] This is certainly not the case, for as Kroeber has stated, "there are [in California] but few clear indications of an association, regional or otherwise, between types of kinship systems and types of social institutions pure and simple . . . . and equally few instances of particular traits of kinship nomenclature according with specific institutions."[68] The same author, in relation to Californian moieties, specifically adds: "the distribution both of types of kinship systems and special traits of kinship designation, fails to agree with the distribution of these moieties."[68] Gifford's later and more extensive work on Californian Kinship Terminologies amply confirms this view.[69]

Benedict's statement that "there seems to be no reason for referring to these designations as moieties,"[70] in regard to the alignment of all Serrano clans to either a wildcat or a coyote division, has been previously discussed. If it were true, as seems to be implied, that the Serrano kinship system departed radically from kinship systems possessed by other dichotomous groups in California there would be just ground for doubting the possession of a dichotomous division among the Serrano. This is certainly not the case as an examination of the central Sierra Miwok kinship nomenclature will readily demonstrate.[71] Since these are perhaps the most characteristic and best known central Californian dichotomous people, they may well serve

---

[65] *Ibid.*, 373.   [66] *Ibid.*, 371.   [67] Benedict, *op. cit.*, 373.

[68] California Kinship Systems, 12:382–383, 1917 (cited hereafter as Kinship).

[69] Present series, 18:7, 246, 1922 (cited hereafter as Kinship).

[70] *Op. cit.*, 371.

[71] Gifford, Miwok Moieties, present series, 12:172–174, 1916 (cited hereafter as Miwok).

for purposes of comparison. Among this group a man uses twenty-nine terms of relationship. Of these, twelve apply to relatives belonging only to his own moiety, nine to relatives of the opposite moiety only, and eight to relatives who may belong to either moiety. A woman among the central Sierra Miwok uses thirty terms of relationship; fourteen of these apply to relatives of her own moiety only, seven to relatives of the opposite moiety only, and nine to relatives who may belong to either moiety according to circumstances. When we turn to the Serrano we find that a man uses forty terms, eleven of which apply to relatives belonging only to his own moiety, sixteen to relatives of the opposite moiety only, and thirteen terms which may apply to members of either moiety. A Serrano woman uses forty-two terms, thirteen of which apply to relatives of her own moiety only, sixteen to relatives of the opposite moiety only, and thirteen to relatives who may belong to either moiety.[72] Among the Miwok then, 27.5 per cent of the relationship terms used by a man, and 30 per cent of those used by a woman may include persons of both moieties; while of the terms used by a Serrano man 32.5 per cent, and by a Serrano woman 30 per cent, are of this type. The fact that a Serrano man uses 5 per cent more kinship terms that include persons of both moieties than does a Miwok man, while between women of the two groups there is identity in this regard, suggests no great difference between the two kinship terminologies. Since Benedict has pointed out that a number of Serrano terms include relatives of different moieties, and that this departs from customary moiety usage, it is significant that in this regard there is no appreciable difference between the former and the undoubtedly dichotomous Miwok. The same lack of exact accord between dichotomy and grouping of relatives holds for other peoples in southern California, but there seems no reason to deny the manifest occurrence of a dual division of society among such peoples because it is not clearly reflected in their kinship terminology. When we find in one or more dialectic units a demonstrable division into two nominal halves, especially when such a division is strengthened by exogamy, these divisions may certainly be referred to as moieties.

The system of kinship classification among the Serrano pointed out by Benedict is undoubtedly important, perhaps the most important single factor in determining alignment of kinship terms, but for reasons shortly to be discussed I am dubious that it is exactly describable as a joking and respect classification. Primarily the dis-

---

[72] Gifford, Kinship, 54–56.

tinction between cross and parallel relatives seems connected with the
fundamental importance of the direct lineage in southern California
social organization.   This point has previously been stressed by
Kroeber.

The characteristics of the southern Californian type of kinship are an enormous
development of reciprocal expression, and a striking reduction of terms denoting
connections by marriage. Perhaps equally important intrinsically is the consistent
recognition of the factor of lineage, as expressed terminologically in the distinction of cross and parallel relatives; but this is not an exclusive southern peculiarity.
All of these traits seem typical also of the systems of the Southwest, with which
region southern California has many cultural correspondences.''[73]

Benedict stresses the point that the Serrano have one term which
includes grandmother's brother, wife's mother's brother, and wife's
father's sister, and another term including grandfather's sister;[74]
also husband's father's sister and husband's mother's brother.[75]   It is
undoubtedly significant that all the relatives in these two groupings
are definitely excluded by either birth or marriage from the direct
lineage of the speaker or the speaker's wife.   They are as Benedict
says "siblings opposite in sex to the direct ancestor [or ancestors]
through whom relationship is traced."[74]   This distinction is carried
into the grandparent generation among Serrano, Diegueño, Cahuilla,
Cupeño, and Luiseño,[76] all of which groups are characterized by
lineages or clans based on the male lineage.

According to Benedict the joking category includes all cross
relatives and the respect category all parallel relatives, which seems a
logical arrangement to distinguish lineal kin from the others.   I was
unable to verify this state of affairs among the Serrano however, for
far from appearing to be an outstanding feature among the very few
Serrano on the Morongo reservation,[77] it seemed obscure, and informants were contradictory in their opinions of the matter.   There is no
doubt that some such division of relatives existed, but the suggested
lines of cleavage seem contradictory, not only between groups but
between individual informants in the same group.   Among the
Cupeño, for example, a woman might make fun of her sister's children
and call them ugly or stupid, and her sister had no right to object;
but it was considered unethical for a woman to joke thus with her

---

[73] Kinship, 378–379.

[74] *Op. cit.*, 373.

[75] Gifford, present series, 18:54–56, 1922.

[76] Gifford, Kinship, 135.   Benedict, *op. cit.*, 373.

[77] Benedict, *op. cit.*, 373.

brother's children or with her own children.[78] This is in direct contradiction to the Serrano system as given by Benedict, wherein a woman should joke only with her brother's children and not with those of her sister.[79] Among the Mountain Cahuilla a man can joke with the sons, but not the daughters, of his father's brothers and his father's sisters; with all grandparents and great-grandparents; with the mother's brother's wife and sons; with the father's sister's husband and their sons; and especially with the husbands of his sisters. He cannot joke with his father's brother or the latter's wife, his mother's sister or her husband, or his brother's wife and their children.[80] This fragmentary list also disagrees with the Serrano scheme given by Benedict, in the lumping of the grandparent generation and the male parallel cousins in the joking category, but agrees in putting the father's brother and mother's sister both in the respect category. Such incomplete data as these are valueless in demonstrating the nature of the division, but they do indicate that the system is not so simple as has been suggested for the Serrano. Since the social organization and kinship terminology of the Serrano agree in all fundamentals with those of the Cupeño and Cahuilla, it is strange that they seem to disagree in the joking relationship.

Benedict's version of the matter has the advantage of simplicity and apparent logic behind it, but is certainly not confirmed by the foregoing data. These data are even less satisfactory in explaining either the application or the significance of the joking relationship. The observations of the present author were contrary to those of Benedict,[81] for neither among the Serrano nor any of their southern neighbors were manifestations of this custom particularly noticed. When questioned, informants were vague in regard to the exact classification of any particular relative, but there seems no reason to doubt that some such categories formerly existed. Later work alone may settle this particular question but enough has been given here to show that neither Serrano kinship terminology nor the division of relatives into respect and joking categories precludes their possession of a dichotomous organization. The bulk of other Serrano evidence testifies to the importance of the moiety.

---

[78] According to Mrs. Salvadora Valenzuela, informant.

[79] *Ibid.*, 372.

[80] According to Jolian Nortes, informant.

[81] *Op. cit.*, 373.

Ceremonial Life: Birth

Very few of the older Serrano survive, and among these I encountered no good informants. Of necessity, therefore, the bulk of the Serrano data were secured from Mrs. Rosa Morongo, who is a member of this linguistic group by marriage and ceremonial affiliation, not by birth. Since Mrs. Morongo has been acting leader of the main Serrano clan for many years she is well qualified to speak in regard to the ceremonies of her adopted people. Much of Benedict's information was received from this same informant and as a result the present account of Serrano ritualism is largely a resumé of her material[82] and that earlier secured by Gifford.[83] The present author's contribution has been to distinguish wherever possible between ceremonial details applying to Mrs. Morongo's native people[84] and to her adopted people, the Serrano. However, since the mǎriña clan in historic times at least, has greatly influenced the neighboring Pass Cahuilla clans and vice versa, the ceremonies of the two groups are very similar. The present list of ceremonies applies directly to the mǎriña Serrano clan and indirectly to the near-by Serrano clans. How closely it duplicates the activities of the extinct northern clans is hypothetical.

Immediately after parturition, mother and child were placed in a heated pit where they remained for about four days, or until the navel cord of the child dropped off. The day following the birth the child's paternal grandparents gave a feast at which presents were distributed to the guests and a cradle board made for the infant. No special restrictions seem to have been placed on the child's father at this time.[85]

Girls' Adolescence Ceremony

Formerly a clan ceremony, waxan,[86] was held for certain adolescent girls. This took place in the dance house and was presided over by the paha of the affiliated clan.[87] A shallow pit was dug and heated with hot stones, and on the removal of the stones the girls were placed in the pit and their bodies covered with sand. Their faces were covered with basketry caps. The sand in the pit was reheated at intervals and the girls remained here for one or more days. When they were removed the paha administered a large decoction of bitter herbs and their hair was washed in the same liquid. They were bathed in warm

---

[82] *Op. cit.*

[83] Present series, 14:178–182, 1918.

[84] The Pass Cahuilla.

[85] Benedict, *op. cit.*, 379.

[86] Benedict, *op. cit.*, 380.

[87] Of the opposite moiety.

water and each girl remained in seclusion under the care of her grandmother for a period of about four days. During this time their faces
were painted daily with certain designs that are not remembered at
the present time. The use of cold water, salt, and meat was forbidden,
as was the stepping on wood, or scratching of the head save with a
special wooden head-scratcher. This public ceremony was held at the
same time as the boys' initiation or jimsonweed drinking. It is said
to have included only the girls of prominent families.[88] Girls from
other families were initiated at a private ceremony including only the
immediate family. The latter form seems to have persisted the longest
and it was possibly merely a later development of the clan ceremony,
for elsewhere in the region the public initiation of all adolescent girls
seems to have been general.

Boys' Initiation or Toloache Ceremony

This ceremony was called tamonin (from tama, to teach), and long
ago seems to have been performed annually. It included only the sons
of prominent families and boys of marked personality. The paha presided over the ceremony and was assisted by the shamans. A decoction of the jimsonweed (*Datura meteloides,* called toloache in Mexican
Spanish) was administered to each boy on the first night, in a hidden
place away from the village. The boys were then taken to the ceremonial house where they danced around a large fire until overcome by
the effects of the drug. They were then laid in rows in the dance
house and allowed to sleep off the effects. At this time they were
supposed to have visions that would guide them in future life. The
nature of the visions received and their import is but scantily remembered by any of the Serrano, and the problem merits more study
among their neighbors than it has yet received. The dancing and
singing continued through three days and nights, and during this
period the older men and the shamans taught the boys various songs.
The tcaka (singer) had charge of this phase of the initiation. The
occurrence of a ground-painting at this time is not remembered by
any of the Serrano,[89] but since variants of this institution occurred
among the Mountain Cahuilla, especially those who had moved to the
San Gorgonio pass, it is possible that similar rites formerly occurred
among the Serrano and Pass Cahuilla but have been forgotten. On
the third day all the boys ran a race and the winner was selected to
be trained for the "whirling" or eagle dance. In the songs sung at

---

[88] Benedict, *op. cit.,* 383.

present by the Serrano clans there are references to the jimsonweed (manitc),[89] but the importance of the cult seems to have been largely forgotten or else it had only a slight hold on the consciousness of the Serrano.

CEREMONIES FOR THE DEAD

Persons that were very sick among the Serrano were removed whenever possible to the ceremonial house where they were doctored by the shamans. Bodies of the dead were prepared for burial by persons hired by the family of the deceased. Within historic times the Serrano buried their dead, usually with as large a number of shell beads as possible. From the universality of the custom among the non-coastal southern Californians it is probable that prior to the influx of Christian ideas cremation was in vogue among the Serrano also.

Destruction of Personal Belongings

Immediately after a death much of the property of the deceased was destroyed. Usually within a month after the burial a special ceremony called mamakwot[90] was given by the family of the dead person. At this ceremony, after a night of singing and dancing, certain selected possessions of the dead were burned.

The Annual Mourning Ceremony

Since this week-long ceremony among the Serrano has been described in some detail by Benedict,[90] and a similar ceremony given by the Palm Springs Cahuilla in which Serrano clans took part is described in the present paper (pp. 122–130), the following summary of events will suffice.

The name for this cycle of ceremonies is not certain;[91] but the last night, on the morning of which the images were burned, was called wakăt, which is probably only a generic term for "feast." The neighboring Cahuilla and Luiseño groups designate this ceremony by a participial form of the verb "to burn," and the Serrano probably did the same. It is said that māriña was the oldest clan and always had precedence in giving such a ceremony; in a like manner all Serrano or Pass Cahuilla clans en route to such a ceremony at Palm Springs would wait at a certain place for the māriña clan to precede them. Among the southeastern Serrano the māriña and aturavīatum clans gave this ceremony on alternate years, each being assisted by the

---

89 Benedict, *op. cit.*, 383.   90 Benedict, *op. cit.*, 374–379.

91 No inclusive term is given by Benedict, Gifford, or Kroeber, Handbook.

mōhīatniyum clan of the opposite moiety. The present-day ceremonial alignment will be discussed later in relation to the Pass Cahuilla.

The ceremony begins on Monday, and the first three days are[92] largely taken up with the preparation of food and ceremonial paraphernalia. It is probable that the clan leader "retreated" at this time to confer with the sacred bundle, as is still the case among the Palm Springs Cahuilla, but the present Serrano clan leaders are vague on this point. A feature of this period is the rabbit hunt participated in by all the men under the direction of the paha, but the affair at present is purely an economic one.[93] Whether it ever had ceremonial significance is dubious.

The Clan Fetish

Wednesday night the matting bundle (muurtc) containing the sacred feathers (vumtc) is brought into the ceremonial house. From the standpoint of the clan (or clans) performing the ceremony this is the most important night of the week. Benedict's description of this event (quoted here, p. 21) is the first clear expression of the fundamental importance of the clan fetish in southern California since that of Boscana.[94] The wider implications of this concept will be treated at length hereafter.

The songs sung at the close of this phase of the ceremony when the fires are relighted, refer to the jimsonweed drinking, and seem to represent all of this rite that has persisted up to the present day.[95]

The Naming of Children

Thursday all children born in the clan during the preceding year were named. Gifts were distributed by the parents of the children, and the ceremony commenced with singing and dancing. The paha carried the child and the name was bestowed by the clan leader. This name was selected from those belonging to the lineage of the father. So far as available information is concerned no secrecy was connected with these names.[96] Since this is contrary to the general scheme in southern California it is possible that our data are inadequate.

---

[92] Present tense refers to those rites still performed, past tense to features that have been discontinued.

[93] A similarly organized rabbit hunt occurred among the Plateau Shoshoneans. Lowie, Notes on Shoshonean Ethnography, Anthr. Papers Am. Mus. Nat. Hist., 20:196, 1924.

[94] Chinigchinich, *op. cit.*, 259–261.

[95] Benedict, *op. cit.*, 375–376.

[96] Benedict, *op. cit.*, 378.

The Ceremonial Eagle Killing

Friday the eagle-killing ceremony was performed, the young birds having been taken from the nest previously. The birds were strangled by the paha, and the feathers used to decorate the images of the dead. This ceremony probably occurred at night, but there are few details on record.

Making the Images

Friday afternoon the images of the dead are made: these are called tü-iv (ghosts).[96a] The immediate family may make the image, but an outsider may be asked to do it, in which case such a person is paid by the family of the deceased.

The Eagle Dance

Saturday the eagle dance (tuwituaim, meaning simply "dance") was performed.[97] The dancer, formerly the winner in the race at the close of the toloache ceremony, was painted with red, black, and white. A feather costume (notably the eagle-feather skirt) was employed, and the dance consisted largely of difficult whirling movements.

Burning the Images

That night the assembled clans sing till dawn. About an hour before sunrise gifts are distributed to the invited clans by the paha. Then the various images of the dead are brought out, usually by a clanswoman of the deceased, but not a member of his immediate family. If a woman outside the clan carries the image she is paid for her services. They dance with the images for about half an hour and then place them on the fire which has been kindled outside the ceremonial house by the paha. Formerly a male relative of the deceased danced with the image, while the paha shot, or pretended to shoot, at him with a bow and arrow. The dancer dodged the arrows, from which the ceremony takes its name wuuv (dodging).[98] At the time of the dance with the death images the bereaved families distribute many presents by throwing them up in the air for the guests to catch.

The entire ceremony closes with the distribution to the invited clan leaders of the strings of shell money. This complex and rather obscure custom will be treated subsequently in relation to the Pass Cahuilla.

[96a] Benedict, *op. cit.*, 377.   [97] Benedict, *op. cit.*, 378.

[98] Informants state that the success of the spirit of the dead in reaching the afterworld depends on the ability of this man to dodge the arrows.

Other Ceremonies

When a deer was killed an all-night ceeremony was held in the "big house." This consisted of singing, dancing, and ceremonial smoking. In the morning the deer was cut up and the meat distributed.[99]

When an eclipse of either the sun or moon was observed a universal shout was raised. All the people congregated in the "big house" and the paha and shamans sang and danced. It was believed that such phenomena were caused by the spirits of the dead eating the celestial body, hence all food was forbidden at such times on the theory that eating would assist the spirits. When the eclipse had ended all the people drank a decoction of bitter herbs, washed their hair in the same liquid, and had a feast.[100]

Shamanism

The Serrano shaman (huremitc) was a "psychically" predisposed person who had acquired his power through dreaming. Such dreams might come normally at night time, during the day in the form of visions, or at the time of the toloache drinking. This power was purely personal, and the main duties of a shaman were curing by sucking, or by seeking the lost soul of the patient and thus restoring health. His equipment consisted of a scratching stick, and a ceremonial wand which symbolized his power.[101] Prior to becoming a shaman a boy must show strange tendencies and have visions. When he had acquired his full power he gave a dance in the ceremonial house before all the people of his local group. Certain of the shamans were believed to assume the form of bears especially, and occasionally other animals.

The subject of shamanism in this general region has been largely neglected. However, the account of Serrano shamanism given by Benedict,[102] of which the above is a very brief summary, and the account for the Cahuilla (which applies almost entirely to the Desert division) given by Hooper,[103] show the general nature of the shamanistic practices of the groups. Since there are still a number of practicing shamans in southern California it is highly desirable that a more detailed study of their methodology be made as soon as possible.

---

[99] Benedict, *op. cit.*, 379.

[100] *Ibid.*, 379–380.

[101] Benedict, *op. cit.*, 382–385.

[102] *Loc. cit.*

[103] Hooper, present series, 16:333–342, 1920. Although the Cahuilla in general are referred to in Hooper's paper, the definite references are practically all to those of the Desert division.

II. THE DESERT CAHUILLA

The Cahuilla in General

The Cahuilla Indians of southern California belong to the great Shoshonean linguistic family and with their western neighbors, the Luiseño, Cupeño, and Juaneño, form one division of the southern California branch of that stock.[104]   Three main divisions of the Cahuilla exist, the Desert, Pass, and Mountain divisions, whose segregation is mainly geographic, though some slight dialectic and rather important cultural differences do exist.

Although the Cahuilla have been written of as a powerful "tribe that once controlled southern California from the Colorado river westward to the Pacific sea,"[105] this seems in the light of recent investigation to be an exaggeration.   Similarly the translation of the name Cahuilla as "master," given by Hugo Reid,[106] has not been confirmed. The derivation of the term Cahuilla is obscure, and it is regarded by the Indians as of Spanish origin.[107]   There is no evidence that the Cahuilla ever were a tribe in the sense of being a united political body, until under the Mexican régime certain groups were amalgamated by the whites to serve as military units.   Prior to Caucasian interference they appear to have been isolated in small, autonomous local groups with no pretense of controlling any other than their local territories.   Since they were the least affected of all the native peoples of southern California by the segregation into missions, they have survived in greater numbers, and to this fact they owe their greater military importance during the early American period in California.

All three divisions of the Cahuilla employ the term īvīat in referring to their own language.   A person who speaks this language is called īvilyūkaleṭ, and the collective term for those speaking the language is īvīatim,[108] or "the Cahuilla-speaking people."   Thus the

---

[104] Kroeber, Handbook of the Indians of California, Bur. Am. Ethn., Bull. 78: 577, 1925.

[105] Barrows, The Ethno-Botany of the Coahuilla Indians of Southern California (University of Chicago Press, 1900), 82.

[106] Indians of Los Angeles County.   Letters to the Los Angeles Star, 1852. Letter No. 1.

[107] Kroeber, Handbook, 693.   The Cahuilla of southern California should not be confused with the Yokuts Kawia tribe on the Kaweah river; nor with the Kiliwas (Cahuillas) a Yuman group of the San Pedro Martir mountains in Lower California (A. W. North, Am. Anthr., n.s., 10:236, 1908).   The spelling Coahuilla used by Barrows is customary, but the pronunciation is Ca-.   There is no connection with the state of Coahuila in Mexico.

[108] This is also the name of one of the Desert Cahuilla clans: present paper, p. 42, and Gifford, present series, 14:191, 1918.

proper term to be applied generally to all the Cahuilla would be īvīatim, a proper name for the group that has not heretofore been given the prominence it deserves.[109]

Since the Cahuilla people were in no sense of the term a unified tribe, but were composed of a large number of independent local groups each differing slightly from their neighbors according to their degree of isolation, the following account strives to show both the differences and similarities of all the groups so designated. For this reason each of the three main divisions will be discussed in as much detail as possible, in order that their place in the general scheme of aboriginal society in southern California may be determined with the greatest accuracy. First in order will be consideration of the Desert Cahuilla.

ENVIRONMENT

The desert groups of Cahuilla-speaking people live on the Colorado desert south of the San Gorgonio pass. Many of the groups in their native state appear to have been scattered along the edges of the desert and west into the Santa Rosa and San Jacinto mountains. Other groups probably fewer in numbers lived along the eastern edge of the desert at the base of the Little San Bernardino mountains. The migration legends and place names of the earliest family homes remembered, originate in the mountains, giving some reason for the belief that at an earlier time the people lived there—later moving out into the desert. The legends involve the flooding of the entire Cahuilla basin, a flood which the Indians declare long ago drove their ancestors up into the mountains, from which environment they returned several generations ago, following the water as it subsided. Floods have occurred in recent times and it is probably such a flood— or at least the subsidence of the forerunner of the Salton sea—that they vaguely commemorate in their stories.[110]

---

[109] The main value of this term lies in distinguishing between Cahuilla and other groups in the field. Since the term Cahuilla has become so firmly fixed in the literature there seems no really valid reason for any attempt to change it.

[110] It is stated on the authority of old settlers that water from the Colorado river reached the Salton sea, causing local floods in the years 1840, 1842, 1852, 1859, 1862, and 1867. In the years 1905–8 occurred the great flood caused by the Colorado river shifting its channel. It is more probable however that the Indian legends apply to the gradual disappearance of the forerunner of the Salton sea, i.e., Blake sea, a brackish lake that previously filled most of the Cahuilla basin. In regard to this E. E. Free states, ''It is probable that the final disappearance of Blake sea was less than five hundred years ago, and the entire existence of the water body can scarcely have been longer. The Indians of the region have a tradition of the previous existence and gradual disappearance of a water body in the basin, and in spite of the notorious untrustworthiness of Indian legends it seems probable that this one has a basis of truth.'' D. T. MacDougall, The Salton Sea (Carnegie Institution of Washington, D. C., 1914), 19–28.

While the information in regard to the mountain habitat of these people is legendary, that in regard to their aboriginal desert villages is still obtainable. The Spanish and Mexican influences east of the San Jacinto mountains appear to have been transitory and nominal, while the American influence in the desert region has been an active force only in the last seventy-five years at the longest. Francisco Nombre, now living at Martinez reservation, was born at that place a year or so before the Mormons settled San Bernardino in 1851. He is the acting chief of the awilem (dogs) clan, and from him was obtained a census of all the towns and clans of the desert region when he was a boy. These data were corroborated and checked by informants from the Torros reservation and appear to be exact. It is to be remembered that such a picture shows only one view of a society which was probably at no time definitely settled. Each clan was apparently in the habit of moving its abode when lack of food or water made it necessary, but undoubtedly the structure of desert society remained much the same until the definite establishment of reservations confined the movements of the people. Barrows[111] has given us such a picture of the desert communities about 1900, and while some of the names he gives for villages appear to be names for localities there is, on the whole, agreement between the old villages and the sites he records.

The essential thing to any community, especially to one living in the desolate environment of the desert, is water, and it is around the natural water holes and artificial wells that the Desert Cahuilla were grouped. It appears to have been possible for several clans to use one water hole or well, and yet to be almost independent of each other in every other regard. Where there was more than enough water for domestic purposes a little farming was carried on, each clan having its allotted area for this purpose. Within the memory of all informants questioned, both corn and wheat were raised in these small patches, and doubtless other vegetables, such as melons, beans, and squash. Francisco was told by his grandfather that before the Mexicans came the Desert Cahuilla had only corn; this they did not raise but traded for with the Yuma Indians of the Colorado river area. The staple foods, however, appear to have been the beans of the various mesquite trees, a great variety of cactus, and similar native plants of the desert.[112]

---

[111] Barrows, The Ethno-Botany of the Cahuilla Indians of Southern California (University of Chicago Press, 1900), 32–35.

[112] See Barrows, *op. cit.*, for a detailed discussion of the many food plants of the Cahuilla Indians.

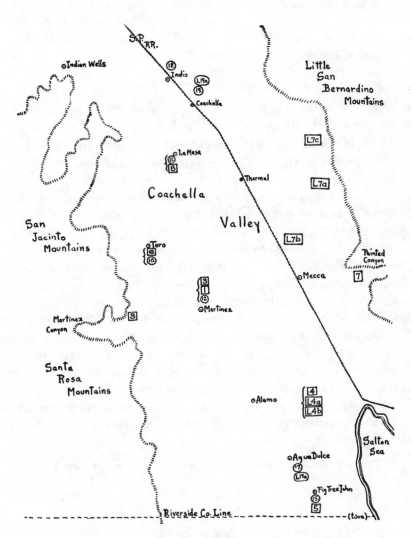

Map 2. Desert Cahuilla Territory.

Excepting such irrigable areas as were owned by the individual clans, the territory in the immediate vicinity of the village was common ground, but beyond this each clan had certain clusters of mesquite trees and small districts in the mountains which they owned and jealously guarded. Within the clan these food-gathering territories were communally utilized, but in case of uninvited incursion of any alien people the owners were prepared to fight. To be able to name all the natural boundaries of the clan territory was necessary for all adults and especially for the net or clan chief. The exact organization and function of the clan will be dealt with after the village grouping of the Desert Cahuilla has been discussed.

In the following lists of Desert Cahuilla clans belonging to the two moieties (tables 3, 4), the lineages bearing individual names (designated by the prefix *L*) are given under the clan with which they were ceremonially united. This list, as well as those of the other Cahuilla divisions, should be compared with the Cahuilla clan list previously published by Gifford.[113] A general statement in regard to this list may be in order. Of Gifford's wildcat clans, number 1 refers to a Serrano group, number 7 to a Pass Cahuilla group, and number 22 to a Mountain Cahuilla group. Numbers 4, 6, 9, and 18 were not known to my informants. Of the coyote clans Gifford records, numbers 1, 4, 5, and 21 were Pass Cahuilla groups, and number 22 a Mountain Cahuilla group. His clans numbers 7 and 10 are identical, and his clan 15 is given as coyote clan 20 in the present list. Coyote clan 2 according to my data is identical with wildcat *L 7a* in the present list, as it was not the clan of Jim Pine, who was a Serrano, but of his wife. Coyote clans numbers 3, 9, 19, and 20 were unknown to my informants. Gifford's other clans, save for differences in orthography, correspond with those in the following lists.

---

[113] Clans and Moieties in Southern California, present series, 14:190–191, 1918.

TABLE 3

Clans Belonging to the Wildcat Moiety

1. awilem, "dogs," at pūichekiva near Martinez. Originally from wilamū in the Santa Rosa mountains.

2. autaatem, "high up," at temalsēkalet near Martinez. Originally from wilamū in the Santa Rosa mountains. Related to clan 1, but a separate ceremonial unit.

3. wantcinakiktum (place name) at pūichekiva, and later īsilsīveyaiutcem in Martinez canyon. At one time dominated by clan 1, but evidently a separate clan. Originally from near atakī in the Santa Rosa mountains.

4. palpunivikiktum, "circle over the water" at palpūniviktum hemkī near Alamo. Originally from atakī in the Santa Rosa mountains.
   L 4a. tēviñakiktum, "round basket," at palpūnivikiktum hemkī. Originally from tevi in the Santa Rosa mountains.
   L 4b. tamulañitcum, "knees bent together," at palpūnivikiktum hemkī. Originally from paliliem hemkī in the Santa Rosa mountains.

5. wantciñakik-tamīanawitcem (place name), "very beautiful," at tūva near Fig Tree Johns. Originally from kīwil, near atakī in the Santa Rosa mountains. Relation to clan 3 unknown.

6. wakaīkiktum, "night heron," at mauūlmiī near Toro. Originally from tcīuk in the Santa Rosa mountains.

7. kauwicpaumēauitcem, "caught by a rock," at maswut helaanut near Mecca. Earlier home unknown.
   L 7a. wavitcem, "many dead branches," at awelpitcava near Thermal.
   L 7b. tūīkiktum (no translation), at tūīkiktum hemkī near Thermal.
   L 7c. panuksē kiktum (no translation), at palaīyil slightly east of Thermal.

8. telkiktum (no translation), īltcuñaloñī near La Mesa.

9. pañakauissiktum, "water fox," at mauūlmiī near Toro. The moiety alignment of this clan is somewhat dubious, but it was said by Palm Springs informants to be the same as that of clan 8.

TABLE 4

Clans Belonging to the Coyote Moiety

10. masūwitcem, "long hairs in the nose," at palhīliwit near Martinez. Originally from īlwukwinet in Los Coyotes canyon.

11. sēwahilem, "mesquite that is not sweet," at iltcuñaloñī near La Mesa. Originally from the Santa Rosa mountains.

12. wantcauem, "touched by the river," at pūichekiva near Martinez. Quite possibly this clan was related to the Pass Cahuilla wanikiktum clan but proof is lacking.

13. wīitem, "grasshoppers," at palhīliwit near Martinez. Originally from ūakī in the Santa Rosa mountains.

14. mūmlētcem, "mixed up," at palhīliwit near Martinez. Originally from ilwukwinet in the Los Coyotes canyon.

15. telakiktum (no translation), at tūva near Fig Tree Johns.

16. mūmūkwitcem, "always sick," at ūlicpatcī near Fig Tree Johns.

17. kaunukalkiktum, "living at kaunukvela," at īvīatim village near Agua Dulce. Originally from kaunukvela in the Santa Rosa mountains.

    L 17a. īvīatum, "Cahuilla speaking people," at īvīatim village near Agua Dulce. This was a subordinate lineage to clan 17; whether it was a late branch, however, is dubious. It may have been the older lineage and may have lost its ceremonial supremacy.

18. wavaīkiktum (place name in Little San Bernardino mountains), at paltēwat near Indio.

19. akawenekiktum (place name in Little San Bernardino mountains), at palsētahut near Coachella.

    L 19a. taukatim (no translation), at palsētamul near Coachella.

20. wēwonicyauam (no translation), at palmulūkalet northeast of Mecca.

DESERT CAHUILLA VILLAGES

The position of the Desert village was determined by the presence of water and proximity to food-gathering areas. Frequently favorable places were occupied by only one clan, and this would seem to have been the earlier condition. At other places where food and water were more abundant several groups might live close together and utilize the same water supply. The relation of such groups to one another varied, and any exact definition of their organization would be subject to exceptions. Often they were related lineages of one clan, who had acquired new names because their immediate relationship had become obscure, and they had moved slightly apart from each other. Where the different lineages were not too distantly related, there was usually one ceremonial head or net. Where they were independent there might be two nets, or as many more as there were distinct clans. The method of government in such a case is illustrated by examples to be given later. A consideration in detail of one such village, and a discussion in general of all the Desert Cahuilla villages and the clan affiliations of each should make this matter clearer.

Typical Village at Martinez

A typical Desert Cahuilla village of fifty-odd years ago called pūichekiva (road-runner's house) was described in considerable detail by Francisco Nombre. The informant lived here from the time he was a small boy until he was about thirty years of age when on account of a continued shortage of water the village broke up. Pūichekiva was located about one mile north of the present Martinez reservation buildings at a point one-third of a mile east of the highway and seven and one-half miles south of Coachella, Riverside county.

At present, as a result of the lowering of the water-table in the Coachella valley, the artificial well from which they formerly obtained their water is merely a dry hole about fifteen feet in diameter and four feet deep, hidden in arrow-weed and cat's claw brush. The mesquite trees which probably determined the location of the village originally have been burned and only blackened stumps remain. Other signs of habitation are faint—scattered piles of blackened rocks from the fireplaces, and a few sherds of red undecorated pottery, alone indicate that forty years ago there was a thriving village here. The area one-half mile to the southwest, where natural seepage provided the two main clans with areas for scanty agriculture, is likewise a sun-baked desert; only the diminution in density of the brush indicates that it was once cleared and cultivated. Map 2 shows the location of the houses, the irregular grouping of the clans, and the straggling nature of the village.

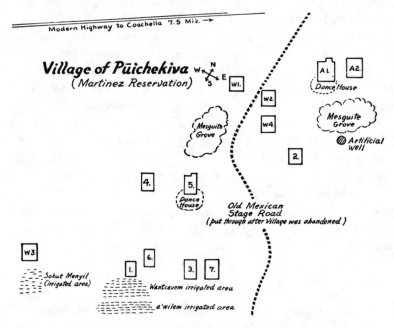

Map 3. Village of Pūichekiva.

Pūichekiva was the oldest name for the village, but it was more commonly called the wantcauem (touched by the river) village, after the first clan to settle there. The wantcauem people according to tradition originally lived in the Santa Rosa mountains. Before coming to pūichekiva they had lived alone at temelmekmekuka (earth?), which was a place three-fourths of a mile west of the highway opposite Martinez, where the Narbonne ranch is now. The two sites were only about two miles apart. The wantcauem clan was joined by the awilem (dogs) clan, which moved here from awilsīlhiwiniva (the willow tree)[114] a place about three-quarters of a mile west of the Martinez reservation buildings, bringing with them another subordinate clan, called wantciñakiktum (a mountain in the Santa Rosas).

---

[114] Originally the awilem clan lived at wilamū, a place in the Santa Rosas near Martinez mountain. Here they had lived with the autaatem clan whose members were relations of theirs. Both clans gathered wild food there and owned the territory jointly.

Where this latter group originally came from is unknown, but later when the village at pūichekiva broke up, they moved alone to Martinez canyon in the Santa Rosas and established a small village called īsilsīveyauitcem[115] (coyote?) where they lived for some time. It is probable that this was their original home before coming to the desert. One man, Pablo Siva, now living at Martinez, is a member of this clan.

The wantcauem clan, when Francisco first remembers it, had seven houses, each occupied by only one immediate family. The relationship of these families is shown in the following genealogy (genealogy 2). The numerals before the names of the individuals indicate their houses as shown on map 3. The Roman numerals signify the successive clan leaders.

GENEALOGY 2

Wantcauem Clan (houses 1–7)

It was said by the informant that hŭnava (4) had not succeeded his father as net because he lacked the qualities desirable. Hence the adult members of the clan had chosen his younger brother tcūva instead. At the time under consideration tcūva occupied the kicumnawit.[116] His uncle tcīvatō was a great pūl (shaman), the story of whose death, told farther on,[117] illustrates the political organization of the village.

The awilem (dogs) clan occupied two large houses each of which contained several families directly related. The occupants of the kicumnawit were as follows:

---

[115] This is the name Gifford gives for his fifth wildcat clan, S. Cal., 190.

[116] Dance house. The term wāmkie, of Luiseño origin, used by the Mountain Cahuilla and all western groups, was never used on the desert.

[117] Present paper, pp. 57–59.

GENEALOGY 3

Awilem Clan (house 1)

I. 1. tōkicnikictciñelnaīī
(green lightning)
+ *mūmlētcem*

- II. pulmicwammama-ī (Pedro Nombre)
  + *masūitcem*
- tahauīīsma (Quattie)
  + *wantcauem*
- sīelsōmitnikic (Antonio Sam)
  + *mūmlētcem*
- tēvenicwīava
  + wantcauem

Here the oldest son succeeded his father as net, which was the generally accepted rule. The case of matrilocal residence in this genealogy was not according to the usual custom of the Desert Cahuilla, but occurred only where the immediate family of the husband was dead, in which case he might live with his father-in-law. The occupants of the second house were as follows:

GENEALOGY 4

Awilem Clan (house 2)

I. 2. pīihutnuminma-ī
+ *masuitcem*

- kwōwethemūma (curlew reaching)
  + *mūmlatcem*
- pīihutyassiī (very active centipede)
- pūtcikiltēvilvēī (Pecho Kintano)
  + *atcatcem*

The respective heads of these two houses were second cousins, as can be seen by a glance at the awilem genealogy.[118] That no rule was observed in regard to single or communal houses can be seen by a comparison of these two clans living in the same village. To anticipate somewhat, it is of interest in regard to the branching off of the lineages, to note that the descendants of the families in house 1 now live apart from those in house 2, and while they recognize each other as relatives, the relationship was very hard to trace. The Nombres and the Kintanos on the Martinez reservation are each grouped separately, and at present usually perform such ceremonies as their annual mourning for lost relatives, independently of one another. This is due in part, no doubt, to the breaking down of the old rules, but it is also due to separation, which was a factor more important fifty years ago than it is today when roads and automobiles make such dis-

---

[118] Present paper, genealogy 6.

tances negligible. To borrow a term from zoology, the "budding off" of the lineages is a process still to be observed, and there seems to be no reason to believe that earlier processes were greatly different.

The wantciñakiktum clan occupied four houses, each of which held one immediate family. The four house-heads were a very old man, and his three grandsons, as shown below.

GENEALOGY 5

Wantciñakiktum Clan (houses 1–4)

```
                                        ┌─ 2. W. Vincente Malouis
                                        │      + masūitcem
                   ┌─ (?) killed        │
                   │      + (?)         3. W. takvic
1. W. tekemsīve    │                    └─    + akawenakiktum
   + (?)           │
                   │                    ┌─ 4. W. amūlmēīkwaiwut
                   └─ (?) killed        └─    + kauisiktum
                          + (?)
```

These were the only members of this clan alive when Francisco knew them. They had joined the awilem people before the latter left their old home at awilsīlhiwiniva (the willow tree), and followed them to their new village. The two sons of tekemsīve had both been killed before the clan came to "the willow tree," but how or when could not be ascertained.

At their old home in the Santa Rosa mountains these people were supposed to have had a net, but on the desert they were under the awilem net, having none of their own. They seem to have been largely dependent on the charity of the awilem people, for they had no agricultural territory, and were given vegetable products by the latter. On the desert the wantciñakiktum people shared the territories of the awilem clan, but they had their own territories at Martinez canyon, in the Santa Rosa mountains, and here they used to go in the spring and early summer to gather edible cactus. It was to the latter place that their three families moved when the village at pūichekiva was abandoned. The wantciñakiktum and awilem clans were not regarded as relatives, but they never intermarried since they belonged to the same moiety, an institution which will be discussed later.

The food-gathering areas of the wantcauem people were mostly in the foothills immediately west of the Narbonne ranch, near their old village of temelmekmekuka. Here at the openings of the cienegas are groves of mesquite trees, and in the canyons themselves grow many kinds of edible cactus. Besides these places they also had a few small clumps of mesquite trees nearer the village. Mountain sheep, deer, and rabbits could be hunted in any locality regardless of territorial ownership, and rabbits especially were often obtained by communal hunts. The awilem clan had gathering territories at their old ancestral home in the Santa Rosas. These they shared with the autaatem clan, whose home was at temalsēkalet and who were regarded as relatives of theirs. Probably these two clans were branch lineages of the same ancestral stock. Their spring migration to the mountains was taken together and they were under the direction of one net while thus united. This leader was the oldest net of the two clans and had the leadership only while the two clans were united. On the return to their desert homes they separated, each under its own leader. Here each clan held its own ceremonials, but the other clan always attended. Likewise, if the one clan was invited to an outside ceremony they brought the other with them. All trace of their exact relationship was lost, but the fact was well remembered, and marriage between the two was taboo on this account as well as by the fact that they belonged to the same moiety. It can be seen by this that the break between these two lineages was more advanced than that between the two divisions of the awilem clan proper, but was similar in its nature.

However, to return to the situation at pūichekiva, the awilem families also had gathering territories around their old village at "the willow tree," and scattered groups of mesquite trees elsewhere. As has been previously mentioned there was an area, one-half mile to the southwest, where natural springs allowed some agriculture. This was mostly owned by the wantcauem clan, but a small piece was owned by the awilem people. Only a few acres in all were arable and here a scanty crop of wheat, corn, beans, and squash were raised, each immediate family growing vegetables in its subdivision of the clan allotment. If this food had been their main staple undoubtedly the arrangement would have been more exact, but natural and not cultivated plants seem to have been the main dependence of the Desert Cahuilla even to recent times.

While this village was perhaps as typical as any other that might be chosen, a consideration of all the villages which existed fifty odd years ago shows that no one case can illustrate accurately all phases of their village organization. Town-dwelling, in a larger sense, does not seem to have been an old institution among any of the Cahuilla-speaking peoples, and these desert towns were in process of formation. Crystallized rules of what might be called municipal government do

not seem to have existed and it is therefore necessary to make a survey
of all the villages to see the many forces which tended toward group
amalgamation, such as need of water, and the equally numerous forces,
such as need of food, which led to dispersal. These forces can best be
discussed after a consideration of all the groups. The following data
show the general social framework of the towns among these desert
groups.

Other Villages

Tūva. The most southerly village on the desert, occupied by the
Cahuillas within the memory of living Indians, was at tūva.[119] This
village was just south of the Riverside and Imperial county line in
the latter county at Fish springs, very close to the Salton sea. Originally the telkiktum clan lived on this site, but its members had all
died when informants first remember the place. This village was
occupied by the wantciñakik tamianawitcem clan. The first word of
this name is a place name for a certain peak in the Santa Rosa mountains. The second term was translated as "very beautiful." This
is the clan of Fig Tree John, a very old and well-known Indian, who
still lives in the vicinity. Gifford[120] gives Palkausinakela as Fig Tree
John's clan name, but this was given as the place name of the site
where Fig Tree John lived later. Near tūva, at a place called
ūlicpatciat, a clan called mūmūkwitcem (always sick) lived before
Francisco remembers; he was told of them, but they, like the telakiktum people, were all dead before he was born. At tūva there was a
spring with enough water for domestic purposes but not enough for
irrigation. Fig Tree John's clan was never very numerous and nearly
all have died. The Mexican surname used by Fig Tree John and his
sons is Razon. About fifty years ago their clan moved to paltūkwic
kaīkaīawit (the first two terms are pal, water, and tūkwic, blue; the
last word was not translated), which was just north of the Riverside
and Imperial county line at a place marked on the Indio Special Map
of the Geological Survey, "Fig Tree John," about two miles north of
their old village.[121] When the clan moved, it had nine houses and
one dance house where the single clan-chief, or net, lived. There was
a warm spring here with enough water for domestic use but none for
agriculture. Lack of water prevented a numerous population in the

---

[119] Barrows (*op. cit.*), applies the name Tova to Agua Dulce, a point a
few miles to the north. As this is the most southerly desert village he mentions it is possible that he was given the name of the older village.

[120] S. Cal., 191.

[121] For location of villages see map 2.

southern part of the Desert Cahuilla territory, and informants stated that the northern groups around Indio and Coachella were always the larger.

Iviatim Village. At Agua Dulce was the īvīatim village and here was also a warm spring. Two clans lived in the village with the spring in the center between the two groups of houses. The kaunukalkiktum clan (kaunukvela, a place in the San Jacinto mountains near Bautiste, kiktum, ''people'' or ''living at''), when Francisco first remembers it, had seven houses, one of which was the kicamnawit or dance house where the net lived. The other clan, or perhaps branch clan, was called īvīatim (a term which the Cahuilla use for a person speaking their language, in other words ''Cahuilla speaking people.'') These people had seven houses, but they had no net nor dance house. They were under the leadership of the kaunukalkiktum net, and formed one ceremonial group with them. Why the village should have been called after the subordinate group is not clear.

Palpūnivikiktum hemkī. Proceeding toward the north, about two miles east of Alamo, was a village called palpūnivikiktum hemkī[122] (water, circling over, living at, territory). There was an artificial well[123] here, in the midst of the palpūnivikiktum houses, which were ten in number including the net's kicamnawit (dance house). This well gave water for domestic purposes but none for irrigation. The palpūnivikiktum clan was said to be the oldest here, its net had nominal control over the two other clans living in the village, and the ceremonies of all three clans were under his supervision. The tamulañitcum (knees bent together) clan had six houses but no dance house. Their houses were roughly grouped together beyond those of the palpūnivikiktum clan. The remaining clan in this village was called tēviñakiktum (round basket) and occupied four houses, also ouside the central group, and the occupants had no independent ceremonial organization. All three clans, or clan and two branch clans, had different localities in the desert where they gathered mesquite beans and the like, but they had one locality in the Santa Rosa mountains, due west of Alamo, called ēova, where all three gathered cactus in the spring and summer. This was regarded as the old home of the original group before the people went to the desert. The three clans

---

[122] See Barrows, op. cit., 26–27, for a description of the desert wells.

[123] The two names given by Barrows, op. cit., 34, Lawilvan or Sivel, meaning cottonwood trees, were not remembered by informants. Palsīkal (small water hole) was given as an old name for this village.

regarded one another as relatives, and intermarriage was not allowed. From circumstantial evidence it would certainly seem that the three clans were lineages of the same original group, and were still ceremonially attached to it.

Pal hīliwit. Two miles south of the Martinez reservation buildings was the village called pal hīliwit (wide water). A large spring here was owned by the mūmlētcem (mixed up) clan. This clan had eight houses, one of which was the kicamnawit occupied by the net. It was regarded as the oldest clan here and had nominal control over the water, the two other clans using it only by permission. This spring furnished water for a little agriculture in a few favorable spots, and was used by the children of all three groups to swim in during the summer. Adjoining the houses of the mūmlētcem clan were seven houses occupied by the masūwitcem (long hairs in the nose) clan. This clan was independent of the former group and had a net and a dance house. The third clan at this place was called wīitem (grasshopper) and at the time under consideration occupied five houses, in some of which several families lived. Like the other two this clan was ceremonially independent, having its own net. As all three clans belonged to the same moiety there was, theoretically at least, no intermarriage. Informants questioned stated that these clans were never related, but lacking genealogies the veracity of this must be left in abeyance.

Temalsēkalet. A village called temalsēkalet (earth crack) was located one-half mile south of the Martinez reservation buildings, at a place which is not within the reservation and is still occupied by members[124] of the group under consideration. This clan was called autaatem (high up) and when the informant first remembers them, they occupied six houses, one of which was the dance house. Having their own net they performed their own ceremonies; their probable early relationship to the awilem clan, and the joint ownership of mountain territory by the two clans, have already been discussed.[125] These houses were grouped around an artificial well, and in several favorable places the individual families carried on agriculture in a small way. Mesquite thickets in the vicinity of the village were owned communally by all the families of the clan.

Pūichekiva. Proceeding from south to north, the next village to be encountered is that of the main informant at pūichekiva (road-

---

[124] August Lomas, one of Hooper's main informants, was a member of this clan. See The Cahuilla Indians, present series, 16:338–340, 1920.

[125] Present paper, p. 48.

runner's house)[126] which has already been described at some length
(pp. 43–49).

Mauūlmiī. At Toro, fifty odd years ago, there was a village called
mauūlmiī. Two clans lived here, the largest was called wakaīkiktum
(night heron) and occupied ten houses, three of which were communal.
As to the other clan there is some doubt. Francisco Nombre said that
it was called kauisiktum (from the rock). A clan of this name lives at
Palm Springs and informants there denied that part of their clan
ever lived at Toro. Alejo Potencio, the net of the Palm Springs
group, said that the clan at Toro was called pañakauissiktum (water
fox), but that they had all been dead a long time. According to Francisco, when he first knew them they had six houses and shared the
well with the wakaīkiktum people. Each of these groups was an independent ceremonial unit, having its own net and dance house. Each
had its own gathering territories and small areas where cultivated
plants were grown. The marriage relationship within this village is
not known, but it is probable that they belonged to the same moiety—
which would tend to make the village exogamous. The wakaīkiktum
people originally lived at tcīuk back in the Santa Rosa mountains,
then at panūksī at the head of a canyon about seven miles south of
Indio, and later came to mauulmiī. The pañakauissiktum clan was
probably the first to live there and dig the well, although the past history and exact status of this clan is far from clear. Thirty years ago
the sēwahilem (mesquite that is not sweet) clan moved here from their
village near La Mesa.

Iltcuñaloñī. At La Mesa, to the west of the highway, was a village
called iltcuñaloñī.[127] This was its later name, its original name being
kelewutkwīikwinut[128] (wood hanging down). Two clans lived here,
the largest being the sēwahilem (mesquite that is not sweet) clan.
The members of this clan occupied one large communal house in which
lived six individual families. These were as follows:

I. ♂ (?) | ♀ (?)

II. pahawut	heul (navel)	tcinkum (crooked)	akasem	lauis (Louis?)
+ *wakaikiktum*	+ *wakaikiktum*	+ (?)	+ *autaatem*	+*autaatem*

[126] Barrows' Sokut Menyil (deer moon), given as name of village at Martinez, is a spot where surface water occurred. It was used by a wantcauem
family for agricultural purposes. See map 3, present paper.

[127] Barrows' Temalwahish (dry earth), which he gives as the village at
La Mesa, was said to be a brushy area one mile south where the La Mesa
people hunted rabbits. The area to the east of the highway from La Mesa
was called tahaukalumal.

[128] Gifford, S. Cal., 190, gives Ekwawinet as the name of this village.

Of the other clan, telkiktum, only one old man wakatīi (cow's udder)
was alive and he lived in a house by himself. This clan was of the
opposite moiety to that of the sēwahilem, and informants stated that
intermarriage had been customary. As long ago as akasem remembered this clan had no net, but wakatīi acted as paha (or master of
ceremonies) for the sēwahilem clan. This approach to moiety reciprocity is an interesting analogy to the practice that prevails among
the Serrano, and is also the only example of the employment of the
term paha among the Desert Cahuilla south of Palm Springs. Whether
this represents a survival of an old custom, or was due to the fact that
wakatīi was the sole survivor of his own clan, is uncertain.

The sēwahilem clan had gathering territories around the village,
and up in the mountains to the west where they went in the spring.
At a comparatively late time the nonhaīam clan moved to this place
from their earlier home at Indian Wells. At this time the latter clan
had seven houses, and while previously they had been under the
atcitcem net at kavinic (Indian Wells) when they moved they
appointed the oldest man of their clan as net and became an independent ceremonial unit.

Maswut helaanut. All the villages heretofore considered were
located west of the present line of the Southern Pacific railroad, but
there was also another line of villages to the east of this artificial
boundary. Maswut helaanut (ceremonial matting spreading) was
the most southerly village in this group and was located in the famous
Painted canyon, about two miles northeast of the modern town of
Mecca. One clan lived here, called kauwicpamēauitcem (caught by
the rock), and when first seen by Francisco Nombre they were occupying twelve houses, several of which were communal. This was the
clan of Cabezon, whom the Mexican authorities made head chief or
captain over the desert groups as well as over those directly west of
the San Gorgonio pass, if desert informants are to be believed. Cabezon was already the head of several other villages or "rancherias"
which were apparently occupied by branch clans of the kauwicpamēauitcem people. It was this fact, probably, together with his personal
ability, that led the Mexican authorities to appoint him as leader over
the hitherto ununited desert communities.

The case is paralleled by similar examples among the Mountain
Cahuilla, where under Mexican control certain clan leaders gained
power over other groups which prior to Caucasian interference had
been completely independent. According to Francisco, the elder

Cabezon was appointed by the Indians themselves, just prior to the advent of the Mexicans, to settle disputes between local groups over territories, women, and blood feuds, which at times led to bloodshed. This, however, is not in agreement with any other informant from the desert or mountains, all of whom agreed that these captains were Mexican innovations and not aboriginal. Francisco said that Cabezon the elder was the first head chief on the desert, and that later he was given "papers" and a horse by the Mexican authorities. The "papers" gave him nominal control over Cahuillas and Serranos on the desert and all native peoples from the San Gorgonio pass to Los Angeles. His nominal jurisdiction did not extend to the Cahuillas or Serranos of the mountains nor to the Luiseño save the group at Saboba. When Francisco was a boy he remembers a band of "Yuma Indians" (probably Mohave) thirty strong who came to obtain a paper from Cabezon appointing one of their members as captain. Cabezon, then a very old long-haired Indian, accompanied these men to Los Angeles to obtain the commission. On the death of Cabezon his authority passed to his son. Considering the fact that Francisco was so positive that Cabezon was the first supreme captain, and the fact that all other informants attributed his position to Mexican origin, it seems most probable that the office was not aboriginal.

Tūīkiktumhemki. Halfway between Mecca and Thermal, and just east of the railroad, was the village of tūīkiktumhemki occupied by the tūīkiktum (no meaning) clan. At the time under consideration it had seven houses, but no dance house and no net. All ceremonies were conducted by Cabezon in the kicumnawit at maswut helaanut. This clan was entirely subordinate to Cabezon's clan, although living several miles away. Like the former group they had food-gathering territories of their own in canyons of the Little San Bernardino mountains to the east. Very close to this place at palmulūlukalet lived the wēwonicyauam clan but the last member of this group died long ago. This clan was of the opposite moiety to Cabezon's group, but their interrelations are not known for they became extinct before any modern informant clearly remembers.

Awel pitcava. Situated about three miles east of Thermal at the foot of the Little San Bernardino mountains was the third village under Cabezon's control. This was the awel pitcava (dogs ?) village, occupied by the wavitcem (many dead branches) clan. They owned six houses but had no net or dance house. All ceremonies of this clan were likewise performed by Cabezon. This group was never large and its members are now all dead. The main food-gathering territories were in the eastern hills.

Palaiyil. The fourth and last of the villages controlled by Cabezon was called palaiyil (water turtle), and was located about three miles northeast of Thermal on the eastern edge of the Colorado desert. This was the home of a small clan called panuksēkiktum, occupying three houses some fifty odd years ago, and now extinct. They had no net or dance house and were likewise dependent on the kauwic pamē̄auitcem clan for all ceremonies. It is highly significant that all these four groups which were ceremonially united were of the same moiety. Marriage between any of these four was not permitted. No data on their exact relationship could be obtained, but it seems probable that some of them at least were collateral lineages of one clan. It is also possible that we might have here the beginnings of a true tribal organization, but in the light of the data on similar groups to the west the former hypothesis seems more likely.

Palsētahut.[129] Farther on to the north, where the Cabezon reservation is now located, was the village of palsētahut (salt water). This place is just east, across the railroad tracks, from Coachella. It was occupied by the akawenekiktum (place name for long ridge in the mountains east of Indio) clan. They had seven houses, and one kicumnawit where the net lived. They were affiliated with a branch of their clan living in the next village beyond. Their territories were around the two villages and toward the eastern hills.

Palsētamul. Near the village of palsētahut, also on the territory now included in the Cabezon reservation, was a village called palsē̄tamul (salt water agave). This village consisted of nine houses owned by a collateral lineage of the akawenekiktum clan. These people called themselves taukatim (?), and were so known to the akawenekiktum people at palsētahut. Outside clans called the inhabitants of both villages by the latter name, however, and the two groups regarded themselves as close relatives. Both belonged to the same moiety. Apparently the taukatim clan was a branch lineage of the akawenekiktum clan, that had moved away and acquired a new name. The akawenekiktum clan proper, at palsētahut, had the net and dançe house and performed all ceremonial functions for both villages. Names of the house-owners some fifty odd years ago were obtained but the informant could not give the relationships of each. He was positive, however, that they were actual blood relatives. The gathering territories of the two villages seem to have been contiguous.

---

[129] This is the same as Barrows' Palsēta at Cabezon.

Paltēwat. The last village occupied by people who are here classified as Desert Cahuilla[130] was one-half mile northeast of Indio, at
paltēwat (water found). The wavaaīkiktum (place name for a canyon
in the hills east of Indio) clan lived here and had seven or eight
houses at the time under consideration. One of these was the dance
house, and was occupied by the net. They likewise were an independent ceremonial group. Their food-gathering territories were
mostly in the vicinity of the village.

Village Summary

While there were doubtless other settlements in this expanse of
territory, which extends from the Salton sea in the south and the Little
San Bernardino mountains in the east, to the Santa Rosa and San
Jacinto mountains in the west and a line between Indian Wells and
Indio in the north, they were small or temporary and were not remembered by informants. The foregoing is merely a cross-section, taken
as nearly as possible to the time the Mormons settled San Bernardino
in 1851,[131] and as such, presents a transitory phase just prior to the
breaking down of aboriginal desert society. The indications are plain
that the male lineage was the unit, and that these units were perforce
joined on the desert by need of water, which was present only in
limited areas. Had this condition been one of extremely long duration it is hard to believe that a more elaborate form of village government would not have arisen, but such does not seem to have been the
case. Either these people differed from nearly all known groups in
not needing any central village political organization, or else, which
is more probable, the formation of these larger villages composed of
several independent clans was a comparatively recent process.

Group Leadership

Where the various groups in a village were only remnants of once
independent clans or where there was reason to suspect that they were
collateral lineages of one clan, there seems to have been one net, or
ceremonial chief. From conditions such as these, true villages and
village chiefs might eventually have arisen, but the evidence already

---

[130] The Palm Springs Cahuilla and surrounding groups are discussed under the
Pass Cahuilla. This has been done for purposes of convenience and because of
certain cultural affiliations to be discussed later.

[131] This arbitrary date was taken because the main informant remembered
that event clearly. His father, who did some work for the newcomers, was
paid in ''sweet salt'' (sugar), and the unique happening was remembered.

presented does not indicate that the Desert groups had attained so stable an organization. Informants questioned knew nothing of village chiefs as such, but always referred to the chiefs as the nets, or clan ceremonial leaders, and where there were several independent clans in the village said there were as many nets as there were clans.[132] Thus it seems evident that the clan was the fundamental unit and was as a rule independent. Village unity seems to have been of the slightest, each clan defending its own areas as best it might. Where affairs concerning the various clans of a region had to be discussed and decided upon, it was done either by an informal meeting of the various nets, or by means of a messenger who obtained the opinions of the various clan heads. Undoubtedly alliances and junctures were effected in the case of attack by a large band of raiders, but such a thing seems to have been rare and modern informants can remember few such occurrences. A case of this kind is mentioned by Hooper,[133] and a similar tale was told me at Palm Springs where I presume she also obtained it. In such a hypothetical case informants, lacking actual knowledge, were doubtful as to the leadership, some saying it would be the oldest net; while as many others said the net never led in war, and that some man known as a bold fighter would have nominal leadership. The actual case related by Francisco Nombre, in which his father killed a malevolent shaman some seventy years ago, probably casts more light on the basis of leadership and degree of unity existing among the Desert groups than can any amount of conjecture. It moreover shows very clearly the utter lack of central organization in the village of pūiche-kiva, at Martinez, which has been discussed at some length previously.

When the informant was a boy of about nine years, the man who lived nearest to the artificial well was a very powerful shaman called tcīvato (goat), belonging to the wantcauem clan. He was a very pleasant old man, with a remarkable beard from which he acquired his name; but he was very dangerous, for instead of curing people he always killed them. According to the informant he was "the greatest pūl (shaman) in the whole world" and he was feared by all the Desert Cahuilla. When all the shamans would gather to show their curing and malevolent powers he always performed last and challenged all pūalem (shamans) to kill him by their powers, but none was able to harm him. This, tcīvato said, was because he had a teaīawa (spirit)

---

[132] The īvīat village previously described seems an exception to this rule, but here the two clans were ceremonially united and quite possibly were collateral lineages of the same original group.

[133] Hooper, *op. cit.*, 355–356.

on every side of him to guard him from hemteteaīawa (their spirits). One of the wantciñakiktum men called amūlmeīkwaiwut (agave eater) once told tcīvato that the latter was killing all the people and that he must stop. Tcīvato only laughed at this, but the next day when amūlmeīkwaiwut was leading a hunting party he was struck between the shoulders and became very sick. The wantciñakiktum people had shamans come from Alamo, Torros, and Martinez, but they were helpless and three days later the victim died. He had been killed by a teaīawa (spirit or pain) sent by tcīvato, and none of the other shamans could suck it out. The latter did not say he had done it, but all the shamans and people knew it was he.

All the people were alarmed at this and two men, one called tcūva, of the wantcauem clan, and a man of the mūmlētcem clan from palhīliwit village, went to see all the clan leaders from the Salton sea to kavinic (a village at Indian Wells). They talked over the situation with each of these and all agreed that tcīvato should be killed. They also discussed who should do the deed, and decided on pulmicwammama-ī (poor will fluttering) who was net of the awilem clan. He was a strong man and very brave. When this was decided, the two delegates returned and told pulmicwammama-ī of his appointment, so that evening he and a shaman of the wantciñakiktum clan named Vincente Malūī, called on tcīvato. They were invited to eat and spend the night there, and accepted the invitations. Tcīvato's wife was away, but two young daughters about ten and fourteen years old were with him. About eleven o'clock when all the family were asleep, pulmicwammama-ī arose, took a long stone pestle, and crushed tcīvato's skull. This he did very completely for he feared tcīvato might not die.

As soon as he saw tcīvato was dead Vincente Malūī went to the body and at the head of the bed he found many small feathers of hawks, ravens, humming birds, and other bird species, with the skin of a gopher snake. When he saw these he knew that they were the materials tcīvato made into teaīawa (spirits or pains). He trampled them into the ground, whereupon, Francisco's father told him, a sound like thunder arose. Vincente Malūī said that tcīvato was dangerous only while awake; when he was asleep he was helpless and so they had been able to kill him. In the morning people from all around came to see the body; the informant and his mother were among them. Later in the morning they put the body on a pile of brush and burned it, burning his house at the same time.

The wife of tcīvato was a wakaīkiktum woman from Toro, where she was visiting at the time of her husband's death. She sent for the children and stayed with her own people. All the nets of the Desert Cahuilla, including the wakaīkiktum net, had consented to the execution and had agreed to annihilate the entire wantcauem clan should any of them seek vengeance. Nevertheless, some of the younger members of the wakaīkiktum group, without the consent of their net, armed themselves and made threats of avenging their kinswoman's husband. The awilem people feared they would be attacked, so each of the clans sent three or four young men armed with bows and arrows to pūichekiva (the informant's village) to guard it against attack. They remained on guard for several days and nights and then as nothing happened returned to their respective villages. No more trouble resulted from the incident.

This example, and others like it, substantiate the words of the informants and show the very small amount of any sort of central authority existing on the desert. The material poverty, peaceful nature, and strenuous food gathering which characterized the southern California Shoshoneans must have contributed to their ability to exist with so little organization. In spite of all these factors, however, informants agreed that life was far from tranquil on the desert, for each little group was suspicious of the other and petty quarrels, usually between individuals, resulted. Vengeance appears to have been largely an affair of the immediate family, and no clearly classified code of blood vengeance or payment for wrongs inflicted was obtained. The interesting and widespread institution of singing songs against enemies in other clans will be presented later in a description of desert ceremonies. The settlement of such quarrels depended on the leaders of the respective clans.

Clan Leadership

The Net

The net acted as ceremonial leader, judge, and to a limited extent as general executive for his clan. Whether or not he led in fighting is very dubious and probably depended on his general qualifications. Theoretically the clan leadership ran in the direct male line, a man being succeeded by his eldest son. Actually the adult members of the clan, of both sexes, decided on the qualifications of this successor, and

might often pass by the legitimate heir for a more capable younger
brother. In case of a net having no adult successors a brother might
succeed, although it was considered more ethical to keep the office in
the same direct line. The qualifications for a net are rather general:
he should be a good speaker, smart, fair-minded, and a good ceremonial
manager. He must know the ritual and traditions of the clan, as well
as the boundaries of all territories owned by them. Informants stated
that a woman could never become net, and no cases of the sort were
obtained. Ownership of property of any sort does not seem to have
been necessary, and there seems no reason to believe that the net was
possessed of more material wealth than any other family head within
the clan.

The Dance House

The office of net is marked by two distinctions, his occupancy of
the ceremonial dance house, and his possession of ceremonial objects
which are rolled up in a sacred mat. At present the dance house or
kicamnawit may be built much in the shape of a modern rectangular
shed with a ridged roof, but it is always made on a greasewood frame
and covered with either arrow-weed or the fronds of the native palm
(*Washingtonia filifera*). In size it varies a great deal. It is distinguished from the ordinary dwelling house by having the front end
enclosed with a semicircular wall of the same material that covers the
house, leaving a space for dancing and a fire. No such round dance
house as that at Palm Springs was seen elsewhere.

The Sacred Bundle

At the back of the house is a small room where the net keeps his
maswut (a mat made of fine mountain grass) in which are kept objects
sacred to the clan, and impedimenta used in their ceremonies. Maswut
is associated with the sea, and two informants translated it as "seaweed," describing it as a mat about three feet wide and four to six
feet long made of tules sewn together. Originally maswut was supposed to be made of tules from the coast, but now they use a sharp-
pointed grass which grows in the mountains. The maswut, the objects
rolled up in it, and the room itself are very sacred, and the latter is
entered ordinarily only by the net and his immediate family. The
use of maswut, or mīsvut, is mentioned in the creation story given by
Hooper[134] for the Desert Cahuilla. Hooper apparently got this crea-

---

[134] Hooper, *op. cit.*, 326–327.

tion story from the mother of August Lomas, now dead, who was a member of the autaatem clan living at temalsēkalet near Martinez. The section referring to the maswut, or as Hooper writes it, mīsvut, is unusually suggestive.

When they were ready to hold the fiesta, Coyote told them he knew what to make effigies of and offered to go to the end of the world to get it. Mīsvut (a seaweed) was what he got. It grew far under the water. It had probably been made in the beginning for this purpose. . . . . During that first fiesta, the Isil people wanted some more mīsvut. When they went to get it, the water bubbled and made a queer noise. It was talking to them, but they could not understand it at first. Soon they understood that Mīsvut was asking them what they wanted. They told him they wanted the big stone, sharvōvōshal, which was to pound things on, more mīsvut, and a pipe made of rock. The mīsvut was always kept rolled up and had a stone pipe in it. Net had given a feast in order to get this pipe, for Mukat had told them that this was necessary. This pipe is used only at fiestas and can be obtained only after the net has given a feast.

This should be compared with the Palm Springs version of the creation[135] to see the even more pronounced affiliation of maswut with the ocean. The rolling up of the stone pipe on the maswut is identical with the case described at Palm Springs,[136] where the sacred objects wrapped up in the ceremonial matting form the center or "heart" of the big house, the distinguishing possession of the net, and therefore the most important possession of the clan. Even today the maswut bundles, belonging to intact clans or religious groups ("parties") formed around a clan nucleus, are regarded as very sacred and cannot be handled by the ethnologist.

The possession of a very sacred object, such as the stone pipe mentioned by Hooper, seems to characterize only certain clans, others either being without similar objects or else refusing to speak of them. All groups however which had a net and formed an independent ceremonial unit, owned a bundle of maswut in which were wrapped eagle feathers and narrow bands made of flicker feathers. Francisco Nombre had such a bundle of maswut in which were kept eagle plumes, the skin of the shoulders and breast of an eagle rubbed very soft with a stone, and a skirt of eagle feathers called elatem. The last object was not used on the desert for the "eagle" or "whirling" dance distinctive of the western Shoshonean groups, but appears to have been a later addition to the bundle and was sometimes presented to the net of another clan on the death of one of his family. Feathers from elatem were also used to decorate the images that were burned. The awilem clan does not seem to have owned any specially sacred object,

---

[135] Present paper, pp. 130–143.   [136] Present paper, p. 128.

such as their relatives of the autaatem clan had in the sacred pipe. This object may have been lost, or again the possession of such an object may denote the clan which represents the oldest line of direct descent from the original ancestral group. This latter theory is purely hypothetical, for the clans are so broken up at present, and the maswut concept so hard to obtain from any but the oldest people, that a comparative study of clan relationship and contents of ceremonial bundles appears impossible. This maswut concept was found to apply not only to the Desert Cahuilla but also to every other Shoshonean group investigated by the present author—that is to all divisions of the Cahuilla, the Serrano, the Luiseño, and the Cupeño. In each of these groups it was associated primarily with two things, the ceremonial impedimenta of the clan chief and the making of figures for the image-burning ceremony.

Only the main factors concerning the leadership of the clan among the Desert Cahuilla have been given, but the more detailed aspects of the position can be best brought out by a study of the ceremonies among these and neighboring groups. These points are discussed in their order but it seems well at this place to discuss the remaining officials of the immediate groups under consideration.

The Paha

The paha,[137] already mentioned, was known at Palm Springs, and by all groups to the west, where he is associated with the boys' initiation or manet dance, at which the jimsonweed drinking plays a prominent part. This ceremony was not performed at all on the desert, where it is called "the war dance" for no very obvious reason. Whether the term paha was generally used by any of the desert groups south of Indian Wells in aboriginal times is open to some doubt. Francisco Nombre, by far the best informant interviewed, said that the term paha was not known by his clan, or by those south and east of Martinez, and in the course of three weeks' intensive questioning never contradicted himself on this point. Other informants from these extreme southeastern groups confirmed him in this regard. On the other hand, Jolian Lopez, a sĕwahilem clan member from Toro, said that his clan as long as he remembered had always had a paha from a clan of the opposite moiety. This suggests the system of reciprocity between intermarrying clans common to Serrano, Cupeño, and

---

[137] The word paha appears to be of Luiseño origin, meaning a snake called the Red Racer (*Coluber flagellus frenatus*). The term has the same connotation among the Cupeño, and among the three Cahuilla divisions.

Luiseño as well as Cahuilla. There is no doubt that the term paha[138] was known to the villages around Coachella; but it also seems equally clear that the villages south and east of there were without such an official or title.[139] According to Jolian Lopez and akasem Levi, both of the sēwahilem clan, the paha was sometimes chosen by all the people, and each clan had its own. This clashes with the actual case cited, but they could reconcile the two versions only by saying that wakatīi (the paha from the other clan) was chosen on account of his fitness, not because he belonged to a clan of the opposite moiety. A paha, according to these two informants, must be a man of forceful personality who can maintain order at all ceremonial functions. He must be feared by all people, for to disobey his instructions would bring death to some one in the group. He notified outside parties of ceremonies performed by his clan, gathered food from all his members, and supervised its preparation and division to guests. On his death it was customary, but not obligatory, to appoint a son or close relative in his place. As in the case of the net, the paha was always a man, never a woman.

The takwa

Hooper, in her description of the mourning ceremony at Palm Springs, speaks of the ceremonial official designated as takwa being employed on the desert. This title is not employed among the desert groups south of Indian Wells, and many of these people do not know the term. Francisco Nombre had never heard it, but said that some relative of the net, either male or female, divided the food among the guests. This person had no special title, but guests on entering and seeing the division taking place would say "takwac nikul," meaning "he or she is dividing food." This division of food is always the main duty of the takwa in the mountains and it is highly probable that the special title arose from this general expression still retained on the desert. Jolian Lopez and akasem Levi, the two informants who told of the paha, both said that the takwa as a special assistant was not known south of Indian Wells, but was so distinguished at Palm Springs and among the Mountain Cahuilla.

---

[138] Gifford, S. Cal., 187, states that each group or clan among the Cahuilla had a paha. This is due to the fact that the term has come to be applied to the ceremonial assistant in general, in spite of the fact that the actual duties of the paha were usually highly specialized.

[139] Hooper, *op. cit.*, 328, also makes no distinction, in regard to possession or non-possession of a paha, between all the Cahuilla groups. Her description of the duties of the paha, however, applies to Palm Springs only.

The Pūalem

The shamans[140] or witch doctors, called pūalem, were in no sense clan or tribal officials, but undoubtedly exerted a strong influence on the groups with which they lived or came in contact. The case already cited of tcīvato, the malevolent shaman at Martinez, is a good example of this. According to informants, shamans are born, not made. When a youth was six or seven years old he would have sick spells which would be doctored by a shaman (pūl), who would understand that the boy was to become a pūl himself.[141] Later when the boy has grown up to an age of seventeen or eighteen a vision comes to him in the night, without his seeking it, and tells him to dance before the people the next night. For three nights he dances before all his clan in the kicumnawit and all the people know he is a pūl. After that he performs all the duties of a shaman, curing sick people by sucking "pains" or "spirits" from their bodies. This subject has been treated more fully by Hooper,[142] but it merits a more extensive study than it has yet received as there are still a good number of practicing shamans on the desert and their esoteric methodology would be extremely interesting. The concept of imitative and contagious magic is strong, and many of the troubles and feuds among these people arose over alleged bewitching of people or food crops. The shamans play a considerable part in the various ceremonies, determining whether occasions are propitious or not, and singing their own songs and dancing their special dances at others. The fundamental characteristic of the shaman however is individualism, and each one has his own songs, dances, cures, and methods of poisoning or bewitching. Not every clan has a shaman and there are no rules in regard to their numbers. There seems to be no feeling that the possession of this power is inherited by a shaman's son, nor were any cases of women shamans recorded. The shaman rarely or never is the man who must remember the songs and traditions of the clan, this duty belonging primarily to the net.

[140] Hooper, *op. cit.*, 333–339, gives a longer account of shamanism on the desert.

[141] I do not believe that such spells are connected with epilepsy or any congenital defect, for of the six or seven desert shamans seen all appeared to be physically normal.

[142] *Op. cit.*

The Hauinik

A voluntary assistant in this last duty was called hauinik or singer, and this name included people of both sexes. Among the desert groups there was no special ceremony to teach the boys to sing, but those who enjoyed it or had natural abilities in this line would listen to the old people until they had learned all the songs. When they had done this they were called hauinik. Older informants on the desert spoke very sadly of the fact that none of the younger people nowadays cared to learn the songs, saying that when they died the songs would die with them.

These were the officials, if such they might be called, of the most southeasterly of the three Cahuilla divisions. It can be seen that, aside from the clan head or net, there was really no person of authority among them. Life was localized, and the slight power was centralized in the patriarchal or family head. Such a loosely organized society was undoubtedly subject to much shifting about, and the personality of the various nets and shamans must have played a great part in determining the troubled or peaceful nature of life among the people. Opposed by outsiders, villages or geographically contiguous clans seem to have had some slight feeling of sharing a common cause, but any definite organization or tribal sense seems to have been lacking.

THE ORGANIZATION OF THE CLAN

In the course of the foregoing external description enough has been said to give a fairly good idea of the importance of the clan, and its relation to the other phases of aboriginal desert life. It has been stated that all members of a clan traced their descent through males from a common ancestor,[143] and a careful investigation of genealogies bears this out. In its complete form the Desert Cahuilla social unit consists of a direct line of male descent, in which theoretically at least the oldest son succeeds his father as head, and the clan includes all collateral lineages for an uncertain number of generations back. Females born in this group are included, and always maintain their clan or lineage name, although on marriage they become ceremonially affiliated with the husband's clan. Since strict patrilineal descent prevails, the children of such women belong to the husband's clan.

---

[143] Gifford, S. Cal., 187.

GENEALOGY 6

Awilem Clan

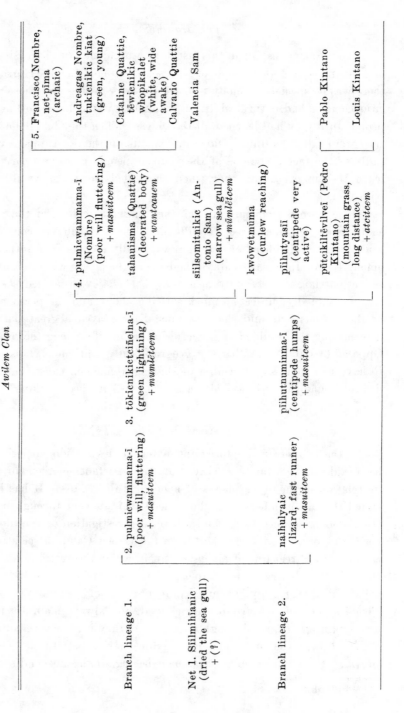

The exact nature of the woman's affiliation to the husband's clan is not entirely clear, but she seems to become an integral part of its ceremonial activity. How much contact she maintained with her own clan was dependent on the distance separating her husband's village from her home village. A clan among these peoples, then, included in its ceremonial activity all people born into the group, and women who were married into the group. As a considerable sexual dichotomy prevailed in regard to the more esoteric duties in the clan, the woman's part seems to have been largely that of gathering, preparing, and serving food, although certain of the older women sang and danced at most ceremonies. It is possible of course that remnants of almost extinct clans may have been assimilated or adopted into other active clans, but no cases of this sort were noted among the Desert Cahuilla, and considering the strictness with which they cling to their paternal names it seems improbable. The "party," or religious organization of unrelated clans, found among the more westerly peoples (the Luiseño especially), does not seem to have been known on the desert. This "party" organization seems to have been due to disintegrating mission influences to which the Desert Cahuilla were not subjected.

The composition of one apparently typical Desert Cahuilla clan, the awilem, "dogs," at pūichekiva, is shown in genealogy 6. Two main lineages that of late years have been conducting separate ceremonies, compose this clan. The split between the two apparently occurred at the latter village where the ancestors of the Nombres, Quatties, and Sams lived in one communal house, and the ancestors of the Kintanos in another. These families live on the Martinez reservation but conduct independent ceremonies, though they sometimes unite for larger "fiestas." All vaguely knew that they were relatives, but the exact relationship was only remembered by one man, Francisco Nombre, the hereditary awilem leader. With his death all exact knowledge of the relationship will vanish. This situation is probably identical with a great number of other such separations or divisions of collateral lineages, and indicates the way in which separately named lineages, and in time, new clans, are formed. It is highly probable that the autaatem clan is another offshoot of this same stock, for the groups regard each other as relatives and formerly united in food-gathering expeditions to their old mountain territories under awilem leadership. But here all actual trace of relationship has been obscured by time. Other more fragmentary genealogies bear out the male lineage composition of the clan, but none shows so clearly the division of the lineages and the recent assumption of English and Spanish names. Most of the latter were given during the early period of white contact, in many cases while the Southern Pacific railroad was being built across this part of the desert and the natives were employed as laborers. Such names are today transmitted in modern European style.

Examples of Nominal Separation and Ceremonial Affiliation

A condition occurring at temelmekmeka, the village where the wantcauem clan formerly lived, is worthy of note. The name of this clan as already stated means "touched by the river," and according to informants from Martinez, part of this clan were several times washed out of their homes by cloud-bursts in the San Jacinto mountains which swept down Martinez canyon. This portion of the clan came to be nicknamed wanicōcem, or "washed out." Later this term came to be applied only to the females of the group and girl babies especially were called by this title. This suggests the Serrano custom of giving different group names to the men and the women in the same clan,[144] and is somewhat analogous to the Colorado river Yuman clan system where the clan name is borne by the women in the clan. Whether this name was applied to the women married into the clan as well as those born into it, was not positively remembered, but was believed to be the case. Likewise the men of the wantcauem clan were in the habit of gathering their best mesquite beans and taking them to the wanikiktum clan near malkī (Banning) at White Water. Therefore the other clans near the wantcauem clan often called the men of this clan "wanikiktum" and the women "oem." In the light of this last information, it seems quite possible that the wantcauem clan was a branch of the wanikiktum clan, the "wani" or "washed out" portion of both names applying to floods of the White Water river. More information from either of these two groups would probably clear the matter up. The use of such nicknames, however, is of importance in showing the possible application of Yuman sex-limited clan names, as well as the prevalence of nicknaming among all these groups.

A somewhat simpler case of clan division occurred within the memory of Francisco Nombre, when the akawenekiktum clan at palsētamul (near Coachella) divided, one branch moving to a near-by.

---

[144] Gifford, S. Cal., 180–181.

site, and assuming the nickname taukatim (no translation). The former group retained the clan leader and dance house and carried on all ceremonies for both villages. Only the two clans concerned recognized the two names; all other clans termed the inhabitants of both villages akawenekiktūm. The two divisions concerned, and outside clans as well, regard the two as being related to each other. Both divisions are apparently extinct, so genealogies could not be obtained.

This seems a clear case of lineage division, probably due to crowding, and informants said that such occurrences were formerly common. For this reason there were certain affiliations between separate groups, so that when one was invited to an outside ceremony they always brought the other, and both participated in the same ceremonies. The four separate lineages, each occupying a village, which were all under the leadership of the central kauicpamēauitcem clan, thus acted as one unit in all ceremonial affairs. Such may have been the relationship between the kaunukalakiktum clan and the īvīatim lineage at the īvīatim village near Agua Dulce. In this case, however, the fact that the village was known by the name of the subordinate lineage, which also meant ''Cahuilla people,'' makes it extremely doubtful whether the active lineage was in reality the oldest. It is quite possible that the ceremonial leadership, due to personnel, may have passed from the original lineage to the more active younger branch. Similar cases of linkage existed at the palpūnivikiktum hemkī village, near Alamo, at pūichekiva near Martinez, and at palsētahut, previously discussed, near Coachella. Such related or collateral lineages might live in the same village, or in near-by villages, but the nature of the relationship was usually considered to be one of blood, and not of marital or ceremonial affiliation. The fact that such ceremonial groups usually consisted of persons of the same moiety is strong verification of the native belief. Complete genealogies would of course be highly desirable in all these cases, but as most of the people concerned are dead there is little chance of obtaining them. Certainly the Desert Cahuilla do not seem to have stressed moiety reciprocity in ceremonies as was the case among the Luiseño, Serrano, Cupeño, and to a certain extent the Mountain Cahuilla; and as a result ceremonial linkage between clans was usually due to blood relationship. To say that the sole basis of all such Desert Cahuilla groupings was remote relationship would be unwarranted, but it seems probable in most cases. Geographic contiguity and consanguinity of the branch lineages actually forming one ceremonial clan would be expectable.

The Moiety Among the Desert Cahuilla

As is the case among most of their western neighbors, all the clans of the Desert Cahuilla are grouped in two major divisions, called respectively the wildcat (tūktum) and coyote (istam) people. In late aboriginal times prior to white interference there seems to have been a strict rule of marriage to prevent endogamy in either group. All informants agreed that prior to the last generation a coyote person might only marry a wildcat person and vice versa. At present the rule has no force but the custom seems to have held until recent times. Out of twenty-eight actual cases of marriage recorded,[145] twenty-six were in accord with the rule of moiety exogamy, and two included the pañakauissiktum clan whose moiety affiliation is doubtful. This is strong confirmation of the schematic pattern given by the informants. The feeling against marriage within the moiety was very strong and, unlike most of the neighboring dichotomous groups, informants said that the rule held even with people who spoke another language, should they marry among the Cahuilla. Thus a Cupeño or Serraño man would have to marry according to his moiety if he came to live with the desert people. As none of the actual cases show such inter-tribal[146] marriages it is impossible to verify this statement, but the informants were very emphatic in affirming it.

When asked the reason for this dual division informants are naturally at a loss. Some said that for an istam to marry an istam would be like relatives marrying and therefore would be highly improper. Others said that the rule had "been from the beginning" and therefore must be followed. Hooper's creation story tells of this division,[147] as does the Palm Springs creation story given here.[148] A comparative study of these two stories shows that there is really a division of nearly all nature between the two creators, one half belonging to the older mūkat who is tūktum, and the other half to the younger temaīyauit who is istam. This is very similar to the dual division of the universe among the Miwok although the classification is not so clear-cut as in the latter case.[149] Informants stated

---

[145] The majority of these cases are to be found in the clan and village genealogies already presented.

[146] The word tribal is here used for convenience to denote a different linguistic group, not a unified political group such as the word usually implies.

[147] *Op. cit.,* 327.

[148] Present paper.

[149] E. W. Gifford, Miwok Moieties, present series, 12:142, 1916.

that all animals and birds were thus members of one or the other moieties according to their respective creators. Lists of these however are difficult to obtain at present although the short list from Palm Springs shows this classification to a slight extent.[150] This seems to indicate that the personal names of the individuals were governed by their moiety affiliations, for these names are based on natural objects which of course belong to either the istam or the tūktum division.

Thus when another clan is invited to a ceremony at the house of an istam clan, they sing the following song on entering:

> selim, selim (California woodpecker)
> Built a beautiful green hemkī (place)
> All is moving around.[151]
> suwalwal (great blue heron)
> anawut (?)
> tamaswut (grebe).

Thus everyone hearing the song knows that the dance house is owned by an istam clan, for these birds are of the istam moiety. The names of the birds have nothing to do with the personal names of the owners of the house but merely indicate the moiety they belong to.

Likewise when the visiting clan enters the dance house of a tūktum clan they also sing a similar song.

> kwowit (shore bird, probably curlew), pumūis (cormorant)
> Built a beautiful green hemkī
> All is moving around.
> kwōwit, pumūis.

These words are chanted over and over again, and show the moiety of the people who own the dance house. At the annual mourning ceremony similar moiety songs are sung, to the accompaniment of much wailing in memory of the dead people. It can be seen that there is no very clear distinction between classes of birds or animals in placing them in one or the other moiety categories, for the birds in both these cases are water birds.[152] The informants however insisted that the two moieties were thus designated by the different birds, but refused to give a fuller list on the ground that only a few distinctive names were remembered and were always used in this connection.

---

150 Present paper, p. 109.

151 Denoting festivity and action.

152 It must be remembered that though these Cahuilla are a desert people they live close to the Salton sea where water birds of many species gather.

Another song, identical to one sung by the Mountain Cahuilla, was sung as a joke, usually to the children. An istam person would sing:

> tūkut tūkū weña peīelic tcūn
> pīke lilima eweīapē!
> *Wildcat, having his arrows in a bag,*
> *Does not look good to us.*
> īsil tahat īsīveña peīelic tcūa
> pīic atacama aaīepī.
> *Coyote, brave man, having his arrows in a bag,*
> *Looks very good to us.*

Each of these lines is chanted over and over, with a rising and falling cadence as many times as desired. This sort of joking between the moieties was a common thing, but according to informants was always good-natured and did not have the sting or vituperative quality that the enemy songs the clans sang against each other possessed.

According to Francisco Nombre, the four oldest animals were great pūalem or shamans; these were hūnwit (the California grizzly bear), iswit[153] or tūkwit (the mountain lion), tūkwut (the jaguar),[154] and īsil (the coyote), who was the youngest. The first three were created by mūkat and were tūktum; the last, īsil, was created by temaīyauit and was istam.

No data in regard to any actual moiety organization were secured, and there are no indications of moiety chiefs or officials of any sort. Gifford has stated that moiety reciprocity occurred in the making of the images for the mourning ceremony,[155] but according to my informants such was not usually the case. Various clans were invited for different nights of the week-long ceremony, and the clan which was

---

[153] The term iswit is used by the Mountain Cahuilla at present as a synonym for tūkwit or mountain lion. The Desert Cahuilla say that it means ''wolf'' but no informant questioned had ever seen this animal in the flesh. Dr. Joseph Grinnell, in 1925, told me that so far as he knew no wolf had ever been taken west of the valley of the Colorado river or south of the Tehachapi. Mr. Joseph Dixon has since examined the skin of a timber wolf, reputed to have been killed in San Diego county, and is inclined to regard it as an authentic record.

[154] The inclusion of this species agrees with information from the Diegueño received by C. Hart Merriam, Journal of Mammalogy, 1:38–40, 1919–20. See also, W. D. Strong, Journal of Mammalogy, 7:59–60, 1926. The Desert and Mountain Cahuilla use the term tukwut for the jaguar (*Felis onca*). Only the old men knew of the animal. Francisco Nombre gave a description of tūkwut, that does not admit of any other species, saying that it was a cat larger than the mountain lion, with round spots and a long tail. Its tracks were larger than the mountain lion's and it was regarded as more dangerous. The last animal of this species he remembered, was killed back of Palm Springs about 1860, by an Indian who was attacked while stalking deer. Francisco saw the fresh, spotted hide, and the long curved claws which were used for a dog collar. Similar skins were presented to his father for use in the image-burning ceremonies of his clan. More data on this animal are given under Hunting Rules.

[155] Present series, 14:187–188.

invited on Saturday night made the images. According to Francisco
Nombre and other informants, the moiety affiliation of this clan was
of no importance. It might be a related group; for example, the
awilem clan usually made the images for the autaatem people and vice
versa. Both of these were naturally in the same moiety. However, it
might be a clan which was affiliated by intermarriage in which case
moiety reciprocity would seem to be employed, but this is mainly a
matter of chance. To say that moiety reciprocity never occurred
would therefore be incorrect, but that it was a generally recognized
and universal desert custom seems contrary to the data at hand.

To sum up the place of this dual division among the Desert
Cahuilla, it appears that regulation of marriage is its primary function, distinction of clans in regard to names and for purposes of joking
being secondary. Theoretical considerations in regard to its wider
significance will be discussed hereafter.

MARRIAGE

As has been previously shown, moiety exogamy was an essential
factor in regulating aboriginal desert marriages, and the actual cases
bear out the schematic pattern very strongly. Even more important
to the native was avoidance of marriage with either maternal or
paternal relatives so far as known. Other rules seem to have been
lacking, and marriages might occcur between people in the same
village, if both moieties were represented there, or between separate
villages. Propinquity seems to have been the main factor in this
regard. Actual cases show a few marriages between the Palm Springs
people and those around Martinez, but informants stated that in the
old days the people south of Indian Wells never married persons from
the groups around Banning, while the groups south of Martinez did
not as a rule marry with the Palm Springs group. This was not a
set rule but was due, informants said, to the distances involved. It is
of course not at all probable that such marriages never occurred for
there was some intercourse between all the desert groups, but the
twenty-eight actual cases show no such distant marriages. Likewise
marriages with the Serrano around Mission Creek or the Cupeño of
Warner's ranch, do not seem to have been at all common.

Theoretically, at least, people from these two linguistic groups
would have to marry according to their moiety should they marry
Desert Cahuilla individuals; that is, an islam (coyote) Cupeño man

must marry a tūktum (wildcat) Cahuilla woman, and a wahīyam
(coyote) Serrano man would have to marry a tūktum Cahuilla woman.
Whether this was actually the case I do not know for no old cases of
this sort were discovered. Neither the Cupeño nor the Serrano have
this feeling in regard to marriages outside their own linguistic group.
The situation in general was very similar to that of our own society,
where people that are in contact with each other naturally tend to
marry while those farther away and less well acquainted do not, but
there was no rule against such unions should chance or personal
inclination defeat distance.

A man would never marry a girl from his father's clan, primarily
because of the nominal relationship and the fact that their moiety
would be the same. He could however marry a girl from his mother's
clan provided she was not a close relative of his mother. This at first
glance seems to cast doubt on the actual relationship of all the clan
members for these marriages were not uncommon. On second consideration however it is obvious that in a clan including all collateral
branches for five generations back, there would be a considerable
number of individuals who would be fourth or fifth cousins and therefore according to a strict blood-family interpretation, not actual
relatives. It was with these individuals that marriage was possible.
Patrilocal residence was the general rule, but cases of matrilocal
residence did occur, especially where the immediate family of the
man was dead. Informants were unanimous in agreeing that the
children were always given the clan name of the man, even in the
hypothetical case that he was the sole survivor of his clan and living
with his wife's people.

Children might be betrothed in infancy in which case presents
of food, baskets, and game, were exchanged between the two families
at frequent intervals. It was more common, however, for them to
wait until the boy was seventeen or eighteen years of age and the girl
twelve or thirteen or perhaps older. Then the match was arranged
between the respective parents. The boy's mother goes to the mother
of the girl she has selected for her son, and tells her that she desires
the girl to help her do her work and to gather mesquite beans. At
this time she takes no presents. The girl's mother asks time to consult with her husband; if he agrees they both consult the wishes of
the girl. The mother is mainly influenced by her feeling for the
boy's family, the father by the food-gathering and hunting abilities
of the prospective son-in-law, and the girl presumably by her feeling

for the boy.   The father of the girl if the match is satisfactory notifies the boy's father.

A female relative, not the mother of the boy, goes with presents to the bride's home and brings her back to the house of her future parents-in-law, where she leaves her outside.   This relative then calls the boy's mother who leads the girl into the house, and seats her with her face in a corner, and her back to the boy's family whose members have been assembled at a feast.   The girl's family in order not to embarrass her and to let her become acquainted with her new relatives, stay away.   The boy is brought in and seated beside the girl, likewise with his back to the assembled relatives.   Food is given them and they are left there to get acquainted.   Not until they begin to talk to each other are they allowed to leave this position.   There were no special songs and no dancing on this occasion, although as many relatives of the boy as the immediate family could feed were invited. The mother-in-law gave the girl no advice or counsel as she had already received this before leaving, from her own mother.   That night only one cover was allowed the bride and groom, for otherwise, my informant said, they might be too shy to sleep together.   In the morning the girl's mother-in-law shows her the duties that she must perform and she becomes a working part of the household.

If it happened that the girl was unhappy she might run away to her parents.   The mother-in-law would go and get her back once or twice but if the girl persisted she was allowed to remain, and her family returned the presents they had received.   If a girl had no children within a period of two or three years and the husband was willing, his parents would return the girl to her home.   At any time the girl might leave, in which case presents were returned; but if there were children the latter remained with the man's family and no presents were returned.

Up to within the last fifteen years thirty dollars in American money was the regular price paid for a girl.   Now they say contemptuously that a girl is only worth ''a paper,'' to wit, the marriage license.   A girl baby is now referred to as ''a paper.''

If a man married an elder sister and was good to her and gave food and presents to her family, he might be given the younger sister should the older one die.   This was done by the parents of the girl so as to keep the boy in the family, and was not compulsory.   Likewise a woman might marry her dead husband's brother,[156] but this

---

[156] Hooper, *op. cit.*, 354, says that a widow might only marry her husband's older brother.   I unfortunately obtained no data on this point.

was entirely a matter of choice. Two cases were remembered where a man had more than one wife. In the first case the man married a woman whose young cousin came to live with them. The first wife was old and weak and asked the younger cousin to stay as her husband's second wife so that she could help around the house. As the young cousin liked the husband she did so, all three living together in agreement. In the other case an older sister had had no children although she had been married many years. She asked her younger sister to come and live with them as a co-wife. The husband had several children by this second wife. No other cases of plural wives were remembered by desert informants.

A similar tale to that recorded by Hooper[157] was also told me, I suspect by the same informant, Francisco Nombre at Martinez, who said that in the old days about which his grandfather told him, a man might go to a girl he desired and take her, fighting off her relatives with his bow and arrows. Should the girl refuse him saying he was too old, he would kill her, for that was a deadly insult. This is in the nature of a legend but is interesting as a repetition of Hooper's information.

HUNTING RULES

As before stated the four most important animals were regarded as shamans, and when any of them were killed a night of singing and dancing in their memory must occur. The grizzly bear (hūnwit) was called hempūwitcū, translated as great-great-grandfather, the mountain lion (tūkwit or iswit) was a relative of uncertain degree, the jaguar (tukwut), and especially the coyote (īsil), were great shamans, but not relatives. When the tracks of a bear were encountered, the older men and women very respectfully asked him to go back to the hills and to hide, lest they be forced to go after him. Many years ago a small party on their way toward Los Angeles encountered a female grizzly and two cubs, near the modern town of Beaumont. The oldest man talked to the bear and told her that they meant her no harm, and as she was a relative of theirs she should not bother them. The mother bear thereupon went peacefully on her way. Shortly before this a bear that had killed two people near Cahuilla was killed by a party of Palm Springs Indians. All that night they danced and sang over the body, just as the people near Martinez did over the body of a deer.

---

[157] *Op. cit.*, 355.

About fifty years ago an Indian back of Palm Springs, while stalking a deer with a deer's head disguise, was attacked by a jaguar which he killed. The claws of this animal were very large and were used to make a dog collar; the skin was saved to decorate images of the dead. Francisco Nombre said that people from Cahuilla (the town of pauī in the San Jacintos) several times brought jaguar skins down from the mountains as gifts at his grandfather's fiestas. These skins he described as considerably larger than those of the mountain lion with black spots on a tawny background. The tracks of the jaguar, he said, were fairly common in the canyons of the eastern Santa Rosas, and he often saw them although he never saw a live jaguar. The male's tracks were much larger than a mountain lion's, while the female's track was about the size of a large male mountain lion's. This assumed sex difference may be a pure rationalization but he was firm in his belief that most of the tracks attributed to the jaguar were very large. The old people made a regular practice of following mountain lion and jaguar trails in order to uncover and eat the remains of deer which these animals buried. Aside from the more or less accidental case at Palm Springs, no record of the jaguar's or mountain lion's attacking anyone was secured. The grizzly, on the other hand, was regarded as very dangerous and when a man-killing individual came into the neighborhood the men of the interested clans joined together and in a group hunted him down. It was considered better to run the bear out of the country than to kill him. Otherwise the bear was unmolested.

When an individual killed a deer he took it to the net's house, i.e., the dance house. If there had been no recent death in the clan all the people would collect and sing all night, eating the deer in the morning. If it was the first deer killed after a death in the clan, the net would take the deer and give it to the clan living closest to him. These people would then sing all night before eating the deer. Part of this deer was usually given to the slayer. When a coyote or wildcat was killed by a younger man he let it lie where it fell, and on returning to the village he would tell some old man or woman of its whereabouts. The old person would then go and get the game and use it as he pleased. Only very old people could utilize these two animal species.

The first deer a young man killed was given to the clan of his mother. On the communal hunts for rabbits and small game a boy never took his own kill home, but gave it to some other family, usually

his mother's. Parents could not eat the game killed by an unmarried
boy. Should the boy eat his own game, or even eat off of the utensil
on which it was cooked he would probably die. When a boy was
about to marry his father told him that he must provide game for the
girl's parents. When he was first married his parents prepared his
game for the girl to eat; they might eat what she left. Later the
parents and their married son could safely eat game killed by the
latter. The husband alternated in providing game for his own and
his wife's family. These rules were regarded as vital and had considerable vogue up to late times. Modern sicknesses are now laid
by the old men to the non-observance of these and a great many other
food taboos.

NAMING OF CHILDREN

The ceremony called hemteūlūwen, was a clan affair and usually
occurred when there were several children of approximately the same
age to be named. It took place in the dance house to which were
summoned all members of the children's clans and the clans of the
children's mothers. The age at which the children were christened
depended on the abundance of food possessed by their families. If
they had enough provisions for a feast when the children were four
or five years old they would have it then, otherwise they would wait
until the children were nine or ten years old. Informants stated that
if a child reached the age of thirteen years without being formally
christened, he went without a name save for such nicknames as he
might acquire. The actual naming occurred about midnight in the
course of an entire night's singing and dancing.

The names to be given were decided upon by the net of the
children's clan, and were those of dead ancestors in the clan. No
name already possessed by a living person might be used. The
knowledge of the clan names is a duty of the net. No one was told
the names until the net, holding the child high in his arms, danced
slowly in the center of the dance house, and suddenly shouted the
name three times. All the people assembled repeated this name. It
was very dangerous and ignominious to have an "enemy" clan get
possession of the names, hence it sometimes happened that a false
name was given at this time, the real name being bestowed in secret
when the child was fourteen or fifteen years of age. The boys were
named for the male ancestors, the girls according to a series of female
names customary in the clan. Examples of these names are as
follows:

Boys' names:

> pīihutnuminma-ī, centipede humps.
> amūlmēikwaiwut, man who eats agave.
> takvic, marksman with a bow.

Girls' names:

> pūtcikilauvaa, dried berry flour (eaten only by nets).
> wīivitavinic, aprons.
> pūtcikil kekūwine, dried berry flour, acorns on cord (bullroarer).

These were names given in the awilem clan and according to my informant were used by no other clan. The girls are usually given names connected with plants or household appurtenances; the boys, animal, bird, or insect names.[158] No exact rule of this sort however seems to be remembered. Several older informants stated that the moiety affiliation of the individual was indicated by the name but, as before stated, an exact or exhaustive dual classification of names was not secured.

The acquisition of new names was not limited to children, for a man might receive a new name at the same time that his child was given its first name. This was to show his greater dignity and importance. In this manner a man might receive as many as five names. Thus Francisco Nombre was named netpīma (an archaic term) as a child, when his oldest daughter was named he was called nentahemiñahīwinut (with the nets), and later when his third son was named he was called nentiniña pakhalwic (gone in among the nets). This name is not indicative of the sex of the child christened, and while the father is known by this name he also retains the others, especially the name he received as a youth. A boy was never given his father's name or vice versa.

It does not appear that any one of the several names a man might receive was more sacred than the others. So-called "enemy" clans hearing any of these names would incorporate them into their songs, to the mortification and danger of the owner of the name. Even though the individual had already changed his name, songs were sung about any old or new name discovered. After the names were

---

[158] Hooper, *op. cit.*, 349, states that songs about plants were sung when a girl was named, and about animals for a boy. My informants did not mention this, but a survey of the names secured shows a marked tendency to give names according to this system. Among the Paviotso of the Great Basin the majority of girls were named after flowers (Lowie, Notes on Shoshonean Ethnography, Anthr. Papers, Am. Mus. Nat. Hist., 20:272, 1924). In a list of nineteen eastern Tewa personal male names given by J. P. Harrington, only two connote flowers or plants; while of twenty female names sixteen of them are plant or flower names (Am. Anthr., 14:476, 1912).

given presents of food, baskets, deer skin, or rarely, ceremonial matting were given to the invited clans and in the morning they returned home.

CEREMONIAL DEFORMATION

All the girls of a clan were tattooed on the chin when they were in their tenth or eleventh year. To this ceremony was invited the clan of the mother, and the actual tattooing was performed with a cactus thorn by the mother's sister. A black (tūl) paint obtained in trade from the Yuma Indians was put in the scratch. A design consisting of straight lines or angles was used. According to informants there was no moiety distinction in the design. Boys of approximately the same age, sometimes a year younger, were also decorated at this time. These boys, not necessarily the net's sons but of promising material, had the nasal septum pierced and three links of deer bone inserted in the opining. Later these boys had their ears pierced with cactus thorns. The piercing of the nose was called multavavepī, that of the ears for both sexes hemnakalmūmhanwin. The decorating of the boys in this manner was only done on rare occasions when a boy of great promise appeared and when his clan was able to afford such a ceremony. Such boys, said my informant, nearly always became famous as leaders or hunters, and the bearers of such distinctions were honored even among the Mohave and the Chemehuevi. The tattooing of the girls, however, and the piercing of their ears, was a regular ceremony. This ceremony was accompanied by a night of singing with a feast. Should the holes pricked in the ear lobes fail to stay open they were not reopened again. These customs have long gone out of vogue and I did not see actual evidences of any of the above-named practices among the present population.

ENEMY SONGS[159]

There seem to have been two main times for the singing of enemy songs between the clans. These were after the tattooing and nose-piercing ceremony just described, and after the naming ceremony for children. While informants gave these two occasions as the formal time for such rivalry between assembled clans, or for the singing of one clan against an absent clan, it would appear from other statements that such singing contests might break out at any ceremonial

[159] Hooper, *op. cit.*, 345, gives several examples of such songs, but does not mention where they were obtained.

gathering where the so-called "enemy" clans might come in contact. The descriptions of these affairs are vivid and animated. The singing often ended in a hair-pulling or free-for-all fight between the women, but the men according to Francisco Nombre never came to actual blows. The net of the ceremonial house, with his assistants, always kept the peace as far as the men were concerned. Fig Tree John, whose tales seem to me more picturesque than accurate, is said to tell of such affairs where several people would be killed before morning, but all informants with whom I actually talked denied this.

Usually two clans would sing, the one against the other, encouraged by the other people who might be there. One man assisted by several women would dance and sing songs using the names of rival clan members and heaping ridicule on them in any way possible. The man usually led and the women followed. The clan thus sung about might after a few minutes ask to sing, in which case they were granted their turn and answered their enemies in the same manner. The moral victory went to the clan which sang the most songs using personal names and ridiculing their rivals. In the heat of the contest individual women would try to sing each other down, often ending in direct vituperation or personal combat. Large crowds assembled where such a contest was expected and in anticipation of such an event new songs were composed and practiced by the rivals. Such a verbal battle might last through an entire night, the rivals taking turns in singing and dancing until one or the other relinquished the field through exhaustion.

Lines for such rivalry in the desert seem to have been mainly geographic, the clans of one locality singing against the clans of another locality. For example, the awilem clan usually sang against the clans or branch clans under Cabezon, located to the east of Coachella. In this manner the rivalries were usually between groups less often in contact and not to any great degree interrelated by marriage. Such rivalries in more ancient times may have led to open warfare, but it would appear more likely that they sublimated such warlike tendencies as the people may have possessed into more harmless channels.

Girls' Adolescence Ceremony

This ceremony called hemelūniwen, is said to have been performed individually for each girl at the time of her first menses. The girl's father would notify the net of the occurrence and the net would send for the clan to which the girl's mother belonged. They came that evening and assisted in the ensuing ceremony. A fire was built before the net's house; when the ground was thoroughly heated the fire was removed and a hole dug about as long as the girl and about two feet deep. Into this was put arrowweed, then the girl, and then more arrow weed, over which hot sand was poured. All night long the girl's clan and the guests danced and sang around the pit, the hot sand being renewed at intervals. In the morning the girl was taken out of the pit by her mother and washed in warm water. A white paint or powder made from a mineral obtained in the mountains was put all over her head.

For a period of two or three weeks after this she was kept under strict surveillance. She was not permitted to wash in or drink cold water, or to eat dry food, salt, or meat. Should she hit or touch any person she might cause the individual suffering from rheumatism or paralysis. A wooden "comb" was provided to scratch her head with, for should she use her fingers it would cause dandruff and loss of the hair. According to Francisco Nombre there was no harm in her looking at things, for her glance did not bring bad luck. Especially must she stay close to her home all through this period. These rules applied thereafter to all her menstrual periods, and her health and that of her husband depended on her care in obeying them. Above all, she must never touch her husband at such a time. When a girl had passed through this ceremony the first time she was eligible for marriage.

Hooper gives several other details[160] concerning this ceremony but does not give the exact locality to which they apply, the main differences from the above account being her statement that the ceremony lasts three nights, that the pit is heated by stones, and that there was a similar ceremony at the second menstruation when the girl's chin was tattooed. In regard to the latter, no informant questioned by me remembered such an occurrence as a second ceremony and the two oldest informants were sure that the chin was tattooed at an earlier time as previously described.

There was no boys' adolescence ceremony practiced by the Desert Cahuilla, according to my informants; this was a westerly ceremony occurring among the Mountain Cahuilla and their neighbors, called by the people of the desert the "war dance." Francisco Nombre told me that once in his grandfather's time the awilem clan tried

---

[160] *Op. cit.,* 347–348.

this mānet or "war dance," but the people became sick and it had never been tried again. He, and all other desert informants, were positive that it had never been regularly used on the desert.

CEREMONIAL KILLING OF EAGLES

Eagles' nests which might be built in the mountain territories of these groups belonged to the clan owning the nest locality, and were carefully guarded. When the eagles began to frequent the nest, a guard was stationed on a near-by eminence to watch and protect them. The clan was notified when the eggs were laid and a feast was held. When the watcher observed rabbits and other game being taken to the nest, or saw that the young birds had become well feathered out, he notified the net who was regarded as the actual owner of the birds. A party of five or six men would then go to the nest to obtain the young. If there had been a recent death in the clan the trip would be sad, at other times there was singing and rejoicing and a feast and dancing would mark their return. The young eagle or eagles would be put in a cage in the net's house and would be carefully fed by all his relatives. When the young birds had attained their full plumage a fiesta was prepared and all neighboring clans were invited.

The clan owning the eagle would invite one other clan in to sing the songs specially relating to the eagle and to his death. All the other clans would join in the singing and dancing. Young and old joined in this ceremony and the dancing and singing lasted all night. The eagle was rolled in the ceremonial matting, maswut, and carried in the slow circular dance by members of the net's immediate family. In the early hours of the morning "the eagle would scream and die," probably killed by gradual compression of his lungs. The body was then carefully laid down by the fire and the dancing stopped. All the people wept and wailed loudly in sorrow at the eagle's death.

In the morning the eagles were skinned and the feathers kept by the net. The bodies were buried in the cemetery where the people were buried. It may be presumed that prior to any Christian influence the bodies were burned, but informants were vague on this point. The skin was rubbed with a stone until it was very soft, and then put away with the net's ceremonial impedimenta, rolled in maswut. Sometimes a skirt of the tail and wing feathers was made which was called elatem, and this was kept in the ceremonial bundle. It was

not used in the elaborate "whirling dance" of the more westerly
Shoshoneans but was worn at the eagle-killing.   Young eagles, or
elatem, might be given to closely allied clans in case of a death among
their members.   This usually occurred when the deceased was a relative by blood or marriage to the net giving the eagle.   Such gifts
however seem to have been rare.   Feathers which were saved after
the eagle-killing ceremony were used to decorate the images of the
dead and were burned with them.

Francisco Nombre told me that in his grandfather's time the
eagle ceremony had been rare and very simple, but in his father's
time it had become more customary and elaborate among the desert
clans.   He added that stories of the eagle and respect for the bird had
always been common among the people of the desert.

Ceremonies for the Dead

At one time, according to desert informants, it was customary to
quietly burn the house and body of the deceased the morning after
the death.   The burning of the body was called pemtcūtwem, and
of the house hemtcūstanwen.   Now, the body is buried shortly after
death, but the burning of the house and personal possessions of the
deceased does not occur until a week later.   Prior to the burning,
members of the clan of the deceased and such other clans as come
with presents, sing all night.   According to one of the desert informants, in the old days food was so scarce and the difficulty of giving
the mourning ceremony a year later so great, that the relatives of
the deceased avoided this first ceremony by quietly burning the corpse
and its possessions before news of the death traveled.   The spot where
the bodies were burnt was called tūlwenive or niskicweniva, "where
they burnt the bodies."

About one year after the death of an individual, occurred the
image-burning ceremony, hemnūkwin, or, as the burning itself was
called, nūkil.   This ceremony was usually so arranged that it would
include mourning ceremonies and image-burning for more than one
person.   The ceremony lasted one week.   To it were summoned all
clans related to the deceased by marriage, and all the clans who had
brought presents to the clan of the deceased at the time the dead
person's possessions were burnt.   Each clan was invited to arrive on
a specified night in order not to have too large a crowd for the entire
time.   The ceremony begins on Monday, and for the first three nights

the shamans (pūalem) of the local clan and near-by clans dance in order to find out whether the time is propitious, and to communicate with the spirits of the dead and propitiate them. Thursday night an invited clan led by their hauinik or singer, sings all night long. Friday night another clan repeats this ceremony. On Saturday night the clan invited to come at that time sings all night, some of them making the images of the deceased which are to be burned in the morning. According to my informants, there was no definite rule in regard to the clan which made the images. Their moiety made no difference whatsoever, but the fact that they had been invited for Saturday night made them automatically the makers of the images. The songs sung at this time are said to be about a number of shore birds, especially those whose feathers were used in the ceremony. At this time each clan on arriving sings its moiety song. Also a sad song about the death of mūkat, lasting nearly all night, is sung if the deceased is a man. If a woman is being mourned for, a song about menyil (the moon) and her ascent to the sky is sung.

The images are made to represent the dead persons and are about five feet high with long narrow bodies. The bodies were originally made of reed matting, the ceremonially important maswut, and were dressed in deer skins. Men were always represented with bow and arrow, women with baskets decorated with eagle feathers. Likewise the image of a man was decorated with an eagle-feather headdress provided by the net. Many ornaments or decorative skins and feathers were attached to the images, but were usually taken off by the members of the invited clans before the actual burning occurred. The modern images are dressed in European style and the body framework is made of wood.

Early Sunday morning the images are carried out of the dance house by close relatives of the deceased, while other relatives distribute food and presents to the guests. The images are carried around the kicumnawit (dance house), and taken to the place of burning, niskicweniva, where they are put on the fire and burned. As soon as they are completely burned the ceremony is at an end and the guests depart. According to native theory the dead, whose images have been burned, are not further to be mourned for and their names are not to be mentioned.

The Migration Legend of the Sewahilem Clan

Told by Akasem Levi (sēwahilem) at Torres, January 25, 1925, through Gabriel Costo, interpreter. Akasem said that his father told him the story, having learned it verbatim from his father.

Aswitseī (eagle flower) stopped first at Happy Point (near Indian Wells) where he left the imprint of his elbows and knees in the rock. From there he came south along the San Jacinto mountains to a place west of Toro; he was weeping and he pushed a hole in the ground with his staff which is still there. Then he settled at kōtevewit (in the mountains), and here he brought out the tobacco which he carried. A man named kauicwīkil lived near there on the edge of the desert. Aswitseī went to visit him, when he got there he sat down and stayed all night. He was changed so that he looked very old and wrinkled. In the morning aswitseī went to a spring and bathed. He remained there a long time and no one could find him.

Now kauicwīkil had a beautiful young daughter, and he told her to go to the spring and look for their guest. When she got there she saw aswitseī, who was now changed into a young, good-looking man. The girl fell in love with him; she went back to the house and sat on his bed, refusing to move from it no matter how hard her father tried to make her do so. Then aswitseī came back and they all laughed. He married her and stayed at kōtevewit. Kauicwīkil had no food except cactus which he ate raw, so aswitseī told him to get some wood and bake mescal stalks. The former did so but did not cook it well and so aswitseī told him to bake it for two nights and a day. Aswitseī was a great hunter and killed all kinds of game. Later he had a son, who grew up quickly while his father was away, but kauicwīkil killed him.

Soon, however, there was another son named teaīwimitcī, who grew up to be a young man. His mother then told him that he would have had a play-mate except for his grandfather's cruel deed. So teaīwimitcī killed his grand-father. This enraged the relatives of kauicwīkil and they planned to destroy aswitseī and his family. The latter heard of this and he sent his wife and son away to the desert. Led by kauichotelīwut, his enemies surrounded the house of aswitseī in three rows and called to him to come out. He did so, for his house was on fire, but he dodged so rapidly that no one could hit him though all shot at him. He got through the three rows and then as he had a bow but no arrows he leaned on it and wept. Then he found the tracks of his wife and his mother-in-law. The former had had another child while she was running away. So they all wept together and settled at tūva (near Agua Dulce). Here although they had no food they managed to live.

Soon however their enemies, led by kauichotelīwut, came to the spring to gather wood for bows. Aswitseī hid in a cave but his enemies found the two women and the baby. [It is not clear what happened to these various sons.] The grandmother told kauichotelīwut that the child was a girl and lay on it so that they could not see it was a boy. They had hidden the tracks of aswitseī, but his enemies saw some food they had thrown out of the cave and knew there was a man there. They told him to come out and when he did they did not kill him but listened to his story.

Then aswitseī and his wife had another son whom they called netamnaka (big chief). He was the ancestor of the sēwahilem people. Then they had two more sons whom they called respectively sūetpūleve (fallen star) and kislamnet (money chief). From the cave at tūva they moved to naīalwawaka (near Martinez). Here they all lived with aswitseī. One day an eagle came over the village; he tried to light on the houses of the eldest sons but could not, so he finally lit on the house of kislamnet, who always owned the eagle after that. There was at this time a very mean man in the family who was called sūetpūleve; like the white people he was always trying to get other people's land. He left the village however, and moved away into the desert. So did kislamnet, who was also mean and fought with all the other brothers. Later he came back and set fire to the houses of netamnaka and sūetpūleve.

Then these two families moved away to kāvinic (Indian Wells), but soon they moved back to Torres. They were married and had many children. A tribe from the mountains came and killed nearly all of them, but it began to rain, so some of aswitseī's people survived. Then the water from the south began to rise and all the people moved ahead of the water toward Palm Springs. They settled near kāvinic, which the water did not reach. Here they lived for some time; then the water began to go back, gradually at first and sometimes rising again. All the people separated along the edge of the water to catch fish.[161] The ilwawaka people called themselves wakwaīkiktum, and the sasañē people called themselves sasañakiktum (this is an extinct clan). The sēwahilem people also went off by themselves. Of the latter four men were alive: netpakiva, the father, and three sons, esūtūlikic (grandmother black louse), hauitemnomiī (quail across mountains), and kelyicanūka (cold ear). The three sons went fishing and the youngest built the fire, but his two brothers gave him none of their fish. They invited him to come with them again but he refused. He told his father how his older brothers treated him and they both wept. Then they went away together and hid. The next morning the two older brothers returned and could not find their father. They were puzzled and the older brother said, "kelyicanūka has told our father how we made him build the fire but gave him no fish to eat, only the net to hold." So they left the place and went away to the southeast and joined other people who lived there. The father and son came out of hiding and following the retreating water they finally came to temalamnaka where they lived. From these two were descended all the present sēwahilem people.

---

[161] Along the western border of the desert next to the foothills of the San Jacinto and Santa Rosa mountains are located a number of small stone pens about six to twelve feet long. These are locally known as "fish traps," and it is claimed they were once used for this purpose when the Cahuilla basin was flooded. The local Indians corroborate this story in their legends, and Akasem Levi told me that the "fish traps" west of Martinez formerly belonged to the awilem clan. As Francisco Nombre, of the latter clan, had made the same statement previously on the basis of his clan myths, the independent confirmation of Akasem is interesting. This method of impounding fish employed by the Papago is mentioned by Lumholtz, New Trails in Mexico, 258, 1912; also for the Tarahumare: Unknown Mexico, 400, 1902.

III. THE PASS CAHUILLA

Environment

The above designation has in general been loosely applied to those peoples who lived in the vicinity of the San Gorgonio pass and spoke the Cahuilla language, in contradistinction to the Desert Cahuilla already described and the Mountain Cahuilla of the Santa Rosa and San Jacinto mountains. The same condition of small, localized, and independent clans prevailed among these people as among the Cahuilla of the Desert, hence they were in no sense a united tribe and their boundaries must depend on those of the small groups taken as belonging to this division. These are shown in map 4. The inclusion of the group at Indian Wells and the two clans near Palm Springs is more or less arbitrary, for these three groups seem at an earlier time to have really represented a ceremonial unit which might well entitle them to the designation of the Palm Springs Cahuilla. Present-day ceremonial affiliations and a general community of cultural traits seem however to link them to the people of the Pass rather than to those of the Desert, so for purposes of convenience I have thus grouped them.

Lacking any political unity or true tribal organization among the Pass Cahuilla we have therefore only one criterion for distinguishing the local groups as such, and that is their language. In the San Gorgonio pass proper two main languages are spoken, the Cahuilla and the Serrrano, both of the Shoshonean stock but each very distinct. At present the remnants of the Pass peoples are in large part gathered together on the Morongo Indian reservation near Banning, and the groups are consequently very much mixed. Added to this is the fact that even in pre-Caucasian times their ceremonial affiliations were based more on propinquity than on language, and as a result the data in regard to such intermingled groupings are usually far from clear. Three things then should always be borne in mind—first, the language spoken by any one clan, second, the actual territory it occupied, and third, the groups with which it was ceremonially united. When this is done a much clearer vision is possible, for any attempt to deal with the local groups as parts of larger political units or tribes almost invariably leads to confusion. Considerable literature in regard to the linguistic affiliation of the peoples under discussion is extant, and largely because of the above stated difficulties it is quite contradictory. I have already discussed this problem in the consideration of the Serrano, so it will be unnecessary to more than refer to the discussion here. In this section, wherever possible I have treated only the Cahuilla-speaking groups, save where their ceremonial relations with groups speaking other languages make departure from this rule necessary. As the other linguistic groups are treated in turn, it will be possible to view the area as a whole and to see clearly the relations between all the groups concerned.

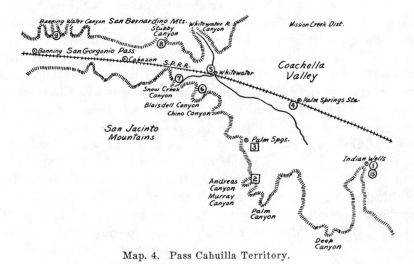

Map. 4.   Pass Cahuilla Territory.

The Cahuilla Indians of the Pass proper are very few in number at present and most of the clans are extinct or represented by only a few survivors, often young people who have little actual knowledge of the past. Fortunately there are among the few old people alive several splendid informants, and to them I am indebted for the following data. Most of the information pertaining to aboriginal conditions in the San Gorgonio pass was obtained from the following people: Alejo Potencio, net of the kauisiktum clan at Palm Springs; Rosa Morongo, acting kīka of the māriña clan of the Serrano, but daughter of the net of the pisatañavitcem clan near Banning, therefore a Cahuilla by birth;[162] Jesusa Manuel, a Mountain Cahuilla woman who married a Serrano man of the atūravīatum clan, now

---

[162] See present paper, p. 10, for discussion of Mrs. Morongo's linguistic affiliations.

living on the small San Manuel reservation near Redlands; and Alec' Arguello, who with his son Alexander Arguello, are the last survivors of the Cahuilla who lived in the San Timoteo canyon. The last two now live at Crafton, California.

The main outlines supplied by the above informants were checked and filled in by other informants at Palm Springs and at the Morongo reservation near Banning. In the course of the winter's work it became more and more clear that a study of these Shoshonean groups to possess full value must be based on the individual village or clan, rather than on any larger grouping, because generalities based on any one locality were apt to lead to erroneous conclusions. Therefore in the present account I have endeavored to show to which particular place the particular description applies. Because so many of the clans are extinct or represented only by younger people, the carrying out of this ideal in its entirety was impossible, but it is an end which has been sought for and which yields the most accurate results. In regard to the very complex problem of ceremonial affiliations, it is necessary to bear in mind the fact that the information of any one informant usually gives only one cross-section, which must be fitted in time and space with that of other people questioned. In the last sixty-odd years, especially, the alignment of groups has been subject to much shifting through the rapid disappearance of native conditions. It is therefore usually erroneous to give any grouping as static and established. With this factor in mind I have roughly classified the data under this head in three groups which comprise first the ceremonial affiliations now existing, secondly the conditions which existed in the youth of the informants questioned and which might be called the last phases of the aboriginal state, and lastly those vague data transmitted by their ancestors to the present informants which give us a hint as to still earlier conditions. Following is a list of the clans, past and present, among the Pass Cahuilla.

TABLE 5

Pass Cahuilla Clans

1. atcitcem, "good," coyote moiety, located at Indian Wells; not active at present. Belonged to the old grouping *A*.[163]

2. paniktum, "daylight," wildcat moiety, formerly located in Andreas canyon; not active at present. Belonged to the old grouping *A*.

3. kauisiktum, "from the rock," wildcat moiety, located at Palm Springs; is active at present. Belonged to the old grouping *A*.

4. haviñakiktum, "deep water hole," coyote moiety, located at Palm Springs station; not active at present. Belonged to the old grouping *B*.

5. wanikiktum, "running water," coyote moiety, located at Whitewater bridge originally, but now on Morongo Indian reservation; active at present. Belonged to old grouping *B*.

6. wakiñakiktum (place name north of Cabezon), coyote moiety, located in Blaisdell canyon; not active at present. Belonged to the old grouping *B*.

7. tetcanaakiktum (place name for peak south of the Pass), coyote moiety, located in Snow Creek canyon; not active at present. Belonged to the old grouping *B*.

8. paluknavitcem (place name northwest of Whitewater station), coyote moiety, located in Stubby canyon; not active at present. Belonged to the old grouping *B*.

9. pisatañavitcem (place name in Banning Water canyon), coyote moiety, located in Banning Water canyon; not active at present. Belonged to the old grouping *B*.

10.[164] costakiktum (no meaning), coyote moiety, located in San Timoteo canyon; not active at present. Belonged to the old grouping *C*.

11. natcūtakiktum, "sand," coyote moiety, located in San Timoteo canyon; not active at present. Belonged to the old grouping *C*.

12. pauatīauitcem (village in San Jacinto mountains), wildcat moiety, located in San Timoteo canyon; not active at present. Belonged to the old grouping *C*.

13. tepamōkiktum (no meaning), wildcat moiety, located in San Timoteo canyon; not active at present. Belonged to the old grouping *C*.

14. temewhanic, "northerners," wildcat moiety, located in San Timoteo canyon; not active at present. Belonged to the old grouping *C*.

15. nonhaīam (no meaning), coyote moiety, located originally at Indian Wells, moved to the desert; not active at present. Belonged to the old grouping *A*.[165]

---

[163] This heading shows the ceremonial affiliation of the clan fifty or more years ago.

[164] Clans 10–14 are all Mountain Cahuilla people, who came to the vicinity of San Bernardino and Riverside as a guard against more distant raiding tribes in 1846. For further discussion of this point see present paper, pp. 6, 7.

[165] Clan 15 seems to have moved to the Desert many years ago, and has already been discussed in relation to the Desert Cahuilla.

CEREMONIAL AFFILIATIONS OF PASS CLANS

As the list of Pass Cahuilla clans (table 5) indicates there were originally three main groupings of a ceremonial and, as will be shown later, of a cultural nature, among them. The first group comprised clans 1 to 3, which were affiliated, with the kauisiktum clan at Palm Springs as their center.[165] Next came the Cahuilla of the Pass proper, clans 4 to 9 which were grouped with the Serrano māriña clan as their ceremonial and in part cultural center. Finally, there were the Mountain Cahuilla clans 10 to 14, who seem to have been affiliated with the Luiseño and intrusive Cahuilla groups at Saboba, as well as with other Mountain Cahuilla clans. These Cahuilla clans of the San Timoteo pass[166] were late arrivals at the San Bernardino mission and therefore cannot be considered as a true Pass people. They will be discussed more fully under the heading Mountain Cahuilla. Such were the conditions existing sixty-odd years ago.

Today there exists only a fragment of the old organization, but it appears to contain in its essentials nearly all the characteristics which were once common to a vast area and to a much larger number of groups. Lines of cleavage have changed, the number of ceremonies performed has been reduced, and details of ritual discontinued, but the actual framework of the old society is still in existence though it will probably disappear with the present generation. The main, and in fact only, general manifestation of the old life occurs at the mourning or image-burning ceremony which each of the four active ceremonial units performs once every two years. To these ceremonies the other three still active clans are always formally invited, and with them come many of the other Cahuilla and Serrano whose ceremonial groups have disappeared, as well as visiting Luiseño, Cupeño, and a few of the Yuman Diegueño from the south.

These four active ceremonial units, two Cahuilla and two Serrano, are the last ceremonially intact groups of the people speaking either language, save for the few clans of the Cahuilla in the desert who hold their own smaller ceremonies. Thus they comprise in their activities practically all that is left of the ceremonial life of the once very numerous Serrano and Cahuilla peoples. The author was fortunate enough to be at Palm Springs in February, 1925, when the kauisiktum clan of that place gave their biennial week-long ceremony which is

---

[166] Barrows, *op. cit.*, 33.

described in detail later. It was possible at that time to observe the organization in operation and to get information in regard to the existing units which still carry on the religious and ceremonial life of the people.

At Palm Springs there is one active clan as well as a goodly number of people from other localities without ceremonial affiliations, who take part in all but the most intimate ceremonial functions of this clan. This is the kauisiktum clan, with Alejo Potencio as its net or ceremonial chief,[167] having a large ceremonial dance house called kicamnawut in which the net lives. As a result of their proximity, ceremonies at Palm Springs draw many of the Desert Cahuilla who do not go to similar affairs at Banning or Saboba. This same condition prevailed to an even greater extent in aboriginal times, a fact stated by both Palm Springs and Desert informants.

On the Morongo reservation near Banning are three active clans; two Serrano and one Cahuilla. The Cahuilla clan has been strongly influenced by the Serrano, to the extent that nearly all of its songs are in the Serrano language. As a result the members of the clan are bilingual to a considerable extent, although their own language is Cahuilla. The name of the clan is wanikiktum, and the wife of Juan Costo (a Mountain Cahuilla man) is the acting head or nuut.[168] She is said to be the oldest person in the direct line of descent of nuuts in the clan, but her exact relationship I could not determine. Mrs. Pablo, the wife of a wanikiktum man, is the oldest survivor of the paniktum clan of the Cahuilla clan originally located in Andreas canyon near Palm Springs. She has a small dance house on the Morongo reservation but it is used for small gatherings and singings only. The paniktum clan at present consists of only about eight persons, and they cannot afford large ceremonies. Hence Mrs. Pablo is affiliated with wanikiktum clan, while the remainder of her clan are affiliated with the Palm Springs kauisiktum group.

The two Serrano clans now located on the Morongo reservation are the māriña and the atūravīatum groups. The most powerful of

---

[167] At Palm Springs there is also a head man who acts as the nominal leader of all Indians on the reservation. He is elected by all the people assigned to the reservation and acts as a go-between for them with the government, or outside parties. His actual power appears, however, to be very limited and there is no evidence that such an office existed prior to its instigation by the white people who needed a temporal head to deal with. This office was held by Lee Arenas, a half-breed, at the time of my visit. He was in no way connected with the ceremony except in cases of disorder.

[168] The Pass Cahuilla term for ceremonial leader or clan head. It is very similar to the Cupeño nut, and the Luiseño nōta.

these is the māriña or Morongo, whose acting head or kīka is Mrs. Rosa Morongo, a Pass Cahuilla woman from pīhatapa near Banning, who succeeded her husband Captain John Morongo who had been a very influential kīka. The importance of this clan has been shown in the section on the Serrano, but at this point it is well to note that its present head is a Cahuilla woman. Sharing the dance house with the latter is the atūravīatum Serrano clan with Miguel Savatco as its kīka. The following list shows in condensed form the main features of the present day grouping.

TABLE 6

Modern Ceremonial Groups of the San Gorgonio Pass

Name:[169]	kauisiktum	wanikiktum	māriña	atūravīatum
Reservation:	Palm Springs	Morongo	Morongo	Morongo
Language:	Cahuilla	Cahuilla	Serrano	Serrano
Songs in:	Cahuilla	Serrano	Serrano	Serrano
Leader:	net	nuut	kīka	kīka
Dance House:	kicamnawut	kicamnawut[170]	kitcaterate[170]	kitcaterate[170]
Sacred Matting:	maiswut	maiswut	muurtc	muurtc

The situation becomes more complex when one considers the ceremonial groupings of fifty or more years ago. Here three main groupings of Pass clans stand out, but the individual clans were much more numerous and their interrelations more intricate. In order to give a clearer idea of their ceremonial linkage it is necessary to give the data pertaining to the ceremonial exchange of shell money, past and present.

CEREMONIAL EXCHANGE OF SHELL MONEY

The modern exchange of shell money is fairly clear, although a certain amount of secrecy still surrounds it. Each of the four active ceremonial groups has several strings of shell beads which are kept by the clan chief, usually in association with the sacred bundle of the clan. The kauisiktum clan at Palm Springs call these strings witcū, and the shell money itself hīssavel or mūketem. The pisata-ñavitcem clan, who lived in the Banning Water canyon, called one

---

169.The first two clans are given in the list of Pass Cahuilla clans, as numbers 3 and 5. The other two clans are listed with the Serrano.

170 Also called wamkite, from the Luiseño term wamkic, used also by the Mountain Cahuilla and Cupeño. The term for ceremonial house is always a combination of the words, ''large'' or ''big,'' and ''house.''

string nuutska and many strings nuutskum. The Serrano clans
called the money uk', or mūketem which appears as a general term
used by all these peoples irrespective of language. The Mountain
Cahuilla clans, both at pauī in the mountains, and sahatapa in the
San Timoteo pass, called the money by the latter term.

There are two main classes of this money. The one called witcū
by the Palm Springs Cahuilla is a piece four times the distance from
a man's forehead to the ground in length, which is given to the
leader of each invited clan at the close of the image-burning ceremony. This is given a cash value of fifty cents. The other called
napanaa by the same people is worth twenty cents, and this appears
to have been the basic unit of shell money value. This was sent to
any clan leader when a death occurred in his clan by all other clan
leaders hearing of it.[171] The length of this piece is determined by
wrapping it twice around the left wrist, carrying it under the thumb
and twice around the fingers halfway to the tips, and back over the
palm to a spot on the mid-wrist four inches from the posterior end
of the palm. This spot, called tcic'hīinut, was formerly placed on
the inner mid-wrist of the clan leader when he took office. It was
done by the paha, who using a string of money as a measure, tattooed
in the mark with a cactus thorn and inserted charcoal. The mark on
Alejo Potencio's wrist was about one quarter of an inch long by half
as wide, showing blue under the skin. According to Potencio such
a mark was once characteristic of each clan leader of the groups to
the north and west, but not to those of the Desert Cahuilla where the
exchange of shell money did not occur.[172] The long string of shell
money, witcū, is given to the leaders of the three invited clans at
the close of the image-burning ceremony. A similar piece is returned
by each when his clan gives a ceremony to which the others are
invited, thus keeping up a perpetual exchange. I was unable to
learn exactly how many pieces of this witcū are in circulation, but it
is obvious that there must be several such pieces in the possession of
each of the four ceremonial units.

According to Alejo Potencio, the shell money was received for the
Palm Springs clan by his grandfather who received it from the
Serrano at Mission creek. They got it from the Gabrieleño, who in

---

[171] There were undoubtedly regional limits within which each circle of
exchange existed, but they are not remembered by present-day informants.

[172] Du Bois mentions that one of the old chiefs of the Luiseño had a tattoo
mark on his left wrist, the meaning of which she could not discover. Present
series, 8:92, 1908.

turn received it from Santa Catalina island. The inhabitants of
Santa Catalina island were called pipīmurum, and the island pipīmul.
Alejo's grandfather told him that the shell money was brought across
from Santa Catalina island on tule rafts to the San Fernando people,
who distributed it among the inland groups. There was another
kind of money called somitnektcum "the small ones," composed of
little shells which were much more valuable than the present large
shell money. All these pieces of small shell money were lost before
Alejo was old enough to remember them.

According to Rosa Morongo none of the Serrano or the Pass
Cahuilla knew where the shell money came from. One night it suddenly appeared. Alec' Arguello, last survivor of the Cahuilla who
lived in the San Timoteo pass, said that the mūketem, shell money,
was brought to Juan Antonio, the Mountain Cahuilla captain who
brought the Cahuillas to San Bernardino, by kānuk,[173] a very old
chief of the San Fernando people, who also brought new songs and
ceremonies. This happened before Arguello was born, and he was
told of it by his father. Such is the data on the origin of the shell
money exchange among these groups west of the San Gorgonio pass.
The evidence is fragmentary, but points indubitably to the Pacific
coast peoples as the source of the system.[174] Whether the system
among these inland peoples was purely aboriginal must be decided
later.

EARLIER GROUPINGS OF THE PASS PEOPLES

The data on older groupings and the ceremonial exchange occurring between them is very complex and equally fragmentary. With
the disappearance of the Gabrieleño, Fernandeño, and Chumash, the
central factors of the problem have apparently been wiped out. Hence
a complete reconstruction of the ceremonial exchange system is impossible. However, bearing in mind the fact that conditions among the
Pass people were peripheral it is possible with care to obtain an idea
of the state of affairs which must once have existed farther to the
west. Two sorts of ceremonial shell money exchange seem to have
existed among the Pass Shoshoneans. First the exchange of the long
strings of shell money called witcū by the Palm Springs group, which
still occurs among the four active clans today. Secondly the older
exchange of smaller strings of shell money called napanaa by the

---

[173] Mentioned by Hugo Reid, Los Angeles Star, 1852, Letter no. 6.
[174] See Kroeber, Handbook, 564.

Palm Springs group, which died out many years ago, but apparently once existed on a very wide scale. We will consider each type of exchange in order.

This first sort of exchange in former times as at present, seems only to have existed between groups who participated in each other's ceremonies. About fifty years ago three different groups of this kind existed among the peoples of the Pass. The present alignment, which has already been discussed, has arisen through the breaking down of these three large earlier groups and the assembling of the few surviving units into the present-day ceremonial union.

Fifty-odd years ago, according to Alejo Potencio, the Palm Springs people did not actually participate in the ceremonies of the Cahuilla clans to the north or of the Serrano to the northeast. There were three clans in the vicinity of Palm Springs who formed one unit and who always attended each other's ceremonies, exchanging the long pieces of shell money, witcū. These are indicated by the letter *A* in the list of Pass Cahuilla clans (see p. 91). Of these the kauisiktum clan at Palm Springs appears to have been the most influential and is the only clan keeping up its ceremonies today. The atcitcem clan at Indian Wells, kavinic, and the paniktum clan of Andreas canyon, were the other two who shared in the ceremonies of this group at Palm Springs.

The clans of the Cahuilla, northwest of Palm Springs, were ceremonially connected among themselves and with the māriña clan of the Serrano.[175] This last clan according to Mrs. Rosa Morongo often brought the other Serrano clans with them to Pass ceremonials, but the Cahuilla clans were linked by exchange of shell money (witcū) only with the māriña, and not with the other Serrano clans. The oldest grouping in the Pass proper, remembered by Mrs. Morongo, included the haviñakiktum, wanikiktum, wakiñakiktum, tetcanaa-kiktum, paluknavitcem, and pisatañavitcem clans of the Cahuilla, and the mārina clan of the Serrano. Of these only the wanikiktum and the māriña clan survive as groups today. Mrs. Morongo said that when she was a girl living near Banning, the māriña clan was regarded by all others as the oldest, and when a number of the Pass clans happened to be going to Palm Springs they all waited at a point north of that place for the māriña clan to precede them. Such a statement might arise from undue pride in the clan of which she is now head, but the fact that the surviving Cahuilla clans today sing

---

[175] Indicated by the letter *B* in the list of Pass Cahuilla clans, table 5.

mārīña songs in the Serrano language shows the great influence of the latter and bears out Mrs. Morongo's testimony. This was the second of the older groupings in its bare outlines, though there were probably other alliances within or with other clans outside of the territories listed, knowledge of which has disappeared with the clans themselves.

The third ceremonial grouping will be discussed later in the section on the Mountain Cahuilla, for all these clans (numbers 10 to 14)[176] were from the mountains and had their own affiliations before they moved to the vicinity of San Bernardino. Thus when they moved they still maintained the ceremonial exchange of shell money with the other Mountain Cahuilla clans and with the Luiseño "parties" at Saboba. The data concerning this group, obtained from Alec' Arguello at Crafton, will be given when the Mountain Cahuilla are discussed.

Besides the previously discussed organization based on actual participation in the same ceremonies, and marked by the exchange of witcū (long strings of shell money) between the united groups, there seems to have been a looser form of union which was discontinued many years ago and may now only be reconstructed with great difficulty. It was customary, as has already been mentioned, for all the clans north of Palm Springs irrespective of linguistic differences, on hearing of a death in another clan to send one string of shell money to the leader of that clan. This smaller string of money was called by the Palm Springs Cahuilla, napanaa. Thus there would seem to have existed a loose ceremonial union between all the Cahuilla, Serrano, Luiseño, and Gabrieleño clans who inhabited the territory from the San Gorgonio pass west to the Pacific ocean.

The data in regard to this exchange are rather contradictory, but of a nature to make it appear certain that in former times such an institution existed. According to Alejo Potencio, the Palm Springs Cahuilla clan would send such a string of money to the leader of any clan between that place and the San Gabriel mission whenever a death occurred in such a clan. This was about seventy years ago, when the informant was a mere youth. At this time lelmus was chief of the gravelinos, or kisīanōs, as the Gabrieleño were called by the Cahuilla. The napanaa was always carried by the paha, and he sometimes took it to the nearest clan which at that time was the haviñakiktum clan at Palm Springs station. The paha of the latter clan would take

---

[176] Designated as old grouping *C* in the list of Pass Cahuilla clans, table 5.

both strings of money to the next clan, and so on. Thus a string of shell money from each group would be relayed on until they arrived at the village of the deceased, where they were presented to the ceremonial leader of the deceased's clan. One year later when the image-burning ceremony for the dead person was held each string was returned to the clan that had sent it. Those clans which were close by received theirs personally, while those farther away were sent theirs. It was customary for the paha or person who brought this shell money to receive ten cents in cash for each string of shell money from the ceremonial leader to whom he brought them.

Mrs. Rosa Morongo was not very clear in regard to the ceremonial exchange in former times, and did not make the distinction between the two types of shell money. She said, however, that when she was a girl shell money was sent by her father to any group having a "big house" and a kīka, whenever a death occurred in such a clan. This exchange extended as far as San Gabriel to the west, Saboba to the south, and Twenty Nine Palms to the east. Exchange of shell money at the close of the biennial mourning ceremony was according to the "older groupings" already shown,[177] and was not nearly so all-inclusive as the just described exchange occurring at the time of death.

It is very probable that the ramifications of this older system and its clearer distinctions are only hinted at in the foregoing account. Due to its esoteric nature and because of the lapse of time involved since it was in active operation, clearer accounts could not be obtained from the informants questioned. From the data here presented, and from other material to be given later in connection with the Cupeño, I am inclined to believe that while the medium of exchange was aboriginal its spread to these Pass groups occurred in mission times, perhaps in part reproducing an earlier condition among the coastal people. The fact that such an exchange was unknown to the Desert Cahuilla seems to support this conclusion. Fragmentary as the data on these early conditions are, they suffice to give one a clearer understanding of the bonds between the many small groups, and to explain the modern institutions which have arisen on the fallen framework of the old structure.

[177] List of Pass Cahuilla clans, table 5.

ORGANIZATION AND NATURE OF THE CLAN

In regard to clan organization, the Pass and Desert Cahuilla seem to have been almost identical. The Pass clans, however, seem to have lived in comparative isolation and not in villages composed of several clans or individually named lineages as did the Desert Cahuilla. As nearly all the original Pass clans have disappeared, detailed data on each group cannot be obtained, but the information in regard to the clan near Palm Springs, combined with that on the Cahuilla clan near Banning, gives a fairly complete picture. There is little reason to believe that the intervening groups differed in essentials from their near eastern and western Cahuilla-speaking neighbors with whom they were intimately associated.

The kauisiktum clan at Palm Springs has a short migration legend which was told me by Alejo Potencio, the net, to account for their present location. It gives the boundaries of the kauisiktum clan, which the informant assured me, was the oldest of these three affiliated clans.

Very long ago a great net who had three names hīwinut (flying), temewhawewunelwic (standing to the north), and kauiskīauka (no meaning), brought his people to watcicpa (Redland junction), and then named himself waswatcañanet and waswatcanayaik. From here he took them to īva (a hot spring just north of Saboba), where he again changed his names to īvañanet and īvañayaik. Then he moved them to kekliva (a mountain just north of Saboba),[178] where he changed his names to keklivanet and keklivayaic (fast runner). Here, while looking for his new home, he named aīakaīc (San Jacinto peak). From kekliva he took the people to panyik (mouth of Andreas canyon), on a stream called milyillilikalet and near this place he found some painted rocks called tekic. He told his people that these rocks were already painted when he came there. From this spot he named all the places that marked his new territory.

To the east he named a small hill sēwitckul (Murray hill), and to the west he named the canyon ēit (Murray canyon). Farther to the west he named palhilikwinut (near head of Murray canyon). Then he named tēvin' imulwiwaīwinut (a flat rock with mortar holes, at mouth of Palm canyon), and halfway up the canyon paskwa a hot spring (rock mortars here also), and then tatmīlmī (the south end of Palm canyon). Another place sewī, near here, was the southwestern boundary.

The next place he named was sīmūta (more rock mortar holes, about five miles west of Palm canyon), and proceeding north and westerly he named pīnalata, kalahal (a flat), tcial (a hill northwest of Palm canyon), kaukwicheki (a stream where hunters and acorn gatherers camped) and pūlūkla (a hill to which hunters would sing in the dance house in order to have deer sent them).

---

[178] Here according to Alejo Potencio, the kauisiktum clan left part of their ceremonial impedimenta, present paper, p. 120.

Thence still northwest to aīakaic (San Jacinto peak), and finally to yauahic (a place just south of Blaisdell canyon). This marked the northwestern limit of his territory.

Going southeast from Murray hill he named taupakic (probably Cathedral canyon, where they gathered mescal), konkistū-uinut (a place near Indian Wells), and alhauik (a hill south of Indian Wells, perhaps Indio mountain). This was the southeastern boundary mark.

From milyillilikalet and tekic (mouth of Andreas canyon) coming north along the eastern edge of the mountains bordering the desert, he named kauissimtcem hempkī (hill four miles south of Palm Springs), temukvaal (a low hill on edge of desert near here, where a man watched when they hunted rabbits), tekelkukuaka (mesquite grove slightly to north), kakwawit (mouth of Tahquitz canyon), kauiskī (two superimposed rocks in Tahquitz canyon from which the kauisiktum clan takes its name), mīaskalet (white rock on hillside in Tahquitz canyon), and palhanikalet "water falling down," name of Tahquitz falls.

Proceeding still to the north, he named iñvitca (a green place north of Tahquitz canyon), tepal (farther north), tūīval (a rocky point just west of the Mission Inn), tetcavī (a large rock fifty yards farther north), and pūllūvil (the large smooth rock cliff at Dry falls). Three large rocks north of here he called kauistanalmū, hauiñenin, and hauītalal; still farther in the same direction he named a hanging rock waīvas (meaning "yell"), malal (north point of Chino canyon), and kistcavel (at point where second bridge on highway from Palm Springs to Whitewater is located). The first rocky point beyond this bridge he called pīonvil, the second point teūamul, and the third point, almost at Whitewater station, he called tama. Between these points occur three large rocks which he named for his three dogs, the first awelmū, the second niñkicmū, and the third paklic. Near the point farthest to the north he named īvawakik (a sharp hill south of Cabezon) which he went inside of, leaving his people. He then became a rock on the summit of this hill which marks the northeastern boundary.

The paniktum clan was located in Andreas canyon with its side canyons north as far as hunwit hekik, a point on Tahquitz creek. Their boundary ran south to the northern rim of Murray canyon. The boundaries of the kauisiktum clan surrounded all the former clan's territory. It is probable that these two clans were originally one, for informants said they regarded each other as relatives. Likewise they belonged to the same moiety. Genealogies to clinch the matter could not be obtained so it must rest in abeyance.

The atcitcem clan had territory in the immediate neighborhood of Indian Wells, called kavinic. Definite boundaries were not obtained.[179] They were of a different moiety from the two former clans and

---

[179] Francisco Potencio, younger brother of Alejo, told me that the paniktum clan was the first to come to this vicinity. Most of them died long ago. Originally the atcitcem clan had owned Palm canyon but as they usually married with the kauisiktum clan, they had given Palm canyon to them as a gift. The old town located in the canyon, and once occupied by the atcitcem clan, was named tatmīlmī.

commonly married members of both. Hence it is probable that their connection was of a political and social nature rather than one of kinship. A fragment of mythology relating to the supposed history of these and the other true Desert Cahuilla clans was told me by Alejo Potencio.

In the beginning these people were created far away, then following their leader they came to a point near kavinic (Indian Wells). Here the leader, aswitsēī (eagle flower), went to sleep and slept for one hundred years. Then his dog barked and woke him up. He called this dog mahalic (looking for creatures). His people had gone while he slept and they were south of kavinic on the desert, and were having their first hemeūlūniwe (girls' adolescence ceremony), for two girls hunal sesive and hunal papase. This was the way the people came to be down in the desert.

Then aswitsēī came up to the mountains at kavinic where he leaned against a rock leaving the marks of his elbows and knees. He looked toward maūlmiī (Toro), then he climbed up the mountain and lay down watching the people, leaving the marks of his elbows and ribs. As he came down he slipped leaving the print of his hand in the soft rocks. Near kavinic was a palm with which he talked. He desired to become a palm himself, but failed to do so.

The above is only a fragment but is interesting for two reasons. First as being part of the longer origin myth of the sēwahilem clan (pp. 86, 87), and secondly as a repetition of the story given by Gifford.[180] Furthermore it aptly illustrates the slight changes which occur in all myths and other social phenomena between group and group of the Cahuilla and their neighbors. Each story varies with the clan telling it, hence an authority in one clan will nearly always say that a story told by the authority in another clan is not right in its details.

At an early time the nonhaīam (no meaning) people lived with the atcitcem clan at kavinic. About sixty-odd years ago, according to Francisco Nombre a Desert Cahuilla informant, they had seven houses but no net or dance house. They were ceremonially subordinated to the atcitcem clan who at that time had ten houses, including a dance house, and a net. Later the former group, which the informant said was related to the atcitcem clan, moved en masse to a new village near kelewutkwīikwinut "wood hanging down" at La Mesa. At this time they appointed their oldest man, whauatiñanaīī, as net, and became a separate clan affiliating with the other Desert Cahuilla clans. A few survivors of this branch clan, called Augustin, now live on the desert reservation of that name. Such branching off and removal of collateral lineages of any one clan must have occurred from time to time, due perhaps to the overcrowding of a small area, scarcity of food, and quite probably of water.

---

180 S. Cal., 188.

Apparently there was only a ceremonial bond between the three Palm Springs Cahuilla clans, for no data or any purely political leadership were remembered. The father of Alejo Potencio told him that once all three of these clans went together to fight with a desert group that had trespassed upon their food-gathering territories. The two parties fought with bows and arrows but no one was killed. (A statement in regard to warfare which seems to be applicable to most of these southern Californian Shoshoneans.) One old man named piwitcem, who led the desert people, dodged all the arrows that were discharged at him so that he could not be hit.[181]

Partly because Palm Springs informants objected to naming dead relatives, and partly because no willing informant well versed in such matters was encountered, genealogies of the Palm Springs kauisiktum clan could not be obtained. It is quite possible, especially in the last fifty years, that this clan has to some extent been recruited from survivors of the paniktum and other Pass Cahuilla groups. The variety of European surnames among those today affiliated in the clan suggests this. Belardo, Chino, Marcus, Potencio, Moreno, and Pete are among these names, and while it is possible that this clan was unusually populous due to the favorable nature of the site, it seems more probable that we have here less of the pure lineage and more of a localized "party" gathered around a lineage nucleus. Lacking genealogies it is impossible to be certain of this, but it seems more likely for this group than for the smaller Desert Cahuilla clans, many of whom even today are able to give the exact relationship existing between all members. How far this condition applies to the other Pass groups it is difficult to ascertain. From statements made by Mrs. Rosa Morongo and the survivors of the wanikiktum clan I am inclined to believe that the Palm Springs condition is unusual and that in aboriginal times a clan organization of actual relatives was the general rule among the Pass Cahuilla. The genealogy of the pisatañavitcem clan (genealogy 7) is definitely that of one male lineage, which accords with the general statements of all informants.

Boundaries of the other Pass Cahuilla clans are largely unobtainable, as in many cases their members are all dead. The central point of such a territory as given in the list of Pass Cahuilla clans is all that modern informants remember. According to Mrs. Rosa Morongo,

---

[181] Except for the bloodless nature of the fight, the above traditional fragment is similar to two such accounts given by Hooper, *op. cit.*, 355–356.

GENEALOGY 7

Pisatañaviteem Clan[182]

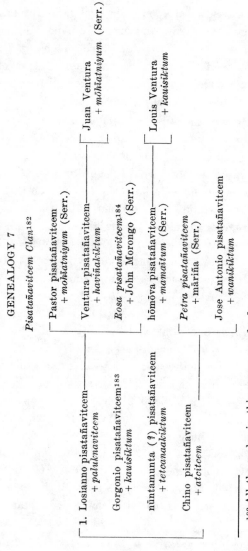

[182] All the males in this group are dead.

[183] According to the informant, the San Gorgonio pass was named after this man. It is more probable that both were named after the same saint.

[184] The informant.

the territory of the pisatañavitcem clan was called malkī, a term for the Banning district, commonly used by all the Cahuilla. This territory was located around the Banning Water canyon, from Hathaway canyon, na'iū, on the west to Millard canyon, tūmawic hema, on the east. The village pīhatapa was located in the first-named canyon. Here her father, Losianno, the nuut, lived in the kicamnawut. When she was a girl there were a good many people here, probably between thirty and forty, all related and belonging to this clan. At present several of her sisters are alive, but none of the men of the clan survive. The clan genealogy (genealogy 7) shows the exact nature of the relationship.

In general it seems that in their organization the clans of the Pass people closely resemble those of the Desert Cahuilla. Primarily they were male lineages, likewise united by possession of a clan fetish, and living each clan by itself. They did not have the necessity for grouping around water holes which existed in the desert. Probably some outsiders have been amalgamated into these clans, especially the Palm Springs group, making really a local band with a strong clan nucleus. The importance of the ceremonial house, the sacred bundle, and the clan head resembles the desert organization. To this the Pass Cahuilla add such features as the exchange of shell money between the clans, as well as other features to be discussed presently.

CLAN LEADERSHIP

The Net

Among the Pass Cahuilla clans the net, as he is called at Palm Springs, or nuut as he is called by the Pass Cahuilla groups to the west, is the ceremonial head and clan leader. As among the Desert Cahuilla the first of these duties is the most clearly defined. Primarily he had in his possession the sacred bundle or maīswut of the clan, and in aboriginal times[185] he lived in the dance house where in a separate compartment was kept the maīswut. This bundle, more fully described in the paragraph on the image-burning ceremony, is the symbolic center of the clan and, as on the desert, is called "the heart of the big house"; that is, of the kicamnawut or dance house. The "big house" is likewise regarded as a sacred place, all-important in the life of the clan.

---

[185] Alejo Potencio, the kauisiktum clan net, lives in the dance house at the present time.

The net presided at all ceremonies, he and his immediate family handled the maīswut, and he knew all the songs and legendary history of his clan. The food gathered for ceremonial "fiestas" was in his charge, and he announced the time when all ceremonies were to take place. Likewise he knew all the minute landmarks of the clan's territory and food-gathering areas.

At all times he controlled the people of his group in a general way, telling them when it was time to gather the various crops of mesquite beans, mescal, and other cactus. He and his family went on these trips and gathered their own supply of the food, but it was customary in the old days for the "big house," or net, to eat the first products of such expeditions. Camping places for the group were usually selected by him. Every day when food crops were being gathered each family was supposed to bring a small amount of food to the "big house" where it was stored. This food was not eaten by the net or his family, but was stored up for later use in "fiestas" or ceremonies given by the clan.

Palm Springs and Mountain Cahuilla informants both said that when a man or woman was worsted in a quarrel the loser took a gift of food to the "big house" and told his troubles to the net. The net would send the paha to bring the other party, and to call all adult clan members to the kicamnawut. A man thus summoned always came, for the "big house" on account of the maīswut was very powerful, and if he did not obey he would take sick and die. A quarrel between people in the clan must be settled at once for talking against people might kill them. When all the people were assembled, the net heard both sides of the argument. He then settled the matter as best he could and gave advice to the parties concerned. This judgment must be obeyed for if it were not the net could kill the disobedient persons by talking to the maīswut about them in a special esoteric language always used for this purpose. This account was given me by Alejo Potencio of Palm Springs, and Jolian Norte a Mountain Cahuilla from Los Coyotes canyon. It seems to indicate that the net of these Mountain and Pass Cahuilla groups was more influential than the clan heads on the desert. Probably this was due to the somewhat more strongly developed maīswut complex among the Pass and Mountain groups. This is shown in the description of the image-burning ceremony in which the maīswut plays such an important rôle.

Among the Pass groups, as elsewhere, the net was an hereditary official, the office theoretically passing from father to oldest son in the same direct line. Actually, the office seems to have passed from the father to his most capable and popular son, with the consent of the clan. Failing a capable son in the direct line the office was taken over by a collateral branch. The ceremonial exchange of shell money brings in a new factor in regard to the duties of the net. He not only kept this medium of exchange, but divided it among the invited clans at the image-burning ceremony and received other pieces at theirs. This has been previously described. The mark for measuring the standard of shell money value that was tattooed on the net's arm is an interesting point. Alejo Potencio, the kauisiktum net, as before stated, had such a mark called tcic'hiinut. This mark he claimed, was originally a distinctive characteristic of every net. Mrs. Rosa Morongo was able to give me no data in this regard, and I did not encounter references to it among the Mountain Cahuilla, but here as in the Pass all the old nets are dead. Since Mrs. Morongo has become kīka of the Serrano band only in comparatively recent years and the old nets of the other Pass clans are all dead, corroborative evidence is hard to obtain. As Alejo actually measured out the shell money given to the three invited groups at the ceremony I witnessed, in exactly the manner he later described,[186] and since all other data received from him were well corroborated by other informants, I am inclined to give his statement in the above case full value.[187] Other aspects of the net's duties are more clearly brought out in the description of Pass ceremonials which is given later.

The Paha

Theoretically, among the Pass Cahuilla clans the paha was an hereditary official, the office passing from father to eldest son. Actually, it appears to have been less so than that of the net, for the office required a special type of man more than one of very special lineage. Probably all the groups from Indian Wells to the north and west had this official with the same title. The paha's duties were in the main ceremonial and he assisted the net at all times. Keeping order and silence at all solemn ceremonies was his particular duty.

---

[186] Present paper, p. 130.

[187] In this regard the old Luiseño chief whose left wrist was similarly tattooed, mentioned by Du Bois, affords corroboration to Alejo's statement. Present series, 8:92, 1908. Kroeber mentions the same method of measuring among the Luiseño; see Du Bois, *op. cit.*, 186.

He saw that each family supplied its quota of food to the "big house" for use in ceremonials, he made all announcements in the village, and he carried the strings of shell money in the elaborate system of exchange that has previously been described. Informants questioned, said that the office of paha had "been from the beginning." As shown in the Palm Springs creation story (p. 134) īsil, the coyote, was the first paha helping the creators in making bodies, tending the elder creator, mūkat, when he was sick, getting the first maīswut, and making the first images. Since that time there has always been a paha. Since a wider survey shows that the title, paha, nearly always indicated the official presiding at the toloache rites, it seems probable that the title was taken over by the Palm Springs Cahuilla from their western neighbors. The same thing probably occurred among the Serrano, but the name of the general assistant among these people has so far always been recorded as paha.

The Takwa

At Palm Springs in the kauisiktum clan, and probably at Indian Wells in the atcitcem clan, a new official appears, called the takwa. The duties of this man are primarily the taking care of food used for clan ceremonials, its preparation, and its division to guests. Likewise he divides all the food, such as mesquite-bean flour, given as presents to the invited clans at the image-burning ceremony. All his family help him in these duties, especially in preparing the food. The desert clans have no such official, but the use of the term takwac nikul meaning "he or she is dividing food," commonly employed on the desert, has been mentioned. Palm Springs informants stated that on the death of the takwa he was succeeded by his son or his nephew. They also added that the takwa had "been from the beginning." Very likely the takwa was the older official whose duties have been in part taken over by the paha, the latter title being nearly always associated with the toloache cult.

Other Officials

The above seem to have been the only clearly recognized officers of the Pass Cahuilla clans, but as on the desert there were pūalem, the shamans, and hauinik, the singers. The description of their duties given for the Desert Cahuilla (p. 65) applies equally well here. The duties of all these clan officers, if such they may be called, are given more fully in the description of the image-burning and other ceremonies described later.

The Moiety Among the Pass Cahuilla

According to the Palm Springs informants the origin of the moiety dates "from the beginning." This is given in the Palm Springs creation story, but the following myth fragment bears directly on the legendary source of the moiety.

After the creation all people, including birds, animals, and trees who were then human, were talking. The lady moon used to take them far away and tell them how to sing and dance when they came back to the dance house. She named one to be net, and made a round house with a fence around it (kic yañic) for him to stay in. Then she made the other party go back and come singing and dancing to the house. She told the net to sing his song also. Those who were coming answered with the same song. She told them always to do this. Then she divided all the people and said these are istam and those are tūktum, and they must sing their own songs. For in the very beginning temaīyauit was istam and mūkat was tūktum and all the things each created belonged to its creator's side.

There is some doubt as to whether the names of children were determined by their clan and moiety affiliation, but Alejo Potencio said that in his grandfather's time this was the case. As even his father was given a Mexican name, it is obvious that detailed data on aboriginal naming are not obtainable today. The following classification of birds and animals into the two divisions was positively asserted. Tūkut, the wild cat; tūkwit, the mountain lion; kauisik, the fox; wilyul, the kit fox; hūnal, the badger; sikawit, the flying squirrel; alwut, the crow; and tamit, the sun, were all tūktum. Isil, the coyote; iswit, the wolf; aswit, the golden eagle; yuñaviwit, the condor; pamūis, the bald eagle; and yuñavic, the vulture, were all istam. Names which included these creatures, Alejo said, were only given to people belonging to the moiety to which the creature was assigned. Likewise each clan had songs including the names of objects or living creatures classed in their moiety, and, as was the case on the desert, these moiety songs were sung by visiting clans when they came to a "fiesta." Such songs were also sung by the clans themselves, thus by hearing certain of the songs of a clan its moiety could be determined.

According to Palm Springs informants the song of the creation, common in a somewhat variable form to all Cahuilla-speaking groups, is divided up between the clans of the two moieties. That is, clans of both moieties can sing from the beginning to the burning of mūkat's body, but the part where īsil, the coyote, takes the heart of mūkat

can only be sung by istam clans. This is a long song-series lasting
all night, about the actions of īsil; how he ran, looked back, lay down,
ate the heart, became sick, and so on. The remainder of the song,
anent the making of images, is the property of both moieties. Thus
the songs of the istam clans are longer than those of the tūktum clans.

In the girls' adolescence ceremony the girls' faces are "sprinkled"
with spots of white clay. There is a tūktum song saying that their
face designs should be spotted. This, according to Palm Springs
informants, was done to girls of both moieties. Among the Cupeño, it
is interesting to anticipate, girls of the wildcat moiety had a spotted
face design, those of the coyote moiety a striped design. It is probable that the Pass Cahuilla once had the same custom, but if so it
is not remembered today.

As among nearly all the other Shoshonean groups where it is
known, the moiety division served primarily in regulating marriage.
According to the Palm Springs informants, in the old days, as was
the case on the desert, people of the same moiety were never supposed
to marry, and very rarely did. In this regard exact data on old
marriages is a prime requisite but due to the great aversion of the
informants to giving information in which individual names are used,
not nearly so many cases of the sort as were desired could be
obtained.[188]

Enough cases were obtained, however, to give an indication of
actual marriage regulation in the kauisiktum clan at Palm Springs.
Of twenty-three actual cases, seventeen were in accord and four were
not in accord with moiety exogamy. Two cases were with groups
lacking or of unknown moiety affiliations. Of these twenty-three
cases, thirteen were old marriages occurring at least forty years ago,
of which twelve were according to the rule of moiety exogamy and
only one was not. The other ten cases had occurred since that time, of
these five were according to moiety exogamy, three were not, and two
were the outside cases already cited. These results corroborate the
statements of informants that in early times moiety exogamy was
quite rigorously enforced among the Palm Springs Cahuilla.

---

[188] The Palm Springs group, especially, and the Pass peoples in general,
have been so stirred up by political and private attempts to secure their
reservation lands in the last few decades, that they are decidedly averse to
giving any information of a personal or territorial nature even in regard to
very old conditions. They fear that such data will be used to oust them from
their present holdings or to assign them to other reservations. When one
considers the history of certain south Californian Indian groups under Caucasian
control he is inclined to sympathize with their suspicions. Nevertheless the
problem of the ethnologist is thereby made much more difficult.

In regard to the Cahuilla clans of the San Gorgonio pass proper, the case was evidently very different. Informants from the groups were unanimous in stating that istam and tūktum were very old names of the groups but were not important as regards marriage. The moiety affiliation was, to quote one informant, like "being a Republican or a Democrat," merely a collective party name but not a division to regulate marriage. In this regard we have the most striking difference between the Palm Springs Cahuilla, who in their strict observance of the moiety bond resemble the Desert Cahuilla, and the Pass Cahuilla who clearly remember the moiety alignment of each clan, but do not practice moiety exogamy.

The few actual cases obtainable among the shattered Pass clans bear out this testimony. From Mrs. Rosa Morongo were obtained twelve cases of marriage in the pisatañavitcem Cahuilla clan, formerly located near Banning. As nearly all the parties included in this list are now dead it is obvious that the situation was not entirely due to recent conditions. Of these twelve, only one case was in accord with moiety exogamy. Seven marriages were with other Cahuilla clans, and of these, six cases were not in accord with moiety exogamy. Five marriages were with members of Serrano clans, likewise having moiety affiliations, and of these, three cases were not in accord with moiety exogamy. The number of cases cited is too small to clinch the matter, but the great preponderance of marriages where non-observance of moiety exogamy was the rule, strongly indicates that this was the prevailing condition among Pass clans. Various reasons for this state of affairs will be discussed later in the section referring to marriage among these groups, but at this time it is most important to note that between the Cahuilla clans near Palm Springs, and those to the northwest in the Pass, a decided difference in the importance of the moiety existed.

In talking to Palm Springs and Pass Cahuilla informants, a few bits of information in regard to the moiety among other linguistic groups were obtained. These are naturally of doubtful value but as there is so little information in this regard extant or obtainable, about the people in question, I give them for what they are worth. Alejo Potencio said that he was told by Gabrielino people that they had istam and tūktum too, but when Alejo gave me the list of groups west of the Pass he was unable to give the moiety affiliation of the few Gabrielino groups mentioned, for he claimed he had never heard their songs and therefore could not tell to which moiety they belonged.

The Gabrielino he called kisīanōs, for they were the first Christians in the region; their language he called arērasa. The Luiseño, whom he called ka-iwīnitum, he said had forgotten istam and tūktum save for a few old men that he remembered in his youth. Likewise they had forgotten part of their earliest songs, hence mūkat was called wīyot, and there was no mention of temaīyauit. This may be pure rationalization, on the basis that what the Cahuilla had their neighbors should have had; or again it may indicate the last fading memories of dichotomous institutions among the people to the west.

MARRIAGE

The regulation of marriage by the moiety bond of each clan has been described in the foregoing section. In brief, it would appear that the Pass Cahuilla clans from Palm Springs south and east followed moiety exogamy, while all those clans to the north and west had moiety affiliations but do not appear to have been strictly exogamous in that regard within the memory of present-day informants. In both subdivisions of the Pass Cahuilla, as we have already noted among the Desert Cahuilla clans, people tended to marry into the groups with which they were in contact as would naturally be expected. No data were obtained in regard to any delimitation of areas or clan groups with whom marriages were permitted, and I strongly doubt that this was ever the case. Originally the moiety controlled marriage, probably among the Pass clans as well as those to the east, but it is a notable phenomena that in the Pass proper all the Cahuilla clans belonged to the coyote moiety, the nearest wildcat clan of their own linguistic group being at Palm Springs. Mrs. Rosa Morongo stated that in her girlhood people of coyote Cahuilla clans were supposed to marry with people of wildcat clans, but that actually it made little difference. Considering the fact that all of these Pass clans were of the coyote moiety, it is easy to see how the moiety control may have broken down simply because there were no wildcat clans conveniently close. Under the old and purely aboriginal conditions, the rule might have held but with the fast changing conditions of the last sixty years it had evidently crumbled. It is also possible that the rule of moiety exogamy had disappeared even prior to the coming of the whites, as it appears to have done among the Luiseño.

How this condition of grouped clans of one moiety only arose in the San Gorgonio pass is, of course, not altogether clear. It seems possible that the various coyote clans of the Cahuilla in the Pass were branches of one or more original coyote clans, sending out collateral lineages that in time became distinct clans. This would be purely hypothetical except for the occurrence of an almost identical state of affairs among the five distinct subdivisions of one original clan among the Mountain Cahuilla in the Los Coyotes canyon. Here the fact of actual relationship between two of the lineages, and the strong probability of a relationship between all of them, is established, yet each subdivision had a separate name. There was, however, one central clan leader, dance house, and sacred bundle. When these lineages left the canyon and scattered, each became a unit by itself. This exodus occurred about fifty years ago due to a severe smallpox epidemic, and the clans were so decimated that they did not continue their ceremonial life, hence it is not possible to state that each division would actually have become a separate ceremonial clan. These data are given more fully in the section on the Mountain Cahuilla, but are mentioned here because the. analogy between the Los Coyotes canyon case and that of the San Gorgonio pass is striking.

Had the break between the divisions in the Los Coyotes canyon case been of a longer duration, and had the ceremonial life of the dispersed lineages of this clan continued after their moving apart, we would have had an identical situation to that observed in the Pass. There are even indications that intermarriage between these related lineages of the Los Coyotes clan occurred after they had moved to village sites somewhat farther apart. Likewise the rule of moiety exogamy was not at all strictly observed by these Cahuilla groups between themselves, or with the Cupeño to the southwest. It is obvious that if this were the method by which new clans arose, the prospering and branching out of an isolated clan would in time tend to surround it with branch clans of the same moiety. Any change causing a break from old traditions would tend to encourage their intermarriage, for propinquity and constant contact would have already paved the way. On the other hand, where clans of two moieties exist in approximately equal numbers, the branch clans would according to chance tend to be about equal in numbers. This is hypothetical and somewhat out of place at this point in the discussion, but is mentioned here because it seems the probable explanation of the Pass Cahuilla condition just cited.

As to the San Gorgonio pass groups intermarrying, the actual cases previously mentioned give some exact information. Out of the thirteen old marriages in the kauisiktum clan at Palm Springs, nine cases of marriage occurred between this clan and clans of the Pass Cahuilla, five of these being with the atcitcem clan.   Between the kauisiktum people and the Desert Cahuilla clans, occurred four cases of marriage.   Of the ten cases of more recent marriages in this Palm Springs clan, seven are with Desert Cahuilla clans, two with Mountain Cahuilla, and one with a Chemehuevi woman.   The indications to be derived from these scanty data are that in early days, while the Pass clans were more intact, Palm Springs people married mainly with these groups, and of these, marriages with the atcitcem clan at Indian Wells were most common.   Later, as would be expected, the Pass clans being so decimated, they married mostly with the more populous Desert Cahuilla clans.   It is probably significant that the few cases of distant marriages came in the later period, modern conditions having tended to eliminate distance.   In the case of the pisatañavitcem clan near Banning all twelve cases were relatively old; these show seven marriages with other Pass Cahuilla clans, and five marriages with Serrano clans near Mission creek.   There seem to have been no clans with which marriage was most common.   It is of course apparent that placing too much reliance on such a small series of actual cases is unjustified, yet such is the paucity of data extant or obtainable that we are justified in making the most of the material at hand.

The actual ceremony of marriage in the Palm Springs clan was quite simple, possessing, however, a few peculiarities differentiating it from the Desert Cahuilla method.   The marriages were arranged by the parents of the boy who selected a desirable wife for him. When a girl was decided upon they took presents of food and baskets to the girl's parents stating their desire for the union.   If the girl's parents were willing they asked the girl, whose willingness was essential.   All parties consenting, the boy's mother brought the girl to the kicamnawut of the boy's clan, where a small feast was prepared.   The father of the boy had told the net, and the paha called all the clan members to the dance house.   The girl's immediate relatives and sometimes her whole clan were invited.   After the feast, an old man of the boy's clan talked to the young couple, telling the boy how he must hunt game for the girl and provide for her and her family.   He told the girl how to care for her husband, how to prepare food so that there should be plenty, and he warned them that they must not quarrel or their children would not be well

brought up. All the assembled people heard this, and the couple
were considered man and wife. The couple then went to the house
of the boy's father where they lived, the boy hunting, and the girl
helping her mother-in-law. If they did not get along well together
the girl returned to her parents, who were not expected to return the
presents previously received. My Palm Springs informants remembered no cases of plural marriage.

Marriage arrangements were much the same among the western
Pass Cahuilla clans, though there seems to have been no ceremony
at the time of the marriage within the memory of the last generation.
Polygamy was rare, and postmarital residence was patrilocal. A
widow often married the elder brother of her deceased husband.

HUNTING RULES

A young unmarried man always took such game as he killed to the
kicamnawut; when a man was married and had a child he then took
it to his own house. If he was living with his father-in-law he gave
the game to him. An unmarried man could never eat anything he
himself had killed, for it would make him very sick.[189] The first
deer a young man killed was taken by his father and mother to the
"big house" with other food as well. The people of the clan
assembled, and a pavūl (bear shaman) sang a song telling the deer
to go to telmekic, the abode of the dead. Then the deer was skinned,
a man holding up the raw hide shouted "he! he! he!" three times,
and blew to the north. The meat was then cooked in the "big house,"
and all the clan ate it except the boy and his parents. As was previously mentioned (p. 100) there was a hill called pūlūkla, near
San Jacinto peak, to which hunters sang in the dance house asking
that a deer be sent to them. They would then go to the spot and if
their prayer was granted they would secure a deer. Such hunters
were called pavūl, and had the power of changing themselves into
bears or mountain lions. Palm Springs informants stated that each
group had these two kinds of shamans, the pūl or curing doctor, and
the pavūl or "bear" shaman possessing the power of becoming an
animal.

When a man or woman met a California grizzly bear in the mountains he called the latter piwil (great-grandfather) and talked sooth-
ingly to him thus, "Beware! Hide yourself far back in the moun-

---

[189] The Luiseño had similar rules and taboos concerning game, especially the
rule against a hunter partaking of meat he had killed. See Du Bois, *op. cit.*, 184.

tains. Your enemies are coming. I am only looking for my food, you are human and understand me, take my word and go away.'' The bear would stop, hold up his paws like arms, then dropping to all fours he would scratch dirt to one side. This meant peace, and he would go away. ''One must never talk about the bear in the night time, for at night the bear travels, and by day he usually sleeps. If you talk about him at night, earth or rocks or mountains tell him what you say. He listens until he hears where you are going to hunt and goes there, so you will surely be killed.''[189a]

Alejo Potencio said that the last grizzly he remembered was killed by white men back of Palm Springs about thirty years ago. Prior to that he saw them several times in the San Jacinto mountains. In regard to tūkwit, the mountain lion, no especial ceremonies were necessary as he never hurt anyone. Palm Springs and Mountain Cahuilla informants both assured me that the Cahuilla and the Chemehuevi could talk to bears in their own language, citing the following instances. Many years ago at a bear and bull fight in Los Angeles, the bear refused to fight and was twice knocked down by the bull. A Cahuilla Indian above the bear on the stockade talked to the bear, saying, ''You must fight and defend yourself, they are going to kill you.'' The bear listened, charged the bull, breaking the latter's neck, and then died of his wounds.

A recent case occurred at Banning when a group of Cahuilla and Chemehuevi Indians laughed at a small bear in a cage. The bear was angry and scratched dirt at them. An old Cahuilla man told the bear to escape to the mountains and the bear listened. That night trying to escape he hung himself with his chain and died. These instances are mainly of interest in showing the close relationship felt between even the modern Indians and certain animals, bears in particular. The widespread feeling of kinship with the animals, common throughout native California, is marked among the Cahuilla.

Boys' and Girls' Adolescence Ceremonies
Manet

Jimsonweed drinking by young boys was not employed ceremonially by the Palm Springs Cahuilla, but Cahuilla clans farther west in the Pass many years ago made use of the ceremony, for Mrs. Morongo states that their songs definitely refer to the custom. At

---

[189a] Concerning the widespread nature of the bear cult it is significant that an old Naskapi hunter, in 1928, made an almost identical statement to me while I was living with that tribe in northeastern Labrador.

Palm Springs the jimsonweed, called kiksawel, was occasionally chewed by adult individuals as a narcotic. Informants stated that in the mountains, shamans obtained dreams by so doing, but on the desert this was never done. A future study of shamanism in the desert may qualify this statement. According to Alejo Potencio, the mānet ceremony came from Santa Catalina island by way of the San Gabriel people, but never reached Palm Springs.

Teaching Boys to Sing

In the winter all the boys of the kauisiktum clan of an age somewhere between six and twelve years were assembled in the dance house to be taught their clan and enemy songs. The paha, who carried a ceremonial quiver, had charge of all the boys and did not allow them to leave the dance house. This ceremony, called wek'lūil, has marked similarities to the mānet ceremony to the west, likewise this ceremonial quiver, called hōkil, appears as a possible derivative of the more elaborate western ground painting which was not used among the Palm Springs Cahuilla. The quiver was made of mountain sheep, deer, or wildcat hide painted in symbolic designs with red and black, and was regarded as specially significant to the boys undergoing instruction. An elder male relative of each boy taught him his clan and enemy songs. The older man sang the songs and the boy followed him, accompanying himself with a rattle. The rattle, called mauūlepūc, was made of an incised gourd filled with palm seeds. There was a wooden handle attached and the whole was carefully painted.

For five or six days this ceremony continued, the elder men taking the boys off separately into the brush in the daytime so that they would not interrupt each other. When singing the boys would kneel and shake their rattles, constantly repeating their songs. At night they returned to the dance house where each boy sang three or four songs in turn. All this time the boys fasted, being allowed only water to drink. In their hair each wore two eagle feathers projecting forwards, and around their waists were belts of twisted grass tightened to serve for ''hunger belts'' as well as breechclouts.

Girls' Adolescence Ceremony

At the same time that the boys were learning their songs, all the girls in the clan, of about fourteen years of age, who had just had their first menses, were initiated into womanhood. This ceremony was called hemeūlūniwe. A pit was dug in the center of the dance house and a fire built in it. When this was thoroughly heated the fire was raked out, the hole lined with hañal (a tall desert grass), and the girl was laid on this, being covered with grass and hot sand. Here, save for brief intervals while the pit was being reheated, she remained for four or five days. In the daytime when the boys were out in the brush practicing their songs, a hauinik (singer) would teach the girls the clan songs while other people danced around the pit chanting. At other times relatives of the girls would teach them the songs they sang against enemy clans on the desert. Like the boys, the girls wore "hunger belts" of braided grass. They had a special wooden head scratcher and were given a decoction of bitter herbs to drink. Under no circumstances could they eat food with salt in it.

On the last morning of the ceremony when both boys and girls had learned all the songs, they were allowed to bathe. They were then painted with dots of red, black, and white over arms and face, in accord with an old tuktum (wildcat) moiety song. This finished the ceremony, for as far as could be ascertained there was no racing or rock painting for either sex.[190]

Naming of Children

Following these boys' and girls' puberty ceremonies there was a ceremony called tēūlūnī'l meaning "name them." At this time all the children of about six years of age were gathered together in the ceremonial house and given their names. An older male relative of the child selected the name, as a rule that of a dead ancestor, and holding the child up in his arms he announced the name to the assembled clan. The people all answered "oh! ho-ho!" and shouted the name. While informants were rather vague in their memories of this old ceremony they stated that the names of the individuals indicated their moiety, for all the animate world was divided into the two classes, hence an animal or plant name must belong to one or the other. Exact verification of this statement could not be obtained from Palm Springs informants, but the short list previously cited gives an idea of such a division. There seems likewise to have been comparatively little attention paid the secret or "enemy" names

---

190 It is possible that these last details were once actively practiced for there are some faded, red, linear drawings on rocks in Andreas canyon, just southeast of Palm Springs, that are very similar to the angular and diamond-shaped designs painted on rocks near La Jolla and Rincon by Luiseño girls at the close of their puberty rites.

by the Palm Springs people but in this, as in the previous case,
I am more inclined to think the long period since such practices
were observed has resulted in the present indifference, rather than
any actual non-observance of the custom under aboriginal conditions.

EAGLE-KILLING CEREMONY

Very long ago the eagle-killing ceremony called aswit pimekniktem
"eagle killing" was performed once a year when young eagles were
obtained.[191] The last ceremony of this sort was performed before
Alejo Potencio was old enough to remember, but he was told of it.
It was very similar to the same ceremony already described which
occurred among the Desert Cahuilla, but there are a few elaborations
or new details which make it worth repeating. The kauisiktum clan
had an eagle's nest located under a white rock on the top of a peak
west of Tahquitz canyon. According to Alejo, "this eagle was
created human, he was made to live near each tribe and be their
eagle." Just before the young eagles could fly the paha was sent
by the net, who actually owned the eagles, with a small party to
secure them. They would climb up just under the nest and shoot
arrows just over it until the young birds became frightened and
fluttered out of the nest. They were then caught, their wings carefully tied down, and were carried to the net's house where they were
placed in a cage. Prior to setting out on this expedition all members
of the clan assembled at the dance house bringing food; they would
then pray to the "Great Spirit,"[192] to the mountain, and to the eagle.
Only after this had been done could they capture the young birds.

While the young birds were kept in captivity they were carefully
fed with rabbits which the boys of the clan hunted for them. When

---

[191] In all cases obtained among the California Shoshoneans it was the golden
eagle (*Aquila chrysaetos*) that was ceremonially killed. The southern bald eagle
(*Haliaeetus leucocephalus leucocephalus*) common to the islands of the Santa
Barbara group, and mentioned by Palm Springs informants, was not so important
ceremonially. At best, birds of this species could only have been stragglers into
the interior, but whether they had the same ceremonial importance here as among
the Chumash, I do not know.

[192] The term "Great Spirit" is employed here because it was the one used
by Alejo. Direct questioning evoked no response in this regard, so whether
this is a reflection of Christianity, or of an early native cult like that of
Chungichnish to the west, I cannot say. Mr. John Gaffey, of San Pedro, an
old friend of Alejo Potencio, told me that the latter used the term amanah
for God, or "great spirit," in connection with the Golardrina herb, which he
said would always cure people bitten by rattlesnakes, except those "whom
amanah had called." The two creators, so far as I could find out, are not
prayed to, and it is possible that there are other deities to whom prayers are
offered.

the birds were fully feathered the ceremony of the killing was prepared for. So far as Alejo had heard, this was a small affair to which
only only one other clan might come, in this case the paniktum clan
from Andreas canyon. All night they danced with the eagles, singing the eagle songs, and in the morning the eagles died. All the
people wept and wailed when this happened. The eagles were carefully skinned; the skin, called pīwic, was carefully preserved wrapped
up in the maīswut bundle of the clan. Feathers from the skin were
used to decorate the images that were burned, but were never given
away. Likewise according to Alejo the young eagles were always
kept by the clan and were never presented to other nets as gifts.

According to Palm Springs informants the "whirling" or
"eagle" dance was never performed at Palm Springs. Alejo Potencio
said that this ceremony, along with mānet and the fire dance, were
all left at kekliva, a mountain just north of Saboba,[193] where according to legend the kauisiktum clan left their original language as well.
The following things they also left there: pōhit (two shoulder decorations of eagle feathers), pōhot (two sticks about two and a half feet
long, held in each hand and beaten together), and tōmīnut (a long
string of eagle, crow, and vermilion flycatcher feathers, similar to the
"sacred feathers" of the Serrano). This is a striking symbolical
representation of the obvious fact that the Palm Springs Cahuilla
possessed less ritual and fewer ceremonies than their western neighbors. Whether it is a record of migration, however, is open to
considerable doubt.

CEREMONIES FOR THE DEAD

As has been already indicated the old life of the Pass peoples, and
for that matter of nearly all the natives of southern California, is
today centered around the ceremonies for the dead and the propitiation of their spirits. Among both the Palm Springs Cahuilla and
the remnants of the true Pass Cahuilla, there has been a marked
tendency in the last sixty years to gather all fragments of old ceremonies, many of which were once unconnected, into a one-week period
of mourning and "fiesta." In this regard, however, it must not be
forgotten that the evidence indicates this grouping of ceremonies
to be rather a characteristic of all mountain Shoshoneans in southern
California, from the Cupeño to the Serrano, and is not entirely
modern. The aboriginal tendency has been greatly accelerated by

---

[193] See clan migration legend, present paper, p. 100.

modern conditions, and today these week-long ceremonies, somewhat erroneously called "fiestas" by the white people, sum up for the Indians all that they remember and cherish of their former life.

There is therefore much of pathos in these attempts to reconstruct that which has gone before, and the wonder of it is that so much of the spirit and color survives at all. To the many white observers at such a ceremony it appears merely a "fiesta" for social purposes, of a somewhat forlorn and incomprehensible type. But to the older Indians it is a hopeless protest against the ruthless hand of time which has wiped out all that once made their lives. More and more these ceremonies assume the "fiesta" nature, for the younger Indians are taking over the ways of their white neighbors and with them the viewpoint of the modern American. To the ethnologist who has been largely under the necessity of reconstructing dead institutions from the words of saddened old Indians, the actual ceremonies such as the author was fortunate enough to witness at Palm Springs, have a very different meaning. Revivified before him he sees and hears many of the things he has talked about with the old men, and for six nights he may catch glimpses of the life that flourished before Cabrillo sailed up the coast of Alta California. In my description of this ceremony I have attempted to give, at least in small part, expression to this feeling. The following are the ceremonies for the dead among the Cahuilla of Palm Springs and the San Gorgonio pass.

Burning the Body

At Palm Springs this was called tcutni'l, "burning the body," and occurred shortly after death. Relatives by marriage, and near-by clans, often came to this ceremony and brought presents for the net of the deceased. At this time the napanaa, shell money, was sent to the net of the deceased by all other nets hearing of the death. If the deceased were a woman, all her ollas, hidden in the canyons or along the ridges where mesquite trees grew, were sought out and broken. At the same time that the body was burned, the house and most of the possessions of the dead person were also burned. For many years, ever since informants actually remember, burial has supplanted cremation, but the destruction of property and even houses by fire, has taken place within quite recent times.[194]

---

[194] E. H. Davis, Early Cremation Ceremonies of the Luiseño and Diegueño Indians of Southern California, Indian Notes and Monographs, 7:103, 1921, records a rite of this kind performed in 1917 by Desert Cahuilla.

Covering the Tracks of the Dead

This ceremony called tcipīnī'l, ''covering the tracks,'' might occur any time after the cremation of the body, usually within a month. The clan of the deceased, and the immediate family especially, brought food to the dance house. Near-by clans, and those who had previously sent presents, were invited to be present. In the afternoon women of the clan dragged bolts of calico around the dance house to ''wipe out the tracks of the dead'' and prevent the return of the spirit. All night the assembled people sang songs to propitiate the dead. At midnight or early in the morning, the relatives of the deceased threw away gifts of cloth, food, and basketry which were gathered up by the guests. These were called wiwitcahuñka, ''anything thrown around.'' At this time any remaining personal possessions of the dead were burned. The visitors, who at this time brought no presents, gathered up their gifts and departed. Both of these ceremonies seem to have been common to all Pass Cahuilla clans.

Burning the Images

This was called nūkil, ''the burning,'' and among the Palm Springs Cahuilla occurred about a year after death. Usually it was held for all deaths occurring within a period of perhaps six months, and several images were burnt. At Palm Springs it usually took place in February, the exact time being set by the clan leader. At the time of tcipīnī'l, ''covering the tracks,'' the net told the immediate family of the dead person to prepare for the large image-burning ceremony. Later the net, through the paha, asked all the clan members to bring tciputmul (large, wide-mouthed baskets) containing their contributions of food to the ''big house,'' where it was stored in anticipation of the coming ceremony. About one month before the ceremony the paha invited all the outside clans to be present and named the exact day. All these things were done in order and the day of the ceremony was never broadcasted prior to the formal invitation to the other clans. This procedure was characteristic of most of the Pass Cahuilla clans, but according to Rosa Morongo each of the most westerly groups that were under Serrano influence formerly performed the ceremony once every two years as is the case at present for all. The Palm Springs clans, like those of the Desert clans previously described, formerly had the ceremony once a year. The time for this ceremony among the western

Pass clans occurred when the constellation of Orion, called pa' tem (mountain sheep) was directly overhead, at which time the māriña clan of the Serrano gave their ceremony, the other western Pass Cahuilla clans following in turn.

In the description of this ceremony, I have combined information obtained before and after, with actual observations made at Palm Springs during the week from February 2 to February 8, 1925, while the kauisiktum clan was performing this rite. During the actual ceremony I was given information by many of the participants, especially Francisco Potencio, Jolian Norte, and Gabriel Costo, the last two being Mountain Cahuillas attending the "fiesta." After the close of the ceremony I talked to Alejo Potencio, the kauisiktum clan leader who had conducted the rites, with Jolian Norte from Los Coyotes canyon as my interpreter. The Cahuilla story of the creation (p. 130) was obtained at this time while it was fresh in the mind of my informant, for nearly all the songs sung for the six nights are concerned with this theme. Hence it is a vital part of the ritual, and reference to it will give the background of much of the ceremony.

The actual rites are all performed in the kicamnawut,[195] a round house with a diameter of about forty feet; the walls are about five feet high, made of odd-sized boards tightly fitted together, and the roof is thatched with fronds of the native palm (*Washingtonia filifera*). At the back of the dance house is a small room where the maīswut is kept, and in front of the house is a board and palm-frond fence forming a considerable enclosure. Here in a small house are stored all the flour, coffee, sugar, and other foodstuffs gathered by the clan for several months previous to the occasion, and fed to the guests during the "fiesta." In this enclosure the cooking and eating takes place during the week, the ritual alone occurring within the "big house." Prior to the ceremony the net, in this case Alejo Potencio, "retreats" within the dance house and talks to no one. Much of this time he spends in the inner room conferring with the maīswut. Meanwhile the paha has organized a rabbit hunt and many jackrabbits and cottontails are brought in as food for both guests and clan members. There seems to be no ceremonial significance attached to this detail at the present time but it may have been more important formerly. The actual division of the food and its preparation are attended to by the takwa and his family, in this case Pedro

---

195 Hooper, present series, 16:328–333, gives a description of the same ceremony at Palm Springs in 1918.

Chino; while the paha, Marcus Belargo, acts as general superintendent. The net seems to take the rôle of priest rather than that of leader, and is not in evidence during the actual arrangements for the performance. It would be almost impossible for an outsider to speak to him for several days prior to the ceremony. This preliminary retirement of the ceremonial leader is a definite part of the ceremony.

Monday evening the people come to the dance house, the women and children sit around the walls with the younger men, while all the older men sit on benches around a fire in the front of the house. None of the invited clans are present at this time but a considerable number of visitors from the desert and other places are already there. Among the older men tobacco is passed around and they smoke quietly, very little is said, but occasionally the paha or some old man will groan and blow up in the air three times, the blowing being accompanied by all in the dance house. During this time the net is not in evidence, being in the room with the maīswut. From the very beginning women, relatives of the dead, cry softly and monotonously—the sound occasionally rising to a wail and then dying down. After about two hours of this, when it is almost dark the shaman of the local clan, Albert Potencio, holding in each hand a bunch of horned owl feathers called tcīatem, rises next to the fire and begins to dance and sing. He dances around the fire shifting his weight from his left to his right foot, and motioning to the four directions with the tcīatem. The song is to the "four little witch-doctors" of the north, temamka kikitum pūalem, the south, kitcumka kikitum pūalem, the east, tamika kikitum pūalem, and the west, kauīka kiktum pūalem, desiring them to find out from mūkat whether the time is right for the ceremony. Likewise he asks the mountains, the sky, night, and day whether it is propitious. In the chorus of this song the kauisiktum clan members join in, with a rising and falling cadence "pa-pī, pa-pī" almost rising to a deep melody, but always just failing and dying down. Then the net, who is with the maīswut in the inner room hears from the little witch-doctors that all is well and the time propitious. When the net joins the group around the fire it is a sign that all is well with "the big house" and the ceremony may proceed.

At this time one of the relatives of the dead comes in with a bolt of cloth which she spreads over the net, to the accompaniment of much wailing from all the women. Then led by the net the people of the kauisiktum clan begin their songs about the death and cremation of mūkat, chanting slowly and in perfect time. The first song is about the "iron wood"[196] from the mountains with which the body must be burned. At this point some one in the audience shouts and makes a great noise at which many people laugh.[197] At the close of each song all present go "hum-hum-ūh!" three times and then exhale "ah!" upward. This is to blow the spirits away from the dance house to the place where they are going.

The next song is about starting the fire, burning the legs, the arms, the intestines, and the head. This is chanted slowly and mournfully. Finally in the song the body is reduced to ashes all but the heart. Here they stop for a few minutes, then the song continues: coyote seizes the heart (several women, much excited, rise and dance in a bobbing weight-shifting manner exhaling their breath sharply in a whistle). Coyote runs to the end of the world and eats the heart, although many creatures chased him. There are many more songs about this, but only an istam clan may sing them. The unidentified joker shouts encouragement and makes loud remarks. All becomes quiet, and nothing but the low sobbing of some of the women can be heard. Then comes a song about the marsh hawk, wesunauwit, who flew away for some kangaroo rats, paīwit, to cure mūkat, but found his father in ashes when he returned. He rolled in these ashes, becoming gray, and flew away to the north. The chorus of this song goes "ho! ho! wesunauwit," repeated over and over.

Each of these songs takes many minutes to sing and there are long intervals between. As it is now very late many of the guests go to sleep in the dance house, where the children have been sleeping quietly in spite of the singing. The dance house is full of smoke, the few oil lanterns and the dim fire giving a fitful light, but around the embers the old men continue the chanting, aided by the women hauiniks who sit behind them. People occasionally pass in or out of the kicamnawut, but they are very quiet.

The next song tells of palmitcawut who followed after the dead mūkat to telmekic, the abode of the dead. For the dead soul the trip

---

[196] This rendering of the songs is very fragmentary, and only intended to give some idea of the amount and quality of each verse in the singing. For the complete creation story see pp. 130–143.

[197] This apparent mocking of the ceremony occurred a good many times. Whether it was a part of the rites could not be determined. There is here a suggestion of the licensed Pueblo clowns who ridicule solemn ceremonial acts. Strangely enough there are stronger resemblances to this feature among the Pomo of north central California, see Loeb, present series, 19:339, 1926.

was short "like an awakening" but for the shaman palmitcawut it was long, and he saw great lizards and tēwelevul, "great devils." Finally he came to where mūkat waited; he desired to find out what the plants that had arisen where mūkat was burned were for. All this is in many songs, or verses, and each is sung several times. The next verse continues "Heat and warmth are from my body, for I am tēwelevul (a great devil)," replies mūkat. The shaman palmitcawut answers "Your heart, your spirit, and your warmth, I cannot come near you, I am afraid, for you are tēwelevul!" Then mūkat says "I begin to remember now, since I died and was burned I had forgotten. All else I told you before I died but not what these plants were for." The shaman answers "Yes, now you remember," and the chanting rises with gorgeous deep swing. As the verses continue, mūkat told palmitcawut that these strange plants were vegetables grown from the parts of his body. He promised to return in three days[198] to his people and palmitcawut went back. On the third night mūkat returned, but all nūkatem (the creation) were asleep, only one man, tceptcikwut, was awake. He gave a loud shout and all nūkatem woke up. They told him he had lied to them, but suddenly mūkat answered with the thunder, and all were very much afraid. This makes up many verses.

Then, while one woman cries in perfect harmony with the chant, they sing "Tukut is crying, all the world is crying for mūkat." All the women weep and wail. One following another the verses are chanted, accompanied by much crying——"Mūūt (the horned owl), kauwmūt (the pygmy owl), are crying for mūkat. All nūkatem (the creation) is crying, all are weeping, the noise is great. Mūūt (the horned owl) and pūc (the road runner) are crying, all are crying for mūkat! All are sick at heart, all are crying, mak'il (the dove) and kwakwut (the duck) are crying for mūkat." Several women are dancing now, there is much laughter for they have left out one song. They give this song in quicker time, and launch out into the last verse with quick rhythm and perfect unison, "tūseko-kalem (the robin), and kō' halem (the quail) are weeping, it is over, it is the end, all is finished."

It is now two o'clock in the morning and many of the group leave, or wrap up in blankets in the dance house. A nucleus of about fifteen or sixteen old people continue the singing. This last song series is, according to Francisco Potencio, in the Yuman language, and is

---

[198] This has a strong biblical resemblance and may be a result of mission influence. It was not mentioned in the creation story told me by Alejo later.

much less animated than the foregoing series.[199] The almost undistinguishable words are chanted in a dreary rising and falling monotone. The songs are about a woman about to have twins which were named xōta and hanī before they were born. At this point in the singing all the women wail loudly and steadily for at least five minutes, covering their heads with their shawls. Then the song continues: the boys have grown up alone, then from the Tehachapi pass came two girls who stayed all night with the boys. The next morning each boy accused the other of having had intercourse during the night and each denied it. To settle the argument they urinated, and as the younger boy could only urinate a short distance it was proved that he had had intercourse. The woman he had slept with became pregnant, and gave birth to twin boys named para and akī. This last event occurred in San Fernando canyon. This song lasts for the rest of the night, being ended just at dawn when the singers disperse to their homes, only Alejo, the net, remaining in the dance house with the guests from other places.

The next night is much the same, more songs of the creation are sung by the local clan, from about eight o'clock in the evening until dawn. More visitors have arrived, especially people from the Torros and Martinez reservations in the desert.

Wednesday evening the local clan continues its singing, after three shamans from the desert have sung their songs and danced, each holding tcīatem of horned owl feathers in their hands. These songs have choruses in which the entire group joins. The first songs sung by the kauisiktum people are about menyil, the moon, and are sung for the dead women. These songs supposedly go to the spirits of the dead women and tell each where to go, how to dress, fly, run, breathe, stand, stop, and what to see. They tell her to wear a headdress, to use the sun as her apron, and the sky as her necklace. This series lasts until about eleven o'clock. Then a series of songs about the sickness and death of mūkat are sung: these songs give advice to the spirit of the dead man. Each verse is ended with the thrice repeated "hum-hum-ūh'" and the blowing up to the sky. As usual the women of the kauisiktum clan weep and wail at intervals.

Thursday evening a group from the Torres reservation sing about half the night, the local clan singing the remainder of the time. This is the first night during which no shamans dance or sing.

---

[199] A Mohave song series, employing the same names and similar incidents, is given by Kroeber, Handbook of the Indians of California, Bur. Am. Ethn., Bull. 78:764, 1925.

Friday night is one of the most important, ceremonially, of the entire week. Before sundown all the people gather around the dance house, more have arrived from the desert, Saboba, and even a few Cupeño men from Pala, hence the place is nearly full. As soon as it is dark the paha makes everyone come inside and sit down; he makes everyone be very quiet. Then he puts out all the lights and extinguishes the fire. All sit quietly in the darkness. Then from the little room in the back of the dance house, Alejo, the net, brings the maĭswut, holding it under his arm. He gives it to the paha who spreads it out in the center of the house. All the members of the kauisiktum clan kneel around this maĭswut, and the men blow smoke over it from their cigarettes, asking it to bless the "big house," to be good to them and all the people. The net talks to the bundle in the maĭswut language, a series of rising and falling monosyllables which no one but the net knows. The slightest indecorum at this time would be very dangerous and all but the net, who talks to the maĭswut, are reverently silent.

At present this maĭswut of the kauisiktum clan consists only of the roll of reed matting. Many years ago there were rolled up in this bundle eagle feathers and the pelvis of a California grizzly bear. This latter was very powerful, and was called yuuknut "frightening." It was perforated, and the paha would whistle on it at this time, a sound that would kill any irreverent or noisy person. The bundle and its contents are called "the heart of the house." Now only the bundle is left.

While it is still dark the net rolls up the bundle and takes it back into the inner room, where it remains until the next ceremony. The fire is rebuilt, the oil lanterns are lighted, and the kauisiktum clan continues its singing of the creation songs until just before sunrise.

Friday evening and Saturday morning the people of the wanikiktum Cahuilla clan and the two Serrano clans arrive. Saturday afternoon the images are completed. These represent the three people who had died within the last year and a half, one man, Francisco Chino, and two women, Marcellina Potencio and Mrs. John Joseph. The images were made of wood and grass, covered with modern clothing, representing the two women and the one man. In the old days the framework of these images was rolled maĭswut, and they were dressed in skins, with eagle feather decorations. Old people of the three visiting clans make these images, and Saturday afternoon when they are completed the women dance with them accompanied by singing and wailing. They are then wrapped in canvas and put away.

Saturday night the three invited groups sing from darkness to
dawn. The maliñakiktum and amnañavitcem[200] Serrano clans sing
from dark until a little after midnight. Their songs are in the
Serrano language sung slowly with considerable approach to melody.
Usually both these groups sing together, but at intervals each sings
its own particular songs. These are based on the Serrano creation
story.[201] One song directed to the dead spirits is as follows: "You
have left this world, you are going to another world which your
creator made for you. Go without coming back, without looking
back, to live forever and ever."

The wanikiktum Cahuilla clan members sing for the remainder of
the night, singing songs in the Serrano language. Just before dawn
they stop. All during this night there are "peon" games in progress
around fires near the dance house. The people wander from game
to game or listen to the singing inside. While the outside clans are
singing, the old people of the kauisiktum clan group together, the
women crying softly, a sound of mourning that forms an undertone
to the whole ceremony within the dance house. Outside, however, the
spirit of "fiesta" prevails and the "peon" games are surrounded by
noisy partisans, while around other fires are gathered social groups
visiting. With the gray dawn the games break up, and all the people
assemble in the dance house enclosure to witness the final ceremonies.

As soon as the singing ceases, the paha and the takwa divide the
flour, coffee, and sugar given to the invited guests. Each woman of
the invited clans receives so many baskets full of the various gifts.
With loud wailings the images are brought out and laid on a canvas
in front of the dance house, and the net prays over them. These
prayers are said to be in a language "from the beginning" which no
one understands but the net.[202] Supposedly these were the songs used
in the first mourning ceremony for mūkat, and have been passed on
from net to net. Then, while the women of the local clan throw
away coins and calicoes, the net, the paha, and the takwa carry the
images around the dance house. With them go women trailing cali-

---

[200] These are terms used by my Cahuilla informants in referring to the mãriña
and the aturavīatum Serrano clans. The Cahuilla term for the Serrano is
ismaĭlem.

[201] Gifford, present series, 14:182–185, gives an outline of this story.

[202] A careful linguistic study of these esoteric, or archaic, prayers and chants
might well reveal the original dialect used, which would be first-hand evidence of
the lines of ceremonial diffusion. Some of them are doubtless mere abracadabra,
but I am convinced that some are actually foreign dialects. They could only be
obtained by one who had secured the entire confidence of the ceremonial leaders,
which can be done with tact.

coes to wipe out all the tracks of the dead. This is done because the tracks around the ''big house,'' which is the ''center of everything,'' are most important, and by wiping them out the others which cannot be found are likewise cared for. The images are then taken to the cemetery and burned. The image of Francisco Chino is carried by Mrs. Susy Arenas, that of Marcellina Potencio by Mrs. Juan Costo, and that of Mrs. John Joseph by Mrs. Matilda Toro. These are relatives of the deceased. In the old days, according to Mrs. Rosa Morongo, a relative, usually a man, carried the image. He would run with it and the paha would shoot at him with a bow and arrow. This was called mamaneka in Cahuilla and wuuv in Serrano, meaning ''dodging.'' The man was paid for this service, and on his success in dodging the arrows depended the fate of the spirit whose image he carried. Today relatives are not paid for carrying the images, but outsiders are. Likewise Mrs. Louis Kintano, who danced and sang all night with the kauisiktum clan, of which she is not a member, was paid for her services.

While the relatives carried the images to the place of burning, Alejo Potencio, the net, and Marcus Belargo, the paha, divide the muketem, shell money. The net measures the string in the manner previously described, and gives it to the paha. The paha calls ''witcū,'' and shouts the name of the party that receives it. First he gave a string to Mrs. Rosa Morongo of the māriña clan, which has no paha at present, then to Miguel Savatco, who is both kīka and paha of the aturavīatum clan, and then to Mrs. Juan Costo, acting nuut of the wanikiktum clan. Each of these took the money and departed. After all this is over, the dead who have been remembered for one year, must now be forgotten.

Palm Springs Cahuilla Creation Myth

As told by Alejo Potencio, ceremonial chief, through Jolian Nortes, interpreter, immediately after the biennial mourning ceremony at Palm Springs, February, 1925.[203]

In the beginning there was nothing but darkness. At times it was lighter but with no moon or stars. One was called tūkmiatahat (female) the other

---

[203] This myth includes the greater number of songs sung at the mourning ceremony. Each sentence given here forms one verse, including much repetition, and the song takes three nights to sing completely. It varies slightly from group to group, and the versions of any two widely separated Cahuilla groups are different in detail though the general motifs are the same. It is a highly impressive and solemn chant, rising at times to rare beauty, but usually sung in a monotonous rising and falling cadence.

tūkmiatelka (male). Sounds, humming or thunder, were heard at times. Red, white, blue, and brown colors[204] came all twisting to one point in the darkness. These were acting all together—twisting.[205] These came together in one point to produce. This ball shook and whirled all together into one substance, which became two embryos wrapped in this placenta.[206] This was formed in space and darkness. These were born prematurely, everything stopped for they were stillborn.

Then again all the lights whirled together, joined, and produced. This time the embryos grew fully—the children inside talked to one another. They asked each other, "What are we? We are eskwatkwatwitcem, and estanamawitum,"[207] for at that time they did not know themselves. While they were in this sack they rolled back and forth;[208] they stretched their arms and knees[209] to make a hole[210] so they could get out.[211] Then they named themselves Mūkat and Temaīyauit.

First their heads came out; they called themselves tcimūluka; both heads came out at once. Then came out their shoulders, ribs, waist, thighs, knees, and ankles.[212] Thus they came out of their house into the darkness, but they were unable to see one another in the dark space. As they sat in the dark Temaīyauit said, "I am older than you, for I first heard the darkness making sounds."[213] Mūkat answered, "No! I am the older for I heard it first." Thus they began to quarrel. Then Temaīyauit said, "What can we do to eat our smoke and blow—aaah! away the dark." Mūkat answered, "Why do you say you are older than I am? Take the pipe[214] from your heart,[215] out of your mouth." So Mūkat took from his heart the black pipe,[216] and Temaīyauit took from his heart the white pipe.[217]

Temaīyauit asked Mūkat, "What will we smoke in it?" Mūkat answered, "Why do you say you are older than I am? We can draw from our hearts tobacco.[218] Then we can eat and smoke it in our pipe." He drew black tobacco[219] from his heart, and Temaīyauit drew white tobacco[220] from his heart. Their pipes were solid, and Temaīyauit asked Mūkat, "How can we open up our pipes to eat and smoke tobacco?" Mūkat answered, "Why do you say you are older than I, if you do not know that with our whiskers we

---

[204] sel wĭl, sel h'eu: red; tēvic wĭl, tēvic he'u: white; tūkic heū, tūkic wĭl: blue: tesit heū, tesit wĭl: brown.

[205] tahūhuñ-sūivee.

[206] tcemsilayaa: our placenta.

[207] Archaic or esoteric. No meaning remembered.

[208] manamanatcemayahī.

[209] wawalwawal-tcemeyahī.

[210] hataniamkavayuul.

[211] tūnaltūnal-tcemeyahī.

[212] sēka, amī, hemhūlūlū, hemees, hemtomī, hemī.

[213] This was their mother's lullaby.

[214] taīuuinumuli, pipe.

[215] tcemsuñ a, from our heart.

[216] uliltunikic.

[217] uliltevicnikic.

[218] pīwut.

[219] pīwut tūlnikic.

[220] pīwut tēwicnikic.

can bore a hole²²¹ through which to draw smoke?''²²² Then the hole was too
big and the tobacco would not stay, but from their hearts they drew out white
and black materials²²³ and made it smaller. All was settled, but they had
no fire.

Then Temaīyauit asked Mūkat, ''How can we light our tobacco to eat and
smoke it?'' and Mūkat answered, ''You still say you are older than I am and
yet do not know how to light your pipe! We can draw from our heart the sun
from which we can light our pipe.'' Then he began to draw the sun; from
his mouth it came, but it slipped through his hands to his feet. Both tried to
catch it, but it was too fast and got away and disappeared. It was lost in
the darkness.

Then Mūkat drew out from his heart the West Light,²²⁴ and Temaīyauit
drew from his heart the East Light.²²⁵ With these Mūkat lit his pipe. When
he smoked the smoke drifted up and formed clouds. He blew it out in spreading puffs, and said, ''This is to eat our hearts and kill our hearts!''

To find out who was the oldest he held up his pipe, saying, ''I am holding
it down.'' Temaīyauit said, ''Where are you?'' looking on the ground.
Temaīyauit tried to find it below, but Mūkat cheated him holding it up in the
air. At last he reached it. Mūkat said, ''You claim you are older but you
are not old enough to know this!'' Temaīyauit smoked until he had had
enough, then he said, ''I am holding it up,'' but he held it on the ground.
But Mūkat knew where it was, and right away reached and took it. This
proved Mūkat was the oldest.

Then they smoked, and Temaīyauit asked Mūkat what they should do next.
Mūkat answered, ''We can draw from our heart the center pole of the world,''²²⁶
and from their hearts they both drew it. ''Lift it up, stand it up, your center
pole of the world, our center pole of the world. Make it stand, your heart
of the world, our heart of the world,'' they said. They put it into the air
but it would not stand. They then drew from their hearts all kinds of snakes²²⁷
to hold the center pole of the world. These they told to hold it but they
could not. Then they put two huge rocks²²⁸ together to hold it but still
it moved.

Then from their hearts they drew all kinds of web-spinning spiders,²²⁹ and
these ran their webs from the top of the pole in all directions, and at last the
center pole of the world stood firm.

Both said, ''It is all still, our heart of the world, your heart of the world,''
and they began to climb up it, saying, ''We, Mūkat and Temaīyauit, are
climbing up!'' Still farther up they sing, ''Mūkat, Temaīyauit, going up, up,
farther up we are going!'' Halfway up the center pole they sing again, and

---

²²¹ penliwalwaane, bore a hole.

²²² penhusossone, to draw on a pipe.

²²³ temalhu uhū, temal pikikī, tūlkūsivivamal (archaic), kanawal tūlawal:
black; tēwic nikic, white.

²²⁴ kauwīkut.

²²⁵ tamīkut.

²²⁶ whīyanahut, translated as the ''center pole of the world,'' or ''heart
of the world,'' and described as a tremendously enlarged shaman's wand,
with which they effect cures and perform magic. It was ''like a Bishop's
mitre'' and symbolized the power of the creators.

²²⁷ palukūwit, temesuwut, all kinds of snakes.

²²⁸hauwaiyauwut and temamlawut.

²²⁹ whalwhalwitem, kuītukwitem.

still singing they come nearly to the top, always calling themselves by name. Then, still calling their names, they reach the top, and sing, ''We, Mūkat and Temaīyauit, are sitting on the top, on the point of the center pole of the world.'' From the top they looked down and saw clouds of smoke[230] rolling up from the place whence they had come.

Tamaīyauit asked where the smoke came from. Mūkat answered, ''It is settling[231] in the place where we were lying and comes from our afterbirth.[232] It is black blood, red blood, fresh blood, smallpox, colds and sore throat, cramps in the back, boils, mumps, hives and itches, inflamed and sore eyes, blindness, acute body pains, palsy and twitching, consumption, venereal diseases, rheumatism, emaciations, swelling of the body,[233] and all other sicknesses.'' All these were the clouds of smoke coming from the place where they came into being. Then Mūkat said, ''We will give power to man or woman, so that each sickness can be cured by someone that has power. These will be the doctors.''[234]

Mūkat was on the west side of the center pole of the world and Temaīyauit on the east side. Mūkat asked Temaīyauit, ''Which direction shall be the oldest?'' Temaīyauit answered, ''We will name that direction where you are now.'' Mūkat then said, ''I am older than you, so first of the directions is the west,[235] then the north,[236] south,[237] and east.''[238] Thus it is that when people come into the ceremonial house they blow west, north, south, and east.

Temaīyauit said, ''How can we make the earth?'' Mūkat answered, ''You see I am older than you, for we can draw the earth from our heart.'' And he drew black earth[239] from his heart, and Temaīyauit drew white earth[240] from his. This earth they put on top of the center pole of the world but it rolled off and was lost. From their hearts they drew all black and all white spiders,[241] who spread webs in all directions. So for a second time they drew black and white earth from their hearts and placed it on the top. To spread this earth they drew forth from their hearts all the kinds of ants[242] who spread out the earth on all sides. To make it faster they drew out two whirlwinds[243] that rapidly completed the spreading out of the black and white earth. Thus was the whole earth made, but it moved and would not stay still. The ants were too light, they could not hold it steady. From their hearts Mūkat and

---

[230] mūlikalipa, hauakalapa: smoke rolling in clouds.

[231] tcemkonive, tcemwenive: settling.

[232] tcemsilayaa: our placenta; tcemkalapī: our afterbirth.

[233] ewul tūlnikic: black blood; ewul selnikic: red blood; ewul palnikic: fresh blood; lūmüil: smallpox; k'ekū: cold and sore throat; tcewiwinut: cramps in the back; tcūklālūnit: boils; pahaīeūlūwinit: mumps or swollen sore throat; kīsawinit: hives or itch; mīwinit: inflamed eyes; tawawinut: blindness; mūwhinut: acute body pain; tawekkūskalet: palsy, twitching; tcatawawinut: consumption; ūūmūwinut: venereal disease; lumīwinut: rheumatism; whawhinut: emaciation; paticwinut: swelling of the body.

[234] pūelem: doctors.

[235] kauikanvic.

[236] temankawie.

[237] kitcamkawic.

[238] tamīkawic.

[239] temul tūlnikic: earth, black.

[240] temul tēwicnikic: earth, white.

[241] kuītūwhitum: black spiders; whalwhalwitum: white spiders.

[242] kūvicniwitum, anwitum.

[243] tenauakatem, kōtīaīalem.

Temaíyauit drew the ocean[244] and placed it all around the world, and likewise they drew out paña tēwelevelum and papakniwitum, the two water demons, and placed them in the ocean. All water creatures they put into the ocean, and, last of all they drew the sacred seaweed mat,[245] the sacred dancing feathers of the doctors,[246] the "water apron"[247] and "water tail"[248] and placed these in the ocean. Thus by their combined weight the last quivers of the earth were stilled, and it was flat as a table.

From their hearts again they drew the sky[249] but it swayed and flapped in the wind. They blew their saliva[250] to the sky and thus made the stars[251] which held the sky in place. Then they put the two whirlwinds at the edge of the earth, and they held the bottom of the sky firmly in place.

The creators determined to make creatures[252] for the earth. Temaíyauit drew coyote[253] from his heart for he was the first assistant.[254] Mūkat drew the horned owl,[255] who could see in the darkness, from his heart. Mūkat had black mud and Temaíyauit white mud to make creatures from, and they each commenced to make the body of a man. Mūkat worked slowly and carefully, modeling a fine body such as men have now. Temaíyauit worked rapidly making a rude body with a belly on both sides, eyes on both sides, and hands like the paws of a dog. The creators worked in the darkness, and the horned owl sat watching them. When a body was finished the owl would say, "M-M-M! It is finished," and coyote would come and put it away, putting those created by Mūkat in one place, and those by Temaíyauit in another. The latter worked three times as fast as the former, and had a great number of crude bodies finished, compared to the few good bodies made by Mūkat. All this took a long, long time.

Finally Mūkat stopped and drew the moon[256] from his heart and it became faintly light so they could see their creatures. Mūkat looked at those made by Tamaíyauit and said, "No wonder you have finished them so quickly, you are not doing good work!" Temaíyauit wished to know why, and Mūkat said, "They have two faces, eyes all around, bellies on both sides, feet pointing both ways and hands like a dog's paws!" Temaíyauit answered, "That is right, it is good, but your work is not good. One face and all parts on one side are not right for they cannot see behind. Mine can see coming and going. Open fingers will let food slip through, mine will hold anything." Mūkat replied, "Yes, but they can draw their hands together and hold anything. Your creatures cannot carry anything for they have no back or shoulders. they cannot hold an arrow to the bow or draw it back, for they are like a

---

[244] pal nūkut.

[245] paña maíswut, a mat that is wrapped around the fetish bundles, and from which images of the dead are made.

[246] paña tcíatum, feathers used by shamans.

[247] paña wíava, significance unknown. An archaic or esoteric term.

[248] paña hekwas, significance unknown. An archaic or esoteric term.

[249] tūkvac, also means "iron," because it is black before the sun comes up.

[250] hemhaña.

[251] sūūwitem.

[252] nūkatem.

[253] īsil.

[254] paha, the ceremonial assistant of the clan chief.

[255] mūut.

[256] menyil.

dog." "But," said Temaīyauit, "there will be no shooting." "Yes, there will be, later on,"[257] said Mūkat.

"But there will be no death," said Temaīyauit. Mūkat answered, "Yes, there will be death." "Then," said Temaīyauit, "if they die, they shall come back." "If they come back they shall smell like dead things," answered Mūkat. Temaīyauit said, "Then they can wash with white clay,[258] and smoke their bodies with burning salt grass[259] and willow[260] and become clean and good smelling." "If they do this the world will be too small," answered Mūkat. Temaīyauit said, "We can then spread it wider." "Yes, but there will not be enough food for all of them," answered Mūkat. "They can eat earth," said Temaīyauit. "But they will then eat up all the earth," answered Mūkat. Temaīyauit replied, "No, for by our power it will be swelling again." This was the end of the dispute.

Temaīyauit was angry because he always lost in every dispute. He said, "I will go to the bottom of the earth, whence I came, and take all my creatures with me, the earth,[261] sky,[262] and all my other creations." Mūkat answered, "You can take yours, but all mine will stay." Then Temaīyauit blew, and his breath opened the earth. His creatures went down with him, all save the moon,[263] the palm,[264] coyote, the wood duck,[265] and a few others. He tried to take earth and sky with him; a fierce wind blew and the earth shook all over, while the sky bent and swayed. Mūkat put one knee on the ground, held one hand on all his creatures, and with the other held up the sky. He cried, "hi! hi! hi! hi!" which is the way all people do now when the earthquake comes. In the struggle all the mountains and canyons appeared on the earth's surface, stream beds were formed, and water came out and filled them. At last Temaīyauit disappeared below, all became quiet, and the earth stopped shaking, but its rough uneven surface remains until today.

Then all Mūkat's creatures became alive. While it was still dark the white people had stolen away to the north, during the time Mūkat held up the sky. The sun[266] suddenly appeared, and all Mūkat's creatures were so frightened they began to chatter like blackbirds each in a different language. Mūkat could not understand any of these, but hearing one man, kīathwasimut, speak the Cahuilla language[267] he pressed him to his side, and let the others run around. This man was the ancestor of the Cahuilla people, and now lives in the abode of the sun,[266] moon,[263] and evening star.[268] Thus only the Cahuillas, speak the original language. Among these creatures was one with red hair[269] and a white clean face; he was cranky and crying, always running about. Mūkat saw this, and he took a long[270] and a short stick.[271] The first he put between the creature's legs like a horse, the second he put in his hand like a whip. Then the creature ran back and forth, going farther and farther away, until at last he disappeared into the north where all his party had gone

---

[257] temal hemūwan: earth, coming to the top; temal paākwan: earth, coming generations.

[258] ūlīwut, tēviwit.	[265] sassēmul.
[259] hañawit.	[266] tamit.
[260] sahawut.	[267] īvīatim.
[261] temal.	[268] sūwut pīniwus.
[262] tūkvac.	[269] ūlika, selnikic: head, red.
[263] menyil.	[270] kelawut, somatikic: stick, long.
[264] mawul.	[271] kelawut, voksekaīpī: stick, short.

before. Then Mūkat put all his creatures into the ceremonial house[272] for it was night. Far away to the north they saw a light, and all the creatures asked Mūkat, ''What is that light in the north which we see now?'' ''Yes,'' he replied, ''those are your older brothers and your younger brothers, your older sisters and your younger sisters. They went away at night. They did not hear me, they did not ask me. They are devils![273] They have four names.''[274]

When the sun arose in the east the dog[275] was talking, but then he became dumb. He knows everything in his heart, but he cannot say one word. The sun came up very hot. Some of Mūkat's children were burned black, some were burned red (well done, well cooked), but in the north where the white people were, it was cold, and they remained raw and white.

The moon was the only woman among all Mūkat's creatures. Every morning she would go away from the ceremonial house to a clean sandy place, where with woven grass string[276] she showed all the creatures how to make cat's cradles. Then she would put one group of people on one side and say, ''You are coyote people,''[277] and the others she would call wildcat people.[278] She told the coyote people to sing against the wildcat people as though they were singing enemy songs. Then the wildcat people would begin to dance; then they would do it the other way around. This was a game. She told them to build a little brush house and put one creature in the house to be chief.[279] Then she told another group to come from far away singing and dancing to the house. This was the way they should do later through all the generations to come. She also taught them to run, jump, wrestle, throw balls of mud at one another, and to flip pebbles at one another from their finger tips. Certain ones she picked out and said, ''You are women. You must grind, and feed these others, who are men, that come dancing to the house.''

At sunset they would return to the ceremonial house, dancing as they came. Among them was one called, tēvicnikictcumelmiī, who always kicked the rattlesnake[280] when he came in. The latter could not play with the other creatures because he could not walk. Mūkat took pity on the rattlesnake and gave him a cactus thorn[281] in his mouth as a fang. When all the other creatures were gone, Mūkat took his ceremonial staff[282] and told the snake to bite it. This the rattlesnake did, but his fang broke off. Then Mūkat pulled out a black whisker and put it in as a fang, but it broke off. So he pulled out a gray whisker, and with this fang the rattlesnake bit through the ceremonial staff and blood came out of it. Mūkat told the snake to bite his enemy and then crawl away to the mountain and stay in his hole. All was ready. When all the creatures came back from their playground tēvicnikictcumelmiī laughed and kicked the snake, which bit him. Tēvicnikictcumelmiī died at once, and

---

272 kicamnawut: translated ''big house.''
273 tēwellevelem.
274 mūwhinut, pahīvawit, kwawinit: archaic; tēwullevelem: devils.
275 awel.
276 witcut.
277 istam: one moiety name.
278 tūktum: the other Cahuilla moiety.
279 net: çlan ceremonial chief.
280 sūwit.
281 īwīul.
282 whīyanahut: shaman's wand. Also ''the center pole of the world.''

the snake crawled away to his hole in the mountain, where he has always stayed since rattling and biting, as the enemy of all Mūkat's creatures.

Mūkat told the moon to have his creatures make bows of wood and arrows of reeds,[283] with no points on them, and to have them stand in two lines and shoot at each other with these arrows. Then Mūkat told them to sharpen the points of the arrows. He then told them to make rock arrow-straighteners[284] and to make arrows of arrow-weed[285] about two feet long, with stone arrow-points.[286] These they were to shoot with short, strong, sycamore bows.[287] He told them to stand in two lines and shoot at one another, but they were afraid because it looked dangerous. Then takwic[288] said, "It is nothing. You cannot die from this," and he stuck an arrow through his body, pulling it out the other side. Then the hummingbird[289] put a quiver[290] on his back, and all shot at him, but they could not hit him for he was too small. He dodged each arrow, and said, "See, it is nothing!" The Arkansas kingbird[291] and then the butterfly[292] did the same, and each said, "See, it is nothing!" So did the crow[293] and the poor will,[294] and they both dodged. Then the vulture[295] tried it but he was too slow; they hit him, and he disappeared. Then the cony[296] wanted to fight them all, and he cried, "Hurry up! Hurry up!" All the creatures began to shoot each other, hunting through the tall grass. Mūkat laughed, and said, "Now they are beginning to kill one another." They shot until both sides were nearly all killed. Then the remainder saw their dead comrades and began to cry loudly. (At this point in the song all women must wail loudly.)

Mūkat looked at the dead people whose bodies were quivering and shaking.[297] Their spirits[298] arose, but their bodies were dead, and the spirits did not know where to go. They looked toward the west, and it seemed to be all clear for them. They went flying to the west. But when they got there there was no gate, they had to stop and come back crying to their bodies. Then toward the north they did the same thing, and to the south, but in vain. They flew to the sky but again in vain. Finally they went to the east where Temaīyauit was. He answered them, "Yes," he said, "you are something. You are great devils.[299] This is what I told Mūkat, that you would die and come back to life, but he always pushed away my word. Thus we created two kinds of

---

[283] hañal.

[284] yēūnapic.

[285] pāhal.

[286] tamanīut.

[287] isiltcukinup.

[288] The fire-ball demon, a great shaman, living on the top of San Jacinto peak.

[289] tūtcil.

[290] mamakwut.

[291] ultēhewic.

[292] malmul.

[293] alwut.

[294] pūlmic, also called the night jar. The Cahuilla say this is the way he got his twisting flight.

[295] yuñavic, the turkey vulture.

[296] ūlut, also called the pika, or little chief hare.

[297] kulūkwit, wekhaūwut, hemtahau: "quivering and shaking are their bodies."

[298] hemtēūlave.

[299] emetēwelevelatūtcem, emeamnaalūtcem: "you are becoming great devils."

clay[300] and two herbs[301] to brush the body and make it clean. Go back again to earth as great devils.'' Hearing this they all hung their heads, and crying and wailing they came back to where their bodies lay. Among the creatures left alive was muntakwut, who was a powerful shaman. He took pity on the dead spirits and with his ceremonial staff bored a hole in the earth, opening the gate of telmekic.[302] When they saw this gate was opened all went below ''sounding their heart,''[303] ''sounding their body,''[304] ''making great breathings,''[305] ''fading away with noise,''[306] ''disappearing forever.''[307] To this place go all the spirits of the dead. This is the way Mūkat tricked and joked with his people.

All the people who were left on earth were very sad, but their teacher, the moon, was still with them. The moon was a naked, white, and beautifully formed woman. She slept apart from all the other creatures. One night Mūkat, who had often watched her, leaned above her and touched her as he passed.[308] Next morning the moon was weak, sleepy, and sore; she felt very sad. She planned to go away somewhere, but before going she spoke to all Mūkat's creatures, saying, ''I am going away, but you must go to the place where you used to play.[309] Go there and play as before. In the evening you will see me in the west, then you must say ha! ha! ha! ha! and run to the water to bathe. Remember this always.'' Then she disappeared and no one saw or knew what became of her. In a short while they saw the new moon rise in the west, and they cried, ''ha! ha! ha! ha!'' as she had told them and ran to bathe.

Some of his creatures now began to plan how they could stop their creator Mūkat from playing more evil tricks on them. They knew that he had told the rattlesnake to kill them, that he had told them to kill one another with arrows, and lastly, that he had mistreated the moon and caused her to leave. So while they were all in the place where the moon had taught them to play they planned to get rid of Mūkat. Then the flicker[310] cried, ''pīūm,'' which meant, ''Don't talk so much but go and poison him.'' All agreed to this, so they planned to watch him at night time. They came into the house dancing, and told tataksil (a little lizard that hides in cracks in the wood) to watch the creator; for the lizard alone was not afraid to watch Mūkat at night. He hid in a crack in the center post[311] while all the others were dancing around it. All night he stayed there, watching.

At midnight, all were asleep as Mūkat had commanded them, save the little lizard who kept watch. Mūkat got up, took his pipe,[312] lit it and smoked,

300 ūliwut, tēviwut.

301 hañaawit, sahawit.

302 ''Neither heaven or hell, but the place where the dead go.''

303 melkelewihemsun.

304 melkelewīhemtahau.

305 tēwoñtalallaī.

306 talalāilyu.

307 n'nēēlu.

308 The informant used these words. They do not make clear what happened, for that was a great sin of the creator.

309 kanīsunwīt, līwīkauwut.

310 tavic.

311 paīinut.

312 ūlī.

blowing clouds of smoke over all his creatures to make them sleep soundly.
Three times he blew smoke over them. Then he set his pipe down, and taking
his ceremonial staff stood up. All the floor of the ceremonial house was covered
with his creatures. First he stepped at their feet,[313] then between their legs,[314]
then next to their arms,[315] then above their heads,[316] and so walked out.
All this time the lizard was watching.

Mūkat went at once to the ocean, where two logs crossed above the water,
and here defecated.[317] Lizard saw him do this, and heard the noise when this
kwaīmūitcī[317] hit the water. Three times Mūkat did this, and each time it was
followed by a sound like thunder in the ocean. Then Mūkat returned into the
house, stepping in the same places that he had coming out, but he did not
see the lizard who was watching. In the dawn all the creatures awoke, danced
around the center post, and the lizard joined them. They all went out to their
sandy playground, dancing. There the lizard told them all that he had seen
that night.

So they planned to poison Mūkat through his own excrement, and they told
the water skipper[318] to stay below the place where the creator sat at night
when he came down to the ocean. He tried to do this, but the great waves
washed him away. Then another small water creature[319] attempted it, but
failed. Finally, the blue frog[320] tried it, and stayed in spite of the ocean's
attempt to drive him away. Here he stayed until midnight, when the creator
came out as he always did. His first kwaīmūitcī hit the water and splashed
but there was no sound like thunder in the ocean, for the frog had taken it
before it hit bottom. Then Mūkat was very frightened, and with his ceremonial
staff felt down in the water to see what was beneath him. He scratched the
frog's back leaving three white marks there. Half of the kwaīmūitcī was left
in the water and all the water creatures scattered it over the great ocean.
Half of it was brought to land, and all the land creatures one by one scattered
it over the earth. Thus it could not be put together again and Mūkat could
not be made well. Mūkat sang to himself, "I felt sick in that water. My
body became cold, swollen and weak. Either this water or my house makes
me sick." All his creatures stayed in the ceremonial house watching him.
Coyote was his nurse, and tended Mūkat. He dug a hole in the ground, made a
fire in it, and then put the creator in, covering him up. Day and night he did
this for Mūkat, and thus he learned all of Mūkat's songs. The others slept all
night so they did not learn Mūkat's songs.

Mūkat grew sicker and sicker, and he called the horse fly[321] to suck[322] his
blood. This was the first time this was ever done. It did him no good. Then
he called the sow bugs[323] and the dragon flies[324] to doctor him. These two

---

[313] hemiña.

[314] pal kicnallalva.

[315] hemkwalmuña.

[316] hemulukna.

[317] paamilyawi, kwaīmūitci: "this tobacco, he eats and drops down."

[318] puñatcauatcau.

[319] pañawawulwawul.

[320] wahaatūkicnikic.

[321] pīpic.

[322] nemaīī: sucking disease from a patient's body.

[323] kumsewhitum.

[324] wakaīullalvawit.

failed, so he tried the water snake,[325] the gopher snake,[326] the red racer,[327] and the king snake,[328] all of whom failed. All of these had only pretended to help him for they all wanted Mūkat to die.

Then he told his creatures to tell the west wind,[329] that belonged to him, to come and help him. The west wind came, like a hurricane, with a great dust storm. Mūkat was afraid, but the west wind went into his body, and for a while he was better; but it was too strong; he was being blown away. He told the white-throated swift,[330] which he named "wind meeter,"[331] to go meet the west wind and tell it to go away for he was afraid. This same thing happened with the north, south, and east winds in succession.

Then he said, "All my creatures[332] have tried to cure me but I am no better. I know now that I am about to die. Perhaps I shall die in the dark of the moon,[333] or in the faint light of the new moon,[334] or during the young crescent moon,[335] or during the older crescent moon,[336] or in the first week of the new moon,[337] or when the moon has a cloudy ring around it,[338] or during the clear half-moon,[339] or when the half-moon has its rim parallel to the earth,[340] or during the full moon when its spots show clearly,[341] or when the full moon comes from the east and is red,[342] or when it begins to wane and one side is flattened,[343] or when it has half disappeared,[344] or during the last dying moon.[345]

All the time Mūkat was sick coyote tended him. When he spat coyote would pretend to take it away, but he would really swallow it, and thus make Mūkat sicker and sicker. Coyote helped Mūkat move from one side to another, from his face to his back, and helped him to sit up. When Mūkat was too weak to spit coyote would lick the saliva off with his tongue. When coyote was away Mūkat called all his creatures, and said, "My hands are growing cold, my heart is growing cold, I shall die soon. When I die coyote will try to eat me, for he is planning to do this while you sleep. Therefore, when I am dead tell coyote to go after the eastern fire[346] which I drew from my heart to light my pipe. When he is gone have hūnāwit[347] and tēkwawit[348] gather all kinds of wood, dig a hole, and prepare to burn my body. Take the palm[349] and with a drill make fire." When the palm, who was a woman, heard this she began to cry and complain that it was unfair to select her from among all the other creatures. But Mūkat continued, "The fly[350] will bore for fire with a drill.[351] Then you can burn[352] me with my creature the fire." That night Mūkat made all his creatures sleep, even coyote, and then he died.

---

[325] pasīwit.

[326] pōkawit.

[327] tatahol.

[328] wiūlwakanawit.

[329] yaīkauinawhit.

[330] sikukwinut.

[331] yaīnamkiwuc.

[332] nenukem, netavum.

[333] sōūmenyil.

[334] tēwi menyil.

[335] sīva menyil.

[336] tcaña menyil.

[337] kaīvu menyil.

[338] kava menyil.

[339] līwi menyil.

[340] tatca menyil.

[341] yelamenyil.

[342] tēvī menyil.

[343] tese menyil.

[344] kavī menyil.

[345] tū menyil.

[346] tamīkut.

[347] The large ancestor of the bear.

[348] The large ancestor of the skunk.

[349] ninmaīwit: one species of palm.

[350] pīpic.

[351] kutmūīvawut: making fire with a drill.

[352] nekwane: also means "eat."

In the morning coyote woke up. He felt Mūkat's heart and knew that he was dead. He said, ''I think it is all over with our creator!'' All the other creatures woke up, saying, ''He is dead! Our father, your father, is dead!'' Then they all cried that there was nothing with which to burn their father, and they asked coyote, because he ran fast, to go after the east light. Coyote went away to the east after the fire. When he was out of sight they prepared the pit, gathered all kinds of wood, and catching the palm tree they threw her down and held her although she tried to escape. The fly took a stick and started to make fire, twirling it between his hands. First came water, then blood, and then fire. With this they kindled the fire, dragged the body of Mūkat to the pile, and put it on the burning wood. It burned.

They all stood in a close circle around the fire. Meanwhile coyote went toward the eastern edge of the world and tried to catch the fire, but it always ran just ahead of him. Finally he looked back and saw the smoke of Mūkat's body burning. ''I thought that might be the way!'' he said, and he came back running very fast. All the people saw him coming, and shouted, ''Here comes coyote! Do not let him in to the fire where Mūkat is burning.'' ''Turn around my brothers and sisters,'' said coyote, ''I am full of tears. Let me in! Let me in! I too want to see my father.'' But they would not let him through. All of Mūkat's body save the heart was burned. Then coyote said, ''I will fly over you,'' and he jumped over their heads into the fire. All Mūkat's creatures pressed the creator's heart into the flames with their sticks, but coyote reached it and scattered blood and fire, so that the people were burnt and pushed back. Then coyote ran out with the heart.

To the east he ran, carrying the heart.[354] All the good runners, mountain lion,[355] wolf,[356] gray fox[357] and kit fox,[358] followed him, but could not catch him. Then he called each by name, and said, ''Stay away! Why do you, my brothers, pursue me?'' Then he talked to the heart of the creator, saying, ''I am carrying you upon the earth, to the edge of the world, to the point of earth and sky, to the bottom of the sky, to the bottom of the world.'' All things tried to frighten him as he ran, but he said, ''I am not afraid of you!'' Then he swallowed the heart.[359] He at once became very sick; he became emaciated and his ribs showed.

Some of Mūkat's creatures who had gone away in search of food for their sick creator returned too late, and found the body of their father in ashes. Among these were sūūwit,[360] elēlēlic,[361] witctcūic,[362] tuīvonpic,[363] the jaguar,[364]

---

[354] There are many more songs about the flight of coyote, but only a clan of the coyote moiety may sing them. Alejo belonged to the kauisiktum clan of the wildcat moiety.

[355] tūkwit.

[356] iswit.

[357] kauwisic.

[358] wilyul.

[359] The Desert Cahuilla say this occurred in the Painted canyon, near Mecca, which accounts for the red stained rocks there.

[360] One of the stars. Also named pahahūwit.

[361] Archaic.

[362] Archaic.

[363] Archaic.

[364] tūkwut.

and the marsh hawk.365 They all cried loudly, and rolled in the ashes. Last of all returned the buzzard, who was slow and returned late. He did not cry, he became dumb, took the skin off his head, and with a stick bored a hole through his beak. After that he was always quiet, he could only hiss.

Then in the place where Mūkat was burned there began to grow all kinds of strange plants, but no one knew what they were. They were afraid to go near the place for a hot wind always blew there. One, Palmitcawut, a great shaman, said, ''Why do you not go and ask our father what they are?'' No on else would go so he followed the spirit of Mūkat. By the aid of his ceremonial staff he followed the trail of Mūkat's spirit although whirlwinds had hidden the trail. In one place were thickets of prickly cactus and clumps of interlaced thorny vines, but at the touch of his ceremonial staff they opened up for him to pass. Far away on the horizon he saw a bright glow where the spirit of Mūkat was leaning against a rock. The creator's spirit spoke, ''Who are you, that follows and makes me move on when I am lying still?'' When the creator's spirit spoke Palmitcawut was dumb and could not answer, though Mūkat asked him several times. Finally he was able to speak: ''Yes, I am that one who disturbs you while you rest, but we, your creatures, do not know what the strange things are that grow where your body was burned?'' Mūkat's spirit answered him, ''Yes, that was the last thing I wanted to tell you, but you killed me before I could do so.'' Then he continued, ''You need not be afraid of those things. They are from my body.'' He asked Palmitcawut to describe them and when he had finished the spirit of Mūkat said, ''That big tree is tobacco. It is my heart. It can be cleaned with white clay,366 and smoked in the big house to drive away evil spirits. The vines with yellow squashes are from my stomach, watermelons are from the pupil of my eye, corn is from my teeth, wheat is my lice eggs,367 beans are from my semen,368 and all other vegetables are from other parts of my body.'' (Thus when any vegetables are gathered and brought to the ''big house'' all the people must pray to the creator.)

Then he said, ''I am in that big house. My spirit is there, my saliva is there. You can move the big house away and always live there.'' They did this and all Mūkat's creatures stayed in the house weeping for their father. Then they began to wonder how they could make the image of their father. Meanwhile coyote was far away, being very sick. At last he took some wet short reeds,369 rolled them into a ball, and swallowed it. Then he vomited up all kinds of disease from his heart. Thus he got well. From far away he heard the people in the ''big house'' talking, planning to kill him when he came back. So coyote came near them and they saw him. He talked gently to them from far away and they listened. He said, ''I have heard you wondering how to make our father's image. I will show you.'' And he gathered all kinds of flowers saying, ''With these we can make the image of our father!'' He was joking with them, making them forget their anger. He brought many kinds of flowers, but by the next morning they would all be dead. All this time he was planning what he should do. At last he remembered that he

---

365 wesunauwit, the marsh hawk, is gray because he rolled in the ashes.
366 yūliwit, tēviwit.
367 nasawam.
368 nenevum.
369 sīmūtum.

must go to the ocean and get paña maīswut,[370] paña hekwa,[371] and paña wīava.[372] So he told the people he was going after these things.

Then he went to the ocean which was far away. That evening he slept at the edge of the earth, and woke up very early thinking it was dawn. He called aloud, asking it not to become light right away. Then he began to sing because the surf was pounding in so hard that he could not go into it. He sang asking the ocean to stop pounding for a little while. Then he went into the water, and got those three things with which to make the image of Mūkat.[373] These three things he brought back to the "big house."

Then he began to make the image of his father. All Mūkat's creatures were crying, and they sang songs as each part of the maīswut was cut and wrapped. Thus the image was made. They sang a song about moving it, standing it up, carrying it to the fire, placing it on the pile, lighting the fire, the smoking, the burning, the crumbling of the last ashes, the last of the burning. Then, covering the ashes with dirt, they sang the last song. All was over.

---

[370] seaweed matting. The wrapping of the clan fetish bundles.

[371] water tail, archaic.

[372] water apron, archaic.

[373] The maīswut was to be cut and wrapped with the other two, but what "water tail" and "water apron" were, no one at present knows. The maīswut is now usually made of tule or reed matting.

IV. THE MOUNTAIN CAHUILLA

ENVIRONMENT

The groups commonly known as the Mountain Cahuilla occupied a large territory in the barren San Jacinto and Santa Rosa mountain ranges, extending from the slopes of Cahuilla and Thomas peaks in the north, to the lands formerly occupied by Luiseño and Cupeño-speaking peoples in the south. It is an area characterized by steep granite ridges and barren rocky plateaus covered with chaparral brush, and affording little encouragement to human occupation. At the higher altitudes occur pleasant little valleys having many oak trees along the streams, and pines and sycamores on the ridges. Game is still abundant for the area is even less inviting to the white settler than it was to the Indian. Hence deer are very plentiful in the mountain meadows, and along the barren cactus-strewn ridges facing the desert the mountain sheep still holds his own. The jackrabbit, brush rabbit, and wood rat among the smaller mammals, and the abundant flocks of mountain and valley quail furnished the native hunter with a considerable food supply. Large as this territory appears on the map, it furnished, as did the desert to the east, few places for extensive habitation. The high mountain valleys and the deep canyons running up from the desert afforded ideal sites for small groups, but as a whole the mountains are very arid and the flora on which the people mainly subsisted is none too plentiful in any one locality. Barrows has given a very graphic description of this area[374] and has shown to what lengths the ingenuity of the Indian went in overcoming these natural handicaps. Although today this territory is much as it was one hundred years ago its Indian occupants are but a pitiful handful. Disease and contact with a culture utterly alien to their own have accomplished what the hard environment could not.

Partly as a result of these environmental conditions the Mountain Cahuilla were geographically divided into small groups of clans, and the customs of these different groups varied slightly under the influence of their neighbors. Likewise the dialect of the Mountain

---

[374] Barrows, The Ethno-Botany of the Cahuilla Indians (University of Chicago Press, 1900), 25–35.

Cahuilla differs to a slight extent from that of the Desert and Pass
Cahuilla, and it is probable that an intensive linguistic study of the
Mountain Cahuilla themselves would show differences between the
more widely separated groups.

Two main groupings according to their location may be observed
among the Mountain Cahuilla, in late aboriginal times, and in the
following account of the varying ceremonials I have thus distinguished them.[375]   To make sharp distinction between these two is

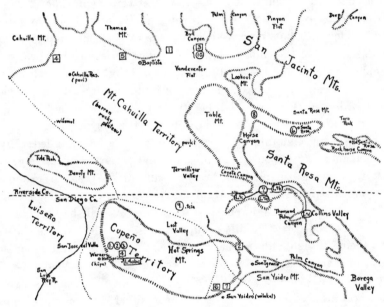

Map. 5.   Mountain Cahuilla Territory.

not entirely correct for there were intermediate and blending groups
between, most of which have perished.   The entire culture of the
southern California Indian, like that of all such closely related
groups, may well be regarded as a liquid medium that flowed more
or less evenly from group to group, thinning out more and more the
farther each cultural influence extended from its source.   Therefore
to make breaks and sharp distinctions between near-by groups is often

[375] Good informants are rather scarce among the Mountain Cahuilla, for not
many of the older Indians survive.   A few of these older survivors, however, and
a small number of intelligent younger Indians who remember the facts told them
by their immediate ancestors, are still available.   Of the former, Mrs. Nina
Coseros, Mrs. Jesusa Manuel, Mrs. Maria Antonio (who died in January, 1925),
Cornelio Lubo, and Alec' Arguello gave me much information.   While of the
latter, Ignacio Costo, Gabriel Costo, Jolian Norte, and Fred Coseros were especially
helpful, both as interpreters and informants.

the necessity but not the ideal of the ethnologist, who desires to show the changing customs of the groups and yet lacks full intermediate data.

The first of these groupings centered mainly in Coyote canyon, and the name Los Coyotes[376] may well be applied to these people. The most southerly village that was occupied by Cahuillas alone, was patcawal at San Ignacio. Originally the people from Los Coyotes, or the wīwaīistam people as they called themselves, used this as a food-gathering and agricultural area. Later, after an epidemic of small-pox they moved there to live, returning to Coyote canyon to gather food. They are thus described by Barrows who mentions the village of Pachawal.[377] Beyond San Ignacio the territories of the wīwaīistam people bordered on the south those owned by the wilakal people located at San Ysidro. The latter are linguistically a hybrid group composed at present of Cahuilla, Cupeño, and Diegueño families in about equal numbers. To the north in the Coyote canyon were located several Cahuilla villages, the central one being called wilīya, and the outlying villages, sauīvil, sauic, and tepana, respectively; the last three were occupied by branch clans of the central group at wilīya. Slightly to the west of wilīya was an old village called tcīa, all of whose inhabitants died long ago. As will be brought out later, these southern Cahuilla groups were in contact with the Cupeño and their Luiseño and Diegueño neighbors, and as a result resembled them in many traits. Save for a mixed group at San Ysidro nearly all this area is now deserted. One or two Cahuilla families live at San Ignacio, but most of the people have either died or moved away to the Cahuilla, Morongo, or Palm Springs reservations.

The second grouping was less centralized, and was composed of the clans near Santa Rosa,[378] and the clans or "parties" located around pauī, now called the Cahuilla reservation. The former places are typical high mountain-stream valleys watered by small swift streams; at Old Santa Rosa, which is situated in a fork of Rock House canyon, were two villages, kolwovakut and kēwel, and at "new" Santa Rosa was the village of sēwīu. Several miles to the northwest was the old town of natcūta, about one-half mile east of Horse canyon. Pauī or Cahuilla appears to have become an impor-

---

[376] The present-day inhabitants of Wilakal at San Ysidro call themselves the Los Coyotes tribe, probably on account of the presence there of several Mountain Cahuilla families from Coyote canyon.

[377] Barrows, *op. cit.*, 34.

[378] This includes both Old Santa Rosa and "new" Santa Rosa.

tant town of the Cahuillas about 1875. No one clan seems to have owned the warm sulphur springs and adjoining territory, for when it was permanently settled the localized clan organization had largely broken down and its inhabitants represented survivors of several of the eastern Mountain clans. At present about three families live at the site of pauī, but all the other Cahuilla families scattered over the Cahuilla reservation come to the warm springs for bathing and laundry purposes. It affords a good example of the effect produced by warm springs in drawing groups together, an example even better demonstrated in the case of the Cupeño clans who were all gathered around the hot springs at kūpa, but maintained their individual clan territories elsewhere.

At the bases of Cahuilla and Thomas mountains, north of pauī about six miles, were located the villages of saupalpa, palpīsa, and pasīawha, which were each occupied by only one clan and represent old individual clan territories. Half a mile southeast of pasīawha was located the old village of pauata, formerly occupied by two clans one representing each moiety. This matter will be discussed later. About three miles southeast of pauī are located mauit and seūpa, both occupied at present, and formerly centers of a single clan territory. Considerably farther to the southeast, on the Terwilliger Flats, was located the town of paukī, which resembled pauī in the variety of its inhabitants, for no one clan appears to have claimed the locality though representatives of at least two clans lived there until the last few decades. While this town was nearer to the Los Coyotes people than to the northern division of the Mountain Cahuilla, its inhabitants nevertheless appear to have been largely recruited from the northern clans. While the above named villages were undoubtedly the largest in the area there were many smaller dwelling sites where the combination of water and acorns or other food supplies made living possible. Every spring, grove of oaks, prominent rock, arroyo, or cienega has its individual name among the Cahuilla, and out of this welter of place names the foregoing villages stand out as old clan homes or permanent dwelling sites.

To the northwest down the Baptiste canyon, the territories of the Cahuilla met those of the Luiseño clans whose village was at Saboba. To the northeast their territories approached those of the Palm Springs Cahuilla, and to the west[379] and southwest the desolate

---

[379] The village of wīasmul, shown on the map, was located at a small sulphur spring about four miles southwest of Cahuilla. It was occupied by people of clans 2 and 4, but was the original clan home of neither.

chapparal-covered plateau, strewn with crumbling granitic rocks of all sizes and swept by cold winds in winter, seems to have been largely uninhabited until the Luiseño territories around Pechanga, Temecula, and Pala were reached. The location of all these Mountain Cahuilla villages is shown in map 5, where the clans are likewise located according to the numbers given in the following list of Mountain Cahuilla clans (table 7).

TABLE 7

Mountain Cahuilla Clans

1. tepamōkiktum or iswitim (wolf), wildcat moiety. Clan home at pasīawha.
2. hōkwitcakiktum (place name), wildcat moiety. Clan home at hōkwitca.
3. pauatīauitcem (place name), wildcat moiety. Clan home at pauata.
4. apapatcem (place name) or nalgāliem (no meaning), wildcat moiety. Clan home at saupalpa.
5. temewhanitcem (northerners), wildcat moiety. Clan home at palpīsa.
6. costakiktum (place name), coyote moiety. Clan home at sēwīa.
7. wīwaīistam (wīwaī, coyote-people), coyote moiety. Clan home at wilīya. Name of group used collectively.
   7a. nauhañavitcem (people living in center), coyote moiety. Clan home at wilīya. Subdivision of 7.
   7b. temewhanvitcem (northerners), coyote moiety. Clan home just north of wilīya. Subdivision of 7.
   7c. tepaīyauitcem (place name), coyote moiety. Clan home at tepaña. Subdivision of 7.
   7d. sauicpakiktum (place name), coyote moiety. Clan home at sauic. Subdivision of 7.
   7e. sauīvilem (place name), coyote moiety. Clan home at sauīvil. Subdivision of 7.
8. natcūtakiktum (place name), coyote moiety. Clan home at natcūta.
9. tcīanakiktum (place name), coyote moiety. Clan home at tcīa.
10. pauatakiktum (place name), coyote moiety. Clan home at pauata.

THE SHIFTING OF THE GROUPS

The locations of the Mountain Cahuilla clans through divers causes have been subject to more changes in the last sixty-odd years than have those of either the Pass or the Desert Cahuilla. These changes have not been entirely due to Caucasian influence for it is probable that long before this influence became felt the people were subject to western cultural influences that tended to uproot the early condition of isolated clans in favor of town groupings such as characterized the

Cupeño, Luiseño, and Gabrieleño. The two towns of pauī and paukī
are examples of such tendencies working in conjunction with certain
mission influences that, coming in later, tended in the same direction.

The primary change effected by the mission fathers seems to have
been in regard to leadership among the Indians under their control.
Needing some temporal head to make responsible for the acts of the
people they appear to have selected the most prominent or forceful
of the clan leaders and given each the title of "El Capitan." One
of these leaders was appointed over each district, the district usually
corresponding to one linguistic area, and under him were appointed
an "alcalde" and a "juez" for each village, whose duties seem to
have resembled respectively those of a constable and justice of the
peace in a modern American town. It is not certain who the first
captain of the Mountain Cahuilla was, although informants stated
he was appointed by the priests at the San Luis Rey mission, hence
the records of this mission might well settle the matter. Juan
Antonio, a costakiktum man, was probably one of the first. During
the troublesome times between 1845 and the treaty of Cahuenga in
1847, the Cahuilla under Juan Antonio sided with the Mexicans
against the Luiseño who appear to have favored the American
invaders. In 1847 at Aguanga there took place a battle between the
Cahuillas under Juan Antonio and the Luiseño under Manuelito Cota
and Pablo Apis, which resulted in an overwhelming defeat for the
Luiseño.[380] This is often referred to as the "massacre" at Aguanga,
and Luiseño informants still state bitterly that the Cahuilla were
treacherous to those who should have been their allies. Exactly what
the facts were is hard to determine at this late date, and is a problem
historical rather than ethnological. At this time the more isolated
Mountain Cahuilla clans were the least broken down by mission and
other Caucasian contacts of any California natives under Mexican
control, hence they were probably the only spirited fighting units
among the so-called "Mission Indians." For this reason they were
evidently treated as allies by the Mexican authorities, who had scant
respect for the pitiful neophytes of the already secularized missions,
that had lost their own culture and not acquired that of their conquerors. Thus to the Cahuilla, the American forces under Kearney
and Stockton were invaders, while to the broken peoples of the
missions they appeared as liberators. The "massacre" at Aguanga
was the natural result of such a situation.

---

[380] H. H. Bancroft, 22:617.

In the year 1846, just prior to the aforementioned fight, several clans of the Mountain Cahuilla under Juan Antonio moved from their mountain homes first to the vicinity of Riverside, then called Jurupa, where the village of pūlatana was established. Later their village was moved to sahatapa in the San Timoteo canyon near El Casco. These clans were probably moved down by the Mexicans as a guard against the Colorado river and other raiding peoples. Bancroft states that from March to August, 1846, there were,

> Indian affairs, showing frequent alarms at rumors of invasion from the Colorado River bands, with several expeditions from the San Bernardino region. On one occasion 18 Indians were killed at San Francisco rancho, having revolted after being captured. It was at one time resolved to station a guard at the Cajon. Six Yuta families came to Jurupa to settle.[381]

The term "Yuta" is ambiguous but may apply to the members of the costakiktum, pauatīauitcem, tepamōkiktum, natcūtakiktum, and temewhanic clans of the Mountain Cahuilla, led here by Juan Antonio. Ignacio Costo was told by his grandmother that about seventy or more years ago either the Chemehuevi or the Paiutes of Utah raided San Bernardino and stole many horses and cattle. The Mexicans asked the Mountain Cahuilla for aid and a united force pursued the marauders to the Cajon pass where they were brought to bay and all killed. Ignacio's grandfather was wounded in the leg during the fight. It was shortly after this episode that the Mountain Cahuilla clans moved to the vicinity of San Bernardino as a guard.[382] As the San Bernardino mission had not been reoccupied by neophytes after the Indian troubles of 1834,[383] the two villages of pūlatana and sahatapa were settled in 1846 by Mountain Cahuilla clans only, although originally the territory had probably belonged to the Gabrieleño.[384]

Among the signers of the unratified treaty of 1852, between the United States and the Luiseño, Cahuilla, Serrano, and Diegueño Indians,[385] Juan Antonio of "Cooswoot-na" signs himself as "Chief" of the Kah-we-as, and "Juan Bautista (Sahat) of Pow-ky" follows,

---

[381] H. H. Bancroft, 22:624.

[382] Möllhausen mentions three or four families of Kawia Indians held in a state of peonage on an estate some miles west of the mouth of the Cajon pass in 1854. Wanderungen durch die Prairien und Wüsten des Westlichen Nordamerika, 1860, p. 439.

[383] H. H. Bancroft, 21:631.

[384] This point is open to question. It has been previously discussed.

[385] At Temecula, January 5, 1852. Publicly reprinted by U. S. Senate, January 19, 1905.

as one of the village heads or alcaldes. The latter thus signs for "Sahat" (sahatapa) and "Powky" (pauki) showing the connection between the mountain town and the later of the two pass towns near San Bernardino.[386]

In the fifties occurred a great smallpox epidemic which wiped out this settlement of Cahuillas, then located at sahatapa in the San Timoteo canyon, killing among others Juan Antonio himself. The few survivors either returned to the mountains or scattered out among the Pass or Palm Springs Cahuilla groups. Juan Antonio was succeeded as captain by Manuel Largo, a temewhanic net. About the year 1875 Manuel Largo assembled all the younger people of his own and other eastern Mountain clans and brought them to pauī (Cahuilla). Only the old people who refused to leave stayed on in their former clan homes. About this same time a smallpox epidemic swept through the wīwaīistam groups located in the Coyote canyon, killing a great number of people including nearly all of the children. As a result, all the houses in the several villages were burnt, and the survivors moved to the village of patcawal at San Ignacio. Prior to this epidemic, however, the sauicpakiktum branch clan had already divided and moved to the villages of sēwīu and kēwel at "new" and Old Santa Rosa respectively. While the sauīvilem branch clan, members of which had intermarried to a considerable extent with the Cupeño, had also moved to kūpa at a somewhat earlier time.

Manuel Largo was captain for a considerable period, at one time being taken to San Francisco and presented with a flag and credentials confirming his leadership under American rule. He resigned his commission later and was succeeded in office by Fernando Lugo, a hōkwitcakik man, elected by all the people at Cahuilla. This captain died at Saboba about 1905, and the office was discontinued.

From the foregoing it seems obvious that the Mexicans, and later the Americans, by supporting the more powerful clan leaders, brought the Mountain Cahuilla from a cultural phase where the isolated clan system was just beginning to break down, into an almost tribal state

---

[386] There is a possibility that the Mountain Cahuilla were invited to come to the San Gorgonio pass as a guard during the San Bernardino Indian troubles of 1834–36. Bancroft, 20:630, notes Indian raids on San Bernardino in 1835, and the pursuit of the raiders by one Ramirez with a mixed force of Mexicans and Indians. Nothing is known of the results of this expedition. He also mentions that most of the rancherias in the mountains were in arms to repel invasion by more distant tribes. However, since Mrs. Nina Coseros and Alec Arguello both maintained that Juan Antonio had led the movement, the year 1846 seems much more probable for the settlement of the Mountain Cahuilla clans near Riverside and San Bernardino.

such as had been already attained under aboriginal conditions by the more westerly Luiseño, Gabrieleño, and most probably the Chumash villages. The finer details of this process are brought out in the following sections of this paper.

History and Organization of the Mountain Clans

The unit of Mountain Cahuilla social organization was the same as that of the Desert and Pass Cahuilla groups. As has already been indicated, the Desert Cahuilla clans were grouped in towns at places where water was available, but the similar breaking down of clan isolation among the Mountain Cahuilla seems to have come about through other causes. This tendency toward centralization was so accelerated by Caucasian influence that it is difficult at this late time to clearly draw a line between the aboriginal and the recent historic stimuli. It is clear that at one time all clans were isolated and politically independent; most of the clan names are those of places where they once lived,[387] and each clan up to recent times had its own food-gathering territories, usually around their old homes. These clan homes were occupied in the winter time, and in the summer the clans seem to have traveled from one food-gathering area to another, or settled in the larger mountain towns such as pauī or paukī. In the spring the canyons toward the desert offered an abundance of cactus while in the autumn the acorn groves of the higher mountains were visited. Every favorable site for such operations was claimed by one clan or another, the intervening barren areas belonging to all.

The towns of pauī at Cahuilla and paukī at La Puerta were later manifestations of the grouping tendency, the former being settled about 1875 and the latter at a slightly earlier date. By the time this occurred many of the clans had already lost their ceremonial independence and a system of "parties," such as has long been noted among the Luiseño, had arisen. The largest clans, under the most dominating leaders, held onto their ceremonial bundles and performed their ceremonies. The clans that had given up their own ceremonial independence participated in the greater part of these affairs, and regarded the leaders of the active clans in much the same way as

---

[387] Certain of the names of clans have no meaning at present, for the existing members have forgotten the place for which the clan was named. The name costakiktum, or Costo as the family is called, is an example of this. Juan Antonio a costakiktum chief signed the unratified treaty of 1852 for "Coos-woot-na," evidently the old place name from which the clan took its Spanish-sounding name.

they had once regarded their own. As will be brought out later, each active clan leader possessed maĩswut, or the sacred bundle, and it was the possession of this fetish bundle that formed the heart of the clan and its surrounding "party."

Considering first the northern groups of the Mountain Cahuilla only, the situation seems to be as follows. No informant remembered the time when every clan was an independent ceremonial unit. That such a condition once existed is apparent from the identity of the Mountain clans in all essentials with those of the Desert and the Pass, and is of course strengthened by the strong traditional belief of all informants that such was the state of affairs among their ancestors. According to Gabriel Costo, on the basis of information obtained from his father, about seventy-five years ago there were four ceremonial units or "parties" among these northern clans. The nets were Manuel Largo, a temewhanic man already mentioned as a later captain; Pomosena, a hōkwitcakiktum man; Juan Chappo, a pauata-kiktum man; and Tomas Arenas, a natcūtakiktum man. Each of these clans participated in the others' ceremonies, and in those of the five "parties" then at Saboba, most of whom were Luiseño in linguistic affiliation. Besides this active participation in the others' ceremonies an exchange of shell money, mūketem, was maintained between all these groups, the several Cahuilla clans near Banning, and the kauisiktum clan at Palm Springs as well. This exchange occurred when a clan member died, and all other clan leaders sent a string of money to the net of the deceased; it did not involve participation in the ceremonies of the other clans. The costakiktum clan under Juan Antonio, the great captain or "Chief of the Cahuillas," seems to have lost its individuality as a ceremonial unit and affiliated with the temewhanic clan for the various ritualistic performances. The tepamōkiktum or iswitim clan seems likewise to have lost its inde-pendence and to have affiliated with the hōkwitcakiktum clan for ceremonies.

The tepamōkiktum people, Lubos, and the hōkwitcakiktum people, Lugos, were undoubtedly branches of the same stock, the nickname iswitim, "wolf," being applied to both of them. The temewhanic, or "northerners," were probably a branch lineage, just as the teme-whanvitcem or "northerners" of the Los Coyotes canyon were a branch lineage living slightly to the north of their parent stock. It is not clear, however, of what clan the temewhanic people were origin-ally a part. The costakiktum people, of the opposite moiety from them, seem to have come under their ceremonial influence through intermarriage. The pauatīauitcem and the tcīanakiktum clans were apparently too reduced in numbers even at this time to form independent units. The apapatcem clan seems to have been the last Cahuilla clan to persist as a ceremonial unit,[388] but at this early time it does not seem to have been in existence. Occupying one of the most northwesterly points reached by the Cahuilla-speaking people it was probably a collateral lineage of one of the older Mountain clans that had acquired a new name.

The information obtained from Alec' Arguello gives us a glimpse of the conditions some seventy years ago among those clans that moved to San Bernardino under Juan Antonio. Five clans, costa-kiktum, pauatīauitcem, tepamōkiktum, natcūtakiktum, and teme-whanic were represented there, just prior to the great smallpox epidemic. There were, however, only two ceremonial units, the hōkwit-cakiktum under Pomosena as net and Manuel Antonio as paha, and the temewhanic under Marsē as net and Tciperosa as paha. Each of the groups had a dance house and a sacred bundle of maīswut. The other clans present participated in the ceremonies of these two. Thus two active clans stayed in their mountain homes, and two active clans moved to the west side of the San Gorgonio pass. Contrary to what one would expect, the two latter clans survived the epidemic in sufficient numbers to still carry on their ceremonies when the survivors had reassembled in the mountains once more, while the former pair of clans apparently gave up their ceremonial activities of their own volition.

Thus, when Gabriel Costo first remembers for himself some forty or fifty years ago, there was only one active clan at pauī (Cahuilla). This was the hōkwitcakiktum clan under Pomosena who had survived the San Timoteo pass epidemic. The latter had for his paha, Domingo Ringlaro, or Nortes, of the temewhanic clan. Thus, while the two clans had fused into one "party" they were still active ceremonially, whereas the other Mountain clans had one by one given up the old customs because of decrease in numbers and the growing Caucasian influences. On the death of Pomosena, the hōkwitcakiktum people also gave up their activities. The apapatcem clan, located north of Cahuilla at saupalpa, carried on ceremonies in their dance house until fifteen years ago; then Augustine Apapas sent all his shell money to Alejo Potencio, the kauisiktum net at Palm Springs, and asked that

---

[388] This clan still survives at Saboba today, see Gifford, present series, 14:205.

the ceremonial exchange be discontinued. At the close of his last mourning ceremony he took the maīswut of his clan and buried it in a cave several miles north of Cahuilla. This marked the end of all Mountain Cahuilla ceremonies. Since then the Apapas people, now living at Saboba, have affiliated themselves with local Luiseño parties but no more ceremonies have been held in the mountains.

The definite disposal of the mūketem, shell money, and the maīswut or sacred bundle of the clan, is an interesting and suggestive phenomenon. It demonstrates primarily a custom of ceremonially disposing of the clan fetish when conditions have so changed as to make its further employment useless, and shows how strongly its importance was felt even to the end. With its burial the old days were over but the "heart of the big house" was protected from sacrilege.[389] The transfer of the shell money to an active clan may very well show, on the part of this clan ending its ceremonial existence, the same desire to pass on its customs to more active groups, that actuated the Chumash, Fernandeño, and Gabrieleño in bringing their shell money gratis to the San Gorgonio pass and the Mountain clans. This event has been discussed in relation to the exchange of shell money among the Pass Cahuilla and Serrano, and seems to be best explained in the aforementioned manner. The probability is strengthened that long before any interior people were involved in this exchange, it had flourished in an even more elaborate form among the coastal peoples who later, crushed under mission and Mexican domination, passed on their customs to the more intact groups of the Serrano, Cahuilla, and Cupeño-speaking peoples.

The foregoing discussion shows the way in which independent lineages or clans fused into "parties," similar to those of the Luiseño, and then, among the Mountain Cahuilla, gradually disappeared. The ravages of smallpox, bringing about conditions that caused the younger people to leave for more favorable localities, and the replacement of aboriginal by modern ideas, have all contributed to their disappearance. Compared with the period characterized by the localized clan, if one may judge by its wide distribution in southern California, this period of change and decay was very short.

Such data as may be obtained in regard to the clans among the Mountain Cahuilla show them to be identical in basic organization

---

[389] The burial or definite disposal of a clan fetish when there is no person to inherit it occurs among various Pueblo groups. It has been mentioned at Zuñi by Kroeber, Zuñi Kin and Clan, Anthr. Papers Am. Mus. Nat. Hist., 18:174, 1919. And at Laguna by Parsons, Laguna Genealogies, *ibid.*, 19:221–222, 1923.

with those of the Pass and the Desert Cahuilla. The following
genealogy (genealogy 8) shows the relationship of all the natcūtakiktum male clan members at sēūpa at the time Maria Antonio, a
hōkwitcakiktum woman, married Charles Arenas, a natcūtakiktum
man, some sixty years ago. At the time of her marriage she lived at
pauī, going to her husband's home at sēūpa to live. Sēūpa is a small
valley in the Cahuilla reservation, marked by a pleasant spring surrounded by willows and cottonwoods, and having several small fields
now growing alfalfa and grain. The men of this clan were as follows:

GENEALOGY 8

Natcūtakiktum Clan

1. Stēewin Arenas

    5. Remundu Arenas

2. Calistro Arenas   6. Tomas Arenas   9. Charlie Arenas   10. Lee Arenas
   (net)   (net)

    7. Vincente Arenas

    8. Curri Arenas

3. Enselmo Arenas

4. Havian Arenas

Each man who was head of a family, that is all but 1 and 4 who
were unmarried and 2 who was dead at the time the informant moved
there, had an individual house. They used the surrounding valley
communally, as they did food-gathering territories owned by their
clan in the vicinity and farther east near the old town of natcūta
where they had formerly lived. At present only 9 and 10 survive
with small families, all the rest having died. This decline, described
by Barrows, is even more sadly noticeable among the Mountain
Cahuilla today. Writing some twenty-five years ago he makes the
following statement:

The decline in this population is extremely rapid. They have been steadily
decreasing for several generations and the end now seems almost in sight.
Villages, which ten years ago, when I first visited them, seemed reasonably
well inhabited, now number scarcely half as many souls. On every side stand
abandoned jacales or crumbling little adobe huts destitute of occupants. A
sombre stillness broods over these little communities. Occasionally a woman's
figure, bent under her food basket, appears returning over the hills, or a horse-
man rides in and out among the cattle that continue to browse where jacales
and granaries once stood, but there is no evidence of active life or of a
population holding its own.[390]

---

[390] Barrows, *op. cit.*, 82.

To return to the consideration of the clan itself, the temewhanic
clan at about this same time (genealogy 9) shows a similar condition—
a few survivors, all related, living in different houses at the clan locale,
in this case palpīsa on the southern slope of Thomas mountain. All
the men indicated in this genealogy are dead, and their few
descendants scattered.

GENEALOGY 9

Temewhanic Clan

saavil Nortes (net)	Tomas Nortes
Juan Bonifacio	Manuel Largo (net)
Domingo Nortes	

One other situation remains to be discussed among these northern
Mountain clans and that is the old village of pauata and its inhabitants. At one time two clans lived here, both taking their names from
this village or locality. These were the pauatakiktum clan belonging
to the coyote moiety and the pauatīauitcem clan of the wildcat moiety;
the fact of their belonging to different moieties yet occupying the
same site from which both apparently derived their names, is unique
among Cahuilla clans in so far as the existing data are concerned.
According to informants, marriages between the two clans were permissible and had occurred, yet informants stated that they were at
one time related. When questioned as to the propriety of such relatives marrying, they explained it by the fact that one group was
tūktum, the other istam. How this situation arose they could not
explain. The pauatīauitcem clan is practically extinct, and no member of the pauatakiktum clan was encountered, hence genealogies
could not be obtained. The pauatakiktum clan moved to the village
of paukī, where about fifty years ago they had ten or twelve houses
and one dance house. The natcūtakiktum clan lived with them there,
as did a few of the pauatīauitcem families. Other pauatīauitcem
families moved to pauī and to sahatapa. As previously stated the
village of paukī is now abandoned, and the few survivors of the two
clans under consideration are scattered. The theoretical implications
of this situation are discussed later in relation to the moiety.

Turning now to a consideration of the southeastern Mountain
Cahuilla clans, collectively designated as the Los Coyotes people, we
find another somewhat anomalous situation. This was briefly touched
on at the time the many clans, all of the coyote moiety, in the San

Gorgonio pass were under consideration.[391]   There were five lineages here, that collectively called themselves the wīwaĭistam people, according to tradition, after a man, wīwaĭīsil, who originally lived at wilīya. The term wilīya applied both to the central village site and to the whole of Los Coyotes canyon, but the former was also called nethekī or "net's place."   At this central village lived the nauhañavitcem, "those living in the central place" lineage; and they were said to be nentem, "belonging to the big house," and having the net.   A short distance to the north lived the temewhanic, "northerners," lineage who were relatives of the central group but lived apart from them.   In this group the office of kutvavanavac was hereditary.   The other similarly related branch lineages were the tepaĭauitcem people at tepana, "stone water tank," who had the office of hauinik, or chief singer, hereditary in their group; the sauicpakiktum people at sauic; and the sauīvilem people who lived at sauīvil and had the office of manet-dancer hereditary in their line.   These places were all close to wilīya as may be seen in map 5.   According to native belief all these groups were once one, the wīwaĭistam people, but because certain families through lack of food at the central village moved to outlying localities they acquired their new names, retaining however their ceremonial alliance with the central group.   Apparently we have here a situation ostensibly similar to the parties of the northwesterly Mountain Cahuilla and the Luiseño, but arrived at by an absolutely opposite series of events.   While the latter parties were groups of broken down clans gathered around one intact clan nucleus, the groups at Los Coyotes were parts of a formerly prosperous clan that had sent out colonies which were still united through the ceremonial power of the maĭswut and the "big house."   Today the decimated nature of this group gives it exactly the appearance of one of the western "parties," and if the actual relationship of the groups were not remembered it would probably be erroneously classed as such.

To obtain a complete genealogy of these groups in their present shattered condition was impossible, but such fragments as were obtainable bear out the words of the informants.   When the genealogy of the temewhanic branch is considered, their relationship to the tepaĭyauitcem clans appears in the following manner.

---

[391] Present paper, p. 113.

GENEALOGY 10

Temewhanitcem and Tepaíyauitcem Clans

Generation 1 (ego)

Jolian Norte (inform.)[393] + Chemehuevi

Matilda Norte + Patricio Torte

Generation 2 nena

Augustine Norte + apapas

Casmiro Norte + waniktktum

Manuel tepaíyauite[393] (unmarried)

Generation 3 neka

Gregorio Norte[392] + palpūnivikiktum

Vincente Norte + pauaiauitcem

Manuel Norte + pauaiauitcem

asevíu (unmarried)

Santiago tepaíyauite + palpūnivikiktum[392]

Generation 4 nepü

met (gopher) + (?)

Lineage 7e (?) Sauivilem

(?) + (?)

Lineage 7b Temewhanitcem

Generation 5 nañaa

(?) + (?)   (?)

Lineage 7e Tepaíyauitcem

Generation 6 niül

liika + (?)   (?) + (?)

(?)

392 The palpūnivikiktum woman in these two cases is the same; she was first the wife of Gregorio Norte, then of Santiago tepaiauitcem.

393 These two men are the sole survivors of this group. They live at Banning.

The informant in this case, Jolian Norte, appears on the extreme right. The terms appearing above the genealogy with each generation are the kinship terms that he calls each of his paternal ancestors by. Thus Augustine is nena (father), Vincente is neka (grandfather), and met is nepū (great-grandfather) to Jolian. Here his remembrance of his direct ancestors stops, but at the time he was a small boy there was a very old man, liīka, shown in the extreme lower left corner of the genealogy, who was a brother to Jolian's great-great-great-grand-father. Jolian's father, Augustine called liīka, nañaa, the term for great-great-grandfather, which may be translated as "from the begin-ning." Hence Jolian had no term to apply to liīka save niūl (little brother) while liīka called Jolian nepas (older brother). As liīka was younger than Jolian's great-great-great-grandfather, he was a "younger" brother to Jolian, and not an "older" brother. This was well remembered by the informant because all his people said it was very unusual, and laughed a great deal that a mere baby should be an "older" brother to such an extremely old man. This has two important implications: first, it shows that seven generations ago the temewhanic and the tepaīyauītcem clans were one; and in the second place that the Cahuilla normally record only six generations, cases like the above being so rare that no special term for great-great-great-grandfather is employed.

Very few informants even remember the term nañaa, the term nepū (great-grandfather) being the last one commonly known. Little emphasis is put on remembering one's genealogy, the opposite idea of forgetting the dead being stressed, and it is easy to see how branch lineages or clans may vaguely remember that they are related although all actual knowledge of the connection is lost. In a like manner, were the data available, the remaining wīwaīistam clans in all probability could be shown as one basic stock. The following genealogy shows all of the nauhañavitcem clan that are remembered.

GENEALOGY 11

Nauhañavitcem Clan

```
                                   ┌─ Valencia Segundo
                                   │     + tepamōkiktum
          ┌─ Casmirio Segundo      │   Maria Antonio
          │     ( or nauhañavitc)─ │     + hōkwitcakiktum
          │   + hōkwitcakiktum     │
          │                        │   Anita
          │   Santiago Segundo     │     + īsilsīva  (Desert wildcat clan)
          │     + (?)              │
          │     + īvīatim          │   Petra
  (?)─────┤                        └─    + tepamōkiktum (Cornelio Lubo)
          │
          │   Florianno Segundo    ┌─ Tomas Segundo
          │     + (from desert)    │     + kauisikiktum
          │                        │
          │                        │   Bernardo Segundo
          │                        └─    + īsilsīva
          │
          │   Martin Segundo       ┌─ George Segundo
          └─    + palpūnivikiktum  └─    + sauicpakiktum (1)
```

Apparently this central lineage had been isolated for some time as the informant could trace no actual connection with anyone in this group, although they were definitely believed to be related. The lower right-hand case of marriage in the above genealogy took place after the sauicpakiktum clan had moved to Old Santa Rosa, and the definite relationship of the group had become obscured. Nevertheless the old people objected strongly to the marriage and when George's wife died on the birth of their second child, they attributed it to this breach of marriage custom. A similar case occurs when the very brief sauicpakiktum "genealogy" is considered.

GENEALOGY 12

Sauicpākiktum Clan

Manuel Torte (or sauicpakik)   Patricio Torte
  + wakaīkiktum   + Matilda Norte (temewhanvitc)

This branch lineage was nearly extinct when the informant first remembers it. The two men shown above were the sole survivors in the male line at Old Santa Rosa when Patricio married Matilda Norte, a temewhanvitc woman from patcawal, where her lineage were then living. All the old people of the wīwaīistam clan objected to this marriage as they did to the other endogamous marriage just mentioned, and after a few years Augustine Norte, Matilda's uncle, taking advantage of Patricio's mistreatment of his wife, made them separate. Both these cases were in large measure due to the breaking down of moiety and interlineage marriage rules under modern conditions, but they also show how the relationship of branch lineages is soon forgotten once they become somewhat isolated in space. The relationship of all sauīvilem lineage members remembered and their probable relation to the temewhanvitcem lineage, is as follows:

GENEALOGY 13

Sauīvilem Clan

```
7b ⎡ met temewhanvitc)                                      ⎡ Chris sauīvil
   ⎢     + (?)                                              ⎢    + panuksēkiktum
7e ⎢ (?)              Andreas sauīvil——Sylvester sauīvil    ⎢
   ⎢    + (?)              + (?)              + hōkwitcakiktum ⎢ Joe sauīvil
   ⎣                                                         ⎣    + kauisikiktum
```

The informant Jolian Norte (temewhanvitc), called Andreas, neka (grandfather or grandfather's brother) and Sylvester, nekum (paternal uncle); Vincente Norte and Andreas sauīvil, being cousins of the same generation. Just what degree removed they were, the informant was unable to say, but it is probable that met (temewhanvitc) and the father of Andreas sauīvil were brothers, making the sauīvilem lineage a later collateral branch of the temewhanvitcem lineage. This possibility is also indicated in genealogy 8. Such were the relationships existing among the branch lineages of the Los Coyotes people, who composed the most southerly Cahuilla-speaking clan.

In summing up the data in regard to the social organization of the Mountain Cahuilla of both the north and the south, it is well to note that in both the unit was the localized male lineage, many of which in the north had become fused into parties through the union of broken down clans, and in the south had formed one large clan through the branching out of a central clan into separated lineages still ceremonially dominated by the parent stock—an interesting example of convergent evolution from dissimilar causes. In the former case the clan fetish bundle served to unite alien lineages into one party, and in the latter case to hold many collateral lineages together in one clan.

LEADERS AND CEREMONIAL OFFICIALS OF THE CLAN

Unlike the situation among the Desert Cahuilla, the Mountain Cahuilla in the course of the last century were profoundly affected by Caucasian contacts and as a result had fused into an almost tribal organization under their captains, who were called takwinūinavac or takwī in their own language. The two foregoing sections have shown how this state of affairs was brought about and have given sufficient data in regard to these later officials to show their general character. Underlying these later manifestatiins, however, were conditions basic-ally similar to those of the other Cahuilla divisions previously dis-cussed, wherein the following clan officials were the most important.

The Net

The first of these was the net, originally the hereditary leader of each clan, as was the case among both the Pass and Desert Cahuilla. His place in the social scheme was very similar to that already shown in the discussion of the Pass clans (see pp. 105, 106). His position was inherited, and he lived in the ceremonial dance house having in his possession the ceremonial bundle, or maīswut, of the clan. As was the case among the Pass Cahuilla he was a judge and settled disputes among his clan members. To his house, i.e., the dance house, were brought people that were very sick and here the shamans attempted to cure them. During the ceremonies the net might lead the singing, as Pomosena (hōkwitcakiktum) used to do, or he might not as was the case with Manuel Largo and Juan Chappo. This was entirely dependent on the natural aptitude of the individual net, and I strongly suspect that leadership in such warfare as formerly occurred was determined in the same way. The Mountain Cahuilla net, like the other Cahuilla nets discussed, was primarily a priest and a patriarch not a war leader.

The Sacred Bundle

With the almost complete disintegration of the Mountain clans information in regard to this maīswut complex has largely dis-appeared, but the following data indicate that it was fundamentally the same for all the Cahuilla. The apapatcem clan maīswut, the final disposal of which has been previously described, consisted of a mat of reeds called sēyil, in which were rolled elatem, the eagle feather skirt, and several whistles made of eagle bones; with these were also

kept the shell money of the net. Ordinarily this maīswut was hidden
in a cave among the great rocks on the road between Cahuilla and
Bautiste. The night before the ceremony this was brought to a place
near the dance house and hidden by the takwa, who ordinarily had
charge of the sacred bundle, although nominally it was owned by the
net. Quite possibly there were other objects included in this bundle,
but the above were all that were known to my informant, Gabriel
Costo.

Among the Cahuilla clans that moved to the vicinity of San
Bernardino there were two active groups, each of which had maīswut.
According to Alec Arguello the contents of the maīswut bundle
(usually made of sēyil, a mountain reed, among these clans) of each
was the same, and consisted of the following articles: elatem, the
eagle-feather skirt; pōhot, two sticks about two and a half feet long,
which like the former object were employed in the "eagle dance";
bone whistles (the names of which the informant had forgotten); and
melawhic the "bullroarer," consisting of a smooth flat stick about
two feet long tied in the middle with a string. The paha blew on the
whistles, and a man called tcauinitem whirled the bullroarer over
his head; the sounds which these produced might only be heard by
grown people and, according to Fred Coseros, a Mountain Cahuilla,
children who by chance heard these sounds were caught by the paha
and put into the inner room of the wamkic with the maīswut, and
were in a very dangerous situation. Their parents had to make considerable gifts to the net in order to secure their release.[394] Another
very sacred object in this bundle was a long string of red-shafted
flicker feathers that were hung around the dance house at the time of
the mourning ceremony. These were called tatcanetem.[395] Equal to
them in sacredness were temhul, a truncated smooth rock about one
foot long with the large end deeply serrated, and taīawūkūl, a smooth
curved stick about fourteen inches long. Neither of these two objects
seems to have had any definite use but were "from the beginning,"
and were very sacred to the clan. The other objects included in this
bundle were called tcīatem, and consisted of pointed pieces of wood
about one foot long to the top of which were lashed rattlesnake rattles,
around these were flicker tail feathers, and outside of this the white

---

[394] This custom also applied to the Serrano, Benedict, *op. cit.*, 376, and present
paper.

[395] See p. 120 for the term tōminut used by Alejo Potencio for such a string
of sacred feathers, which he claimed were left near Saboba long ago during the
migration of the kauisiktum clan to Palm Springs. They are also similar to
both Serrano and Luiseño "sacred feathers."

inner down of the golden eagle. Around the base was wrapped a rattlesnake skin which in drying bound all the plumes together. These were carried in the hands of the various dancers. Lastly there was pīwic, a plumed headdress of eagle down in the form of a band to tie around the head. It seems probable that there were differences between the two clan bundles but if so they were not remembered by Alec Arguello.

The net of the wīwaiistam clans at Los Coyotes canyon likewise had a sacred bundle called maiswut which was kept in the dance house. It consisted of the usual woven reed mat, the reeds in this case were themselves called maiswut and came from the coast. In this were rolled pīwic, long strings of flicker, eagle, horned owl, barn owl, and burrowing owl feathers, which were sacred and were hung up in the big house only once a year at the mourning ceremony. Besides these there were in the bundle elatem, the eagle-feather skirt, tciatem, short pointed sticks with flicker and horned owl feathers on the ends, and the mūketem, the shell money of the clan. Likewise there was included mēūlakpic, the ceremonial bull roarer.

The foregoing ceremonial impedimenta will be mentioned later in connection with the Mountain Cahuilla ceremonies, but the elaborate composition of these sacred bundles or clan fetishes is shown by the lists, fragmentary though they probably are. These bundles were the symbolic centers of the original clans, and later became the ceremonial centers of the "parties" which arose from the broken-down clan organization.

The Paha

While the Pass Cahuilla seem to have given various duties to the man they called paha, among both northern and southern Mountain Cahuilla the office was primarily associated with the jimsonweed drinking or manet ceremony. The northern Mountain clans had the takwa as general ceremonial assistant, while the southern clans gave the same person the title of kutvavanavac. For the Desert, Pass, and northern Mountain Cahuilla it seems very probable that the takwa was once the only assistant to the clan leader, and that the term paha was adopted through the infiltration of ideas connected with the toloache cult which had spread from west to east. The two offices persisted side by side but in each case there was an older local term of limited distribution for the general ceremonial assistant, while the word paha was identical for all groups, with the same symbolism connected with it in every case.

Among the northern Mountain Cahuilla clans while the paha was employed primarily in the manet ceremony, he was also the net's messenger in the exchange of shell money between the various groups. In the former ceremony he combined keeping order with joking, for if any one went to sleep when he (or she) was singing, the paha would pour water or drop red-hot coals on him, to the amusement of all onlookers. He always led in the ceremonial blowing that was employed to waft the dead soul to the abode of the dead. At manet he supervised the entire ceremony and administered the toloache drink to the youths. Whenever there were announcements to be made the paha attended to them. He was respected by all the people and seems in part to have maintained this respect through their fear of his personal powers or charms. Such joking as he employed seems to have been ceremonial, and acting the clown seems to have been part of his duty. The term paha among the Desert Cahuilla is sometimes translated as "funny man," but beyond that their knowledge of the term seems rather vague.

Kutvavanavac

The southern Mountain Cahuilla or Los Coyotes people employed the term kutvavanavac instead of takwa and this official had many duties. He ordered the men to hunt and the women to prepare food and cook when a ceremony was in order. When a deer was killed the hunter would tell the kutvavanavac, and he would send other young men out to bring it to the dance house. All ceremonial fires were lighted, and all ceremonial blowing was begun by him. When he was told to do so by the net he went to a hill near the village and called "ha-a-a-a! Bring your tcipitmul (flaring mouth basket) to my house!" and all who heard him had to obey. He called the dance house "my house" because it belonged to all the clan, and all the people could so refer to it. During the ceremonies he constantly moved about the "big house" maintaining order and making all present blow to waft away the spirits of the dead. Like the paha among the northern Mountain clans, the kutvavanavac was in part a joker and did many things to make the people laugh during the ceremonies and at other times. Prior to the "eagle dance" he announced its performance by making a great noise with the bullroarer. The term kutvavanavac is very similar to kutvōvōc employed by the Cupeño in designating the same official, and may be of Diegueño origin.

Takwa

The takwa among the northern clans had much the same duties. At manet he had charge of the preparation and division of food, and at all other ceremonies he seems to have held the same sort of position as the kutvavanavac among the southern clans. These duties will be brought out in connection with the ceremonies to be described later. Greeting the invited guests was one of his main duties; when they were first sighted he would run to greet them shaking a gourd rattle, called paa-īl. The guests, singing and dancing, would follow him back to the wamkic.

Hauinik

Among the lesser and more specialized ceremonial performers of the Mountain Cahuilla there were several that apparently were unknown to the Cahuilla of the Desert and perhaps to those of the Pass as well. The first of these was a special hauinik, or singer, whose duty was the singing of the song of the creation. During any ceremony at which this song was sung the hauinik would kneel in the dance house near the fire and sing the song from beginning to end. He was not supposed to move even for natural functions as that would hurry the song, hence he might remain immovable for two days and a night until the song was ended. Such a singer among the Los Coyotes Cahuilla was a very old man līīka tepaīauitcem (previously mentioned as the great-great-great-great-uncle of Jolian Norte, a Los Coyotes informant, genealogy 10). This man was reputed to be a very wise man; his hair was gray and hung to his waist, he wore only a breech-clout, and he was reputed to be the only man in the mountains who knew the entire creation song in all its ramifications. He was barely remembered by Jolian Norte, for he died when the former was a small boy, perhaps fifty years ago. The male dancer (or dancers) who danced the eagle or "whirling" dance among the Mountain Cahuilla were likewise unknown to the Desert Cahuilla and apparently to the more southerly Pass Cahuilla clans. They were men who had shown especial aptitude in their manet ceremony as boys, but if they had any especial title it was not remembered by my informants.

The Manet Dancer

The ceremony of manet, or jimsonweed drinking, involved another official in its performance besides the paha. This other ceremonial performer among the northern Mountain Cahuilla was called tcauini-tem, and among the southern Mountain Cahuilla tcenenvac. Both of these had the same duties which consisted of leading the novitiates in dancing, whirling the ceremonial bull roarer, and keeping women and children away from the dance house at this time.

Shamans and Shamanism

The part played by the shamans or pūalem in the life of the Mountain Cahuilla is at this late date hard to determine. There have been no active shamans in the mountains for many years, but from the vague data obtainable there would seem to have been at one time a considerable shamanistic cult. Among the northern Mountain Cahuilla there are stories of contests between shamans, when all the noted shamans would assemble and see which had the most power. One shaman would go apart from the group and walk toward the others while all would attempt to kill him with their spirits (teaīawa, translated as "pains" or "spirits"). Should he fall "dead" each in turn, using his own esoteric methods, would try to bring him back to life. The one who succeeded was acknowledged by all as both slayer and resurrector, and acknowledged as the one having the most power.[396] As to the means whereby a man became a shaman there was no agreement among northern Mountain Cahuilla informants. Some said he acquired his power through visions obtained at manet or by subsequent jimsonweed drinking; others said that the shaman was born with the power and that visions were unnecessary. The actual facts are nâturally unobtainable at this time in the mountains, but an intensive study of the Desert Cahuilla shamans, many of whom are still active, would yield information in part applicable to all Cahuilla groups.

The southerly Mountain Cahuilla informants were more definite in this regard saying a shaman always acquired his power at manet, or by a subsequent drinking of the jimsonweed decoction, when dreams came to him revealing his particular methods. An acquisition

---

[396] Similar shamans' contests among the Yokuts of south central California are described by Kroeber, Handbook, 506–507.

at the time of a definite supernatural guardian does not seem to have occurred, methods of curing and performing miracles, not guardian spirits, being secured through dreaming. These southern shamans had certain ceremonial duties such as dancing on the fire to put it out at the close of the fire dance, and killing the eagles by their "spirits" or by imitative magic at the eagle-killing ceremony. These ceremonies will be discussed later. The shamans' usual method of curing was by suction, by which means they claimed to draw out small stones, insects, and other foreign objects from the patient. Apparently no stigma was attached to a shaman who failed to cure a patient. Shamans, however, were often killed when it was believed that they were malevolent and were killing people or harming the food crops. Thus it is probable that occasionally a shaman was believed to have intentionally done harm rather than good to a patient under his care. But it was generally believed that such shamans killed from the population at large and did not use their malevolent powers on their own patients. As among the Pass Cahuilla, certain shamans were supposed to be able to change into various animals, especially into bears, in which form they did much damage and sometimes killed people.

The following is the story of a malevolent shaman at Los Coyotes canyon, told in the words of my informant Jolian Norte.

My grandfather's father named met (gopher) was a great pūl (shaman) who claimed to be God. He could catch bullets in his hands, pull up tobacco from the ground, and see the child in the sun. At one time he was taken by the priests, whipped and locked up, but he became a little child and they were frightened and let him go. Then he bewitched many people and killed them, so his daughter asked the people to kill him. All the wīwaïistam people at wilīya talked the matter over and decided that morūī, a bear pūl (shaman) should kill him. It was in summer and the watermelons were ripe; as met was sitting down eating one of these, morūī came up behind him and hit him over the head with a digging stick, but he could not kill him. All the other people then piled rocks over met and finally he died.

Shamans among the southern California groups seem to have frequently paid with their lives for their power over their contemporaries.

The Moiety and Marriage Among the Mountain Cahuilla

Among the Mountain Cahuilla the moiety grouping of all the clans into either a wildcat or a coyote division was primarily an arrangement for regulating marriage and had considerable effect up to the last generation, which has now broken away from the old rule. Among all the Cahuilla groups information on the moiety is much harder to obtain than information on the clans, which appear as basic and of more importance in the social consciousness of the people. As even the clans among the Mountain Cahuilla have largely gone to pieces in the last century, it is obvious that detailed knowledge of the moiety classification has suffered to a greater extent. Even the mythologic origin of the moiety has been forgotten by many of the older people in the mountains, for with the lapse of all ceremonies the older myths are rarely revived among them.

One informant, Cornelio Lubo, stated that istam (coyote) people were so named "because they followed the coyote trails." All informants agreed that joking between moieties was common, and quoted the song likewise used on the desert (see p. 72) as an example of this tendency. No special moiety paints were recalled, Cornelio Lubo stating that people of either moiety might employ red, black, or white paint which was put on forehead and cheeks with circle and bar designs. One informant, Nina Cosesos, stated that "long ago tūktum (wildcat) people worshiped the wildcat and would not kill it, so the younger people became tūktum," but I am inclined to believe she was rationalizing, for all other informants denied that the moiety totem animals were sacred. There seem to have been traces of moiety reciprocity between clans in regard to the killing of eagles, and the making of images for the mourning ceremonies. That is, a tūktum clan, usually one related by marriage, would present eaglets to, and make the images for an istam clan, and vice versa. However, this situation was not very clear in the minds of informants questioned. Strong traces of moiety reciprocity being found among the Serrano of the San Bernardino mountains to the north and the Cupeño of the southern Santa Rosas, it seems probable that at one time reciprocity between the moieties was practiced among the intervening Mountain Cahuilla, but the observable traces today are faint.

The case of two clans, one of each moiety, living at the village of pauata and both taking their names from the village is very interesting in relation to the moiety. This situation existed before any informant personally remembers, but since three informants separately made this statement on the basis of what their parents had told them, I believe it to be an actual case. If this condition was as stated, it would appear that the institution of the moiety came to the Mountain Cahuilla at a time when the clan was fully developed. One lineage of the original clan became known as istam the other as tūktum, and their relationship being obscured, marriage between the two was permitted. The example of the five Los Coyotes lineages, which were all collateral branches of one clan, seems a case in point. Lacking tūktum clans in their neighborhood, these branch clans seem to have in at least two cases overlooked their basic relationship and intermarried.[397] Should an idea similar to that of the moiety have reached them at this time it is possible that the one clan might have been divided, with a regular system of marriage between the divisions as the result. Since we are here mainly concerned with what did happen and not what might have happened, it will be well to discuss this matter later in relation to all the data. The theory however appears plausible.

The wīwaīistam groups at Los Coyotes canyon had three names for īsil, the coyote. He was called paya īsil "water coyote," tamīia īsil "sun coyote," and īsil tēvicnikic. "white coyote." According to Jolian Norte, "no one knows why īsil has these three names for there was only one īsil that stole the heart of his father. He was created like aswit (the eagle); he was not born." It was believed among the clans of this group that before a great sickness came, īsil barked from the north, and all the shamans knew of it at once.[398] The shamans would call all the people to the dance house at wilīya, and there they would dance all night to drive away the disease. There are resemblances here to the Dieguēno color association in regard to the wildcat,[399] another point that may well be discussed in the conclusion.

A list of thirty-two actual cases of marriage indicates that the Mountain Cahuilla prior to the last generation observed moiety exogamy in a great majority of cases. These marriages were mostly between the southern mountain clans and were in the main older marriages between individuals now dead; most of them are shown in the genealogies previously given. Where marriages were between Cahuilla and Cahuilla, all three main divisions included, nineteen out of the twenty-four cases were according to the moiety rule. Seven marriages between Mountain Cahuilla and the Cupeño show six marriages not in accord with the moiety bond and only one in keeping with the rule—a small number of cases, but rather forcibly demonstrating the fact that marriages between the different linguistic groups disregarded the moiety bond, whereas marriages within any one linguistic group seem to have followed the rule closely.

---

[397] See genealogies 9, 10.

[398] Kroeber notes that the cry of the horned owl, or the bark of a coyote near a house, is believed by the Luiseño to foretell a death. See Du Bois, *op. cit.*, 182.

[399] See Waterman, present series, 8:333, 1910, and Gifford, S. Cal., 169.

Marriages between the Mountain and the Pass Cahuilla seem to have been common; out of eight cases only one was contrary to the moiety rule. Marriages between the southern Mountain clans and those of the Pass Cahuilla were less common, only three cases being recorded, one case being contrary to moiety exogamy. One comparatively late marriage between a Mountain Cahuilla man and a Chemehuevi woman is the only case of the kind in the present list.

The actual arrangements for marriage among the Mountain Cahuilla were simple. Aside from the regulation against marriage with actual blood relatives or within the moiety, the latter regulation being enforced only by public opinion and fear of ridicule, the choice of mates was unlimited. Childhood betrothals arranged between parents were common, in which case frequent presents to the family of the girl were paid by that of the boy. Where no such arrangement was made, the parents of the boy, when he was about eighteen, selected a girl for him. The girl might be fourteen or fifteen years old. The boy's mother would take presents of venison, acorn meal, or perhaps baskets to the girl's family and make her request. If the girl's parents were agreeable the presents were accepted, and the girl might return with her mother-in-law. There appear to have been no parent-in-law taboos among any of the Cahuilla. The net of the boy's clan then invited all the clan members and all relatives of both the boy and girl to a feast in the dance house, where the takwa prepared and divided the food. The girl was instructed in her new duties by her mother-in-law, and the newly married pair lived with the boy's parents. If they did not get along well together the girl might gather up all her personal possessions and return to her own house, in which case there was no return of presents. No stigma was attached to her and she might marry again at any time. Should a wife be faithless the husband could send her home. There seems to have been no feeling that a husband should fight or kill a wife's lover; he merely let the wife go if he could not or did not care to keep her.

Adolescence and Associated Ceremonies

Girls' Adolescence Ceremony

This was called emeūlūniwe among the Mountain Cahuilla, and last occurred in the mountains forty or fifty years ago. It appears to have been much the same as that practiced among the Desert and Pass Cahuilla. This ceremony usually took place in the late sum-

mer or fall before the winter rains set in and included all the girls
of the clan who had just had their first menses. Apparently it was
not performed for each individual girl, but collectively for all girls
in each clan who had reached this period of life. It took place in the
wamkic in the presence of all the clan members. The girls were
"baked" in the pits for a three-day period during which time the old
people sang. The usual taboo against scratching or touching the body
was in force. For a six-month period after this ceremony salt and
cold food could not be eaten by the girls, a special hot food being
prepared by their mothers. This ceremony among the northern clans
was supervised by the takwa. Among the Los Coyotes canyon clans
this ceremony was concluded by the following ceremony. All the
girls sat in a row in the dance house, while the paha with a red, black,
and yellow painted mortar, filled with water, stood behind them.
The hauinik placed some tobacco in this water and both he and the
paha sang several songs. Then the paha went to one of the girls;
he blew up in the air three times, then he put a ball of tobacco in
her mouth which she swallowed and he gave her a drink of water.
She was then painted all over with red. No memories of any girl's
race, face painting, or rock painting were remembered, but here as
was also the case at Palm Springs, certain of the less decomposed
granite rocks near Cahuilla show faint traces of red designs similar
to those definitely connected with the girls' puberty ceremonial rock
painting among the Luiseño at La Jolla and Rincon.

Manet

Among the Mountain Cahuilla we encounter the jimsonweed or
toloache cult in its central manifestation, to wit, the jimsonweed-
drinking boys' initiation, or manet ceremony. Probably this rite
occurred among the more westerly clans of the Pass Cahuilla but
traces of it there are faint. All the Mountain clans, however, seem
to have had it in a more or less complete form. Informants from the
northern mountain clans said that manet meant "grass that could
talk," but could only be heard by shamans. The Los Coyotes canyon
people claimed that manet "belonged to the water," and that all
manet songs were not in the īviat (i.e., Cahuilla) language but were
in the "ocean language" and no one could understand them. The
songs were sung to the "great witch doctors" who lived on the ocean
floor, and they were prayers for the ocean winds to blow clouds over
the mountains. They believed that "the ocean was above, below this

were all the winds and on the bottom were the great pūalem (shamans) and other monsters.'' The jimsonweed was a great human pūl (shaman) with whom they could talk. Thus among these southern clans at least, and probably among the other Mountain Cahuilla clans, the manet ceremony was held as a prayer when water was short and food scarce, or when an epidemic raged among the people. The pūalem (shamans) were always active at this ceremony. Besides this of course, it was also a boys' initiation rite.

Manet occurred once every few years when the occasion demanded it, or when there were several boys to initiate. The southern clans performed manet in connection with hemwek'lūwil, a three- or four-day ceremony in which small boys from six to ten years of age were taught their own clan songs and their ''enemy songs'' by their fathers. This took place in the wamkic or its environs, and while each boy's instruction was in the hands of relatives they were presided over by the paha. The paha prepared strings of woven reeds called wic, and strings of eagle and flicker feathers which were worn by the dancers. A dancing leader or manet-dancer called tcauinitem was selected by the net as the best dancer to lead the boys. The southern clans called this man tceñenvac. His duties consisted in leading the boys in their dances in the wamkic at night, and during the day in seeing that they practiced their songs in a secluded place away from the village. While the boys were dancing in the wamkic their relatives threw baskets and other gifts over their heads to be gathered up by the guests. The takwa attended to preparation and division of food in this ceremony. This part of the ceremony was watched by clan members and visitors of both sexes.

Then came the esoteric part of the ceremony called kiksawel,'''the drinking,'' which occurred inside the wamkic. No women or children were permitted to witness this; only the men of the clan and the novitiates, youths of eighteen to twenty years, were present. The manet-dancer whirled the bullroarer as a warning to the uninitiated to stay away. The bullroarer was called melawhic by the northern clans and meūlakpic by the southern clans. The net prepared the jimsonweed, ''cooking it'' (meaning probably drying it), and ground it up in a small ceremonial mortar called takic, with a small pestle called paūl. Water was added and the liquid was then put in a red pottery bowl called tesnut kumūīsmul, and the paha gave each boy a swallow. The men in the wamkic then took each boy by the waist and danced around the fire led by the manet dancer. All were naked, and according to

Alec Arguello old people sometimes fell into the fire in the excitement but were not burned. The novitiates became unconscious and were left in the dance house all night. The next afternoon they were taken out of the dance house and hidden in a secluded canyon by the paha. Here they were taught songs while at night for one week they danced every evening. The jimsonweed however was drunk only once.

The drinking of the jimsonweed produces visions, but no especial dream cult or interpretation is remembered by modern informants. One northern Mountain Cahuilla informant said that if any boy saw in his dreams an animal that spoke to him, bad luck for his relatives would result. A southern Mountain Cahuilla informant said that boys at this time "had dreams like pūalem (shamans)" and that anything seen in the vision was their "spirit or friend." Since it is fifty or sixty years since this ceremony took place among the Mountain Cahuilla it is not strange that the details are vague.

The last afternoon of the week the ground-painting or some equivalent to it was made. Alec Arguello said that among the Mountain Cahuilla clans which moved to San Bernardino the following occurred. The paha marked off a special area in front of the wamkic beyond which outsiders could not come. Then coming from the interior of the wamkic he brought a very sacred red, white, and black basket called nēat, which he carried around the space. He then returned it into the inner room of the dance house. This was very important, according to Alec Arguello, but no one knew the meaning of it.[400] The true ground painting must have occurred there however, for Nina Cosesos said she had seen it made three times, once at pūlatana (near San Bernardino) when she was a girl of about 10 or 12 years, once at Saboba, where it was made by a Mountain Cahuilla net, and once at pauī (Cahuilla) when she was about 16 years of age. She is a very old woman, probably between 80 and 90, hence this occurred in the neighborhood of seventy years ago. Her memories were somewhat vague but leave no doubt as to the general nature of the ritualistic performance. The net, in the case last cited, made a shallow pit four or five feet in diameter. In this was placed a "web" of red, pauisvul, black, tūl, and white, tēwic, colors. These colors were made of red ocher, iron oxide, or some similar mineral, a black mineral probably graphite, and white clay. They were arranged like the spokes of a wheel within the pit. The net then explained to the boys who were

---

[400] This is undoubtedly a form of tukmul, or the sacred winnowing basket, used by the Luiseño in their toloache ceremonies. Du Bois, *op. cit.*, 78–79.

being initiated the meaning of the design, but my informant did not hear this. The occurrence of the ground painting at Cahuilla is likewise remembered by Cornelio Lubo when he was very young; but he said that only certain of the old men knew what it meant, the younger people being in complete ignorance. If there was any direct connection of this phenomenon with Chungichnish it was not remembered by any of the Cahuilla talked with. Primarily, manet was a boys' initiation ceremony and when the decoction had been drunk, the songs and dances learned, and the ground painting made and explained, the boys were regarded as men and full-fledged members of the clan. The ceremonial ground painting probably occurred among the southern clans, as it was well known among the Cupeño, their neighbors to the south, but no informants who remembered it among the southern Mountain Cahuilla were encountered.

Ant Ordeal

Among the northern Mountain clans, this ceremony closed with the ant ordeal called hemūnīwe or "stinging ants ceremony." A large pit was dug where an ant's nest had been and many ants were collected in it. Then the young men who had been initiated were rolled naked into the pit and when they came out the ants were brushed off with nettles. Every young man in the clan was supposed to pass through this ordeal once, in order to give him bravery and greater endurance in hunting.

THE FIRE DANCE

Among the southern Mountain clans the manet ceremony closed with the fire dance, called tapasak. A large fire was built outside of the dance house. Both men and women of the clan surrounded it and moved around the fire singing and dancing, sometimes at a fast, sometimes at a slow pace. Then after the dance had become fast and there was much excitement all the men sat down around the fire and pushed it in with their feet. Men did not burn, informants say, but they often became unconscious from the heat, the shamans fanning them with feathers to bring them to. Then all the men changed position and used their hands in putting out the fire. The shamans occasionally jumped into the fire and kicked the coals around with their bare feet, but they likewise did not burn. The women and children stood outside the circle and looked on, chanting the songs for this particular ceremony, which are about ten in number. Finally the fire was entirely extinguished and the ceremony ended. The exact method by which the dancers and shamans handled the glowing coals, like the present-day performances of Desert shamans with live coals, is not known by the uninitiated or in detail by the ethnologist.[401] As has already been suggested a detailed study of shamanism among the Desert Cahuilla would yield much of interest on these points.

The Eagle-Killing Ceremony

The eagle cult manifested itself strongly among the Mountain Cahuilla especially among the southern clans, where as among the Diegueño it was closely associated with shamanistic practices. Among these groups the eagle killing seems also to have been associated with the mourning ceremony for a dead clan leader, although it might be performed by itself as a separate ceremony for the eagle.

Among the northern clans the ceremony occurred in honor of a net (clan leader) or one of his close relatives who had died. In this case, a clan net of another moiety might present the young eagle to the bereaved net, and a year after the death this net would invite the giver of the eagle and his clan to preside at the ceremony. The eagle, which after its presentation had been carefully cared for in the net's house, was taken by the invited takwa, who, carrying the bird, danced at the head of the two clans in the dance house. Finally, sometime after midnight, the eagle "gets dizzy" and dies. Offerings of food were made to the dead eagle. All the people mourned loudly for him, and the takwa removed the primary feathers of the wings and tail to make elatem, the eagle-feather skirt, which belongs to the local net. The local net threw away gifts of food and baskets which the guests gathered up. In the morning the eagle's body, carefully wrapped in cloth, was buried either by the grave of the recently deceased for whom the ceremony was given, or else in the dance house itself. No informant among these northern clans remembered this ceremony personally so the information in regard to it is necessarily sketchy. The name of this ceremony among these northern clans was kēwittawat.

The southern clans of the Los Coyotes canyon called this ceremony aswitīpēmēniktum the "eagle killing." One informant said that "long ago tūtcil (the humming bird) wanted to take aswit's (the

---

[401] See Waterman, present series, 8:327, for a first-hand account of this ceremony among the Diegueño, showing the way in which the fire is actually extinguished.

eagle's) place, but all agreed that he was too small. Aswit was a human being and was placed in the first mountain made, called haui-yauwit and kalalaïwit, so every tribe could own him.'' When an eagle was to be killed among these southern clans all neighboring groups were invited, each for a different night.[402] They sang sad songs and there was a great deal of mourning. The eagle which was in a cage near the net's house ''heard all this and was very sad, for he knew what was going to happen.'' When all the people were assembled on the last evening the fire was extinguished, and the local clan led by the net and the kutvavanavac gathered around the eagle and sang. Then a local shaman took the eagle, holding each leg tight against the bird's breast, and brought it to the fire in the center of the wamkic. Then clockwise the people circled the fire, but back near the walls, dancing and singing while the shaman held the eagle near the fire in the center. Thus all the other shamans could attempt to kill the eagle by their personal power. Some shamans had so little power that the eagle did not even scream, while others made him scream for only a few seconds. This, my informant said, was because they had ''too little electricity,'' a unique description of the supposed psychic power of the shaman. Other shamans in front of the eagle hit their own heads in order to kill the eagle, but while the eagle screamed and shook his body he did not die. Other shamans stood in the fire and pointed at the eagle with ''sticks''[403] to kill him, and the eagle might hang his head for a moment but recovered. Another shaman would ''swallow'' a stick and throw out something to kill the eagle. Thus the shamans may work all night to kill the eagle. If the eagle is alive in the morning, a very improbable situation, they let it go. When it dies all present cry loudly and scatter offerings of acorn meal or other food on the body. The net or kutvavanavac removed the primary feathers and down to make elatem, the skirt, or tciatem, the headdress. In the morning the eagle was wrapped in cloth and buried in the clan burying ground.

There is no doubt that the foregoing ceremony is Diegueño in many of its essentials, but Jolian Norte stated that it was identical with that at Los Coyotes where the shamans supposedly killed the eagle in the manner here described. The Cupeño likewise believed in

---

[402] This description actually applies to a mixed Diegueño, Cupeño, and Cahuilla ceremony at Mesa Grande about fifteen years ago, but my informant Jolian Norte stated positively that the Los Coyotes ceremony was identical.

[403] Waterman, present series, 8:317–318, describes an identical procedure among the Diegueño, and also describes how the eagle is really killed by compression of the lungs and heart by the man holding it.

the killing of the eagle by the shamans, as did both the Diegueño and
these southerly Cahuilla groups. The killing of the eagle by shamans
was also practiced among the Luiseño.[404]

The "Whirling" or Eagle Dance

The "whirling," "morahash," or eagle dance was common to all
the Mountain Cahuilla, and was called pūnil, which was translated
simply as "the eagle dance." The following description applies to
the Los Coyotes canyon Cahuilla ceremony which was, so far as I
could find out, identical with the same ceremony among the northern
mountain clans. This dance among the southern clans might occur at
any time, but was usually given at the close of nūkil, the image-
burning ceremony. There might be several eagle-dancers, usually
specially qualified dancers, but only one dancer danced at a time.
The kutvavanavac would announce the ceremony by whirling the bullroarer (meūlakpic) whereupon all the men and women would form a
circle outside of the dance house. At this time the kutvavanavac
would perform many antics to make the people laugh. There was a
special doorkeeper who, with a pole called nahat, cleared all people
away from the entrance to the dance house. When all was ready this
doorkeeper shouted loudly three times, and all the people echoed him.

The kutvavanavac stepped into the center of the circle and stared
intently at the sun, then the eagle-dancer wearing elatem, the eagle-
feather skirt, pīwitcem, the eagle plumage headdress, and carrying
two short sticks called pōhut in his hands, ran out of the dance house,
knelt in the center of the circle, and stared at the sun for almost a
minute. His face and neck were covered with white clay. Then
hitting the two sticks together to tell the people when to start and to
stop singing, he moved slowly around the circle imitating the actions
of the eagle. Suddenly he began to whirl faster and faster, accompanied by the men and women who were singing and dancing in line
around the circle. His feather skirt straightened out and he kept
whirling, while all the people sang the songs of the eagle dance. At
the last song the kutvavanavac shouts loudly, the doorkeeper opens
the crowd with his pole, and the dancer stops whirling suddenly and
runs into the dance house. This performance may be repeated by
other dancers but only one man dances at a time.

While the two foregoing ceremonies both have to do with the eagle,
they seem unconnected in their performance and probably in their

---

[404] Du Bois, *op. cit.*, 182.

inception. The ceremonial killing of the eagle is apparently an ancient and universal south central Californian custom found among all the groups considered in the present paper. Whereas the eagle or "whirling" dance is a specialized ceremony, apparently an integral part of that loose complex designated as the toloache cult. It is therefore found only among those peoples to which this cult extended; hence peripheral peoples like the Desert Cahuilla did not have the ceremony of the eagle dance although the ceremonial killing of eagles was well known among them.

Mourning Ceremonies

Ceremonies for the dead among the Mountain Cahuilla seem to have been largely identical with those of the Desert and Pass Cahuilla, and add little detail to the data already given for those groups. The ceremonies have not been performed for many years, so most of the detail has been forgotten. These older ceremonies, not being associated with any late cult such as the Chungishnish complex, seem to have been much the same among all the southern Californian groups studied.

As occurred among all these groups in early times, the bodies of the dead were burned according to native tradition; but within the memory of all informants the body of the deceased was buried soon after death. At this time a feast called hemtcipinwe, for all the relatives of the dead, was held and a night of singing followed. Within a week or so after the death occurred hemtcūstanwe—the ceremonial burning of the dead person's possessions. This seems to parallel tcipīni'l "covering the tracks of the dead," among the Pass Cahuilla, for Mountain Cahuilla informants said that this was done in order to send the soul, tawehonaveh, "to the place of the dead." Not only the personal possessions, but also the house of the deceased was burned. Other clans, especially the one into which the dead person was married were invited to this ceremony, and often brought presents of food to the family of the deceased.

To the week-long image-burning ceremony called nūkatem "burn them," neighboring clans were invited, each for a different night. As occurred elsewhere, the local clan sang for the first part of the week, the visiting clans during the latter part. About the middle of the week, after nightfall the maīswut of the local clan was brought from the inner room of the dance house and prayed over by the net

and his family. This was prepared for by the paha, who, with the
bullroarer, signaled for silence. The net and the paha assisted by
shamans then hung the sacred feathers (long bands of horned owl,
barn owl, burrowing owl, and flicker feathers) all around the dance
house. These remained until the close of the ceremony. On Saturday
the images were made, in early times the bodies being made of
maīswut, cut in thin rolls, three to four feet long, with similar rolls
lashed across to form the arms of the image. Extra maīswut
was kept in the dance house for this purpose. At the close of the
ceremony the images were burned outside the dance house and the
shell money was distributed to the invited clan leaders. As has been
previously mentioned, some informants stated that should a clan of
the wildcat moiety give the ceremony, the images were made by a
specially invited coyote moiety clan. Actual cases to bear these statements out are lacking, so while moiety reciprocity in the mourning
ceremony is suggested, it cannot be proved.

Miscellaneous Data

The foregoing ceremonies are the only ones which the Mountain
Cahuilla remember in any detail. There are however a few fragmentary suggestions bearing on ritual and material culture which
seem worth recording at this time. Actual naming ceremonies were
not remembered by informants, for Spanish names have been in vogue
for several generations, but one informant was told by his father that
such a ceremony formerly occurred in the dance house once a year,
when children were given names in secret. Enemy clans desired to
obtain these names for their ridiculing songs. These songs have been
in disuse for a long time, but were once sung at any gathering of a
"fiesta" or ceremonial nature. An example of such a song, sung by
the hōkwitcakiktum clan against the wakwaīkiktum clan of the Desert
Cahuilla, is as follows:

> Minavacum manilyawun new'um
>   wakaīkīkaīk
> temasūwit yaīc kīwit tamauka!

This was translated as "Come on along, you wakaikik person, if you
are able!" These so-called "enemy" clans seem always to have been
those of another district; for example, the Mountain Cahuilla clans
usually sang against clans of the Desert Cahuilla as in the case just
cited, and vice versa. Mild ridicule and not vituperation seems to

have been their main purpose, although in early times there may have been more feeling in them than is now remembered. If there was any connection between these songs and the moiety of the clans concerned it is not remembered. The moiety songs have the same ridiculing character, but seem to possess less social significance than the songs of clan against clan.

The exchange of shell money, mūketem, between Mountain Cahuilla clans has not been given in detail because detailed information is lacking. The northern clans carried on a ceremonial exchange with the Luiseño "parties" at Saboba, and with the Pass and Palm Springs Cahuilla clans. This has already been described (p. 98). The Los Coyotes canyon Cahuilla exchanged shell money with the Cupeño at kūpa (Warner's Hot Springs) and with the people at wilakal (San Ysidro), but Jolian Norte, my best informant on the Los Coyotes canyon group, remembered little beyond the fact that when he was a boy such a ceremonial exchange occurred between the northern and southern Mountain clans.

The wamkic of the northern clans, and the kicamnawut or wamkic, as the southern clans called the ceremonial dance house, was at least in its later stages much like a modern frame house with walls and roof made of arrow-weed (*Artemisia ludoviciana*).[405] There was a semi-circular enclosure in front, and a small room behind where the clan or "party" leader kept his maīswut and other ceremonial impedimenta. According to Cornelio Lubo, on the authority of his grandfather, the old house of the Mountain Cahuilla was called tamikic, and was semisubterranean. A pit about 3 feet deep and 20 feet in diameter was dug, and a central post about 7 feet high erected, from which rafters ran to the edge of the pit. These were first covered with brush and then by a layer of dirt. In his time houses of brush with more or less modern frames were in vogue, but he assured me that long ago the tamikic served both living and ceremonial purposes. The sweat house was called hasluc,[406] and in the mountains was 10 to 15 feet in diameter, 4 or 5 feet high, and covered with brush and dirt. A fire was built in front of the entrance. Its use seems to have been medicinal and not ceremonial, and it was last used about forty years ago, there being one such house at Cahuilla at that time.

---

[405] The last dance house at Cahuilla was burned many years ago. It stood on the site where a small frame house noted as "the home of Ramona" now stands. Supposedly, this is the house where the heroine of Helen Hunt Jackson's novel lived when her Indian husband was killed. I venture no opinion.

[406] Barrows, *op. cit.*, 77, describes the Cahuilla sweat house and its use.

V. THE CUPEÑO

These people occupied a position on the border line between the two great speech families of southern California, the Shoshonean and the Yuman. To the north and west of the Cupeño were the Luiseño and Cahuilla, both of whom are Shoshonean, and to the south and east of the Cupeño were the Yuman Diegueño. Hemmed in by these different groups the Cupeño population contained elements of each. Their speech is fairly close to that of the Cahuilla and it is with them that the Cupeño have had their most intimate contacts. The two dialects are said to be mutually intelligible, but the Cupeño language seems to have added some Yuman elements to its fundamentally Shoshonean construction. Certain of the Cupeño clans appear to have been originally of Diegueño (Yuman) speech affiliation, and as a result many of the Cupeño are bilingual in respect to the radically different Cupeño and Diegueño tongues.

About 1902 the majority of the Cupeño were more or less forcibly removed from their houses at Warner's Hot Springs, and taken to Pala in Luiseño territory. The data here presented were gathered in part by Gifford during a three-weeks' visit to Pala in 1919, and partly by the present author, who during the month of November, 1925, worked with the Cupeño at San Ysidro, Warner's Hot Springs, and Pala. Not knowing at the time this unpublished work by Gifford at Pala,[407] I covered much the same ground that he had already been over, and our notes, in part obtained from the same informants (after an eight-year interval) admirably check and supplement one another. Among other data Gifford obtained a Pala agency census for 1919, and a house-to-house census of the Cupeño prior to their removal from Warner's Hot Springs, as complete as informants could give it from memory. These lists and his other data he most kindly turned over to me, and they are incorporated in the present account. Where our information differs I have so indicated in the text, but on the whole there is almost complete accord between the two accounts. Gifford's notes are more complete as regards the census and personal affiliation of individuals, mine as regards genealogies and ceremonials.

---

[407] Gifford had previously published a preliminary report on the Cupeño, based on short visits in 1916 and 1917, see present series, 14:199–201, 1917.

The village of kūpa at Warner's was famous for its natural hot springs, and as elsewhere these were highly valued by the natives. Legendary accounts[408] tell of a time when the Cupeño were almost exterminated by their neighbors and while the story of the massacre and magical restoration of the people are mythical, it is highly probable that a place so naturally favored as kūpa should have been the scene of considerable struggle for ownership. There is nothing legendary about its seizure from the Cupeño by the whites, and its ownership had undoubtedly been disputed before.

In 1822, a sub-mission was established at Santa Ysabel, and shortly after that a branch was evidently established at Agua Caliente, as Warner's Hot Springs was then called. In 1830, a Spanish or Mexican woman, Apolinaria Lorenzana, called "la Beata," was in the habit of taking the sick from Santa Ysabel to bathe them in the warm springs at Agua Caliente.[409] After the Franciscans abandoned their mission here, the Cupeño moved into the deserted buildings. Several families included in the census lived in these large deserted adobes. Each house was divided among the different family units, each having its fireplace and living section. The main Cupeño informant, Mrs. Manuela Griffith, was born in such a house in 1852, and she had never seen the regular dwelling house of her people. It was described by her parents as a circular, semisubterranean, and earth-covered lodge. When the Cupeño went into their mountain food-gathering territories they made rectangular, double lean-tos of pine bark. They used this type of dwelling under such circumstances until they were removed from kūpa about 1902. When Mrs. Griffith was young nearly all the families were concentrated in the old mission buildings,[410] but later the younger married couples began to build adobe huts for themselves.

Quarrels between the Cupeño and the owner of the land grant, Mr. Warner,[411] led to the insurrection of 1851 and the subsequent retreat of the Cupeño to Los Coyotes canyon, while the troops burned their town.[410] Cavalry under Major Heintzelman pursued the Indians

---

[408] Gifford, S. Cal., 199. Also present paper, pp. 270–273.

[409] H. H. Bancroft, 19:553, n. 20.

[410] In December, 1851, a company of San Diego volunteers burned the Indian village at Agua Caliente, in retaliation for the burning of John J. Warner's house at that place. It is possible that the Cupeño prior to this had had their own homes, but were thus forced to herd together in the old mission buildings after their crude dwellings were destroyed.

[411] In 1840, Agua Caliente was granted to Jose A. Pico, and by a later grant of 1844, to J. J. Warner. The latter seems to have purchased the claim of the former grantee.

to Los Coyotes canyon and brought them back. Five of the ring-
leaders, including Antonio Garra (Kaval) were captured by Juan
Antonio Costakik,[412] a Mountain Cahuilla captain. These were
executed, but the remainder of the Cupeño were allowed to remain in
their old territory until the expulsion of 1902.

Kūpa was very favorably located at the base of Hot Springs mountain (called by the local Indians, Lookout mountain), where there
are beautiful valleys with large oak groves while the ridges are covered
with pines and sycamores. Deer are still abundant, and the Cupeño
must have always had an adequate food supply. To the west the
open valley of San Jose (San Jose del Valle) stretches to a small lake
(now the Henshaw dam) where Luiseño territory began. These flats
were used by the Cupeño for gathering various kinds of weed seeds
and grasses. The warm springs themselves are on a rise at the edge
of the mountain and the hot water not only occurs in pools but actually
forms a good-sized stream. At present the adobe houses used by the
Indians have been somewhat rehabilitated and are used as guest rooms
by the local hotel. The stream where the Indians formerly bathed,
leached acorns, and soaked fiber for baskets, now runs into a swimming
pool and a series of bath houses. Bedrock mortars and other signs of
the old life are abundant, but the Indians are gone.

Villages and Clans

The Cupeño formerly occupied the large village called kūpa at
Warner's Hot Springs, from which they have derived their name, and
a smaller and linguistically more mixed village, wilakal, at San
Ysidro about four miles southeast of kūpa. The two villages were
united by marriage and social intercourse but were apparently
politically independent of one another, and each was the center of a
different clan grouping. Kūpa was always the largest, and was
occupied by four Cupeño clans and one affiliated Cahuilla clan.
Wilakal was, and is today, occupied by two clans, one apparently of
Cahuilla and the other of Diegueño origin. Representatives of all
Cupeño clans lived in both villages but each was centered in only one
of the two towns. The clan and lineage composition of each is given
in the two following tables (8–9).

---

[412] H. H. Bancroft, 29:482, n. 17. Bancroft speaks of Garra as a San Luis
Rey Indian, but my genealogies show him to be a Cupeño. The part played by
Juan Antonio was not remembered by Cupeño informants.

TABLE 8

Clans and Lineages at kŭpa

Clan[413]	Nicknames	Supposed origin	Moiety
1. kavalim (?)	nauwilot (louse), Laws, tcañalañalic ("sprouts"), nŭka ("daughter-in-law"), Gara (Span.?)	Cupeño	Coyote (Islam)
2. pumtumatŭlniktcum	palaut (place name) ("blacktooth")	Cupeño	Coyote (Islam)
3. temewhanitcem (northerners)	witcūat ("fiberstring")	Cupeño	Coyote (Islam)
4. tŭktum (wildcat people)			
L 4a. sivimŭatim ("to strike the sun," or, "face peeling from sunburn")		Diegueño	Wildcat (Tŭktum)
L 4b. aulīatim (auliñawitcem) ("something tied over head?")		Diegueño	Wildcat (Tŭktum)
L 4c. taka'atim (taka'anawitcem) ("peak" or "something sharp")		Luiseño	Wildcat (Tŭktum)

5. sauīvilem ("uncooked" or "unripe"). A Mountain Cahuilla lineage from Los Coyotes canyon affiliated with clan 1, and of the same moiety

TABLE 9

Clans at wilakal

Clan	Nicknames	Supposed origin	Moiety
6. tcūtnikut (place name from ta'mīsuknival, "place where they burned people")		Diegueño	Wildcat (?)
7. tūcvikinvatim (from tūtcil, "humming bird")		Cahuilla	Wildcat (?)

---

[413] The endings im and um are collective plural endings, meaning "people." The endings em and itcem are the same but apparently of Mountain Cahuilla origin.

The information concerning wilakal is much less complete than that in regard to kūpa. Having witnessed the eviction of the kūpa people, the inhabitants of wilakal have no trust in the white man. They believe that by finding out the history of kūpa the white people were able to take their land and they have no desire to be treated in the same way. Hence, in 1925, over twenty years from the time of the Cupeño removal to Pala, it was still impossible to get information concerning social organization at San Ysidro. With adequate time to establish contact and overcome the distrust of the few inhabitants remaining, such information could be obtained, but as is so often the case, time was lacking. Fortunately Gifford obtained from kūpa informants a house-to-house census of wilakal as it was prior to 1902. This census is probably less complete than that of kūpa, where the informants lived, but with additional information obtained by Gifford and myself, it serves to establish the main features of their social organization.

San Ysidro is a lovely mountain valley about four miles southeast of Warner's Hot Springs. A considerable stream flows through it and many oaks grow in the creek bed and up along the ravines. The mountain walls rise sharply and are scantily covered with brush, but the ridges are wooded with pines, sycamores, and scrub oaks. Wilakal is situated on a bare rise in the valley floor marked by a small Catholic chapel and the house of the captain. Above on the hillside, and elsewhere in isolated clearings, are about eight or nine houses. The wilakal people formerly lived in small brush- or tule-covered huts, but at present small, dilapidated frame houses are the rule. For the period between 1865 and 1902 there are twenty wilakal houses on record, but there were probably not many more than half this number occupied at any one time. At present a few brush storage baskets for acorns, small brush outhouses, and mortars give a faintly aboriginal aspect to the site. The people are none too friendly to the casual white man, but it is certain that they have had little reason for being overly gracious. They are known as the ''Coyote tribe'' by neighboring whites and are regarded as renegades from various villages.

POPULATION

The Cupeño population, including both villages, has been estimated by Kroeber at five hundred persons at most.[414] The following data obtained since this estimate was made give considerably more information on the problem than was then available.

Gifford obtained from the Indian agency at Pala a census of that reservation for December 18, 1919. As it serves to bring out several important social facts this census is given in full in census 3 below, but a summary of the data may be given here (table 10).

TABLE 10

Composition of Pala Population in 1919

Cupeño	106
Cahuilla	10
Luiseño	44
Diegueño	22
Various	29
Total	211[415]

In comparing this census with the earlier ones (censuses 2 and 3) it must be remembered that a small Luiseño population already lived at Pala when the bulk of the Cupeño were moved there. Of the forty-four Luiseño given above, twenty-six lived at Pala before the Cupeño came, five came from kūpa, and thirteen came in from other places. It is not certain how many Cupeño remained at wilakal, but there were probably not more than forty, including all other groups represented there. Of the Cupeño listed above, sixty came from kūpa, and forty-six had been born in Pala during the nineteen years of Cupeño residence there. Because of intermarriage with whites, half-breeds are reckoned according to the mother's clan, but formerly strict patrilineal descent prevailed. This must be taken into account in reckoning the pure-blooded Cupeño. The surnames given in the Pala census (3), combined with the house censuses (1 and 2), will give information on such questions.

Gifford in 1919 also made a house census of kūpa and of wilakal prior to 1902, obtaining the bulk of his information from Mrs. Manuela Sivimuat (then 67 years old) and her daughter, Mrs. Salvadora Valenzuela (45 years old). The latter acted mainly as interpreter, but having been born in kūpa, checked her mother's information. In 1925, the present author obtained a set of kūpa genealogies

---

[414] Kroeber, Handbook, 689.

[415] Census 1 shows the method of determining tribal affiliations. This total does not include the people who remained at wilakal after 1902.

from the same informants, and these genealogies, covering the same period, have been added to Gifford's census. The almost complete accord between the two accounts is striking, and with the subsequent checking by other informants, vouches for the accuracy of the completed census. This census covers roughly the period between about 1865 and 1902, or, from the girlhood of our main informant until the Cupeño eviction from kūpa in 1902. These are given in full censuses 1 and 2) but table 11 gives a summary showing the population.

TABLE 11

Cupeño Population between ''1865'' and 1902

	Kūpa	Wilakal
Clan members	280 (including sauīvilem clan)	102
Persons with other names	67	3
Illegal children recorded	20	3
White men	20[416]	1
Mountain Cahuilla	19	12
Desert Cahuilla	3	11
Pass Cahuilla	0	1
Luiseño	1	3
Diegueño	4	2
Distant Indians	4	0
Total: 556[417]	418[418]	138

For this period then, the Cupeño had a total population of 556 persons including aliens of all sorts. It is obvious that in a period of about forty years one generation would tend to disappear and another take its place; hence this total of 556 is considerably larger than the population at any one time during the forty years. Perhaps 400 would be a fair estimate of the average Cupeño population during the period in question.

The above census includes forty-eight persons listed in the Pala census of 1919. The 1919 census (3) lists in all sixty persons who were born in kūpa and the discrepancy of twelve is probably due in great part to modern names in the agency list which cannot be identified with the earlier lineage names.

---

[416] Including one Negro.

[417] Including only those persons who actually lived at kūpa or wilakal. Children who died young, or men who married Cupeño women and took them away, are not included.

[418] In all totals based on the house census, children who died young are not included.

The decline in Cupeño population between say, 1870 and 1919, is marked. In 1919, only 106 pure and mixed Cupeños are recorded, while in the earlier census 382 are mentioned. Allowing for a discount in the latter number, because it covers a period of years, the disproportion is still great. If a similar decline on a smaller scale is granted, between "1870" and purely aboriginal times, then Kroeber's estimate of 500 for the native population seems quite in accord with the facts here presented. Cupeño genealogies (14–22) show how rapid this decline has been, and forcibly demonstrate the increased mortality and sterility coincident with a forced move to an uncongenial habitat. This is discussed more fully in relation to the individual clans.

Evidently the Cupeño population was always heterogeneous. This is natural considering the central position of the group, and the extremely favorable site they occupied. The house censuses 1 and 2 show that during the forty-odd years they cover, forty-two Cahuilla were incorporated in the Cupeño population, and only six Diegueño and four Luiseño. Moreover, this total of forty-two does not include the members of the sauivilem clan who were Cahuilla but have been here counted as Cupeño because of their almost entire removal to and incorporation at kūpa. Of the forty-two, thirty Cahuilla were of the Mountain division, and ten of the Desert division. One rather dubious case of Cupeño intermarriage with Pass Cahuilla exists. Of all the Cahuilla clan groups the one at Los Coyotes canyon was in closest contact with the Cupeño. The list of marriages during the same period (table 12 and genealogies 14–22) shows that this condition was not due solely to Cahuilla women being brought to kūpa, for as many Cupeño women married Cahuillas and moved away as was the case with either Diegueño or Luiseño.

Gifford has pointed out the fact that all Cupeño clans of the wildcat moiety claim to have originally been Luiseño and Diegueño stock.[419] This is an obscure problem and will be discussed later in connection with Cupeño clan organization. The house censuses show far more contact between Cahuilla and Cupeño than between the latter and all other groups. Whatever earlier relationship may have existed between the Cupeño, Luiseño, and Diegueño, is not clearly indicated by the data at hand, but that many Cahuilla people were incorporated in the Cupeño population is certain.

The Pala census for 1919 (3) shows a low proportion of Cahuilla residents compared to both Luiseño and Diegueño. In part this is

---

[419] Miwok Lineages and the Political Unit in Aboriginal California, Am. Anthr., n. s., 28:395, 1926.

due to the fact that children of Cahuilla mothers are naturally considered as Cupeño when their fathers are of that tribe.   Then, as Pala was always Luiseño territory, there was a Luiseño population there when the Cupeño came.   Only five Luiseño moved from kūpa to Pala with the Cupeño; the remainder either had always lived at Pala or came there from other places.   The same is true of the Diegueño at Pala; only three of the twenty-two came to Pala from kūpa.   Pala, being one of the largest Indian towns in southern California, has attracted a good many Luiseño and Diegueño in late years, but the bulk of the population is still mainly of Cupeño stock.

In passing, it may be well to comment on the value of the house census data from the biological standpoint.   Certain inaccuracies are bound to appear in any census based on data of a purely mnemonic character.   Contemporary families of the informants are apt to be more fully recorded than are earlier families.   Families that move away may be forgotten, and the record of children who died young is never complete.   Similarly, the exact order of birth of children is often not remembered.   Errors of this sort came out in comparing the census and the genealogies, but on the whole, from a social standpoint, they are of a trifling nature.

From the standpoint of determining comparative birth and death rates over a period of years, the comparative fertility of various types of marriage, and the exact proportion of the sexes,[420] such factors of error as above enumerated are important.   If it is borne in mind that the house census gives the bulk of the population, not its totality, it may safely be used for other than social determinations.   In any such work it is essential to combine the houses censuses (1 and 2) with the Pala census (3), for no persons born after 1902 are included in the former.

The value of the genealogical method in social studies is too well known to call for further discussion here.   In the following account of Cupeño society, in almost every case the belief of the informant is checked against the actual practice of the community as revealed by the census and genealogies.   Often the rationalizations of informants are as important to the ethnologist and psychologist as are the actual happenings, but it is essential that rationalizations and facts be clearly distinguished.

---

[420] It may be worth noting that in house census 1, of the 280 kūpa members recorded, 137 were males and 143 females; of the 102 wilakal clan members, 55 were males and 47 females.

CENSUS 1

House Census of Kúpa, "1865" to 1902[421]

HOUSE 1

HH 209 Belares kaval
+210 *Guadelupe kalaunakwis* (L)

2d HH 211 Roman kaval
+212 *Tomasa sauivil*

    216 Bonifacio kaval
    +217 *Teresa nauhañavitc* (MC)
    218 Salvador kaval
    +219 *Liberata sivimûat* (h 34)
    220 *Dominga kaval*
    +221 Cleato teûtnikut (rw)

    231 *Leonora kaval*
    +W

    232 *Maria teûtnikut*

    222 *Dorotea kaval*
    223 Jose Antonio kaval
    +224 *Guadelupe auliñavic*
    225 *Cinciona kaval*
    +167 Cinon sivimûat (h 34)——
    (rw)
    226 *Maria kaval* (rh)
    +227 Pedro auliñawic

    233 *Hermenhilda sivimûat* (h 34)
    234 Trincolino sivimûat (h 34)
    235 Gabriel sivimûat (h 34)
    236 Marcos sivimûat
    43 *Nievas sivimûat*
    237 *Trinidad sivimûat**
    238 Tomas sivimûat*
    239 Fermil sivimûat
    240 *Gabriela sivimûat*
    241 *Nogada sivimûat*
    242 *Francisca sivimûat*
    243 Jose Antonio sivimûat
    244 *Maria Juana sivimûat*
    245 *Esperanza sivimûat*
    246 Jose Maria sivimûat

213 *Soledad kaval*
+575 Jose Antonio sivimûat ——
(rw)
+215 Matias teûtnikut

    59 *Manuela sivimûat* (h 34, 36, 37, 39)
    +W

    228 *Candelaria teûtnikut* (h 27, 28)
    229 Antonio teûtnikut
    230 Javiel teûtnikut

---

[421] Symbols used in census: nos. 1–208 refer to individuals listed in Census 3; nos. 214, 286, 519, and 126W not used; +sign = marriage; * = died young; italics = female; HH = house head; rh = went to reside with husband; rw = went to reside with wife; h 1, 2, etc. = listed in houses 1, 2, etc.; ? = name or relationship obscure; L = Luiseño; MC = Mt. Cahuilla; PC = Pass Cahuilla; DC = Desert Cahuilla; S = Serrano; D = Diegueño; W = white man.

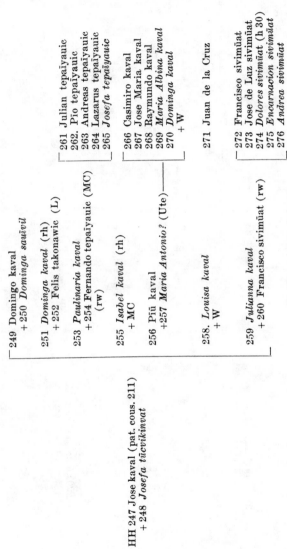

House 2

HH 247 Jose kaval (pat. cous. 211)
+ 248 *Josefa tùcvikinvat*

249 Domingo kaval
 + 250 *Dominga sauïvil*

251 *Dominga kaval* (rh)
 + 252 Felis takonawie (L)

    261 Julian tepaïyauie
    262. Pio tepaïyauie
    263 Andreas tepaïyauie
    264 Lazarus tepaïyauie
    265 *Josefa tepaïyauie*

253 *Paulinaria kaval*
 + 254 Fernando tepaïyauie (MC)
 (rw)

255 *Isabel kaval* (rh)
 + MC

    266 Casimiro kaval
    267 Jose Maria kaval
    268 Raymundo kaval
    269 *Maria Albina kaval*
    270 *Dominga kaval*
      + W

256 Piū kaval
 +257 *Maria Antonio?* (Ute)——

258. *Louisa kaval*
 + W

    271 Juan de la Cruz

259 *Julianna kaval*
 + 260 Francisco sivimūat (rw)

    272 Francisco sivimūat
    273 Jose de Luz sivimūat
    274 *Dolores sivimūat* (h 30)
    275 *Encarnacion sivimūat*
    276 *Andrea sivimūat*

House 3

HH 277 Antonio kaval (pat. cous.
 211)
 + 278 *Malvina sauïvil* (h 34, 40)

    279 Antonio kaval
    280 Jose Luis kaval

House 4

281 *Candida kaval* (auliñawic)
+ 282 auliñawic (long dead)

283 *Martina auliñawic*
+ HH 284 Carlos kaval
(pat. cous. 320) (rw)

288 *Gertrudis kaval* (rh)
+ 289? tepaïyauic (MC)

285 *Miguela auliñawic*
+ W
+ 605 Palegrino sauïvil (rw)

290 *Margarita?*
291 *Carmen?*

292 *Mercedes sauïvil* (rh)
+ 293 Silverio Nolasquez
(Yaqui) (h 27)

287 *Maria Antonio auliñawic*
+ 320 Ortis kaval

294 *Trinidad kaval*

House 5

HH 295 Marianno kaval (bro. 209)
+ 296 *Maria Ignacia sauïvil*

297 *Dominga kaval* (rh)
+ MC

298 *Angela kaval* (rh)
+ PC

299 *Francisco kaval* (h 12)

300 *Tomasa kaval*
+ W

301 *Joaquina kaval* (rh)
+ W

302 Adolf Scholder (h 31)

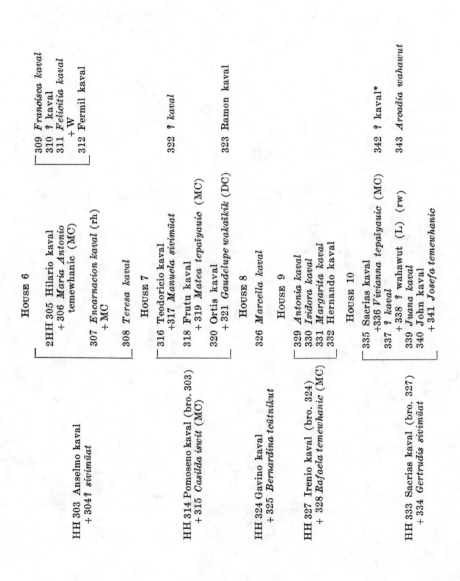

HOUSE 6

HH 303 Anselmo kaval
  + 304? *sivimüat*

2HH 305 Hilario kaval
  + 306 *Maria Antonio temewhanic* (MC)

307 *Encarnacion kaval* (rh)
  + MC

308 *Teresa kaval*

309 *Francisca kaval*
310 *? kaval*
311 *Felicitia kaval*
  + W
312 Fermil kaval

HOUSE 7

HH 314 Pomoseno kaval (bro. 303)
  + 315 *Casilda iswit* (MC)

316 Teodoricio kaval
  +317 *Manuela sivimüat*

318 Frutu kaval
  + 319 *Matea tepaiyawic* (MC)

320 Ortis kaval
  + 321 *Gaudelupe wakaïkik* (DC)

322 *? kaval*

323 Ramon kaval

HOUSE 8

HH 324 Gavino kaval
  + 325 *Bernardina toütnikut*

326 *Marcella kaval*

HOUSE 9

HH 327 Irenio kaval (bro. 324)
  + 328 *Rafaela temewhanic* (MC)

329 *Antonia kaval*
330 *Isidora kaval*
331 *Margarita kaval*
332 Hernando kaval

HOUSE 10

HH 333 Sacrias kaval (bro. 327)
  + 334 *Gertrudis sivimüat*

335 Sacrias kaval
  +336 *Vivianna tepaiyawic* (MC)
337 *? kaval*
  + 338 *? wahawut* (L) (rw)
339 *Juana kaval*
340 John kaval
  + 341 *Josefa temewhanic*

342 *? kaval**

343 *Aroadia wahawut*

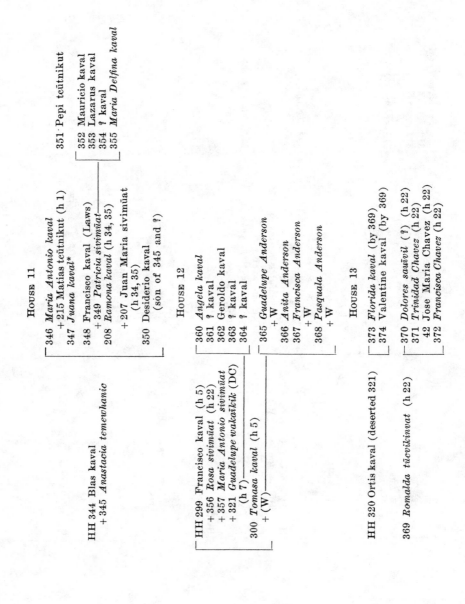

HOUSE 11

HH 344 Blas kaval
 + 345 *Anastacia temewhanic*

346 *Maria Antonio kaval*
 + 215 Matias teūtnikut (h 1)
347 *Juana kaval**
348 Francisco kaval (Laws)
 + 349 *Patricia sivimūat*
208 *Ramona kaval* (h 34, 35)
 + 207 Juan Maria sivimūat
        (h 34, 35)
350 Desiderio kaval
        (son of 345 and ?)

351 Pepi teūtnikut
352 Mauricio kaval
353 Lazarus kaval
354 ? kaval
355 *Maria Delfina kaval*

HOUSE 12

HH 299 Francisco kaval (h 5)
 + 356 *Rosa sivimūat* (h 22)
 + 357 *Maria Antonio sivimūat*
 + 321 *Guadelupe wakaškik* (DC)
        (h 7)
300 *Tomasa kaval* (h 5)
 + (W)

360 *Angela kaval*
361 ? kaval
362 Geroldo kaval
363 ? kaval
364 ? kaval

365 *Guadelupe Anderson*
 + W
366 *Anita Anderson*
367 *Francisca Anderson*
 + W
368 *Pasquala Anderson*
 + W

HOUSE 13

HH 320 Ortis kaval (deserted 321)

373 *Florida kaval* (by 369)
374 Valentine kaval (by 369)

369 *Romalda tūcvikiwoat* (h 22)

370 *Dolores sauūvil* (?) (h 22)
371 *Trinidad Chavez* (h 22)
42 Jose Maria Chavez (h 22)
372 *Francisca Chavez* (h 22)

HOUSE 14

HH 375 Hilario pumtumatülnikie 2HH 377 Piü pumtumatülnikie
+376 *Eleria sivimüat*   +378 *Marcellina sivimüat*

379 *Francisca pumtumatülnikie* (rh)
+380 Jolian tepaïyauie (MC)

381 Domingo pumtumatülnikie
+217 *Teresa nauhañavite* (MC) (h 1)

382 Pedro pumtumatülnikie
+357 *Rosa sivimüat*
+383 *Tresenda taka'at*
+384 *Catalina nauhañavite* (MC)

385 *Maria pumtumatülnikio* (rh)
+386 Jose Maria müut (L)

387 *Maria Ignacia pumtumatülnikie*
+388 Leon sivimüat (h 22)

389 Jose Cecelio pumtumatülnikie
+358 *Maria Antonio sivimüat* (h 12)
+390 *Josefa tepaïyauie* (MC)—

392 *Dominga pumtumatülnikie*
393 *Jacinta pumtumatülnikie*
394 *Teresa pumtumatülnikie*
22 Mariano pumtumatülnikie
18 *Felicidad pumtumatülnikie*
395 Raymundo pumtumatülnikie

396 *Encarnacion Rodriguez* (h 36)

391 *Cruza pumtumatülnikie*
+W

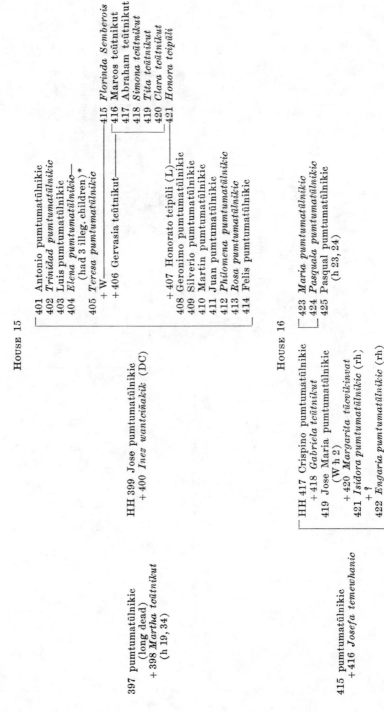

House 15

397 pumtumatûlnikie (long dead)
+398 *Martha teûtnikut* (h 19, 34)

HH 399 Jose pumtumatûlnikie
+400 *Inez wanteñakik* (DC)

401 Antonio pumtumatûlnikie
402 *Trinidad pumtumatûlnikie*
403 Luis pumtumatûlnikie
404 *Elena pumtumatûlnikie* (had 3 illeg. children)*
405 *Teresa pumtumatûlnikie*
+W
+406 Gervasia teûtnikut

+407 Honorato teipûli (L)
408 Geronimo pumtumatûlnikie
409 Silverio pumtumatûlnikie
410 Martin pumtumatûlnikie
411 Juan pumtumatûlnikie
412 *Philomena pumtumatûlnikie*
413 *Rosa pumtumatûlnikie*
414 Felis pumtumatûlnikie

415 *Florinda Semberois*
416 Mareos teûtnikut
417 Abraham teûtnikut
418 *Simona teûtnikut*
419 *Tita teûtnikut*
420 *Clara teûtnikut*
421 *Honora teipûli*

House 16

HH 417 Crispino pumtumatûlnikie
+418 *Gabriela teûtnikut*
419 Jose Maria pumtumatûlnikie (W h 2)
+420 *Margarita tücvikiwvat*
421 *Isidora pumtumatûlnikie* (rh)
+?
422 *Engaria pumtumatûlnikie* (rh)
+?

423 *Maria pumtumatûlnikie*
424 *Pasquala pumtumatûlnikie*
425 Pasqual pumtumatûlnikie (h 23, 24)

415 pumtumatûlnikie
+416 *Josefa temewhavic*

HOUSE 17

HH 426 Clara sivimūat
(pumtumatūlnikie)

427 Cosbi pumtumatūlnikie
+ 418 Gabriela toūtnikut
(h 16 later)

428 Juan pumtumatilnikie*

HOUSE 18

429 ? temewhanic (sauīvil)

430 Mercella sauīvil
+ HH 431 Merchol temewhanie

432 Maria Esperanza temewhanie

HOUSE 19

433 Melicati temewhanic
? temewhanie (long dead)
+ 434 Angela auliñawic

HH 435 Juan Angel temewhanie
+ 436 Matea tepaīvauic (MC)
+ 398 Martha toūtnikut
(h 15, 34)
436 Josefa temewhanie

437 Cinciona temewhanic (h 32)

HOUSE 20

438 Trista wacipanakwis (taka'at)
(L)

HH 140 Nicolas taka'at
+ 439 Justa toūtnikut

440 ? taka'at*

HOUSE 21

HH 441 Felis taka'at (bro. 140)
+ 442 Dominga kaval

443 Trisanta taka'at
444 Roman taka'at
+ 445 Isidora sauīvil
446 Bautisto taka'at
447 Maria Adelina taka'at

448 Rafael taka'at
449 Bautisto taka'at
450 Nicolas taka'at
451 Marta taka'at
452 Luis taka'at
453 Parfiro taka'at
454 Florida taka'at
455 Angela taka'at
456 Rufine taka'at
142 Julianna taka'at (rh)
+ W

HOUSE 22

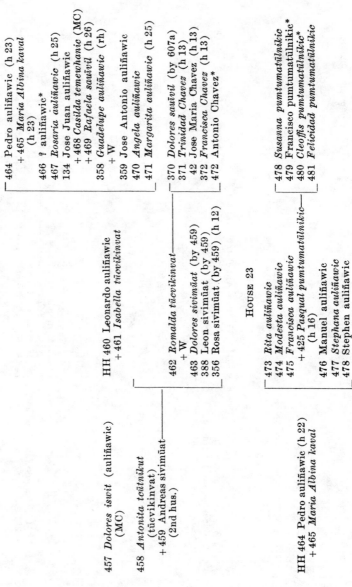

457 Dolores iswit (auliñawic) (MC)

458 Antonita tcütnikut (tücvikinvat)
+459 Andreas sivimüat (2nd hus.)

HH 460 Leonardo auliñawie
+461 Isabella tücvikinvat

462 Romalda tücvikinvat
+W
463 Dolores sivimüat (by 459)
388 Leon sivimüat (by 459)
356 Rosa sivimüat (by 459) (h 12)

464 Pedro auliñawie (h 23)
+465 Maria Albina kaval (h 23)
466 ? auliñawie*
467 Rosaria auliñawie (h 25)
134 Jose Juan auliñawie
+468 Casilda temewhanic (MC)
+469 Rafaela sauivil (h 26)
358 Guadelupe auliñawie (rh)
+W
359 Jose Antonio auliñawie
470 Angela auliñawie
471 Margarita auliñawie (h 25)

370 Dolores sauivil (by 607a)
371 Trinidad Chavez (h 13)
42 Jose Maria Chavez (h 13)
372 Francisca Chavez (h 13)
472 Antonio Chavez*

HOUSE 23

HH 464 Pedro auliñawie (h 22)
+465 Maria Albina kaval

473 Rita auliñawie
474 Modesta auliñawie
475 Francisca auliñawie
+425 Pasqual pumtumatülnikic (h 16)
476 Manuel auliñawie
477 Stephana auliñawie
478 Stephen auliñawie

478 Susanna pumtumatülnikie
479 Francisco pumtumatülnikie*
480 Cleoffis pumtumatülnikie*
481 Felicidad pumtumatülnikie

HOUSE 24

HH 425 Pasqual pumtumatülnikie
(h 16, 23)
+475 *Francisca auliñawie*

478 *Susanna pumtumatülnikie*
481 *Felicidad pumtumatülnikie*
482 Antonio pumtumatülnikie*
483 *Loreta pumtumatülnikie*

HOUSE 25

HH 367 *Rosaria auliñawie* (h 22)
+ W

471 *Margarita auliñawie* (h 22)
+ Negro

469 Jose Antonio auliñawie
(h 22)

156 Manuel Romero
153 Julio Romero
484 *Dolores auliñawie* (by ?)
485 *Victoria Richly*
+ ?

486 *Margaret Ortega*

HOUSE 26

HH 134 Jose Juan auliñawie
(h 22)
+ 469 *Rafaela sauivil* (h 26, 40)

487 Isidoro auliñawie*
488 Luis auliñawie
489 *Dolores auliñawie*
490 *Francisca auliñawie*
491 Enrique auliñawie
492 Calistro auliñawie

HOUSE 27

HH 293 Silverio Nolasquez
(Yaqui) (h 4)
+ 292 *Mercedes sauivil* (h 4)

493 Salvador Nolasquez
+ 228 *Candelaria teütnikut*
(h 1, 28)
108 Ramon Nolasquez
109 *Carolina Nolasquez*
494 Ignacio Nolasquez
114 *Claudina Nolasquez*
+ 459 Andreas sivimüat (h 22)

115 *Felipa Nolasquez*
(kept name of 114)

House 28

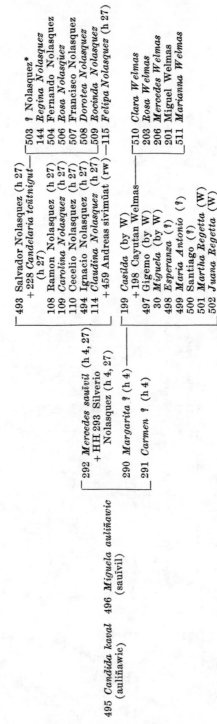

495 *Candida kaval* (auliñawic) 496 *Miguela auliñawic* (sauïvil)

292 *Mercedes sauïvil* (h 4, 27)
+ HH 293 Silverio Nolasquez (h 4, 27)

290 *Margarita* ? (h 4)

291 *Carmen* ? (h 4)

493 Salvador Nolasquez (h 27)
+ 228 *Candelaria teütnigut* (h 27)

108 Ramon Nolasquez (h 27)
109 *Carolina Nolasquez* (h 27)
110 Cecelio Nolasquez (h 27)
494 Ignacio Nolasquez (h 27)
114 *Claudina Nolasquez* (h 27)
+ 459 Andreas sivimüat (rw)

503 ? Nolasquez*
144 *Regina Nolasquez*
504 Fernando Nolasquez
506 *Rosa Nolasquez*
507 Francisco Nolasquez
508 *Dorotea Nolasquez*
509 *Rocinda Nolasquez*
—115 *Felipa Nolasquez* (h 27)

199 *Casilda* (by W)
+ 198 Cayutan Welmas

497 *Gigemo* (by W)
30 *Miguela* (by W)
498 *Esperanza* (?)
499 *Maria Antonio* (?)
500 Santiago (?)
501 *Martha Regetta* (W)
502 *Juana Regetta* (W)

510 *Clara Welmas*
203 *Rosa Welmas*
206 *Mercedes Welmas*
201 Miguel Welmas
511 *Marianna Welmas*

House 29

512 Juan Diego tcütnikut
+513 Diega (tcütnikut)

HH 514 Jose Maria sivimũat
+515 Mercholla tcütnikut

516 Sylvestra sivimũat
+95 Adolfo Moro (Northern Indian)

517 Triselda Moro
518 Andrea Moro
+124 Ambrosio sauivil (h 40) —— 528 Rosa sauivil*
+520 Joe sivimũat (h 34, 35) —— 529 Charles sivimũat

521 Matilda Moro*
522 Damacio Moro*
98a Domingo Moro
+373 Florida kaval (h 13)
+99 Nicolasa isvit (MC)
530 Benedicia Moro
531 Francisco Moro
532 Antonina Moro
533 Marcellina Moro
534 Petra Moro
100 Annie Moro
535 Gregorio Moro

523 Adelina Moro
524 Macedonia Moro
96 Andres Moro
525 Rita Moro
526 Anita Moro
1 Celsa Moro
+527 Pedro apapas (MC)
2 George apapas
536 Virginia apapas*
3 Claudia apapas
4 Dovidia apapas
537 Sylvestra apapas*
5 James Edward apapas

House 30

HH 274 Dolores sivimũat (h 2)
+538 Francisca mitcax (L)
+431 Marcella sauivil (h 18)

539 Casalaria sivimũat
540 Tomasa sivimũat*
541 ? sivimũat*
542 ? sivimũat*

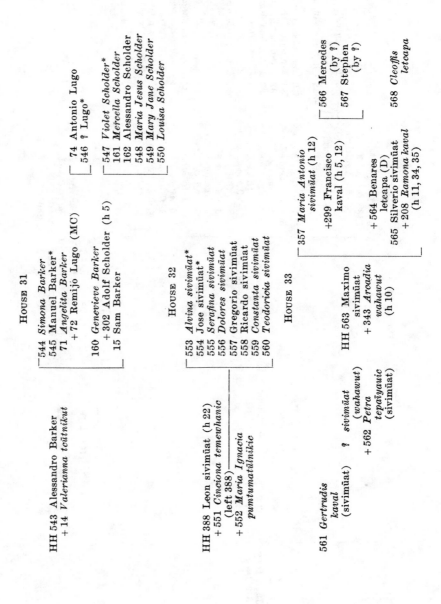

HOUSE 34

HH 569 Leonardo sivimŭat
+570 *Leonarda* (*sivimŭat*)

2 HH 571 Francisco sivimŭat
+572 *Barbara nauhañavito—*
(MC)

577 *Eustacia sivimŭat* (rh)
+578 Seferino tŭcvikinvat
579 Alberto sivimŭat
580 Asisquilo sivimŭat
+581 *Victoria tŭcvikinvat*
582 Pablo sivimŭat
583 Rufino sivimŭat
584 Antonio sivimŭat
+277 *Malvina sauívil*
(h 3, 2nd marriage)
585 Juan de la Cruz
sivimŭat
586 *Matilda sivimŭat*
207 Juan Maria sivimŭat
+208 *Ramona kaval* (h 11)
587 Miguel sivimŭat
167 Cinon sivimŭat (h 1)
+225 *Cinciona kaval* (h 1)

234 *Trincolina sivimŭat* (h 1)
235 Gabriel sivimŭat (h 1)

573 Fermin sivimŭat
+574 *Martha tcŭtnikut*
575 Jose Antonio sivimŭat
+213 *Soledad kaval*

+576 *Maria iswit* (MC)

59 *Manuela sivimŭat*
(h 1, 36, 37, 39)
588 *Martina sivimŭat**
589 *Tiburcia sivimŭat**
590 Bautisto sivimŭat*
349 *Patricia sivimŭat* (h 11)
219 *Liberata sivimŭat* (h 1)
220 Vicente sivimŭat
+591 *Encarnacion Rodriquez*
(h 36)
520 Jose (Joe) Domingo sivimŭat
(h 29)
592 *Romana sivimŭat*
593 Sylvestro sivimŭat
594 Pedro Pablo sivimŭat
595 Luis sivimŭat

HOUSE 35

```
 ┌ 584 Antonio sivimūat (h 34)
 │   + 277 Malvina saúivil (h 3, 34)
 │ 207 Juan Maria sivimūat (h 34)
 └   + 208 Ramona kaval (h 11, 34)
```

HOUSE 36

```
HH 596 Javiel sivimūat (bro. 569) —— 598 Manuela sivimūat
   + 597 Javiela?                     591 Encarnacion Rodriquez
                                          (left 220, h 34)
```

HOUSE 37

```
                         59 Manuela sivimūat
                            (h 1, 34, 36, 39)
 ┌ HH 215 Matias teūtnikut    230 Javiel teūtnikut (by 215)
 │    + 213 Soledad kaval         (h 38)
 │                                + 599 Francisco Chavez (h 38)   52 Mareos teūtnikut (h 38)
 │                            600 Francisco teūtnikut (by 215)
 │                            601 Manuel teūtnikut (by 215)
 └                            602 Julianna teūtnikut (by 215)
```

HOUSE 38

```
52 Mareos teūtnikut

HH 230 Javiel teūtnikut (h 37)
   + 599 Francisca Chavez (h 37)
```

HOUSE 39

```
 ┌ 603 Salvadora Griffith (rh)
 │    + 187a Santos Valenzuela (D)
 │ 189 Claudina Griffith (rh)
 │    + W
 │ 192 Catherine Griffith (rh)
 │    + W
 └ 604 Christina Griffith*

59 Manuela sivimūat
   (h 1, 34, 36, 37)
   + W
```

HOUSE 40

HH 605 Pelegrino sauivil
(bro. 212, h 1)
+ 606 *Josefa wantciñakrik* ADC)
607 Enrique sauivil
607a Jose sauivil

445 *Isidora sauivil* (h 21)
608 Adolfo sauivil*
124 Ambrosio sauivil (Ortega)
117 Jesus sauivil (Ortega)
+ 118 *Jacinta baipa* (D)

431 *Marcella sauivil* (rh)
+ 274 Dolores sivimüat (h 2, 30)
125 Juan Bautista sauivil (Ortega)
469 *Rafaela sauivil* (rh)
+ 134 Jose Juan auliñawic (h 22, 26)
278 *Malvina sauivil* (h 3, 34)

609 Marcos sauivil*
610 Fidel sauivil*
611 *Teodoricia sauivil*
612 *Rebecca saaivil**
613 Valentine sauivil*

HOUSE 41

HH 42 *Jose Maria Chavez* (h 13, 22)
+ 43 *Nievas sivimüat* (h 1)

614 *Angelita Chavez* (rh)
+ Pima Indian
615 *Maria Chavez**
616 *Rosalie Chavez*
617 Santos Chavez
46 *Amelia Chavez*

CENSUS 2

House Census of Wilakal, "1865" to 1902[422]

W. HOUSE 1

HH 1W Juan Diego kaval
+ 2W Madelena tepaiyauic (MC)

  3W Maria Benita kaval
  4W ? kaval*
  5W ? kaval*

W. HOUSE 2

HH 6W Marcos tūcvikinvat
+ 7W ? sivimüat

  8W Concepcion tūcvikinvat
  9W Crescentio tūcvikinvat
  + 10W Josefa awilem (DC)
  419 Jose Maria pumtumatūlnikie
  + 10W (on death of 9W)

    11W Susanna tūcvikinvat
    12W Inocentia tūcvikinvat
    + ?
    13W Eduvicis tūcvikinvat
    14W Salome tūcvikinvat*
    15W Maximo tūcvikinvat*

  16W Crispino pumtumatūlnikie
  + 17W Martha teïtnïkut
    (Wh 3)

W. HOUSE 3

  21W Stephen tūcvikinvat
  + 384 Catalina nauhanavito
    (h 14)
  22W Lino tūcvikinvat (Wh 8)
  + 23W Guadelupe wantciñakik
    (DC)
  24W Jose tūcvikinvat
  + 25W Maria wantciñakik
    (DC) (Wh 11)
  26W Maria Antonio tūcvikinvat
  27W Maria Gracia tūcvikinvat

    32W Refugia tūcvikinvat
    33W Geronimo tūcvikinvat
    34W Felicidad tūcvikinvat
    35W Nicolas tūcvikinvat
    36W Raymundo tūcvikinvat
    37W Manuel tūcvikinvat

  28W Stephen tūcvikinvat
  29W Esperanza tūcvikinvat
  30W Natividad tūcvikinvat
  31W Simon tūcvikinvat

HH 19W Jose Ignacio tūcvikinvat
+ 20W Dolores tcïtnïkut

+ 17W Martha teïtnïkut
  (Wh 2)

18W Obego
  pumtumatūlnikie

422 Symbols identical to those in Census 1. W = Wilakal. Plain numbers refer to Census 1.

W. House 4

HH 425 Pasqual pumtumatûlnikie (h 16)
+ 32W *Refugia tûcvikinvat* (Wh 3)

38W Pio pumtumatûlnikie*
39W Eduardo pumtumatûlnikie

W. House 5

HH 40W Cervantes sivimûat (Wh 20)
+ 34W *Felicidad tûcvikinvat* (Wh 3)

41W *Felicitia sivimûat*
42W Rocentio sivimûat
43W *Lucy sivimûat**
44W Silverio sivimûat
45W Felix sivimûat

W. House 6

46W Gabriel wiit (D)
+ 47W *Nievas teûtnikut*

HH 35W Nicolas tûcvikinvat
+ 48W *Eusebia wiit* (D)

49W ♀ tûcvikinvat
50W ♀ tûcvikinvat
51W ♀ tûcvikinvat
52W ♀ tûcvikinvat
53W *Pia tûcvikinvat*
54W *Flora tûcvikinvat*
55W ♀ tûcvikinvat
56W ♀ tûcvikinvat

W. House 7

57W *Victoria ciwi* (teûtnikut)

HH 37W Manuel tûcvikinvat
+ 58W *Dominga ciwi* (L)

59W ♀ tûcvikinvat*

W. HOUSE 8

32W *Refugia tücvikinvat*
33W Geronimo tücvikinvat
34W *Felicidad tücvikinvat*
35W Nicolas tücvikinvat
36W Raymundo tücvikinvat
37W Manuel tücvikinvat

60W Conrado tücvikinvat

HH 22W Lino tücvikinvat (Wh 3)
+23W *Guadelupe wantcinakik* (DC)
24W Jose tücvikinvat (Wh 3)
+25W *Maria wantcinakik* (DC) (Wh 11)

W. HOUSE 9

63W Juan tücvikinvat
64W *Teresa tücvikinvat* (rh)
+65W Felipe tcütnikut (Wh 16)
66W *Victoria tücvikinvat*
67W Claudio tücvikinvat
68W Bautisto tücvikinvat
69W Salvador tücvikinvat
70W Ricardo tücvikinvat

HH 61W Martin tücvikinvat
+62W *Dolores costakik* (MC)

W. HOUSE 10

73W *Tomasa tücvikinvat*
74W *Margarita tücvikinvat* (rh)
+75W Jose Maria pumtumatülnikie (Wh 16)

HH 71W Manuel tücvikinvat
+72W *Isidora tcütnikut*

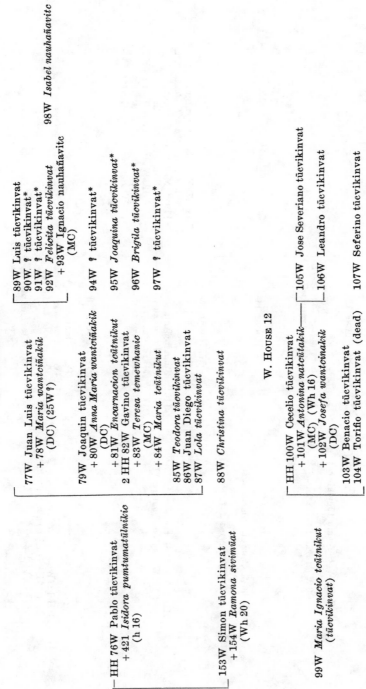

W. House 11

HH 76W Pablo tücevikinvat
+421 Isidora pumtumatülnikio
(h 16)

77W Juan Luis tücevikinvat
+78W *Maria wantcíñakik*
(DC) (25W ?)

89W Luis tücevikinvat
90W ? tücevikinvat*
91W ? tücevikinvat*
92W *Felicita tücevikinvat*
+93W Ignacio nauhañavite
(MC)

94W ? tücevikinvat*

95W *Joaquina tücevikinvat*

96W *Brigila tücevikinvat*

97W ? tücevikinvat*

98W *Isabel nauhañavite*

79W Joaquin tücevikinvat
+80W *Anna Maria wantcíñakik*
(DC)
+81W *Encarnacion teütnikut*
2 HH 82W Gavino tücevikinvat
+83W *Teresa temewhanie*
(MC)
+84W *Maria teütnikut*

85W *Teodora tücevikinvat*
86W Juan Diego tücevikinvat
87W *Lola tücevikinvat*

88W *Christina tücevikinvat*

153W Simon tücevikinvat
+154W *Ramona sivimüat*
(Wh 20)

W. House 12

99W *Maria Ignacio teütnikut*
(*tücevikinvat*)

HH 100W Cecelio tücevikinvat
+101W *Antonina natcütakik*
(MC) (Wh 16)
+102W *Josefa wantcíñakik*
(DC)

105W Jose Severiano tücevikinvat
106W Leandro tücevikinvat

107W Seferino tücevikinvat

103W Benacio tücevikinvat
104W Torifio tücevikinvat (dead)

W. House 13

HH 107W Seferino tŭcvikinvat
(Wh 12)
+ 3W Maria Benita kaval
(Wh 1)

108W Joaquina tŭcvikinvat
109W Loreta tŭcvikinvat (rh)
  + 110W Honorato wŭt (D)

W. House 14

HH 60W Conrado tŭcvikinvat
(Wh 8)
+ 111 Francisca ? (PC)

W. House 15

HH 111W Luis tcŭtnikut
+ 112W ? wĕwonicyauam (DC)

113W Juan tcŭtnikut
  + 114W Vivianna ? (W)
115W Marcelino tcŭtnikut
116W Marcellina tcŭtnikut

117W Francisco tcŭtnikut
  + 118W Martha natcŭtakik (DC)
119W Mariano tcŭtnikut
120W Bautisto tcŭtnikut
  + 121W Anna nauhañavite (MC)
122W Amelio tcŭtnikut
123W Bernadina tcŭtnikut (rh)
  + ?

W. House 16

HH 124W Juan tcŭtnikut
+ 101W Antonina natcŭtakik
(MC)

65W Felipe tcŭtnikut (Wh 9)
  + 64W Teresa tŭcvikinvat
125W Valerianna tcŭtnikut
  + W
406 Gervasio tcŭtnikut
  + 127W Victoria tŭcvikinvat

128W Mercedes tcŭtnikut*

129W Rocinda tcŭtnikut

W. House 17

130W ? *tcīyalyñawhic* (D)

HH 131W Manuel *tcūtnikut* (Wh 19) + 132W *Isabel temewhanic* (MC)

133W *Milina tcūtnikut*
134W Francisco *tcūtnikut*
135W *Victoria tcūtnikut* + 136W Juan de Mati *sīwi* (L)

137W Pomoseno *sīwi* + 138W *Nicolasa wanteñakik* (DC)
139W *Dominga sīwi* + 198 Cayutan Welmas (W)
140W *Portacia sīwi* + 141W Felipe nauhañavite (MC)
142W *Juliana sīwi*
143W Mateo *sīwi* + 144W *Lola wanteñakik* (DC)

145W Alfredo Welmas

146W ? *sīwi**

W. House 18

HH 145W Alfedro Welmas (Wh 17) + 147W *Patrea tōbak* (L)

148W Cirilio Welmas
149W Julian Welmas

W. House 19

151W Trincolino tcŭtnikut
+ 109W *Loreta tŭcvikinvat*
    (Wh 13)
84W *Maria tcŭtnikut*
    (Wh 11) (rh)
+ 82W Gavino tŭcvikinvat
    (Wh 11)
17W *Martha tcŭtnikut*
    (Wh 2, 3) (rh)
+ 19W Jose Ignacio tŭcvikinvat
    (Wh 3)
81W *Encarnacion tcŭtnikut*
    (Wh 11) (rh)
+ 79W Joaquin tŭcvikinvat
    (Wh 11)

HH 131W Manuel tcŭtnikut
    (2nd family)
+ 150W ♀ *kaunukalakik* (MC)

W. House 20

154W *Ramona sivimŭat*
    (Wh 11) (rh)
+153W Simon tŭcvikinvat
    (Wh 11)
155W Jesus sivimŭat ——————(several children)*
+ 156W *Maria naahañavite*
157W *Refugia sivimŭat*
158W *Josefa sivimŭat*
40W Cervantes sivimŭat (Wh 5)
159W Jose sivimŭat
+ 160W *Andrea pauatakik* (MC)

HH 151W Juan Diego sivimŭat
+ 152W *Vivianna tepaiyauic*
    (MC)

CENSUS 3

Pala Census for the Year 1919

Compiled by E. W. Gifford from the Pala agency records, December 18, 1919,
with the addition of tribe, village, moiety, and clan data from native
informants,[423] per E. W. Gifford and W. D. Strong

No.[424]	Name	Age	Sex	Relation	Village	Moiety	Clan[425]	Tribe
1	Apapas, Celsa	44	F	Widow	kūpa	–	?	Cu.
2	George	25	M	S	kūpa	C	apapas	Ca.
3	Claudia	23	F	D	kūpa	C	apapas	Ca.
4	Dovidia	19	F	D	kūpa	C	apapas	Ca.
5	James Edward	17	M	S	kūpa	C	apapas	Ca.
6	Celestina	6	F	D	kūpa	C	apapas	Ca.
7	Ardillo, Camillo	32	M	B	Old Pala	–	keñic (Ardea)	L.
8	Febridad	46	F	B	Old Pala	–	keñic (Ardea)	L.
9	Thecla	43	F	B	Old Pala	–	keñic (Ardea)	L.
10	Francisco	70	M	W'r	Old Pala	–	keñic (Ardea)	L.
11	Robert	25	M	S	Old Pala	–	keñic (Ardea)	L.
12	William	29	M	S	Old Pala	–	keñic (Ardea)	L.
13	Damicio	32	M	S	Old Pala	–	keñic (Ardea)	L.
14	Barker, Valarianna	76	F	Widow	kūpa	?	tcūtnikut	Cu.
15	Sam	43	M	S	kūpa	C	kavalim	Cu.
16	Blacktooth, Pasqual	64	M	H	kūpa	C	pumtum	Cu.
17	Francisca	54	F	W	kūpa	W	auliatim	Cu.
18	Felicidad	22	F	D	kūpa	C	pumtum	Cu.
19	Loretta	17	F	D	kūpa	C	pumtum	Cu.
20	Augustin	14	M	S	kūpa	C	pumtum	Cu.
21	Susanna	27	F	D	kūpa	C	pumtum	Cu.
22	Blacktooth, Marianno	35	M	H	kūpa	C	pumtum.	Cu.
23	Lizzie	30	F	W	San Felipe	–	?	D.
24	Peter	5	M	S	Pala	C	pumtum.	Cu.
25	José Cecelio	3	M	S	Pala	C	pumtum.	Cu.
26	——, ——	1	F	D	Pala	C	pumtum.	Cu.
27	Brittain, Margarita	63	F	W	kūpa	W	aulīatim	Cu.
28	Freeman, Juana (half white)	23	F	D	kūpa	W	aulīatim	Cu.

[423] Information obtained from native informant, Mrs. Margarita Brittain, and others.

[424] Numbers are those of agency register. Additions to agency register have ''a'' suffixed.

[425] The tribe of the individual is the same as that of the father. If the father is white, then the tribe and clan is that to which the mother belongs.

CENSUS 3—(*Continued*)

No.[424]	Name	Age	Sex	Relation	Village	Moiety	Clan[425]	Tribe
29	August	1	M	GrS	kūpa	W	aulīatim	Cu.
30	Brittain Miguela	41	F	D	kūpa	W	aulīatim	Cu.
31	Mane Antonio	33	F	D	kūpa	W	aulīatim	Cu.
32	Santiago	32	M	H	kūpa	W	aulīatim	Cu.
32a	Flora	—	F	W	Pichanga	–	?	L.
33	James F.	5	M	S	Pala	W	aulīatim ?	Cu.
34	Joseph Frementius	7	M	S	Pala	W	aulīatim ?	Cu.
35	Margarita	6	F	D	Pala	W	aulīatim ?	Cu.
36	Paulina	3	F	D	Pala	W	aulīatim ?	Cu.
37	Beltran, Sinforosa	19	F	GrD	Old Pala	?	?	L.
38	Calac, Evorista	38	F	W	Old Pala	?	?	L.
39	Castillo, Adelina	31	F	GrD	Old Pala	–	?	L.
40	Chapulo, Trincolina	40	F	D	kūpa	–	?	D.
41	Chavez, Antonio	44	M	B	kūpa	W	tūcvikin.	Cu.
42	Jose Maria	53	M	H	kūpa	W	tūcvikin.	Cu.
43	Nievas	51	F	W	kūpa	W	sivimūat	Cu.
44	Angelita	31	F	D	kūpa	W	tūcvikin.	Cu.
45	Rosalie	20	F	D	kūpa	W	tūcvikin.	Cu.
46	Amelia	16	F	D	Pala	W	tūcvikin.	Cu.
47	Christina	15	F	D	Pala	W	tūcvikin.	Cu.
48	Tomas	14	M	S	Pala	W	tūcvikin.	Cu.
49	Sylverio	10	M	S	Pala	W	tūcvikin.	Cu.
50	Chutnicut, Francisco	47	M	H	kūpa?	?	tcūtnikut	Cu.
51	Chutnicut, Frank Howry	1	M	S	Pala	?	tcūtnikut	Cu.
52	Marcos	30	M	B	kūpa	?	tcūtnikut	Cu.
53	Chuparosa, Cecelio (dead)	104	M	W'r	wilakal	?	tūcvikin.	Cu.
54	Freeman, Florence	8	F	D	Pala	?	?	?
55	Regus	6	M	S	Pala	?	?	?
56	Garland, Blastro	29	M	H	San Felipe	–	?	D.
57	Alessandro	1	M	S	Pala	?	?	?
58	Garcia, Ramon	27	M	B	Old Pala	–	?	L.
59	Griffith, Manuela	67	F	Widow	kūpa	W	sivimūat	Cu.
60	Golsh, Albert	33	M	H	Old Pala	–	?	L.
61	Golsh, ———	-	M	S	Old Pala	–	?	?
62	Golsh, ———	-	M	S	Old Pala	–	?	?
63	Lancaster, Frances	57	F	Widow	Old Pala	–	?	L.
64	Apemanio	22	M	S	Old Pala	–	?	?
65	Amelia	20	F	D	Old Pala	–	?	?
66	Annessetta	18	F	D	Old Pala	–	?	?
67	Guadelupe	26	F	D	Old Pala	–	?	?
68	Lachuza, Jose Juan	61	M	W'r	kūpa	?	?	?
69	Leo, Anselmo	75	M	W'r	kūpa	–	?	D.
70	Linton, Magdalena	40	F	Widow	kūpa	–	?	?
71	Lugo, Encarnaciona	76	F	Widow	Old Pala	–	?	L.
72	Remijio	45	M	H	Pauī	C	hōkwitc.	Ca.
73	Angelita	47	F	W	kūpa	C	kavalim	Cu.

CENSUS 3—(*Continued*)

No.[424]	Name	Age	Sex	Relation	Village	Moi-ety	Clan[425]	Tribe
74	Antonio	19	M	S	Pala	?	hōkwitc.	Ca.
75	Nemisio	13	M	S	Pala	?	hōkwitc.	Ca.
76	Stephen	7	M	S	Pala	?	hōkwitc.	Ca.
77	Ramon	56	M	B	Old Pala	?	?	?
78	Escolastica	54	F	B	Old Pala	?	?	?
79	Maria Niquela	47	F	W	?	?	?	?
80	Lugo, Eustarkio	64	M	H	?	?	?	?
81	Lyon, Willie	31	M	H	kūpa	C	kaval	Cu.
82	Florian	3	M	S	Pala	C	kaval	Cu.
83	Willie Jr.	2	M	S	Pala	C	kaval	Cu.
84	Mechac, Marcos	69	M	W'r	Puerta Cruz	–	hilelba'	L.
85	Jose Maria	85	M	H	Puerta Cruz	–	hilelba'	L.
86	Mystica	20	F	D	kūpa	–	hilelba'	L.
87	Juan	33	M	H	kūpa	–	hilelba'	L.
88	——————	3	M	S	Pala	–	hilelba'	L.
89	Frank	32	M	B	kūpa	–	hilelba'	L.
90	Rebecca	26	M	Widow	kūpa	–	hilelba'	L.
91	Rafael	6	M	S	Pala	?	tcūtnikut	Cu.
92	Agatha	4	F	D	Pala	?	tcūtnikut	Cu.
93	Faustine	3	M	S	Pala	?	tcūtnikut	Cu.
94	——————	1	M	S	Pala	?	tcūtnikut	Cu.
95	Moro, Adolpho Sr.	83	M	H	kūpa	?	?	?
96	Andrew	39	M	B	kūpa	?	?	?
97	Adolpho Jr.	29	M	B	kūpa	?	?	?
98	Charles	22	M	B	kūpa	?	?	?
98a	Domingo	?	M	H	?	?	?	?
99	Nicholasa	43	F	Widow	?	?	?	Ca.
100	Agnes Annie	21	F	D	kūpa	?	?	?
101	Catherine	14	F	D	kūpa	?	?	?
102	Nejo, Jose	87	M	H	San Felipe	–	?	D.
103	Josepha	79	F	Widow	San Felipe	–	?	D.
104	Jose Jr.	47	M	S	?	–	?	D.
105	John	4	M	GrS	Pala	–	?	D.
106	Felicidad	26	F	D	?	–	?	D.
107	Nogales, Jose	39	M	H	kūpa	C	pumtum.	Cu.
108	Nolasquez, Ramon	47	M	B	kūpa	C	sauīvil	Cu.
109	Carolina	45	F	B	kūpa	C	sauīvil	Cu.
110	Cecelio	43	M	B	kūpa	C	sauīvil	Cu.
111	Rafael	35	M	B	kūpa	C	sauīvil	Cu.
112	Salvador	58	M	W'r	kūpa	C	sauīvil	Cu.
113	Rosinda	27	F	D	kūpa	C	sauīvil	Cu.
114	Claudina	39	F	W(168)	kūpa	C	sauīvil	Cu.
115	Felipa	17	F	D	Pala	C	sauīvil	Cu.
116	Louis	14	M	S	Pala	?	?	?
117	Ortega, Jesus	46	M	H	kūpa	C	sauivil	Cu.
118	Jacinta	44	F	Widow	Santa Ysabel	–	?	D.
119	Evarista	19	F	D	Pala	C	sauīvil	Cu.

CENSUS 3—(Continued)

No.[424]	Name	Age	Sex	Relation	Village	Moiety	Clan[425]	Tribe
120	Juan de Mater	13	M	S	Pala	C	sauīvil	Cu.
121	Francisco Javiel	11	M	S	Pala	C	sauīvil	Cu.
122	Cecelia	9	F	D	Pala	C	sauīvil	Cu.
123	Gregory	7	M	S	Pala	C	sauīvil	Cu.
124	Ambrosio	50	M	B	kūpa	C	sauīvil	Cu.
125	John	42	M	H	kūpa	C	sauīvil	Cu.
126	Nellie	28	F	Widow	San Jose	—	?	D.
127	Maria Magdalena	8	F	D	Pala	C	sauīvil	Cu.
128	Bitus	6	M	S	Pala	C	sauīvil	Cu.
129	Ferdinand	3	M	S	Pala	C	sauīvil	Cu.
130	Josephine	4	F	D	Pala	C	sauīvil	Cu.
131	Owlinguish, Petronilla	13	F	Orphan	Pala	W	auliñawic	Cu.
132	Christina	9	F	Orphan	Pala	W	aulıñawic	Cu.
133	Lucretia	8	F	Orphan	Pala	W	auliñawic	Cu.
134	Jose Juan	75	M	H	kūpa	W	auliñawic	Cu.
135	Rafaela	48	F	Widow	kūpa	C	sauīvil	Cu.
136	Henry	20	M	S	kūpa	C	sauīvil	Cu.
137	Louis	30	M	B	kūpa	C	sauīvil	Cu.
138	Quashish, Marcelino	69	M	H	kūpa	—	?	L.
139	Josepha	59	F	Widow	?	—	?	L.
140	Peña, Nicholas	37	M	B	kūpa	W	taka'at	Cu.
141	Cornelius	33	M	B	kūpa	W	taka'at	Cu.
142	Johnson, Juliana	26	F	Widow	kūpa	W	taka'at	Cu.
143	Portillo, Florencio	32	M	H	San Felipe	–	?	D.
144	Regina	35	F	Widow	kūpa	C	sauīvil	Cu.
145	Dominga	8	F	D	San Felipe	–	?	D.
146	Rita	6	F	D	San Felipe	–	?	D.
147	Josephine	5	F	D	San Felipe	–	?	D.
148	Magdalena	2	F	D	San Felipe	–	?	D.
149	Quitac, Lucas	33	M	H	San Felipe	–	?	D.
150	Francisca	45	F	Widow	San Felipe	–	?	D.
151	Reiter, Andrea Moro	49	F	Widow	kūpa	?	?	?
152	Robles, Remijio	30	M	B	San Felipe	–	?	D.
153	Romero, Julio	31	M	H	kūpa	W	auliñawic	Cu.
154	Garcia, Cinciona	30	F	Widow	Old Pala	–	?	L.
155	Roberts, Julianna	45	F	Widow	kūpa	?	tcūtnikut	Cu.
156	Romero, Manuela	31	F	Widow	kūpa	W	auliñawic	Cu.
157	Salazar, Maria	69	F	Widow	Old Pala	–	?	L.
158	Sebastian	20	M	S	?	?	?	?
159	Albino	24	M	S	Old Pala	–	?	L.
160	Scholder, Genevieve Barker	39	F	W	kūpa	C	kaval	Cu.
161	Marcella	19	F	D	kūpa	C	kaval	Cu.
162	Alexander	18	M	S	Pala	C	kaval	Cu.
163	Joseph Abraham	13	M	S	Pala	C	kaval	Cu.
164	Virginia	10	F	D	Pala	C	kaval	Cu.
165	Bernice Genevieve	6	F	D	Pala	C	kaval	Cu.

CENSUS 3—(*Continued*)

No.[424]	Name	Age	Sex	Relation	Village	Moiety	Clan[425]	Tribe
166	William	4	M	S	Pala	C	kaval	Cu.
167	Sivimuat, Sinon	89	M	W'r	kūpa	W	sivimūat	Cu.
168	Gabriel	50	M	H(14)	kūpa	W	sivimūat	Cu.
169	(number not used)							
170	Sivimuat, Esperanza	41	F	Widow	kūpa	W	sivimūat	Cu.
171	Zenobia	37	F	Widow	kūpa	W	sivimūat	Cu.
172	Soto, Benicio	39	M	H	Puerta Cruz	–	?	L.
173	Melvina	40	F	Widow	kūpa	C	sauīvil	Cu.
174	Duro, Juan	23	M	S	Old Pala	–	?	L.
175a	Catherine	20	F	sD	Old Pala	–	?	L.
176	Ramon	10	M	sS	Old Pala	–	?	L.
177	Pico, Joe	8	M	Orphan	Old Pala	–	?	L.
178	Scott, Filemino	37	M	H	Old Pala	–	?	L.
179	Ramona Golsh	28	F	Widow	Old Pala	–	?	L.
180	Marian	6	F	D	Old Pala	–	?	L.
181	Ethel	3	F	D	Old Pala	–	?	L.
182	———	1	F	D	Old Pala	–	?	L.
183	Trujillo, Esperanza	34	F	Widow	kūpa	W	auliñawic	Cu.
184	Vivianna	12	F	D	Pala	–	?	L.
185	Albino	9	M	S	Pala	–	?	L.
186	Delfrida	6	F	D	Pala	–	?	L.
187	Florian	3	M	S	Pala	–	?	L.
187a	Martha	3mo	F	D	Pala	–	?	L.
188	Valenzuela, Salvadora	45	F	Widow	kūpa	W	sivimūat	Cu.
189	Claudina (H)	26	F	Widow	Mesa Grande	–	?	D.
190	Nadine Helen	1	F	D	Pala	–	?	?
191	Mojado, Catherine Valen	24	F	Widow	Mesa Grande	–	?	D.
192	Francis	4	M	S	La Jolla	–	?	L.
193	Lucille	3	F	D	La Jolla	–	?	L.
194	Ortega, Margaret	23	F	Widow	kūpa	W	auliñawic	Cu.
195	Ortega, Guadelupe	7	F	D	Pala	?	?	?
196	———	2	F	D	Pala	?	?	?
197	———	1	M	S	Pala	?	?	?
198	Welmas, Cayutan	59	M	H	Portuguese			
199	Casilda	46	F	W	kūpa	W	auliñawic	Cu.
200	Rufina	21	F	D	kūpa	W	auliñawic	Cu.
201	Miguel	18	M	S	Pala	W	auliñawic	Cu.
202	Jose Juan	14	M	S	Pala	W	auliñawic	Cu.
203	Rosa	11	F	D	Pala	W	auliñawic	Cu.
204	Serafina	8	F	D	Pala	W	auliñawic	Cu.
205	Philip	28	M	S	kūpa	W	auliñawic	Cu.
206	Merced	26	F	D	kūpa	W	auliñawic	Cu.
207	Sibimoat, Juan Maria	68	M	H	kūpa	W	sivimūat	Cu.
208[426]	Rámona	65	F	Widow	kūpa	C	kaval	Cu.

[426] One number, 169, not used. Four extra "*a*" numbers. Total: 211.

The Organization of the Clan

The mythical origin of the kūpa clans appears in the latter part of the kūpa decimation and revival legend.[427]   This is given in complete form below, but that part concerning the origin of the clans is repeated here.

Kisil-pīwic and his mother, having destroyed their enemies, were alone at kūpa.

His mother was grinding acorn meal when from the west she saw two women approaching. She called to her son, telling him that two persons—women not warriors—were approaching. The women came to a patch of wild currants and hid there. So kisil-pīwic sent his mother to bring them to kūpa. She found the girls and asked them if they were not afraid. They replied that they were not. Then the mother said, ''You have come to carry wood and water for me.'' She took the two sisters, who were from taka'at (base of Smith mountain in Luiseño territory), and brought them to her son. He married both of them.

First the older sister had two sons, then the younger sister had one son. When the sons of the elder sister grew up they married sivimūatim women. These were southerners from tūuhut and tūcvulī (about six miles south of kūpa). The son of the younger sister married an aliñawitcem woman from solūkma (near wilakal). Each of those families also had children.

The oldest son and his wife were very good to kisil-pīwic; the others were not. This made the old man very angry and he called all his descendants together. Then he said, ''This is my eldest son; his name shall be kaval—he will see farther and own more land than all others.'' Then to the second son he said, ''Build your house away at sitcñil (place under thorny bushes), and call yourselves pumtumatūlnikic (black tooth), for you are stingy and must live there.'' To the third son he said, ''Go to the north and call yourselves temewhanitc (northerner).'' Thus, from the beginning, all the kūpa people were close relatives.

The above legend states that kisil-pīwic and his sons intermarried with one Luiseño clan and two Diegueño clans, all three of whom belonged to the wildcat moiety, whereas the three clans founded by the sons were of the coyote moiety. The legendary genealogy of the kūpa clans is as follows:

Mythical Kūpa Genealogy

kisil-pīwic (Cahuilla?)
    + ♀ taka'atim (Luis.)

> 1st kavalim (Cu.)
>   + ♀ sivimūat (Dieg.)
> 1st pumtumatūlniktcum (Cu.)
>   + ♀ sivimūat (Dieg.)

    + ♀ taka'atim (Luis.)

1st temewhanitcem (Cu.)
    + ♀ aulīatim (Dieg.)

---

[427] The two Cupeño women who told this legend belonged to the sivimūat clan.

According to informants the three wildcat lineages in clan 4 (see table 8) have always been united under one head, lineage 4*a* usually having the chief, although lineage 4*b* has had several recorded leaders of the group. Lineage 4*c* seems to have always been under the domination of one of the others. According to tradition the sivi-mūatim people who did not unite with the other Cupeño remained at tūuhut and continued to talk the Diegueño language while the kūpa branch spoke Cupeño.

The ancestors of the three coyote clans (1–3) were supposed to have originally come from San Ignacio and to have spoken Cahuilla. According to theory their founder kisil-pīwic gave all the lands to his oldest son, the first kaval, and he in turn allotted parts to each of the other clans. The sauīvilem clan members are Mountain Cahuilla from San Ignacio who came to kūpa only about three generations ago, intermarried with the kavalim clan, and shared their lands with them. The two main Cupeño informants, Mrs. Griffith and Mrs. Valenzuela, claimed that clans 1 and 2 were considered as close relatives and could not marry, but that either clan could marry into clan 3. They explained this dissolution of the moiety bond on the grounds that the ancestors of clans 1 and 2 were full brothers as shown above in the legendary genealogy, and that their descendants always lived very close to one another, while clan 3, although supposedly founded by a half-brother, had its home territory farther away. This assumed correlation between propinquity and consanguinity apparently played a rather large rôle in determining marriage and other regulations. It will be discussed in more detail later.

There is no clan origin myth on record for the village of wilakal. It seems certain however that the tcūtnikut clan (no. 6) was of Diegueño origin. Even today their songs and rituals are in that language. The tūcvikinvatim clan (no. 7) on the other hand seems to be of Cahuilla origin, and their ceremonies are conducted in that language. Whether either of these clans belonged to either of the moiety divisions is not positively known. Gifford has stated that both belonged to the wildcat moiety,[428] and such is the general opinion of kūpa people. When the actual cases of marriage involving these two clans are considered, it appears that there are more marriages not in accord with such a moiety alignment than are in accord with it. Moreover, there are several cases of intermarriage between these two clans in comparatively early times. This is not characteristic of any

---

[428] Present series, 14:193, 1918. Am. Anthr., n. s., 28:395, 1926.

of the other dichotomous groups we have considered except certain of the Pass Cahuilla clans where the moiety ruling had become almost obsolete. As later discussion will show, the people at kūpa considered the moiety bond rather lightly, yet their marriages are much more in accord with it than are those at wilakal. Evidently wilakal was on the border of that area where dichotomy prevailed and it seems possible that neither clans 6 or 7 belonged to one moiety or the other.

The clan genealogies at kūpa reveal much the same social situation as prevailed among the Cahuilla but the clans appear to have been larger and more stabilized. The genealogy of the kavalim clan (genealogy 14) covers five generations, the three male survivors being now men of middle age or more. The relationships of the various branches of the clan are indicated by the lines, question marks indicating persons in the line of descent whose names were not remembered. Those relationships where connections are established through unremembered ancestors are not so hypothetical as they may appear, for they are based on the degree of relationship said to exist between the parties concerned. The indications are that five generations ago the kaval lineage might have been reduced to one family. This is a possibility, but it is much more probable that the collateral branches extend farther back than the reconstruction indicates. On the other hand there seems no reason to doubt the fundamental lineage nature of the group. In nearly all cases the degree of relationship, usually cousinship, was remembered by the living people and no persons were encountered in the various censuses or genealogical lists who did not show some degree of relationship to the main line, which on account of its completeness may be taken as that from Antonio kaval down to Mauricio and Lazarus Laws. The latter surname marks an interesting series of name changes from kaval, nicknamed Garra, through kaval, nicknamed nauwilot, to Laws, which is a refined pronunciation of nauwilot or louse. The genealogy shows clearly how nicknames acquired by individuals may later be applied to lineages or clans. One individual, Antonio, was nicknamed Garra, but this name seems to have disappeared. Two of his sons (299, 344) were nicknamed nauwilot, and this name, today translated Laws, was passed on. Another son (211) was nicknamed tcañalañalic, or sprout, and this name passed on to his son. Likewise one of Antonio's cousins (247) was nicknamed nūka, or daughter-in-law, and this name was also passed down in his line. The above nicknames according to informants were in the main acquired by amatory episodes which excited the mirth of the people. The importance of the custom was shown especially well by the five branch Cahuilla lineages at Los Coyotes, which acquired their individual names in this fashion. Luiseño data from La Jolla, to be given later, show the same process. In the light of these cases we may without undue theorizing assume that had any branches of the kaval clan been forced to move away on account of food scarcity or other causes, they would in the course of a few generations have become known by the above or similar nicknames, while the name kaval would in time become unknown to them. How often this has happened in the past to the clans we are considering can naturally never be known, but it is a process which may be seen going on among the groups under consideration.

A brief study of the kavalim genealogy gives a striking illustration of the way in which the numbers of the clan have fallen off in the last two generations. Of the fourteen men in the next to the last generation one man is alive. Of the last generation only five are on record, and of these only two are known to be alive. One generation has practically seen the extermination of the largest and most powerful Cupeño clan. The same state of rapid decline is shown in all the other kūpa genealogies, where the high mortality and sterility of the groups is striking. It affords a clear example of a decline in population due to a new and uncongenial environment. From contemporary accounts it would seem that the same fate quickly befell the natives transplanted to the missions in earlier times. The Cupeño as a whole were not taken away under the old mission régime, but the later forced move to Pala greatly accelerated a decline already under way. The causes for the marked sterility, which more than infant or adult mortality is bringing about the decline of the native southern California population, are easy to guess at. But exactly how they operate in a biological way is almost entirely unknown. One of the reasons for including all the Cupeño census data in the present paper is the hope that they may be of value in attacking this and similar problems.

To return to the clan situation at kūpa, the kavalim clan had three male members known to be alive in 1919, pumtumatūlniktcum clan six, temewhanitcem clan nine, tāka'atim lineage two, sivimūatim lineage two, auliñawitcem lineage three, and the sauīvilem Cahuilla clan eight. This last clan, as the genealogy shows, has only been at kūpa for four generations, having moved there from Los Coyotes canyon in Cahuilla territory. As no recent census of wilakal was obtained, it is not possible to determine exactly what proportion of the persons in the two wilakal clan genealogies survive at present. The genealogies (21–22), which are less complete than those of kūpa clans, indicate nevertheless that much the same decrease in population has occurred at both villages.

The genealogy of the pumtumatūlniktcum clan (genealogy 15), differs in no essential from that of the kaval clan save that there seems to have been less tendency for collateral branches to acquire nicknames. There are fewer collateral branches, which may in part account for the scarcity in nicknames. The lineage nature of the group is clearly demonstrated by the genealogy. The last clan of the coyote moiety, the temewhanitcem, is represented by only three males, one paternal uncle and two brothers (genealogy 16). These men are all dead and the clan is now extinct. According to the Cupeño division of lands (to be discussed later), this must once have been an important group, but these few survivors are all that informants can remember today. The genealogies give no clear evidence bearing on the reputed relationship between these clans and the kāvalim clan.

The Mountain Cahuilla sauīvilem clan also represents one lineage (genealogy 18). Women of this clan márried men of the kavalim clan, and the group under Ambrosio sauīvil seems to have moved from Los Coyotes to kūpa under the auspices of the kavalim clan who shared their food-gathering areas with them. They are better represented in Pala today than are most of the true Cupeño clans.

The Cupeño lineages of the wildcat moiety (genealogies 17, 19, 20) offer nothing new or unusual in their individual organization. The taka'atim genealogy (17) is clearly that of one closely united lineage, showing few collateral branches and no tendency toward nicknames. According to informants this is a related branch of the two following lineages, but the genealogies shed no direct light on this statement. The sivimūatim lineage, like the kavalim clan, consists of many collateral lines of descent evidently having a common origin many generations back. One branch had acquired the name Moro as a pseudonym, but in the main sivimūat has persisted as a family name to the present time. Four generations back from the present finds four collateral lines still in existence, and it is clear that their convergence must have occurred at least two generations before this. Informants claim that the line in which Francisco sivimūat (571) appears (see top of genealogy 19), is related to the auliñawic lineage in the following genealogy (20), but the exact degree of cousinship could not be given. It is probable, though not demonstrable by the

genealogies at hand, that common ancestors to both these lineages
would be found in the fourth, fifth, or sixth generations back from
the present. The auliñawitcem genealogy (20), already referred to,
is clearly that of one lineage. There is thus some probability but no
positive proof that the informants are correct in their claims that the
three wildcat lineages were once one family, and were thus related
by a blood as well as a clan and a moiety bond. The striking fact
that both clan and moiety coincide will be discussed later.

As has been previously stated no genealogical or detailed information was obtained at wilakal, and as a result the genealogies of the
clans at that place compiled from information furnished by kūpa
people are incomplete. The tūcvikinvatim genealogy (21) however
shows the lineage nature of this clan, with no more gaps in the relationships than occur in most of the kūpa genealogies. The tcūtnikut
genealogy (22), if such it may be called, leaves much to be desired,
for there is no reliable information in regard to the exact relationship
of the various collateral branches. The number of these branches is
not greater than that of the other Cupeño clans which are known to
be of a lineage organization, and there is reason to suppose that with
more information their relationship to each other would appear.

In general it appears that the three coyote moiety clans are
reputed to be of one stock but cannot be demonstrated as such by the
genealogies; whereas the three wildcat lineages are likewise reputed
to be of one stock and their genealogies purport to show where the
connecting links occur, but do not demonstrate them with any degree
of exactness. When the various lineages of certain Desert and
Mountain Cahuilla clans were considered, such reputed clan relationships were actually demonstrated (see genealogies 6 and 10). But in
each case the separation of collateral branches in the lineage to form
separate clans occurred within five generations. Among the Cupeño
the clan organization seems more stable and as a result the earlier
connections between lineages are more remote and harder to trace.
Clan number 1 (see genealogy 14) extends back five generations in
the genealogy, and would probably require one or two generations to
reduce it to one family (i.e., father and sons). Clan 2 (genealogy 15)
extends back five generations, and would likewise require one or two
generations to reduce it to one family. Clan 3 (genealogy 16) shows
only a fragment in its genealogy, the line being practically extinct.
Lineage 4*b* (genealogy 20) extends back only three generations,
though there may have been collateral branches which had become

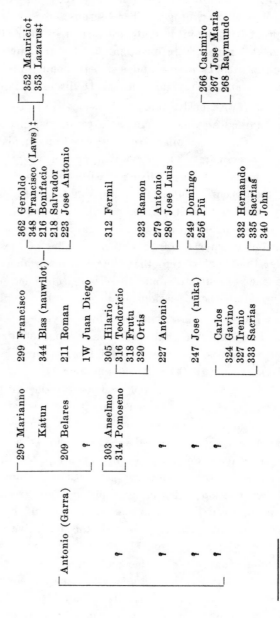

GENEALOGY 14

Kavalim Clan[431]

[431] Numbers are from censuses 1, 2, 3. ‡, individual known to be alive. Names in parentheses are nicknames.

GENEALOGY 15

Pumtumatúlnûktcum Clan

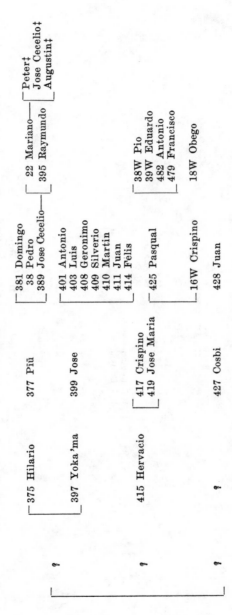

GENEALOGY 16
Temewhanitcem Clan

```
?  ———  431 Merchol
           435 Juan Angel
433 Melicati
```

GENEALOGY 17
Taka'atim Clan

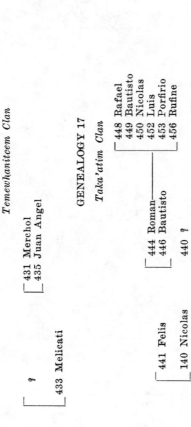

```
444 Roman  ———  448 Rafael
446 Bautisto     449 Bautisto
                 450 Nicolas
                 452 Luis
                 453 Porfirio
                 456 Rufine
440 ?
441 Felis
140 Nicolas
```

GENEALOGY 18
Sauivilem Clan

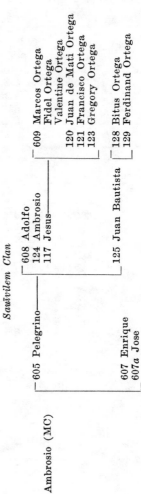

```
Ambrosio (MC)
605 Pelegrino  ———  608 Adolfo
                    124 Ambrosio  ———  609 Marcos Ortega
                    117 Jesus            Fidel Ortega
                                         Valentine Ortega
                                         120 Juan de Mati Ortega
                                         121 Francisco Ortega
                                         123 Gregory Ortega
                    125 Juan Bautista  —  128 Bitus Ortega
                                         129 Ferdinand Ortega
607 Enrique
607a Jose
```

GENEALOGY 19

Sivimūatim Clan

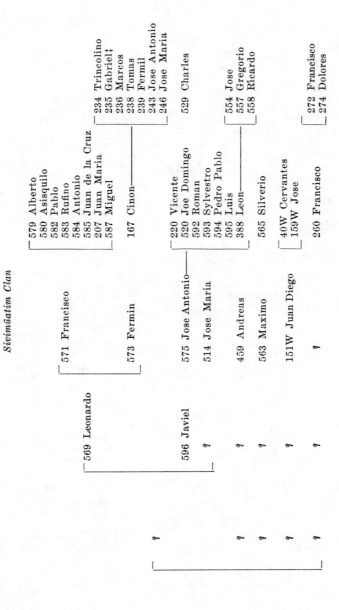

GENEALOGY 20

Auliñawitcem Clan

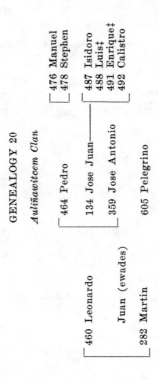

GENEALOGY 21

Tucvikiwvatim Clan

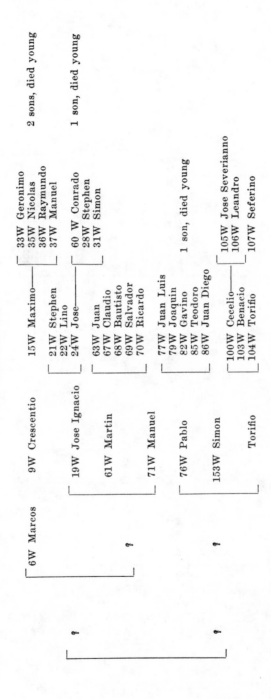

GENEALOGY 22

Teñtnikut Clan

512 Juan Diego

? 11W Luis

113W Juan ———— 117W Francisco
115W Marcellino   119W Marianno
                   120W Bautisto
                   123W Amelio

? 124W Juan

65W Felipe
406 Gervasio ———— 416 Marcos
                  417 Abraham

? 131W Manuel

134W Francisco
151W Trincolino ———— 229 Antonio

?

215 Matias ———— 230 Javiel
                    Francisco
                    Manuel
                367 Pēpī

52 Marcos‡

?

221 Cleato

extinct by this time. The same is true of lineage 4c (genealogy 17).
It is possible that both these lineages branched off from lineage 4a in
this or the preceding generation, but if so the exact connections have
been forgotten. Lineage 4a (genealogy 19) extends back four generations and would undoubtedly have required at least two or three
more generations to reduce it to a single family. It is thus patent
that the individual lineages were more tenacious among the Cupeño
than among their northern neighbors.

The Cupeño, almost in the center of the area under consideration
and occupying an unusually productive and favorable ecologic niche,
appear to have been the most stable of any of the groups so far considered in maintaining their lineage groupings. In no other essential,
however, does the Cupeño clan seem to have differed from that of
their neighbors, among many of whom the reputed early relationships
between individual lineages can be established by genealogies.

The Clan Fetish Bundle

The masvut, or clan fetish bundle, was as important among the
Cupeño as among the Cahuilla. It consisted of a roll of matting about
six feet long by three feet wide made of fine pointed mountain reeds
called sulyil.[429] In this bundle were commonly placed the paviut, a
crystal-headed wand; ūlat, the eagle-feather skirt; keñhut, strings of
shell beads; tcīatem, eagle-down headbands; aiilem, turtle-shell
rattles; and other ceremonial impedimenta. The contents of the
bundle with the addition of ceremonial gifts were called numhut,
which is translated as "treasure." This bundle was highly venerated,
and strips of the matting were formerly employed as frames for the
images burned at the mourning ceremony. The masvut bundle was
ordinarily kept rolled up, and was hung in a dark corner of the clan
leader's dwelling, which was also the ceremonial house. The clan
leader was the only person permitted to touch it, and on his death it
was taken by his successor. Portions of the numhut or "treasure,"
and strips of masvut were given away to other clan leaders at important ceremonies, but the original bundle wrapping was always retained.
When the numhut, or the masvut, was moved for any purpose, women
accompanied it to "feed it" acorn meal. These women seem to have
been those who had married into the clan as well as those born in it.
The masvut food was called penut kāwa, apparently an archaic term.

---

[429] According to Gifford, S. Cal., 198, this matting, which he calls "masbat,"
is made of *Epicampes* grass.

Each clan of the coyote moiety formerly had a masvut bundle, but there was only one wildcat moiety or clan bundle. This bundle was formerly in the sivimūatim lineage, but later was transferred to the auliñawitcem lineage. The taka'atim lineage seems never to have possessed the bundle and the ceremonial leadership thereby implied. Details concerning the transfer of the bundle and leadership would be of great interest, but they do not seem to be obtainable at this late date. Moreover the importance of the sacred bundle, priest, and ceremonial house was not fully realized by either Gifford or myself at the time we did most of our work with the Cupeño, and many details concerning the complex may still be obtainable that were then overlooked.

It is this complex that arbitrarily separates the clan, as the term is here employed, from the pure lineage as defined among the Miwok by Gifford.[430] As the southern California clan may only consist of one small lineage that possesses the complex, this distinction may seem too arbitrary; but as this clan may also consist of several only remotely related lineages, as among the Mountain Cahuilla and Cupeño, the distinction in terms seems justified. When one speaks of separately named lineages that together form one clan, the two terms are essential. While the sacred bundle, priest, and ceremonial house complex is also "the heart" of the "party," that organization, as it is composed of unrelated lineages and is not exogamous, will not be confused with the clan, which is exogamous and held together by kinship as well as ceremonial bonds.

THE STATUS OF THE MOIETY

A tendency not to take the moiety division of Cupeño clans seriously prevailed among all the Cupeño questioned. They say that the division was just a legend and really had little value. They claim that none of the three wildcat lineages at kūpa could intermarry, because they were all blood relatives, and not because they were of one moiety. Correspondingly, kaval and pumtumatūlnikic people may not marry because they are close relatives, but either may marry with temewhanic people because the latter lived farther away and were less closely related. Theoretically the two wilakal clans are assigned to the wildcat moiety, but actually they seem to have been little affected by any regard for the moiety. There is no clearly expressed belief in any eponymous moiety ancestor.

---

430 Am. Anthr., n. s., 28:389, 1926.

"In the beginning," it is said, "coyote was a person; so was wild-cat. They married. Wildcat was a woman, coyote a man." Another story says that coyote was lazy,[432] and when he hunted only killed crickets and frogs. His wife was a wildcat. She got sick when she ate them, but coyote did not. A wildcat man however married a coyote woman and he killed rabbits and quail which they both ate.[433]

Formerly when a wildcat was brought into the village by hunters, all the girls of the islam (coyote) moiety gathered in a circle around it, and sang the following song:

> "tūkutūma-a-a-! (wildcat)
>   mūtīhut-a-a-a! (short, bob-tail)
>   uhmūtihut-a-a-a! (flat-faced)
>   tūkut nahanic!" (wildcat, old man)

Each line was repeated three times. When a coyote was brought in, all the girls of the tūktum (wildcat) moiety sang:

> "īsilim-a-a-a! (coyote)
>   sīvihut-a-a-a! (lean)
>   tcīīhut-a-a-a! (sneaky)
>   īsil nahanic" (coyote, old man)

The animals were then taken to the clan leader's house and divided up in the same way as a deer or any other game animal. Obviously there was no taboo on eating the flesh of the moiety animal.

In the boys' and girls' initiation ceremonies, neophytes of the coyote moiety were painted with stripes, those of the wildcat moiety with spots. The colors used were red and black, and the custom of differential marking, as among the Cahuilla, was associated with the commands of the moon in mythical times. This ritual, it is said, was especially connected with pukuvyahil, the feather dance, which informants say was given the temewhanic clan by the neighboring Luiseño.

One of Gifford's informants stated that the moiety originated at a meeting in ancient times at kūpa, when some of the old men said they would be tūkut, and the others said they would be īsil. The same informant said that tūktum people called the wildcat nūpīwī, which approaches the Cahuilla term "my great-grandparent," and the islam people designated the coyote in the same manner. All the Cupeño, he added, called the bear by the same term. Neither Mūkat nor Tumaī-yauit, nor the sun or moon, were definitely aligned with either of the

---

[432] This is the opposite of the coyote moiety characteristics given Gifford by a Cupeño informant at Banning, present series, 14:192, 1918.

[433] This suggests a southern Diegueño story of coyote and wildcat, recorded by Spier, present series, 20:332–333, 1923.

moieties so far as could be ascertained. The moiety origin myth fragment published by Gifford[434] could not be verified, and appears to be a somewhat garbled version of the Cahuilla creation story. No division of animals or plants into one or the other moieties was remembered by any Cupeño informant questioned.

The house census of kūpa between the years "1865" and 1902 (census 1) lists thirty-four marriages between clan members belonging to that village (table 15). Of these, thirty-two are in accord with the rule of moiety exogamy and only two are not. This demonstrates conclusively that however lightly the Cupeño may at present consider the moiety classification it formerly exerted a strong control over marriages between clans. It is possible that the assumed relationship between clans 1–3, and between lineages 4a–4c (table 8) was the controlling factor and not the moiety at all. But even if this latter view is taken it seems probable that there exists some etiological connection between such an alignment and the moiety classification. This will be discussed presently.

The marriages between wilakal clan members living at kūpa show much less regard for moiety exogamy. Of twelve such marriages involving members of the tcūtnikut clan, seven are in accord with the rule and five are not. Of seven such marriages involving members of the tūcvikinvatim clan, three are in accord with the rule and four are not. Practically all these marriages were with kūpa clan members. There likewise appears to have been no moiety control exerted in marriages between Cahuilla clans and kūpa clans, for of thirty-two such matings, eleven are in accord with the rule, seventeen are not, and four cases are doubtful (see table 15).

At the village of wilakal during this period ("1865" to 1902) there are sixteen marriages between Cupeño clan members on record, and of these only five are in accord with moiety exogamy, while eleven are not (see table 16). When the marriages between wilakal clans and Cahuilla clans are considered (table 14), of the twenty-eight recorded cases, thirteen are in accord with the moiety ruling, fourteen are not in accord, and one case is doubtful. Naturally, since both wilakal clans were assigned by informants to the wildcat moiety, the eight cases of marriage occurring between them were contrary to any rule of exogamy. The actual cases therefore demonstrate that wilakal marriages were uncontrolled by any rule of moiety exogamy, and it may be presumed that if such dichotomy was recognized there at all

---

[434] S. Cal., 192.

it had very slight importance.   More detailed information on the nature of Cupeño marriages will be presented in the following section devoted to that subject, but from the foregoing it is obvious that kūpa was characterized by exogamous moieties, while at wilakal if such a dichotomy were present at all it exerted no influence on actual marriages.

It has been suggested as a possibility that the Cupeño moiety originated through the settlement of the three wildcat lineages with the three original Cupeño coyote clans.[435]   The foregoing data lend considerable corroboration to such an hypothesis.   In the clan formed by the three wildcat lineages we have for the first time encountered an identity between clan and moiety.   Moreover the three coyote clans regarded one another as blood relatives, as did the wildcat lineages, and each regarded endogamous marriages as improper because of assumed kinship rather than as a violation of an arbitrary moiety rule.   The three coyote clans according to their mythology are of Cahuilla origin, while two of the wildcat lineages claim to be of Diegueño origin[436] and the third is said to be of Luiseño origin. Whether the three wildcat lineages are really collateral branches of one parent stock, or whether the third lineage of supposed Luiseño origin was only ceremonially affiliated in the clan and moiety, cannot be positively ascertained.   The fact that the three formed an exogamous group suggests the former explanation, while the fact that the third lineage was always subordinate to the other two suggests the latter.

Be that as it may, the fact that the coyote clans claim to be of Cahuilla origin, while the two most important wildcat lineages claim to be of Diegueño origin has a still further significance.   The Cahuilla group nearest to the Cupeño formerly lived at wilīya (San Ignacio) in Los Coyotes canyon, and consisted of one clan composed of five related lineages collectively called wīwaíistam, named after wīwaíisil, the legendary founder of the clan.   They were known as the "coyote people" from the latter part of their clan name.   The first portion of the name, wīwaíisil, suggests wewal, the Cahuilla term for rain,[437] but this is not certain.   The coyote had a peculiar significance to this

---

[435] Gifford, Am. Anthr., n.s., 28:345, 1926

[436] Mrs. Griffith says that in her mother's time there was a related branch of sīvimūat people who had a Diegueño name.   These lived at matkwai in Diegueño territory, and they always came to sivimūat ceremonies at kūpa.   The Cupeño sivimūat people also went to their ceremonies, especially to those for girls at time of puberty.

[437] Kroeber, present series, 4:79, 1907.

group aside from designating the clan : he was called paya īsil, ''water coyote''; tamia īsil, ''sun coyote''; and īsil tēvicnikic ''white coyote.'' When a coyote was heard barking to the north it was believed to presage a great sickness and special ceremonies were performed by the shamans.[438] These are only fragments of what was evidently once an important concept, but my informant who was one of the last survivors of the group in question, was too young at the time they were driven from their homes by a great smallpox epidemic to know all the details. No such series of associations involving the coyote were encountered among any other Cahuilla group, although the stellar rôle played by the coyote in the creation myth of all Cahuilla groups is well known. It was from Los Coyotes canyon that the ancestors of kisil-pīwic, who in the myth revived the present Cupeño society after its decimation, were supposed to have come.

The Diegueño groups south of Cupeño territory lay stress on the wildcat rather than the coyote, and claim the wildcat as their ''property'' and their ''god.'' The people were believed to be related to the wildcats as to brothers, and there were two wildcats that first told the months of the year. Similarly there is a color symbolism attached to the two wildcats of the east (red) and the west (blue). The coyote is in disrepute.[439] When this Diegueño attachment to the wildcat and deprecation of the coyote is compared to the Cahuilla (especially the wīwaīistam clan) attachment to the coyote and ignoring of the wildcat, the moiety alignment of the Cupeño clans takes on an added significance. It seems very probable that at the unusually favorable site of kūpa, lineages of Cahuilla origin settled first (priority is assumed because these lineages seem to have dominated, and to have owned the largest number of food-gathering territories) and intermarried with one or more Diegueño lineages who also settled there. The animal names most commonly associated with each group were adopted as totems of the two divisions, between which marriage was not forbidden on account of kinship. The spread of these two totemic names to designate intermarrying groups would have been a simple matter, and may account for their application among the Cahuilla, Serrano, and Saboba Luiseño.

Such an explanation, however, does not account for the very widespread custom of dichotomy in southern California and the neighboring areas, but merely appears as a plausible explanation of the par-

---

[438] The situation at wilīya has been previously discussed, present paper, p. 171.
[439] Gifford, present series, 14:169, 1918.

ticular animal designations applied to the moiety in southern California. The roots of the moiety itself would seem to go far deeper, many of the commonest traits associated with the dual division occurring among such distant groups as the Miwok, Yokuts, and their neighbors. This problem has been discussed in a previous publication[440] and need only be referred to at this time.

CUPEÑO MARRIAGES

Formerly Cupeño parents arranged marriages for their sons when the latter were about fourteen years of age. They usually selected a girl of about ten,[441] and obtained the boy's consent to the proposed match. This might be done by either the parents or the grandparents of the boy. One of the grandparents, or parents, would take a gift of rabbits or other food to the parents of the girl and propose the marriage to them. The girl's parents discussed the matter, obtained the opinion of the girl, and if it was agreeable to all took the girl to her new home. If they were poor they went empty-handed, but usually they took baskets and food as presents. The richer the family the more numhut, "treasure," went with the girl. The couple were then taken to the clan leader of the boy's family, and a feast followed. All food at this ceremony was provided by the family of the groom and there was an entire day of feasting, singing, and dancing. The latter family also threw away many gifts consisting of seeds, acorn meal, and baskets for the guests to gather up. At the close of this ceremony the clan leader (nuut) talked to the newly married pair, advising them to be faithful to each other, and to labor so that they might be prosperous. Postmarital residence was commonly patrilocal. In census 1, out of seventy-four cases where postmarital residence was clear, fifty-two cases were patrilocal and twenty-two cases were matrilocal.

The mother-in-law took the girl out to the territories owned by the boy's lineage, or clan, as the case might be, and showed her where to gather seeds, acorns, cactus, and other food plants. She advised her in regard to preparing food, keeping house, and taking care of herself

---

440 Strong, An Analysis of Southwestern Society, Am. Anthr., n.s., 29:45–48, 1927.

441 These ages appear too young, but they were thus given by Mrs. Manuela Griffith whose information in all other regards proved correct whenever checked against actual occurrences. Such marriages however were mostly before her time and it seems more probable that eighteen and fourteen years, rather than fourteen and ten years, would be the average ages at marriage.

as a married woman. For several months the boy's mother provided the bride with ground meal and other food, while the groom took all his game to his parents-in-law. Not until they had a child could they eat meat killed by the husband. After two years if there was no child the wife might be sent home, though if she were a hard worker her new family usually kept her. In former times it is said that a man might have several wives, but no actual cases were remembered. If two married people quarreled, or either was unfaithful, they might separate without any ceremony or return of presents.

Mrs. Griffith's mother, Soledad kaval, told her that if a man desired to marry a girl who professed to be unwilling, he sent a friend to ''drag her.'' This friend would go to the girl's home and stand there with his legs crossed. He would then say to her parents, ''I am sent here to drag this girl,'' whereupon he would seize her by the arm and commence to take her away. If she struggled fiercely her parents would drive the man away, but if she went quietly then all members of the groom's clan would have a great celebration and the wedding followed.

Soledad also stated that a woman formerly would go to a small special shelter in the woods to bear children. After several weeks, when she returned home, any new things in the house were hidden for fear the child might die. After the mother came into the house, her husband was forbidden to eat salt and had to drink warm water just as she did. Early every morning they would bathe the child and paint designs on its face. A special basket, made by the child's paternal grandmother, was used to bathe the child in. After its bath the child was put in a cradle lined with willow bark. These rites were observed for at least one month. Such rules, Mrs. Griffith added, were observed long ago but in her own time were largely neglected. Today the old rules of marriage have almost entirely disappeared among the Cupeño, although they have been only partly replaced by the modern American system.

The following tables (12–16) show the distribution of Cupeño marriages over the period (''1865'' to 1902) covered by the house censuses 1 and 2.

TABLE 12

Total Number of Cupeño Marriages between "1865" and 1902

Kūpa	Wilakal	Between members of the group and:
64	16	other members of the group
62	37	people of near-by groups
19	....	whites
1	....	Negroes
4	....	people of distant groups
150	53	total: 203

TABLE 13

Outside Marriages at Kūpa between "1865" and 1902

	Luiseño	Diegueño	Pass Cahuilla	Desert Cahuilla	Mountain Cahuilla	Wilakal
kavalim	2	1	1	2	12	6
pumtumatūl	1	....	....	1	5	5
temewhan	....	....	....	....	1	1
aulīatim	....	....	....	....	2	1
taka'atim	....	....	....	....	2	....
sivimūatim	2	....	....	....	2	5
sauīvilem	....	1	....	1	1	....
tcūtnikut	....	1	....	....	....	....
tūcvikinvat	....	....	....	1	....	....
Other families	....	1	....	....	1	2
Total: 62	5	4	1	5	26	20

TABLE 14

Outside Marriages at Wilakal between "1865" and 1902

	Luiseño	Diegueño	Pass Cahuilla	Desert Cahuilla	Mountain Cahuilla	Kūpa
tūcvikinvatim	1	2	1	8	5	....
tcūtnikut	2	2	....	2	4	....
pumtumatūl	....	....	....	1	....	....
sivimūat	....	....	....	....	3	1
kāvalim	....	....	....	....	1	....
Other families	1	....	....	2	1	....
Total: 37	4	4	1	13	14	1

TABLE 15

Clan Marriages at Kūpa

	tu.	tcu.	si.	ta.	au.	sa.	te.	pu.	ka.
kavalim	2	3	15	2	3	4	1	0	0
pumtumatūl	1	3	6	1	1	0	1	0	
temewhan	0	1	2	0	1	1	0		
saūivilem	0	0	3	1	3	0			
aulīatim	1	0	0	0	0				
taka'atim	0	1	0	0					
sivimūatim	2	4	0						
tcūtnikut	1	0							
tūcvikinvat	0								

Total marriages: 64; (between kūpa clans: 34; between kūpa and wilakal clans: 19; with saūivilem clan: 12).

TABLE 16

Clan Marriages at Wilakal

	pumtum.	kavalim	tcūtnikut	sivimūat
tūcvikinvatim	3	1	8	3
tcūtnikut	1	0	0	0

Total: 16 (between W clans: 8; between W and K clans: 8).

The foregoing tables speak for themselves, but a brief discussion of certain points they bring out may be in order. Table 12 shows that at kūpa there were more marriages within the village than with outsiders, while at wilakal the situation was reversed. Gifford has assumed that the latter condition was due to both local clans being of one moiety, thereby necessitating village exogamy.[442] The previous discussion of clan intermarriage at wilakal showed that such a rule was not obeyed (see table 16). Half the recorded wilakal marriages were exogamous and half endogamous so far as the two local clans were concerned. The moiety seems to have exerted no control whatsoever. Naturally in a small village like wilakal outside marriage is more imperative than in a larger village like kūpa where there is a wider choice of mates within the village. In all probability it was this factor, and not the moiety at all, that caused the greater number of outside marriages at wilakal. All marriages with alien races or

[442] Am. Anthr., n.s., 28:395, 1926.

distant Indians on record occurred at kūpa. This is probably due to its larger size and greater accessibility to whites, but it may also be due in part to the imperfection of the wilakal record.

Table 13 shows a greater number of marriages between the kavalim and pumtumatūlniktcum Cupeño clans with clans of the Mountain Cahuilla than occurred between any other three groups. This may be attributed largely to the predominant numbers of these two Cupeño clans, and also to the commonly observed fact that once intermarriage between two groups commences it usually increases through the greater social contact. Table 14 shows that the wilakal clans married with Desert Cahuilla clans in almost as many cases as with those of the Mountain Cahuilla. Wilakal is nearer the Desert Cahuilla and both proximity and increased social contact led to more intermarriages with Desert clans. Tables 13 and 14 both show how many more marriages at kūpa and wilakal were with Cahuilla than with either Luiseño or Diegueño. Obviously, as their large proportion in the population indicated, the Cahuilla were in more intimate contact with the Cupeño than were any of their other neighbors.

Table 15, which shows the proportionate number of interclan marriages at kūpa, has been previously discussed in relation to the moiety. In general it appears that kūpa marriages were exogamous as concerned that institution, while wilakal marriages were not. Beside the limitations implied by the moiety, kūpa marriages show no preferential grouping, the larger number of marriages occurring between the most populous clans as would be expected. The two marriages contrary to moiety exogamy are between the kāvalim and temewhanitcem clans, and between the latter clan and the pumtumatūlniktcum clan. Informants explained this by claiming that the temewhanitcem clan was more distantly related to each of the other two than they were to each other, adding that the members of the former clan had once dwelt rather far distant from the others. They seemed to feel that the only impropriety in the matter was the marriage of assumed kinsfolk, but that the relationship was so remote that no important rule was thereby violated. The fact that both clans belonged to the coyote moiety apparently made no difference.

Table 16, previously discussed, demonstrates the fact that no moiety ruling seems to have controlled wilakal marriages. The eight marriages between the two wilakal clans, and three of the eight marriages with kūpa clans, do not accord with the rule. The present data are contradictory to any other moiety alignment possible, as well as to the alignment of both clans to the wildcat moiety, insisted on by kūpa informants. The number of cases is inadequate for complete reliance, but the assumption is strong that any dichotomy prevailing at wilakal was of a very weak nature as regarded control of marriage.

CLAN OWNERSHIP OF LAND

Lists of clan-owned sites in the vicinity of kūpa were obtained by Gifford and the present author. In each case the informants were Mrs. Manuela Griffith and her daughter, Mrs. Salvadora Valenzuela. The two accounts were checked and combined in the following list of sites owned or shared by the various kūpa clans. The list is by no means exhaustive, in fact it would in all probability be doubled or trebled if one were able to go over the ground with one of the older Cupeños. It includes nevertheless the most important food-gathering areas where certain wild crops were most abundant. The greater part of the intervening territory was free to all. The three lineages of the wildcat clan (or moiety) are said to have held their territories in common during recent times, but formerly they seem to have owned individual territories. It must be remembered, in considering the unequal distribution of territories, that some of these were undoubtedly more fruitful than others, so that mere number of sites is no absolute criterion of the amount of produce thus obtained.

TABLE 17

Sites Owned by Kūpa Clans

Designation on map; name of site; clan owning site; remarks.

East Side of Hot Springs Mountain

1k; nañova; kavalim; about 4 m. W. of San Ignacio; acorns gathered.

2k; sūmil; kavalim; camp near nañova; only kavals camped here.

3k (te); pucyukū; kavalim and temewhanitcem; small valley or mountain W. of San Ignacio. Both clans gathered acorns.

4k; somal; kavalim; acorns.

5k; (p.); pauicīva; kavalim and pumtumatūlniktcum (E. W. G.); acorns.

6k (si); macil; kāvilim, part given to sivimūatim (E. W. G.); acorns.

7 (si); sūicpukī (rabbit's house); sivimūatim; five kinds of acorns. Home of mythical black and white rabbit, that stood four feet high, which the kāvals originally brought with the hot springs when they came to kūpa. The kāvilim clan gave this place to the sivimūatim clan; acorns.

8 si; acwitpapauwi; sivimūatim; acorns.

9 si; puic cīva; sivimūatim; acorns.

10 si; huvukta; sivimūatim; acorns.

11 si; sūwilkitci; sivimūatim; acorns.

12p; tūktcīal (wild currant); pumtumatūlniktcum; acorns, seeds, and berries. Bedrock mortars.

13k; hovukta; kavalim; acorns.

14 te; wīatava; temewhanitcem. Lost Valley; weed seed, berries, wild oats.

15 te; patcīkva; temewhanitcem. Near Lost Valley. Acorns and other food.

16 te; tkumla; temewhanitcem; west of Lost Valley. Acorns and other food.

17 te; antimpumki (ant's territory); temewhanitcem; acorns and ant larvae.

18 te; nikic; temewhanitcem; wild squash. The seeds were parched and ground into meal. Pulp used as soap.

19k; acwitputīa; kavalim; eagle's nest here; owned by kavals. Food products gathered by temewhanitcem.

West Side of Hot Springs Mountain

20p; alīma; pumtumatūlniktcum; this clan owned site, but people of all clans camped here in bark huts. There were flat rocks for drying meal, and rock mortars.

21p; paukat; pumtumatūlniktcum; near alīma.

22p; ku'vt (elderberry); pumtumatūlniktcum, near alīma.

23p; kwiñilpūmukua; pumtumatūlniktcum; near alīma.

24 te; kataubani; temewhanitcem; near alīma.

25 te; palavalac; temewhanitcem; near alīma.

26 te (a); būcbuku; temewhanitcem; near alīma. A small part of this site was given to auliatim.

27 te (a); nañaulūk; temewhanitcem; near alīma. A small part of this site was given to aulīatim.

28 te; naxat; temewhanitcem; near alīma.

29 te; wīatava; temewhanitcem; near alīma.

30 te; patcikvū; temewhanitcem; near alīma.

31 te (s); saimal; temewhanitcem; near alīma.

32 te; acwutmimhika; temewhanitcem; near alīma. One-half given to sivimūatim.

33 te; taupavicku; temewhanitcem; near alīma.

34k; kwinsīvitc; kavalim; acorns.

35k; īval; kavalim; acorns.

36k; alwitimpumkī (crow's territory); kavalim; acorns.

37a; picskualī; aulīatim. creek bed below ''crow's territory'' with three kinds of acorns.

38a; suūvickicnut; aulīatim; camped here, and not long ago planted vegetables.

39k (a); kūlilva; kavalim and aulīatim; the latter clan gathered food. Three kinds of acorns.

40k; dilyīhat; kavalim; acorns.

41k; kawickatoli'i; kavalim; acorns.

42k; hilyakali (dripping); kavalim; acorns.

43 ta; upatcikic; taka'atim; creek and oak grove; acorns.

44k; kulūmal; kavalim; acorns.

45k; yūbatcikis; kavalim; acorns.

46k; sukatkavilhi; kavalim; acorns.

47 si; matistampumpkī; sivimūatim; acorns.

48k; kiwiit'ka; kavalim; acorns.

49p; pamat (spring); pumtumatūlniktcum; there were three main springs near kūpa, owned by the kavalim, pumtumatūlniktcum, and temewhanitcem clans.

Vicinity of Kūpa

50p; isval (grass seeds); pumtumatūlniktcum; another spring.

51p; tepalku (water holes); pumtumatūlniktcum; rocky hill near kūpa, where there are mortar holes.

52p; taucaval; pumtumatūlniktcum; place just south of kūpa where ceremonies were held. A large rock here, when touched, was supposed to bring storms.

53; mukwacma (fleas); all clans; small flat where town stood.

54k; palatiñva; kavalim; another spring, nominally owned by kavalim.

55p; palmūlikal; pumtumatūlniktcum; a hot spring.

56 te; ?; temewhanitcem; a hot spring on west side of town.

57k; taucval; kavalim; various summer products gathered.

58k; kūpayatca (bedrock mortars); kavalim; site where present bathhouse stands at Warner's Hot Springs.

Southeast of Kūpa

59p (si); daukī; pumtumatūlniktcum and sivimūatim; hillside where small acorns were gathered; first owned by pumtumatūlniktcum clan and given in part by them to the sivimūatim.

60p; taupamūki; pumtumatūlniktcum.

61k; yumowut; kavalim.

62k; patculic; kavalim.

63p; wiatwatowilut; pumtumatūlniktcum.

64 si; tcamicpakavul; sivimūatim.

65k; waxatcilnakpoiyahiva (frog mounting); kavalim; a small hill.

66p; naktamii; pumtumatūlniktcum; traditional home of clan.

67 si; tuligmal; sivimūatim.

68 si; matistampuki (bats' home); sivimūatim.

69t; paxal; temewhanitcem.

70p (k); kociginix; pumtumatūlniktcum and kavalim.

71p (k); sowalkitcī; pumtumatūlniktcum and kavalim.

72p (k); wixit; pumtumatūlniktcum and kavalim.

Southwest of Kūpa

73; kukditgi; fiesta ground, belonging to all the clans.

74k; wiatpīwit; kavalim; a single large oak tree with long acorns.

75k; paigī; kavalim.

76k; sincmitciswa'; kavalim; a seed-gathering area.

77k; hukicbumu; kavalim; sage and other seeds gathered.

78k; ditsa; kavalim; down on the floor of the valley; a seed-gathering site.

Northwest of Kūpa

79k; sōvaiīhamū; kavalim.

80k; iñva'a; kavalim.

81k; miaulū; kavalim; according to myth this is the site where the ancestors of the Cupeño journeying from the north stopped just prior to founding kūpa.

Northeast of Kūpa

82k; sūklūpa; kavalim; in the valley; greens and seeds.

83k; hunwutpūpali; kavalim.

84k; kukūlimpumki (burrowing owl's territory); kavalim.

85k; tcatimpumki (white owl's territory); kavalim.

86k; packi; kavalim.

87k; tōtikima; kavalim.

88k; salūtki; kavalim.

89k; sikmani'i; kavalim.

90k; saīyil; kavalim.

91 te (si); yildipū; temewhanitcem and sivimūatim.

92k; tauwamal; kavalim; small hill from which mythical ancestors first saw the site of kūpa.

93k; mokwūnimpū; kavalim; here ants were gathered for boys'·"anut" ceremony.

The foregoing list (table 17) indicates that the kavalim clan held the lion's share of the kūpa territory. Out of the ninety-three sites listed, this clan owned wholly or in part forty-six. Thus half of all sites named[443] belonged to only one of the five clans represented at kūpa! This state of affairs tends in some degree to bear out the native belief that the kavalim clan once owned all the territory, later parceling it out to the other clans. Taken into account with the kavalim predominance in ceremonial affairs to be discussed later, this disproportionate ownership of land makes it seem probable that the kavalim clan or lineage was the first to occupy the area, and that the other lineages came later.

The temewhanitcem clan owned eighteen sites, the pumtumatūlniktcum clan seventeen, the sivimūat lineage nine, the aulīatim lineage two, and the taka'atim lineage one. The sauīvilem clan owned none, but its members shared the territories owned by the kavalim clan.

TABLE 18

Shared Territories

	a.	s.	t.	p.	k.
kavalim	4	1	2	4	×
pumtum	0	1	0	×	
temewhan	2	2	×		
sivimūat	0	×			
aulīatim	×				
Total: 16					

According to informants the shared territories resulted from one clan giving to another clan, with which it commonly intermarried, a share of its territory. This may be true for some cases, but in others it obviously does not hold.

---

[443] This list of sites may well be taken as a random sampling, for Mrs. Griffith was a sivimūat clan member by birth, and her daughter being half white, likewise considered herself a member of that clan. There was therefore no reason why they should aggrandize the power of the kavalim clan.

Thus the kavalim clan may have given parts of its territory to the aulīatim and sivimūat clans, and actually, in spite of being of the same moiety, to the temewhanitcem clan because of marriage.[444] But the four territories shared with the pumtumatūlniktcum clan cannot be accounted for in this way. In all other cases where kavalim is not involved, however, the two clans sharing one territory are of opposite moieties. There are too few cases of this sort to draw any positive conclusions, but the fact that eleven of the sixteen shared territories were in part owned by the kavalim clan is significant. It

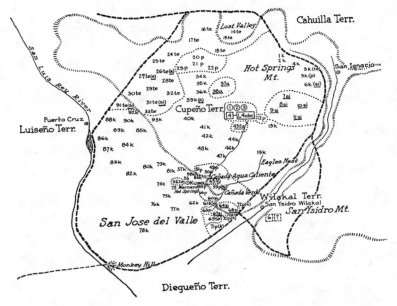

Map 6. Clan ownership of tracts in Cupeño territory. Numbers designate tracts as listed in table 17; letters following numbers: clans owning tracts, as per same table; letters in parentheses: clans with acquired ownership or secondary rights; dotted lines: grouping of tracts, showing tendency to continuity of clan ownership; broken lines: "tribal" boundaries; hachured lines: mountain or mesa edges; numbers in circles and squares: clans or clan groups found in territory, as per text.

adds further evidence to the native claim of kavalim priority and original ownership. Intermarriage, and probably distant relationship, determined the nature of joint ownership of land, while there were undoubtedly other factors which we have not considered.

Only the most productive canyons, oak groves, cactus patches, and seed-bearing areas were owned by the clans. All intervening territories were free to all, and hunting for deer, rabbits, quail, pigeons, etc., was permissible on any territory by the members of all clans. The

Cupeño at kūpa however excluded those from wilakal, as well as neighboring Cahuilla, Luiseño, and Diegueño groups, and these groups in turn excluded all others from their territories.

Map 6 (p. 248) shows the tendency of the sites owned by each clan to cluster in certain areas, and it also shows the impossibility of exactly marking off the territories of one clan from those of the others. They are so intermingled geographically that only an approximation of the land division between them may be shown on a map. Spier first demonstrated this condition among the clans (gentes) of the southern Diegueño,[445] and Gifford confirmed it for the Miwok and other south central and southern California groups.[446] It is certainly the case for the Luiseño and for all three divisions of the Cahuilla. Among the Cupeño this grouping is even more complex, for the clans were centralized in one village and therefore had their food-gathering areas more intermingled. Map 6 gives only the roughest approximation of the location of these areas, and undoubtedly a careful ethnogeographic survey of the area would bring out other unsuspected conditions of land tenure.

CLAN AND CEREMONIAL LEADERSHIP

The Nuut

The head of the Cupeño clan was called nuut, and was the keeper of the masvut bundle. Each clan had a ceremonial dance house which they called wamkic (a Luiseño term), and here the nuut lived and kept his ceremonial fetish bundle hung up in a dark corner. Each of the clans of the coyote moiety had a nuut originally, but the wildcat clans had only one, usually in the sivimūatim lineage. All ceremonies were ordered by the nuut, and he cared for all the food gathered for the various feasts and ceremonies. As was the case among the Cahuilla, he obtained his power from the masvut bundle, and he was likewise supposed to know all the ritual and sacred legends of his clan. The clan leadership ran in the male line within the lineage, usually from father to eldest son, but often an older son who was unfitted for the office was passed over in favor of a younger brother, or an uncle in a collateral line. It was considered essential

---

445 *Op. cit.*, 301, see map, fig. *A*.

446 S Cal., 390–400.

444 In house census 1, there are two cases of intermarriage between the temewhanitcem clan and the two other clans of the coyote moiety.

that the nuut's wife be an active, generous woman able to provide much food and many baskets for the clan ceremonies. It was quite as essential that the nuut be free-handed and generous as that he know all the ritual and be a good song leader. Affairs that concerned the entire village were discussed by all the clan leaders, either personally or through messengers, and in such a discussion the opinion of the kavalim clan leader bore more weight than any of the others. In 1851, at the time of the Cupeño revolt, the leader was Antonio Garra of the kavalim clan, so it is obvious that kavalim supremacy goes back at least that far. The leaders of each clan were consulted in cases demanding joint action, but the kavalim nuut seems to have acted as head in cases of emergency.

In the kavalim clan, Antonio Garra (kaval) is the first nuut remembered. He was before the informant's time, but was remembered because of his prominent part in the Cupeño revolt of 1851. Who succeeded him is uncertain: perhaps Belares Kaval (see genealogy 14).[447] The first nuut whom the informants actually knew was Roman kaval. He was succeeded by a cousin of his own generation, Hilario. Hilario was succeeded by Francisco nawilot, another cousin. Francisco, a very old man, now lives at wilakal, but his ceremonies are, as the Cupeño say, "covered up," which means the life of the clan as a ceremonial unit is ended. In the pumtumatūlniktcum clan the earliest nuut remembered was Hilario pumtumatūlnikic, or Blacktooth. He was succeeded by his son Pīū, who was in turn succeeded by his son, Jose Cecelio. The son of the latter, Marianno Blacktooth, is the present nuut. His ceremonies, like those of all the kūpa clans, are now "covered up." Of the temewhanitcem clan Juan Angel is the only nuut remembered. This clan is now extinct, and as far back as informants can remember no more than three male members were alive. When Juan Angel died the few survivors of his clan went under the leadership of Pīū pumtumatūlnikic. When Pīū was too young, and Hilario was too old to give ceremonies, the pumtumatūlnikic clan went for a brief time under the leadership of the temewhanitcem nuut. Evidently these two clans were closely united.

Of the three wildcat lineages, Leonardo sivimūat was the earliest nuut remembered. He was succeeded by his son Francisco sivimūat. During this period the auliñawitcem lineage, as well as the taka'atim lineage, were under sivimūatim leadership. On the death of Francisco

---

[447] Reference to genealogies 14–19 will show the relationship of all these clan leaders.

sivimūat, Leonardo auliñawic became nuut, but the exact reason for
this shift of leadership from one lineage to the other is not remembered by informants.   He was succeeded by his son, Jose Juan
auliñawic, who in 1925 lived in Pala.   The taka'atim lineage, within
the memory of all informants, has never had any nuut, but has been
under the ceremonial control of either the sivimūatim or the
auliñawitcem lineages.

The sauīvilem clan, Cupeño informants say, may have had its own
leaders at Los Coyotes canyon, but at kūpa was always under the
control of the kavalim nuut.   We have previously discussed the situation at wilakal, Los Coyotes canyon.   Most of the tcūtnikut clan
members living in kūpa were under the pumtumatūlniktcum nuut,
but when Matias tcūtnikut died the pumtumatūlniktcum nuut, then
Jose Blacktooth, gave no mourning ceremony for him, so his disgruntled relatives transferred their allegiance to Jose Juan auliñawic,
nuut of the wildcat clan.   This recent happening illustrates particularly well the very loose bonds of the affiliated clan or ''party'' organization based entirely on ceremonial grounds, not on kinship as was
the case in former southern Californian organization.   Such tūcvikinvatim clan members as lived at kūpa retained their ceremonial
attachment to their own clan at wilakal.

From the foregoing account it can be seen that no exact rule of
descent in regard to clan leadership prevailed.   In each of the coyote
clans it tended to pass from generation to generation in the male line
of each clan lineage, while in the three lineages of the wildcat clan
it passed from one lineage to another, but so far as present data are
concerned always excluded the third lineage.

The Kutvōvoc

The clan leader's ceremonial assistant was called kutvōvoc; similarly the ceremonial assistant of the southern Mountain Cahuilla was
called kutvavanavac.[448]   This office was hereditary, passing in the
lineage as did the clan leadership.   In most ceremonies the kutvōvoc
of another clan was employed: if kavalim gave a ceremony the
sivimūatim kutvōvoc would preside, but when any other clan gave a
ceremony the kavalim kutvōvoc was employed.   This reciprocity will
be more fully discussed as each ceremony is considered.   The kutvōvoc

---

[448] Similar to the term kutcut (clan chief) of the northern Diegueño. Gifford,
present series, 18:173, 1918.

must be a man of commanding presence, with a loud clear voice for announcing events and for singing. He was usually believed to have supernatural powers and the fear thus inspired helped him in keeping order. The kavalim and pumtumatūlniktcum clans each had a kutvōvoc, but as far back as informants remember the temewhanitcem clan did not. All the clans of the wildcat moiety had only one kutvōvoc, usually in the sivimūatim clan. It was possible for the clan leader to be both nuut and kutvōvoc. This was the case in the kavalim clan when Roman kaval held both offices.

The Paha

Beside the kutvōvoc, the Cupeño employed the paha in the manet ceremony. This ceremony the Cupeño say was given to the kavalim clan by the Luiseño at Puerta Cruz. At first only this clan had a paha and performed the manet ceremony, but later it was shared with the pumtumatūlniktcum clan, and about sixty years ago on the death of a kavalim paha the ceremony was given to the sivimūatim clan as well. The paha symbolized, among the Cupeño as among the Luiseño, the red racer snake, and was painted half red, half black to represent the supposed sex colors of this reptile. The term paha means red racer. As the clans generally united for the manet dance, there were usually three pahas employed at the ceremony, each clan or clan group providing one. This officer was originally appointed by the nuut, and often a shaman whom the people feared was given the position. If a relative of the incumbent showed ability in this line he might succeed to office, but there seems to have been no regular rule of descent.

There were other persons who had special duties in ceremonies or led in certain songs, but they were not given titles and may best be discussed in relation to the particular ceremonies.

Shamans and Shamanism

Formerly there were many shamans at kūpa. One man of the temewhanitcem clan (name not remembered) was able to change himself into a bear and in such guise killed many calves. He likewise transformed himself at certain ceremonies in order to frighten the people. All shamans were called pūlum. Individual dreams or physical peculiarities usually led a person to become a shaman, and all those that are remembered seem to have been men. They cured afflicted persons by sucking out the disease. This disease was often exhibited by the shaman as a red snake (species?). Toothache was believed to be caused by a worm in the tooth which the shaman sucked out. Other worms which caused the lungs to dry up were supposed to cause tuberculosis. A shaman was believed to have unusual powers to hear and to understand all sorts of natural phenomena, and each had special "powers" in him which he could throw into an enemy. Unless the shaman withdrew this "power" the enemy would die. Even today the Cupeño are very careful not to allow any of their hair to remain where a malevolent shaman might secure it and do them harm. It was considered especially dangerous to find a stray hair in the basket in which a newly born child was washed. Certain shamans were supposed to be able to induce a good crop of acorns or to blight the crop. Such power was purely individual, and while the shaman undoubtedly had much influence in the society to which he belonged, he was never a formal official as such. Shamanism and religion in general merit a great deal more study in southern California, and in the outlying districts many data are still obtainable.

RITUAL AND CEREMONY

The Calendar

The summer and winter solstices were determined by two or three old men who carefully observed the rising and setting of the sun. They "screamed out" when the longest and shortest day of the year arrived. Their position in the social scheme does not seem to have been official, but was regarded as necessary by all the people to indicate the time for gathering certain foods and giving certain ceremonies. The exact calendrical time for most of the ceremonies is not remembered by informants. The calendar was created by Mūkat. The eight pairs of periods are obviously not moon months. The ending -mal on the first of several name pairs may denote "present" or "little"; -yil on the second name in several pairs may mean "past."

1. tovakmal. Acorns, getting black
   tovakic.
2. tasmoimal. Everything coming up, greens ready to eat.
   tasmoiyil.
3. taupakmail. "Summer." Everything ripening, plenty to eat.
   taupakic.
4. tausumbakmaiyil. Ripening of grass seeds.
   tausumlaxic.

5. pakumoimal. Wild cherries ripe and gathered.
   pakmoiyil.

6. nimoimal. Acorns ready to pick (December, the month when the eagle
      is supposed to die).
   nimoiyil.

7. novanomal. ''kwinil'' acorns gathered.
   novanwut.

8. soimaimol. Finishing month (month in which the Luiseño Wīyot died).
   somēyil.

Naming Ceremonies and the Singing of Enemy Songs

A special ceremony called pumtaulūninwin, for naming children, might be given by any clan having several children to name. There was no special time for this ceremony. A clan of the opposite moiety was always officially invited to attend this affair, usually one with whom the clan giving the ceremony was much intermarried. All relatives of the children's mothers were likewise invited and usually the other kūpa clans came without any special invitation. The naming took place at night in the privacy of the wāmkic to prevent any of the so-called ''enemy clans'' learning the names for use in their ''enemy'' songs. Children were named by the nuut, or by elderly male relatives, and were usually given the names of dead ancestors in the male line.

Mrs. Griffith's mother, Soledad kaval, was named paumuau matcauhanut; the first word is a place name near Mesa Grande, the second word means ''bowed head.'' Roman kaval was named hūnwut tōvicnikic, ''bear white''; Leonardo sivimūat was named ''pakānic,'' blackbird; and Pīū pumtumatūlnikic was named tauval pūic, ''thunder road-runner. Other male names were aswit tōvicnikic, ''eagle white''; kūpa ñayawit, ''kūpa fast runner''; and kūpa whīwinit, ''kūpa standing.''

At this time the nuut appointed a special man to pierce the ears of the boys with a sharp chamise thorn. Mrs. Griffith's grandfather had such pierced ears, and the informant remembered seeing Cahuilla from Los Coyotes canyon with large holes in their ear lobes and nasal septa, in which were placed sprigs of arrowweed.

At this ceremony ''enemy songs'' were always sung. The kavalim clan sang against the natcūtākiktum and pauatakiktum clans of the Mountain Cahuilla, and the pumtumatūlniktcum clan did the same. The temewhanitcem clan sang against the watic clan (?) of the Diegueño. The sivimūatim and taka'atim clans sang against the melisatim clan of the Luiseño (near the Henshaw dam), and the auliñauitcem clan sang against the takanawhic clan of the Luiseño who also lived near kūpa. Each clan would take turns during the night in singing their songs. These songs were sung at other times but the name-giving ceremony was considered a particularly appropriate time.

Girls' Adolescence Ceremony

This ceremony called aulūninil occurred once a year, usually in November or December. The Cupeño initiated all girls at about the age of nine or ten irrespective of whether they had had their first menses or not. Each of the coyote clans had such a ceremony, but the sivimūatim lineage held one ceremony for all the other wildcat lineages. The wilakal clan members living at kūpa returned to wilakal for their ceremony.

The nuut of the clan performing the ceremony would notify the parents of all girls of the right age, and tell them to prepare food and gifts for the ceremony. When all was ready the nuut would send the kutvōvoc to notify all the other clans. That night all the people assembled in the wāmkic of the clan giving the ceremony. The nuut notified them who the girls were that were to be initiated. Piles of food were assembled in the center of the wāmkic, one for each of the visiting nuuts. The nuut giving the ceremony then gave one pile to each of the visiting leaders who divided it among their clan members.

In the morning the kutvōvoc took more food to all the invited clans. The duration of the ceremony depended on the amount of food to be distributed. Certain clans, especially the pumtumatūlniktcum people, were reputed to be very stingy and to give only short ceremonies. When all the food was distributed the kutvōvoc went to a near-by hill and called all the people to the wāmkic. All the neophytes were put in a near-by house and covered up. The kutvōvoc dug a long pit in the center of the wāmkic and his wife gathered a great amount of soft pungent weeds. A fire was built in the pit and when the earth was hot the fire was raked out and the pit lined with the weeds. Then one at a time the kutvōvoc brought out the girls all covered up and placed them in the pit. Meanwhile his wife had boiled a certain weed called wikwut in water, and gave each girl a cup of this to drink. If a girl from another clan was included in the group she was served first. The girls were covered with the weeds.

Presents were then thrown out on the floor and the kutvōvoc shouted three times, whereupon all the guests scrambled for the presents. All day the girls lay in the pit, while the women of the clan sang special songs over them. Later the women sang the enemy songs of their clan, and often the women of the other clans joined in. In the evening the girls were taken from the pit, it was reheated, and they were returned to it. When the sun went down the singing of enemy songs ceased and all present ate outside the wāmkic. That night the men sang enemy songs and the women danced. In the morning food was again distributed. The ceremony might continue for a week, during all of which time the girls were supposed to remain in the pit. They were fed acorn gruel and given warm water to drink. Often visiting clans brought eagle feather skirts, ūlut, to the clan nuut as presents; these and strings of feathers were hung on the walls of the wāmkic during the ceremony.

At the end of the prescribed period the girls were taken to the house of the kutvōvoc, and while here were given gruel and warm water; meat and salt were especially forbidden. Usually after a week they returned to the wāmkic and food was once more passed out to all the guests who had again been summoned. The women sang during the day and the men at night.

Then the kutvōvoc and his assistants arranged the ground-painting, terehaīut, in the center of the wāmkic. This was made of white clean sand, black charcoal dust, yellow seeds, black seeds, and red powdered iron oxide (from certain springs). The red color represented blood. The painting was in the shape of a circle, usually about twelve feet in diameter. In the center were three holes, the center one representing the heart of the universe. On each side of these were the figures of Mūkat and Tumaīyowit; each had a ''walking stick,'' tcaīlakpic, and a pipe, itcit. Around them were figures representing their people.

The kutvōvoc brought in each girl. He took her around the painting, explaining all the symbols to her and especially warning her that she must obey all the rules she had just learned during all future menstrual periods. As each girl was brought in her parents scattered presents for the guests.

The kutvōvoc told the girl that some of these symbols would protect her, others would kill her if she did not obey all the rules.[449] He put a small piece of dried meat into her mouth and she pretended to

---

[449] This strongly suggests the Chungichnish cult, but the actual name of Chungichnish seems to have been applied directly to the raven, and so far as can be learned today did not mean a definite deity or cult.

spit one piece into each of the three holes. The kutvōvoc grunted three times, and she spat the meat into the center hole. If the saliva landed without getting stringy it was a good sign, but if not it showed that the girl had already broken one of the rules. Each of the girls went through this performance.

The kutvōvoc then put them in a row in the center of the dance house. He brought in a fine basket called wakpic, and a fiber brush with which he brushed all the leaves from the girls' hair into the basket. Then wreaths of the same punget weed were put on their heads, bracelets of a weed called wic were put on their wrists and ankles, and a woven reed belt was put around the waist of each. The kutvōvoc then filled a hollow arrow-weed tube with the leaves he brushed from the girls' hair, and followed by the girls he went to a certain warm spring where one palm tree grew. He buried the arrow-weed tube in the mud here, and took the wreaths and ornaments from their waists and ankles to another place where he deposited them. Special wreaths of human hair were put on their heads, and similar ornaments on their wrists. All the people gathered together and the boys of the village raced over a course of about half a mile. They were followed by the younger women, and then the newly initiated girls raced over the same course. The course ended at some rocks and here the girls painted rectilinear designs with red iron oxide. This ended the main ceremony.

The girls' mothers took them home, and each morning for one or two months they bathed their daughters very carefully in the warm springs. Each girl continued to fast over this period and had a special stick to scratch herself with. Her face was painted black and red, in spots if she belonged to a wildcat clan and in stripes if she belonged to a coyote clan. Different designs were put on each day with black on a red background. These designs were put on with a sharp stick dipped in grease and paint. There was a design for each day, and when a girl had used up all the designs her period of probation was over. It was essential that the designs be kept fresh and not mussed up. After all the designs had been used the girl was allowed to eat meat and salt again, except during her menstrual periods.

The Feather or Whirling Dance

This ceremony, called pukuvyahil, was given to the temewhanitcem clan by Luiseño from nulūlva (about six miles northwest of Puerta Cruz) and was given by that clan to the other Cupeño groups. It might be performed at any time of the year and included boys and girls of all clans ranging from sixteen to twenty years of age. The pahas of the various clans took the initiates to a secluded place away from the village and taught them to sing and dance. All the songs were in the Luiseño language. The kutvōvoc stayed in the dance house and prepared the food for the ceremony. One boy or girl sang and danced at a time, and eagle-feather skirts were worn in a whirling dance. When they had learned the songs and dances the paha brought them back to the wāmkic, and all the people assembled outside. The kutvōvoc shouted the name of the boy or girl who was to dance, and then one of the two pahas shouted "hou-ou-ou!" and kicked on the wall three times; the paha outside answered in kind, and the first paha rushed out of the house and fell prone in the center of the dance enclosure. Both pahas then whirled bullroarers, aïil, and the dancer wearing ūlut, the eagle-feather skirt, and pachīa, a headdress of eagle down with horned owl and eagle feathers erect in it, circled the dance enclosure three times. The boys and girls were painted, and when dancing carried a red stick about a foot long in one hand and a black stick in the other. They dashed these together when they wanted the singing faster. Outside the circle were the bulk of the guests, all slowly dancing clockwise; inside the circle were the singers, and before them were the two red and black painted pahas, swinging bull roarers. In front of these and inside the circle of dancers each boy and girl danced, one at a time, whirling and squatting until exhausted. When the dancers crowded in, one of the pahas with a long pole widened the circle.

Boys and girls of coyote clans had stripes of red and black clay painted all over their bodies and faces, those of the wildcat moiety had spots all over their bodies. The Cupeño say that this is the way the dance came to them from the Luiseño. After all the children had danced and sung their songs, there was a general feast. As might occur at the end of any ceremony, they often danced out the fire at the close of the feast. This was called tēpaset.

The Manet Dance or Boys' Initiation

Originally this dance was given the kavalim clan by Luiseño from Pichanga. Some of the songs in the Pichanga dialect the Cupeño understand, but other songs in the San Gabriel language they do not understand. Formerly the kavalim clan initiated all the Cupeño boys but later the ceremony was performed by the other clans as well. It was called manet pannil, "the drinking," and might occur at any time. If a raven, kawialwut, or a crow, alwit, was heard cawing near the village the man who heard it took a basket full of food to his nuut, and a manet dance was held for three nights. The raven was also called tcingitcnic and was believed to bewitch people, hence the manet dance, which was very sacred, was held to prevent him from doing evil.[449a]

Youths ranging from ten to eighteen years of age were given jimsonweed or manet. The Cupeño called the jimsonweed in their own language nakta-muluuc. The nuut gathered all the boys who were to be initiated and sent them away from the village with two pahas to watch them. The jimsonweed was prepared in secrecy by the clan paha, the roots being pounded in a special mortar, tamyaic, and soaked in water. The nuut administered a cup of this decoction to each of the boys and then after painting their faces they were brought into the wāmkic. No one but men might be present when the drink was administered. When the boys were all in the wāmkic they danced in a circle around the fire until they became unconscious from the combined effects of heat and drug. A large fire was kept blazing by the kutvōvoc. In the morning they were all sent out of the village again. Girls of about the same age were likewise sent away from the village at this time under the guardianship of an old woman who taught them various songs. Both girls and boys were painted as in the feather dance and were not allowed to eat salt. Sons of clan leaders wore eagle down, pīwic, in their hair.

When the boys had learned all their clan songs, the kavalim clan giving the ceremony, and all the invited clans, assembled in the kavalim wāmkic. All the various nuuts sat together, as did the members of the clan giving the ceremony, while the others were more or less mixed. Informants denied that people of the two moieties sat or danced on different sides of the dance house.[450] They said that this was only done "in play" and never in a serious ceremony like manet. It is only possible to conjecture whether this joking moiety division of dancers is a survival of a once seriously observed custom or not. Certainly in Cupeño society as we know it, it seems to have had no importance. A sand-painting, identical in all details with the one described for the girls' puberty ceremony, was made, and the symbolism of the painting was explained to each boy by the kutvōvoc.

[449a] Sparkman, present series, 8:218, 1908, states that the Luiseño also called the raven by this name.

[450] See Gifford's statement, present series, 14:197, 1918.

At this time the rules which he must observe as a man were given him, and he was shown certain of Mūkat's creatures which would punish him if he did not obey them.[451]

When the ground painting was made, a rectangular pit about 5 by 3 feet and 3 to 4 feet deep was dug. A design of a crude human figure with arms extended was made of twine in the bottom of this pit. This figure was called the wānawut; and three flat stones were placed in the pit, one below the feet, one in the center, and one above the head of the wānawut. When the kutvōvoc had explained the ground painting to the boy he led him to the wānawut pit and explained its symbolism. This symbolism does not seem to be very clearly remembered at the present time, but informants agreed that the pit represented the boy's passage through life and the figure death. When the kutvōvoc completed his lecture the boy spat into the center of the figure. Then kutvōvoc shouted "So and so's son is coming," and called "ha-a!" three times. The boy jumped onto the first stone in the pit, then to the second and squatted a moment, then to the third, and then jumped out of the pit. Should be falter and step on the wānawut it indicated that he would die young. When a boy completed this ordeal successfully all the people shouted and sang. This rite was performed by the older boys from fourteen to sixteen years of age. It was called tcīawinwa wānawut, "jumping over the wānawut."

This dancing and singing at night were repeated at the wāmkic of the pumtumatūlniktcum and sivimūatim clans. There were three nights of dancing at each. Each day of the dance the parents of every boy being initiated carried a winnowing basket, levatimal, full of acorns to the kavalim nuut. The kavalim nuut, or whichever nuut was giving the ceremony after the kavalim clan relinquished their exclusive claim to it, gave food to the kutvōvoc who distributed it to all the other clan leaders. Each afternoon at about four o'clock, the clan giving the ceremony provided a feast for all the other clans. It was essential that their nuut be personally present to see that all the guests received a sufficiency of food, for if he stayed away the guests would be disgruntled. On the last afternoon of the ceremony the kutvōvoc brushed the hair of each boy who had drunk the jimsonweed, and put the brushings into an arrow-weed tube. As in the girls' puberty ceremony this tube was buried in the mud at a certain spring.

---

[451] No clear exposition of these rules was remembered, but they probably differed only in detail from the Luiseño advice given the boys in the same ceremony. See Sparkman, present series, 8:221–224, 1908.

Then the boys all ran a footrace and the winners were regarded as especially promising young men. On the last evening the presiding nuut thanked his clan members for going hungry that he might give the ceremony, and the kutvōvoc gave a short speech which ended the occasion.

The Ceremonial Eagle Killing

There appears to have been one golden eagle's nest in kūpa territory on Hot Springs mountain at a place called aswit petia, eagle's nest. This site was owned by the kavalim clan and the eagles were likewise its property. In the spring men were sent to watch the eagles, and when the young birds were hatched and the natal down was being replaced by the juvenile plumage the watchers reported the event to the kavalim nuut. The nuut then invited the pumtumatūlniktcum and the temewhanitcem clans to aid him in securing the young bird. A large party proceeded to the cliffs above the nest and a man was lowered on a rope to get one and sometimes two young birds, which he brought up in a carrying net. As the returning party neared the village signal fires were made to warn the villagers of their approach. The eaglet was formally given to the kavalim nuut at the wāmkic, and immediately all the kaval people began to throw out gifts. At this time should any other person desire any possession of a kavalim person he could take it and the owner was not supposed to object. Certain presents were given the invited kutvōvoc, and these he distributed to the guests in honor of the eagle. Races were held and the fastest runner carried the young bird. A cage about five feet high was made of willow branches and here, next to the kavalim wāmkic, the eagle was kept. The kavalim nuut told the kutvōvoc that he wished ''to feed the eagle,'' and the latter organized a rabbit hunt in which all men in the invited clans participated. Two days and nights of dancing and singing followed and each night the kutvōvoc fed all but the kavalim clan, who were the hosts. Then for some time the young eagle was carefully fed until he had assumed almost full adult plumage. During this time there were no special ceremonies but there was much feasting and social activity.

When the eagle was almost grown the kavalim nuut would assemble his clan and tell them that he wished to kill the eagle in memory of the kavalim dead. They usually agreed to this and much food and gifts of all sorts were prepared. All the other clans were invited to the kavalim wāmkic for a certain night. When they had assembled the kutvōvoc placed a pile of food and gifts before each invited nuut, and the kutvōvoc of each clan divided the gifts between the families. The young eagle was wrapped in masvut, the ceremonial matting, and brought from the interior of the wāmkic while all present sang or cried loudly. A kavalim man carried the eagle dancing around the fire in the wāmkic. Other kavalim people followed him, all wailing. They all wore extra clothes which the guests were allowed to take from them as they danced. All through the evening the dance continued at intervals. Between times the various clans sang their enemy songs. Then the dance with the eagle continued to the accompaniment of special "eagle-killing" songs. These songs tell how aswit, the eagle, is grieving and crying for the people. All the people whose relatives had died within the year weep and wail, throwing away many presents. Before dawn a man with strong wrists takes the bird and by compressing its lungs kills it. The various shamans however are supposed to have killed it by their magical powers, the one who was performing his incantations at the time it died being considered the most powerful. Then the mourning of all was redoubled, a special song translated "the eagle is ended, all is over" being sung. The body is given to the nuut who removes most of the skin, the tail and wing feathers as well as the down being very valuable. The next morning the body wrapped in masvut was buried in the wāmkic.

The eagle was thus sacrificed in memory of the dead, and because it was the most sacred and valuable of birds the respect paid the deceased was all the greater. Cupeño informants did not believe that the eagle carried messages to the dead as did the Luiseño, though this may have been an earlier belief.

The "Nuut's Road" and Its Implications

If none of the kavalim clan had died during the year, the young eagle might be taken but was not killed by them. The nuut would assemble the clan in the wāmkic and they would decide which clan should be given the eagle. It was given to a clan, usually of the opposite moiety, in which several deaths had occurred during the year. The kavalim clan usually gave such presents to one of the three kūpa wildcat lineages, but it might be given to neighboring wilakal, Cahuilla, Luiseño, or Diegueño clans.

There appears to have been a regular exchange of gifts whenever a death occurred, between all these groups. This was called sūlakil, the nuut's road. But the gift of the eagle was an addition to this system. When it was decided which clan was to receive the eagle, food and gifts to accompany the bird were gathered, and led by the kutvōvoc the bearers of the present proceeded to the wāmkic of the recipient clan. Here they were met by the kutvōvoc of this clan, who had already been notified, and who gave a present of food, basketry, and sometimes shell money in return. The donors returned home the next day after a feast. This second clan then issued invitations to all others and proceeded to have the eagle-killing ceremony. If they did not wish to give such a ceremony they might give the eagle to another clan. In the same way neighboring clans sometimes brought an eagle to the kūpa clans.

The true sūlakil or "nuut's road" was evidently the southern equivalent of the elaborate shell money exchange in the north which has already been discussed. Whenever a death occurred in any of these southern clans, irrespective of their linguistic affiliation, the neighboring clans, especially if they had intermarried with the clan in question, sent a present of numhut, "treasure." This gift took the form of kenhut, shell money; ūltum, eagle-feather skirts; various ceremonial objects; and sometimes masvut, the ceremonial matting. There was a regular system for such exchange, but its details have been forgotten. A length of three and a half feet of shell money was always included. Informants agreed that this shell money, kenhut, was received long ago from the San Gabriel people, whom the Cupeño called temankammalyem. The recipient of such a gift did not return it at the time, but at his clan's annual mourning ceremony about a year later invited all the clans who had sent gifts, and returned the exact amount of shell money with the addition of food and other presents.

The presence of this ceremonial gift exchange among these southern clans, as well as among those in the vicinity of San Gorgonio pass, makes it seem almost certain that in aboriginal times the western half of southern California was practically one ceremonial unit. It particularly emphasizes the lack of cohesion between the linguistic groups, or as they have erroneously been called "tribes," as compared to the bonds of unity established by intermarriage and common ceremonial activities. Obviously the clan in its larger sense, ranging from the small single lineage to that composed of several ceremonially united lineages, was the political unit in the area. Between these units, each of which probably represented a village, there was a network of economic and ceremonial connections, only the faintest records of which may be obtained today.

First Ceremony for the Dead

When a member of any clan died a ceremony called pisatūil was held the night following the death. The nuut of the clan that had suffered the loss had his kutvōvoc gather food from all clan members, and then notify the leaders of the other clans in the village. That night all the invited clans assembled before the wāmkic bringing presents. All that day the members of the mourning clan brought food contributions to the wāmkic, and when all the guests were assembled, the nuut, accompanied by three men, went inside and brought out the gifts which they piled before the fire. If the loss had been in the kavalim clan the pumtumatūlniktcum and temewhanitcem clans were notified first, and the kutvōvoc of the former of these two clans announced to the others those for whom the kavalim people were mourning. The presents were distributed and the kavalim clan sang their songs for the first part of the night, then the other clans sang one after another for the remainder of the night.

In the morning food was distributed to the guests, after which the kūtvōvoc organized a rabbit hunt in which all the men participated. When they returned a big fire was blazing and the rabbits were prepared by the kutvōvoc and his assistants. Women of the clan prepared more food and another feast was served in the wāmkic. All participated in this save members of the clan giving the ceremony. After this feast the nuut of the mourning clan thanked all the people for coming and "suffering in the cold night" for his sake. The kutvōvoc answered him, and the guests departed. Formerly the body of the deceased was burned immediately; at the present time it is buried within a few days.

In the foregoing account the feasting seems to play such a prominent part that the, thanks of the clan leader to his guests at the end of the ceremony seem uncalled for. It must be remembered however that the main part of the ceremony lies in the night-long singing. One who has sat up all night at such a ceremony in winter, enlivened only by the mournful chanting and the weeping of the women, will understand it better. There is little of the proverbial "Irish wake" about the ceremony, yet the older Indians seem to enjoy it. It is however more the joy of a chronic church-goer than that of a reveler.

Second Ceremony for the Dead—Burning the Possessions

If the clan of the deceased is well provided with food, this second ceremony called sūuchumnil, "burning the possessions," might follow the first within a few days. This however rarely happened, for two such ceremonies at once would be apt to make any clan destitute. Usually a few days after pisatūil the clan leader called all the members to the dance house. At this time he took down his masvut bundle, and divided the numhut it contained into piles, one for each of the various clan leaders that were to be invited. The family of the dead assembled the clothing, baskets, and other possessions of the deceased that were to be placed on the fire, while the other clan members agreed to gather food for the ceremony. Some time after this when the requisite supplies had been gathered, the nuut told all the clan the exact day for the burning.

The kavalim nuut, if it was one of his members that had died, notified the sivimūatim kutvōvoc who presided at the ceremony. According to informants the calling in of another clan was usually based on marital relations with that clan; hence if the moiety rule was observed, as it was at kūpa, moiety reciprocity would have resulted automatically. However when the pumtumatūlniktcum clan asked the kavalim kutvōvoc to preside there was no such reason involved. Throughout many of the Cupeño ceremonies the exact nature of the reciprocity is not altogether clear, but the question must be left in abeyance so far as the present data are concerned. If more details of the daily economic life of the people were obtainable the reciprocal relationships between the groups might seem much more logical than they do at present.

The invited kutvōvoc summoned all the other invited clans to the ceremony. All the members of the host clan with their various bundles assembled with the guests in the wāmkic. The nuut of the host clan then went to the nuut of the reciprocal clan and whispered to him for some time, after which the latter arose and announced the family names of the dead for whom the ceremony was given. All the numhut, which was divided up and placed in piles on the masvut matting, was then distributed to the invited clan leaders. This numhut included baskets, eagle-feather skirts, and ceremonial wands called pavīut which were cross-shaped, colored red, and decorated with shells on one side. This material was carefully put aside by the recipients.

Food was then distributed in a similar manner, and cared for by the kutvōvoc of each clan. The masvut matting was left on the floor and the bundles which were to be burned were placed on it.

Hosts and guests sat in a circle around the fire and commenced the songs for the dead. At this time more gifts were thrown around the wāmkic. One man, called toūvac, then sang a song which informants say is very long and very old. It told the soul to go fast, to go swiftly, to go down, down. Then to go up, to go east, to go way down into the darkness, and at last to come up into the clear place to happiness. Another man sang a long song, slowly and sadly. The songs are about death and darkness; then they describe the many kinds of wood used in burning the body. Each singer accompanied his song with a tortoise-shell rattle called aīil, and a few people danced slowly as he sang. Finally late that night all the songs were finished. All rose and the bundles were put in a large basket. The invited kutvōvoc took this and danced clockwise around the fire three times, then he threw it on the fire. All present wailed loudly at this time and threw many possessions into the fire.

The remainder of the night was spent in singing "enemy songs," for all the enemy clans were believed to be rejoicing that deaths had occurred at kūpa. This rejoicing had to be warded off by singing or it would harm the people. Each clan took turns singing against their particular enemies. In the morning all dispersed.

Final Ceremony for the Dead—Burning the Images

About a year after a death, or sometimes later in order to include other persons who had died, the nuut had his kutvōvoc summon all the clan to the wāmkic. In silence he unrolled the masvut bundle and spread out the numhut it contained. Then he told the people when nañaukalan, "the image-burning," was to occur. All that night clan songs were sung, and in the morning the people dispersed to prepare for the coming ceremony with its accompanying feasts and giving of gifts. When all was prepared the proper clan was notified (kavalim, if the wildcat clan gave the ceremony, and vice versa), and their kutvōvoc invited all the other clans.

For three days all feasted and sang. Each morning there was a communal rabbit hunt, while in the afternoons the women sang and at night the men continued the songs. Later in the week materials for the images were gathered by the kutvōvoc of the reciprocating clan. He made all the bodies of the images out of masvut given him by his nuut. Meanwhile his wife prepared faces of buckskin and wigs of human hair. This took place in the mornings while the men were away on their rabbit hunt. The hair used for the images was obtained from the women of the mourning clan, who either cut it between two stones or burned it off. The faces of such women were also blackened with charcoal. The faces of the images were stuffed with a reed called sīic. White shell beads were used for the teeth and the face was marked out with charcoal. These and all other parts of the images were then rolled in the masvut and tied up.

Early on the last morning of the ceremony (which usually lasted a week) all assembled in the wāmkic. The nuut unrolled his masvut in the center, and all prayed and blew smoke over it. In such ceremonies wild tobacco, called pīvut, was employed. Ceremonial smoking accompanied all serious ceremonies as among the Cahuilla. Then the numhut, which had been previously divided, was given to the various clan leaders. Many songs were sung, most of them identical with those sung during the sūuchumnil ceremony. Late in the afternoon the presiding (invited) kutvōvoc brought in the bundle containing the image material and laid it on the masvut matting which remained spread in the center of the wāmkic. Special songs were sung at this time relating to making the images, and the host clan members threw out gifts for the guests to gather up. This part of the ceremony was called nañawil, "the image-making."

When all the songs were concluded the presiding kutvōvoc picked out four persons, usually men and their wives, to make each image. As a rule these persons were relatives of the deceased whose image they made. Then the kutvōvoc shouted three times and all the persons who were to assemble the images screamed out the enemy names of their clan. The kutvōvoc took a sharp knife and cut open the bundle of masvut containing the material for the images. At this point all the people in the wāmkic shouted "wu-u-u-k" (cut it). This bundle represented the bodies of their enemies.

All the assembled people assisted in making the images. They were roughly made to represent the characteristics of the deceased persons they symbolized. The images of children were made of a similar size, those of renowned clan leaders were decorated with feather skirts and hung with strings of shell money. Men were always indicated by having bows and arrows as well as carrying nets on their backs; women were decorated with rabbit-skin cloaks and valuable baskets. An apron of matting, beads, and a small basket on the head likewise indicated a female. At present, modern clothes and ornaments are put on the images, but formerly the images were painted and dressed in native costume.

The leader of the first group to finish its image shouted for a tortoise-shell rattle (aīil) and followed by all the relatives of the deceased went out and danced around the wāmkic with the image. The others followed and many presents were thrown for the guests to gather up at this time. As they danced with the images they sang one song, constantly repeated:

> "To the north turn it! To the north turn it!⁴⁵² Coyote (īsil) and Wolf (iswit) made it of masvut and hair!"

Chanting this song they danced around the wāmkic, throwing away presents. If the clan was prosperous they went twice, but if they were poor they only circled the wāmkic once. Then they took the images to where the kutvōvoc with a hand drill had kindled a fire of fast-burning brush, and thrust the images into the flames. More presents were thrown over the crowd and the dance continued around the fire. When all the images had been consumed, all gathered close around the fire, the members of the host clan on the inside. Six times they shouted "Bury them!"; then all grunted three times and blew toward the sky. The ashes of the fire were covered with soil and all stood up. The host nuut gave presents to the invited kutvōvoc for his work, and the ceremony was over.

The invited clans returned to their homes, rich with the gifts of the mourners, while the host clan stripped of all its wealth set about the slow task of replenishing its food and ceremonial supplies.

MYTHOLOGY

Cupeño Creation Myth⁴⁵³

"The gods Tumaiyowit and Mūkat created the world and all that is in it. They quarreled and argued as to their respective ages. They disagreed on many things. Tumaiyowit wished people to die. Mūkat did not. Tumaiyowit

---

452 The Cupeño say that the head of a dead person should always face the north. The Luiseño likewise connect masvut and hair in their religious symbolism, see Kroeber, Two Myths of the Mission Indians of California, Jour. Am. Folklore, 19:320, 1906.

453 Gifford, present series, 14:199, 1918, gives an outline of this myth. My informants, Mrs. Manuela Griffith and Mrs. Salvadora Valenzuela, had read this account and objected that it was incomplete. At my request they filled in the gaps, and in the present version I have given Gifford's account marked by quotation marks, with the informants' new material in parentheses.

went down to another world under this world taking his belongings with him (taking with him the children who live under the water). People die because Tumaiyowit died.''

"Mūkat, who remained on earth,'' (told all his children to dance. Rattlesnake was his handsomest son, but all the people teased him. Mūkat became angry, and he gave rattlesnake poison, telling him to bite the most handsome people. He bit ūil, ''cedar tree,'' a very handsome man, and he died. Then Mūkat called the people together and told them how to make bows and arrows without points. But secretly Mūkat put points on the arrows. He told the people to play with their bows and arrows, and pauhit, ''willow tree,'' was killed. The moon was a beautiful young girl who used to paint her brothers every day, but Mūkat made love to her. Her brothers became very angry and the moon was embarrassed and disappeared).

(In the night the spirits of the dead came to visit their fellows, but they missed the moon. They refused to go away, and all the people were afraid but could not get rid of them. Then munkawit, ''a small fly,'' dug a hole, and the people put the bodies of the dead in it and tramped down the earth. Thus the dead could go down to tūlmakic and never return. One day coyote saw the moon's reflection in the water. He screamed, ''Here is our sister who went away from us.'' But the moon was too high to be reached.)

(Mūkat thus) ''finally fell under the ill-will of mankind, because he caused quarreling and fighting. Every evening he put the people to sleep by blowing tobacco smoke from his pipe. When they were fast asleep, he arose stealthily, stepped over them, and went to the ocean to defecate. Each time he heard his excrement strike the ocean floor and he knew that all was well. Three times he would hear the sound. Then he returned. When the people awoke they found him in his place. They tried every possible means to discover when and where the god[454] attended to his natural functions, but to no avail.''

''Finally a very slim lizard hid on the god's cane. The god did not see it. The lizard discovered where the god went and what he did and reported to the people. Then they set the frog to bewitch the god. The frog hid in the ocean, and, as the god defecated, swallowed his excrement. The god, not hearing the usual sound, knew that something was wrong. He poked downward with his cane, which rubbed along the back of of the frog making the marks which we see there today. The god (the creator) Mūkat became ill and died.'' (He lay on his bed, which creaked. When the creator spat, īsil, ''coyote,'' swallowed the saliva. This made Mūkat weaker and weaker. All his children refused to help him although they pretended to. The water snake rolled over him, but it did the creator no good.) ''When ill, he told the people, 'If I die today or tomorrow, burn me. Do not let coyote come near me, for he will do an evil deed'.'' (''Send him to the end of the world to get fire.'' At midnight the creator, Mūkat, died.)

''Upon the death of the god his body was burned. The people sent coyote to fetch wood (fire) for the funeral pyre, for they feared that he might eat the body of the god. Coyote departed. He was away nearly a day. As soon as he left, they started to burn the body. The fire drill and hearth with which the pyre was ignited, were two men. The body of the god was burning when coyote reached the end of the world. He saw the smoke and hurried back. When he arrived at home all of the body had burned except the heart,

---

[454] Creator is more nearly correct.

which the people kept turning to make it burn. When coyote arrived the people were standing close together about the pyre. (Those, like acorn, who were closest to the fire became covered with oil. Coyote) "He said, 'Brother and sisters, let me see this. He is my god (father).' They only stood the closer together, but coyote jumped over them and seized the heart. He ran north, where he ate it. Where the blood dripped there is gold. The people pursued in vain. Coyote looked back as he ran with the heart in his mouth. That is why a coyote when running away always looks back to this day."

"The people who stood around the pyre became trees, some tall, others short. It was over the short people that coyote had jumped. The people pursued coyote northward. Across the mountains in that direction the trees stretch today. They are the people who pursued coyote. Some have been knocked down, just as coyote knocked down the people."

The Decimation and Revival Legend of the Kūpa People[455]

In the beginning there were many people at kūpa. One day they were having the pumtaulūminwin (child's naming and ear-piercing ceremony) for the son of the chief. All were in a cave inside of a big mound when the kitcamkotcam (southerners or Diegueño) attacked them and burned up the mound. Only the wife of the chief and his child, a boy, escaped because the attackers called to her to come out. All the other people were killed and all the houses at kūpa were burnt. This happened at kic-hū-kic (house-short grass-house).[456] The attackers wanted to kill the child but she disguised it as a girl so they let her keep it. Then they tried to persuade her to come with them but she told them she would follow them the next morning and so they departed without her.

Early the next morning she went north toward ūīkut (Saboba) where her relatives lived. These [relatives] were two men, hūvutyet and pa'ul, who had families at Saboba. Soon their children shouted: "There is a woman coming from the south," and the men inside the house said, "It may be our nephew kisil-pīwic (hawk-white down)." The children were sent to fetch her as both men wanted her to live at their house, but she went to hūvutyet's house. They asked her why she had come to them and she answered, "They killed them all." Then they asked if there was no one closer to go to, and she said there was not. All mourned a great while for her relatives and all did many things for her. But she was not satisfied and each day went off by herself to gather seeds.

When the child became older and stronger she carried him on her back in a cradle. Sometimes she left him, leaning the cradle against a tree, and when she returned she would find dead rabbits and wood rats hung on the child's breast. She was very angry, and threw these away, thinking some one was making fun of her. She told this to hūvutyet and he said, "Do not throw away; bring them to me to eat. Then the child will not cry, for he kills them for me."

[455] A somewhat different and less complete version of this myth is given by Gifford, present series, 14:199–201, 1918. In his later notes at Pala he mentions the differences between the two stories. The present version was given in Cupeño by Mrs. Manuela Griffith, and translated by her daughter, Mrs. Salvadora Valenzuela, at Pala in 1925.

[456] This site was a few rods northwest of the Warner's Hot Springs Hotel, where informants say there is black charred earth even today.

The boy grew rapidly, and when very young went hunting with the men and always killed more game than **they** did. When at the time of the new moon they had races he always won. Likewise when they played pumkaupīwin (shinny) he always beat all the others. All the people were becoming jealous of him. His mother observed this and said to him, "Do not go out with these people; you do not belong to them. Your people lived far away but they were all killed." So when the people asked him to hunt, race, or play with them he refused.

Hūvutyet observed that the boy was indifferent to work or play. He asked the mother if she had told the boy who he was. The boy's mother answered, "Yes I told him that these are not his people and that they do not like him. That his home was far away where are his pala tingva (hot springs)." Then the child spoke, "Now I know where I came from, I will go and see my place, my home!" So hūvutyet gave him some numhutim ("treasure" including many strings of shell beads) and a hākut (carrying net) to carry them in. He also gave the boy a long club. Hūvutyet told kisil-pīwic to scatter these beads when he got to kic-hū-kic (house-short grass-house), his home at kūpa. The club (paunapic) was to kill his enemies with, for hūvutyet knew that he must fight. In the carrying net were placed bundles of acorn meal and various seeds for food. Last of all hūvutyet gave him masvut (sacred matting). When all was ready to start the mother sang:

> "Now you are going with your numhut!"
> And kisil-pīwic answered:
> "Nuñ-e Nuñe nu numhut pumūm!
>   Nuñ-e Nuñe nu masvut pumūm!"
> "I am going, I am going, with my numhut—!
>   I am going, I am going, with my masvut—!"

They traveled to the edge of wīatava (Lost valley, near kūpa) and here kisil-pīwic left his mother. He went down into the valley and met many people who looked like southerners. When they saw his long hair they shouted, "Our nephew (tcumūtīma), we fixed him, we bathed him, that is why he is so handsome." Each day he went with them hunting, and always killed the most game, which he gave to them. Then he would return to his mother. She was suspicious and constantly asked him where he had been. He always answered that he had just been up on the mountain from which he could see all over. At last she followed him to tūcvikinvat (Sam Taylor's place, near wilakal), where she saw him with all the people. When he returned to wīatava he brought with him a deer he had killed, and told his mother to eat it. She answered, "Nuuts in the big house, not old women like me, should eat deer meat!" But he insisted, saying, "You must eat it for there is no one else." As kisil-pīwic could not eat the game he had killed himself, she had to eat it.

Kisil-pīwic set out long rows of stone traps to catch wood rats which he brought to his mother. After several days he always found his traps empty and he asked his mother what was robbing them. She said it was probably īsil (coyote), but when he drew a picture of the tracks he found at the traps she told him it was a bear (hūnwut). She told kisil-pīwic to beware for the bear was very dangerous. Instead he hid and waited for the bear, and after a long hard fight killed it with his club. So he told his mother he had killed something with long curved claws, and she said that it must be a bear. "Yes," he answered, "and I am going out to bring it in." He carried the huge animal in on his back and skinned it. He tried to make his mother eat the bear but she refused, saying that only chiefs could eat bear meat. Then he sewed up the skin and blew into it till it was full, and the bear came to life. When his mother saw this she went away to a little hill and looked down the valley. Kisil-pīwic played with the bear as though it were a puppy. He asked his mother if she had seen his bear, and she said she had but that it was very fierce so she had gone away. He told his mother that they were going away, saying, "I am taking my bear for my uncles to see." But before they left, the mother went down to wilakal and told the people there about the bear. When she returned to wīatava her legs were all scratched and kisil-pīwic asked her where she had been. She told him that she had been looking for acorns. "Your feet look as though you had been bathing," said her son, but she denied it, saying that she had washed her feet at sūicpuki (rabbit's home).457 Then they departed with kisil-pīwic leading his bear.

They went north of kūpa to kisil-pūic-pukī (hawk, road-runner home) where there were many stones good for straightening arrows. From here kisil-pīwic looked down on his home.

Soon the southerners found out that he was there and they asked him to go hunting with them, which he did. They said, "We will catch him, we will not get our hands covered with blood." So they asked kisil-pīwic to show them his bear which he kept in his hut. He would only show them the bear's paws and many did not think he had a bear at all. Many people came from the south to help kill him and they surrounded his hut. When kisil-pīwic came out they all shot at him with arrows but he was unhurt. He came out many times, each time differently dressed and acting like a different person. The southerners thought there were many people with him and they decided to attack the next day. Kisil-pīwic then gathered up all the arrows that had been shot at him. The next day when they approached he and his bear met them. The bear killed very many and they all fled, while the mother of kisil-pīwic killed the wounded with his club (paunapic). Two men were caught by kisil-pīwic and these he swung against an oak tree, but he did not kill them. He told them to go tell his aunts that he had killed all the people, and said, "Now I am going back to my place, kūpa." He and his mother scalped all the dead, filling a large carrying net with scalps. While he was carrying these scalps he rested at ūūupūa (where he rested). Farther up the hill he was tired and called this place pahīksava (where he panted); then he went to pūīlima (where they ate), and then to mūkacmū (fleas). Here he took a long robe and fastened all the scalps to it. Last of all he and his mother feasted. Then he went to kic-hū-kic near by and scattered the shell beads. He sang on his father's rock. He was all alone at kūpa; all his enemies were afraid of him.

His mother was grinding acorn meal when from the west she saw two women approaching. She called to her son, telling him that two persons, women not warriors, were coming. The women came to a patch of wild currant and hid there. So kisil-pīwic sent his mother to bring them to kūpa. She found the girls and asked them if they were not afraid. They replied that they were not. Then the mother said, "You have come to carry wood and water for me."

---

457 This site was on Lookout mountain, and belonged to the kavalim clan. A huge white rabbit with black spots, reputed to be four feet high, was supposed to live here. The rabbit and the hot springs at kūpa were reputed to have been brought there by the first kavalim. Many native people, and even some white men, claim to have seen this remarkable rabbit. In each case bad luck followed such a sight.

She took the two sisters, who were from taka'at (base of Smith mountain in Luiseño territory), and brought them to her son. He married both of them.

First the older sister had two sons, then the younger sister had one son. When the sons of the elder sister grew up they married sivimūatim women. These were southerners from tūuhut and tūcvuli (about six miles south of kūpa). The son of the younger sister married an auliñawitcem woman from solūkma (near wilakal). Each of these families also had children.

The oldest son and his wife were very good to kisil-pīwic, but the others were not. This made the old man very angry and he called all his descendants together. Then he said, "This is my eldest son, his name shall be kaval—he will see farther and own more land than all others." Then to the second son he said, "Build your house away at siteñil (place under thorny bushes), and call yourself pumtumatūlnikic (black tooth), for you are stingy and must live there." To the third son he said, "Go to the north and call yourself temewhanitc (northerner)." Thus from the beginning all the kūpa people were close relatives.

After he had sent his other sons away, kisil-pīwic and his oldest son had fiestas to which the other sons were invited. The oldest son had to supply the food, and that is why a kaval is always kutvōvoc and waits on other people at their fiestas.

There was one oak tree with especially big acorns at kūpa (near the present school house), and here kisil-pīwic would dance. Many acorns would fall down for him but for no one else. These he would take to the kavalim women and they would grind them and make acorn meal cakes for him. He would eat these while all his children watched. He would tell them to go in the other direction where the wind had blown down acorns, but he would not give them any of his. The children told their fathers that kisil-pīwic had bewitched the oaks so that they bore acorns only for him. His other sons hid near the tree and when kisil-pīwic danced to make the trees bear, they bewitched him so that the trees would no longer bear for him. Thus he had no food and died. The oldest son made ceremonies for his father and all the other sons and their families came.

VI. THE LUISEÑO

The Luiseño are the most southwesterly of all the Shoshoneans and today their coastal and foothill range is one of the most populous districts in southern California. As it was formerly the center of Spanish mission activity the combined influences have now obliterated all but faint traces of the native culture. Fortunately the Luiseño have received more attention from the ethnologist than the groups previously considered and as a result more is known concerning their former mode of life and their religious beliefs. The culture of the group has been studied most fully by Sparkman, Du Bois, Kroeber, and Gifford,[458] but the details of their social organization have remained somewhat obscure. This is largely inevitable since the long continued alien pressure early disintegrated the social structure of their more westerly villages. However, in the peripheral eastern portions of Luiseño territory certain groups have maintained part of their old organization up until the last generation, and here it is still possible to find a few individuals who remember the native social patterns. The previous consideration of their eastern Shoshonean neighbors, especially of the Cahuilla and the Cupeño, where native life has persisted into the last generation on a larger scale, gives many clues to hitherto obscure or unstressed points in Luiseño organization. It is this new viewpoint, rather than such new data as are here presented, that seems to clear up some of the contradictions existing in regard to the social organization of the groups.

The extent of Luiseño territory is somewhat uncertain but its general contours have been indicated on map 7. The boundaries have been drawn in accord with Sparkman's account,[459] but the clans are more or less arbitrarily assigned to the various sites they have occupied in historic times, and their locations accord with the following Luiseño clan list (table 19). This list is based on that previously given by Gifford[460] but a considerable number of additions and

[458] P. S. Sparkman, Culture of the Luiseño Indians, present series, 8:187–234, 1908. C. G. Du Bois, The Religion of the Luiseño Indians of Southern California, present series, 8:69–186, 1908. A. L. Kroeber, Handbook of the Indians of California, Bur. Am. Ethn., Bull 78, 1925. E. W. Gifford, Clans and Moieties in Southern California, present series, 14:155–219, 1918.

[459] *Op. cit.*, 189.

[460] S. Cal., 203–205.

changes have been made. The sites are probably more nearly correct for the easterly clans which for the greater part have clung to their ancestral homes, but the western clan groupings are in many cases the direct result of mission influence. According to informants there are slight dialectic differences between the speech of the northern Luiseño around Saboba, those in the east around Aguanga, and those of the central and western portion of the territory. The native groups around the mission of San Juan Capistrano had such a distinct dialect that they have been designated in all the more recent literature as the

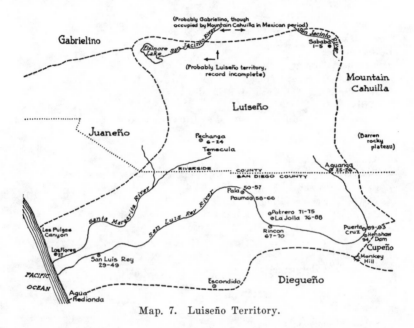

Map. 7. Luiseño Territory.

Juaneño.[461] South of the Luiseño were the Yuman-speaking Diegueño, to the east were the Mountain Cahuilla and Cupeño, and to the north were the Juaneño, Gabrielino, and Serrano. Culturally the Luiseño seem to have been active agents rather than passive recipients, as the following account will demonstrate, but the extent to which they received cultural stimuli from their northern neighbors is unknown because of the early disappearance of the latter groups. There is however strong reason for believing that a large part of the ritualistic detail passed on by them to peoples of the south and east they had themselves received from the Juaneño and Gabrielino.

---

[461] Sparkman, *op. cit.*, 189.

TABLE 19

LIST OF CLANS[462]

Saboba

1. Litcic.* Slipping.
2. Pokhat.*
3. Amurax.* Curled, as the leaves of a plant from the heat.
4. Tcipmal.* A species of owl.
5. Yulotcuwat.* Morning star.

Pechanga

6. Tcauwi.* To chase or scare up game. (Also represented at Rincon. Gifford.)
7. No. not used.
8. Hakyuk.* Hungry.
9. Tcukul.* (Perhaps from tcuki, to fill tight. Gifford.)
10. Eñla.* Salt. A branch at Pala also.
11. Wilix.*
12. Pahanim.* Budding (translated as Brewer blackbird to present author).
13. Oyot.* Thief, robber.
14. Kowak.*
15. Atatci.* Bark of a tree.
16. Tosamal.* A small plant with yellow flowers (*Baeria gracilis*).
17. Kocak.* Sweet.
18. Wavic.* People piling food for fiesta.
19. Cahama.* In the white willows.
20. Makara.*
21. Canat.* Asphaltum.
22. Bahovic.*
23. Totmani.* Rolling stone.
24. Ūhōk. To trot.

Aguanga

25. Atōla. Root.
26. Aīyal. Poison oak.

Los Flores

27. Hōwak. Foam (?).

San Juan (Juaneño)

28. Pōtcavinik. Splash (of water).

San Luis Rey

29. Tuvotwic or Tovotmuc.* Something ground to dust.
30. Atuulu.* A plant growing abundantly.
31. Halixliña or Halusliña.* Walking pigeon-toed or standing stoop-shouldered.
32 Ketekt.* Trousers (?) pulled up short.
33. Siñle.*

---

[462] This list includes many family names, or nicknames, as well as those of the clans or ceremonial and political units. The modern sites under which they are grouped merely indicate the general locality of each in late historic times. See map 7, present paper. Clan names marked with asterisk, from Gifford.

34. Towic.* Ghost.
35. Karik.* From kari'i, to eruct.
36. Pevesañahoiket.* Tule swaying in wind.
37. Keruskat.*
38. Totomal.* Small stone.
39. Saume.* Sound of sea shell at ear.
40. Lavik.* Wilting.
41. Ñonis.* Talking low when sick.
42. Nosis.*
43. Panowa.*
44. Yawahaisan.*
45. Kauwut.*
46. Tovita.* Small rabbit species.
47. Kelita.
48. Mapulis. Sitting in hunched position, hands in front of face.
49. Cuevish.463

Pala

50. Luvakwis.* To wilt or to become dry. (Said to be a branch of the Aīyal clan at Aguanga.)
51. Tcorī.* To roll. (Said to be oldest Pala clan.)
52. Wakpic.* Broom (for sweeping).
53. Sokisla.* To live forever (?).
54. Beēbethe.
55. Octonawa. (otc = cliff.)
56. Pevēsesh. Tule.
57. Tcehaīa. The Pleiades. (Said to be related to the Nasikut clan at Aguanga.)

Pauma

58. Maxlaña.* Fan palm.
59. Kēeñic.* Ground squirrel (a branch at La Jolla also).
60. Coktcum.* Scratch flesh with nails.
61. Pauval.*
62. Ayal.* Knowledge (?).
63. Tcat.* White owl.
64. Sīwak. Awake (a branch at Potrero also).
65. Pavoña.* Feeling a slight pain after a severe one.
66. Cokīcla. Beetle (?).

Rincon

67. Ōmic.* Blood (a branch at Potrero also).
68. Ñasikut. To chip or flake off (a branch at Potrero also).
69. Tcevic. Breaking by pulling.
70. Kewewic. Fox. (Given Gifford by Saboba informant.)

Potrero (Cuca Ranch)

71. Kalak. Sways.
72. Sōvenic. Mischievous. (Same as Gifford's no. 5 at Rincon.)
73. Sūwacic. Afraid.
74. Sūkat. Deer.
75. Amoya. Tired. (Mendenhall's Ranch.)

---

463 Name of Lucario Cuevish, informant mentioned by Du Bois, *op. cit.*, 74.

La Jolla[464]

76. Sūvic.   Rustling.   (Same as Gifford's no. 1.)
77. Tōvac.   To settle in water, like sand.   (Same as Gifford's no. 8.)
78. Akī.   Hole in the ground.   (Same as Gifford's no. 2.)
79. Amagō.   Branch of a tree.   (Same as Gifford's no. 3.)
80. Wassuk.   Stretched.   (Same as Gifford's no. 4.)
81. Awaīū.   Meat beggar.   (Same as Gifford's no. 7.)
82. Acketum.   Bather.   (Same as Gifford's Cuca clan no. 1.)
83. Pakut.   Deep basket.
84. Pamukemal.   (Extinct.)
85. Ūlukuh.   To hide behind.   (Extinct.)
86. Tculūpitcum.   (Extinct.)
87. Puhpūka.   Door.   (Extinct.)
88. Lukutcic.   Mosquito.   **(Extinct.)**

Puerta Cruz

89. Sēpuk.   (A branch of the Amago clan at La Jolla.)
90. Mitcax.   Choked or stuffed.
91. Waxipañawic.
92. Mūta.   Horned owl.
93. Kwacic.

Henshaw Dam

94. Palawhitcem.   Ground fungus or puffball.   (Branch at La Jolla also.)

CLAN ORGANIZATION

According to Sparkman[465] the Luiseño bands or clans[466] inhabited separate villages and were independent of each other.   They had no powerful chiefs but the religious chief of each clan possessed the most influence, all matters pertaining to religion being under his control. The office was hereditary but failing competent successors it might pass out of the direct line of descent.   Women were occasionally allowed to hold this office.[467] The office of chief of the rabbit hunt[468] was hereditary, and the medicine man (shaman) presumably had some governmental power.   Each band (or clan) had its allotted territories, which were occasionally subdivided between the different

---

[464] Gifford's clans, nos. 5, 9, and 10, were not mentioned by my informants.

[465] *Op. cit.,* 190, 215.

[466] Both terms are used apparently synonymously.

[467] Considering the strict limitation of this office to males among the eastern neighbors of the Luiseño one is inclined to attribute this to modern conditions under which the women interested carried on the religious activities.   Juaneño myths however. tell of a chieftainess, and it is possible that this was a western custom.

[468] This was usually the ceremonial assistant or paha.

families composing the band. These clan territories were jealously guarded and trespassing often led to quarrels. Du Bois mentions the clans and speaks of the chiefs being associated with ceremonial objects,[469] but her main concern seems to be with the parties. Gifford[470] deals at some length with the clans, which he considers as male lineages, a point brought out more strongly in a later publication.[471] He notes that certain of these clans have hereditary leaders, but that many of them do not and are often grouped into religious parties. He rightly distinguishes between the clans into which a person is born and the parties which may be joined at will. Kroeber[472] sums up all the above data and concurs most fully with Gifford; he points out that the relation of the chief to the political or territorial group is wholly obscure and doubts that the small individually named families or clans could have been the sole political units. A discussion of the clan organization of the Luiseño at La Jolla, Puerta Cruz, and Pala may throw more light on certain of the problems involved.

At La Jolla four informants gave the bulk of the information; these were Yēla Wassuk, Refukia Wassuk, Juan Antonio Wassuk, and Barbara Awaīū, all very old people. They agreed that there had never been any parties at La Jolla, but that each clan was separate, and formerly each had a nōta, a maswut bundle, and a special dance enclosure built for their ceremonies.[473] No persons having the same clan name could marry, and it was not customary to marry into the clan of the mother unless that group was so large that the selected mate was not considered a direct maternal relative. When Yēla was a girl the sūvic and the tōvac clans lived at Yapitca, one-half mile west of the La Jolla schoolhouse. Each had a nōta and carried on its own ceremonies. Formerly the tculūpitcum clan lived here but they were all dead before her time. At īañaho near the Nelson place, three-quarters of a mile east of the La Jolla schoolhouse, lived the amagō, akī, wassuk, and acketum clans, each clan being an independent ceremonial unit. Formerly the extinct puhpuka clan lived here. At hōlyulkum, the Nelson place, lived the awaīū clan, as well as several families from other clans. The panukemal, luhkutcic, and ūlukuh clans formerly lived here but became extinct before she remembers.

---

[469] *Op. cit.*, 160–161.

[470] S. Cal., 201–214.

[471] Miwok Lineages and the Political Unit in Aboriginal California. Am. Anthr., n.s., 28:389–401, 1926.

[472] Handbook, 685–688.

[473] According to La Jolla informants the native term for clan is kiktum, identical with the Cahuilla term.

GENEALOGY 23

Wassuk and Awaiū Clans[474]

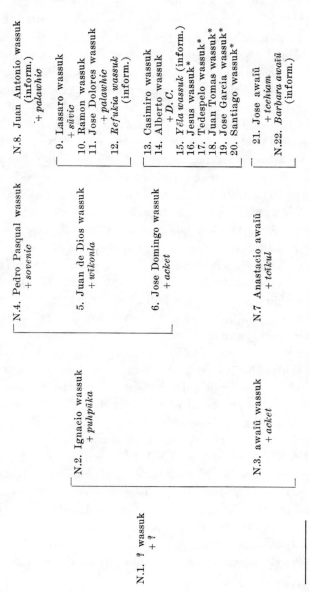

N.1. ♀ wassuk
+ ?

N.2. Ignacio wassuk
+ *puhpūka*

N.3. awaiū wassuk
+ *acket*

N.4. Pedro Pasqual wassuk
+ *sovenic*

5. Juan de Dios wassuk
+ *wikonla*

6. Jose Domingo wassuk
+ *acket*

N.7 Anastacio awaiū
+ *tcikul*

N.8. Juan Antonio wassuk
(inform.)
+ *palawhic*

9. Lassaro wassuk
+ *silvic*
10. Ramon wassuk
11. Jose Dolores wassuk
+ *palawhic*
12. *Refukia wassuk*
(inform.)

13. Casimiro wassuk
14. Alberto wassuk
+ *D. C.*
15. *Yēla wassuk* (inform.)
16. Jesus wassuk*
17. Tedespelo wassuk*
18. Juan Tomas wassuk*
19. Jose Garcia wassuk*
20. Santiago wassuk*

21. Jose awaiū
+ *tcehiam*
N.22. *Barbara awaiū*
(inform.)

[474] N. = nota, or clan leader.   * = died young.   Females indicated by italics.

At señmī, a flat one-half mile southwest of the Nelson place, lived part of the kēeñic and pakut clans. There were several other village sites in the vicinity but the clans that once occupied them had disappeared.

Certain of these clans were believed to be related and always reciprocated in presiding at each other's ceremonies. Thus the ūlukuh, panukemal, and the akī clans were said to be three branches of one stock, the latter being considered the oldest or original clan. It was impossible to verify this assumed relationship since two of these clans are extinct and the third nearly so. Similarly the sēpuk clan at Puerta Cruz was said to be a branch of the amagō clan that had moved away, while the palawhitcem clan at the Henshaw dam was said to be a branch of the wassuk and awīū clans. Since several members of the last-named clans survive, it is possible definitely to establish the relationship between these two groups and to show the way in which the split occurred. Three generations before that of the informants, all of whom figure in the genealogy (genealogies 8, 12, 15, 22, 23), the wassuk clan was at īañaho where the survivors still live. The clan was large and food was scarce, so that awaīū (3) (meat beggar), head of one family, moved away to hōlyulkum where there was room for growing some vegetables and less competition for acorns and other wild products. His nickname was passed on to his children as a family or clan name and they considered themselves independent of the parent clan. Awaīū became nōta, acquired a maswut bundle and gave his own ceremonies, including in his group certain unattached families of Luiseño then living at hōlyulkum. The office passed on to his son (7), and from him to Barbara awaīū (22) who at present regards herself as a nōta although her clan or family is very small. When the wassuk clan had ceremonies the awaīū clan was always invited, and on the rare occasions when the latter had a ceremony, for they were few in numbers and poor, they in turn invited their relatives from īañaho. All the informants agreed that this was the usual way the clans split up, largely through economic pressure. In hard times, therefore, clans that were once large might, in this manner, become subdivided into small family groups. If the head of the family which moved was of importance a new clan was thus established; if not, they returned to the parent group for all ceremonies. The distance between the two groups also played a part in determining whether they became independent or retained their old affiliations.

GENEALOGY 24

Mitcax Clan

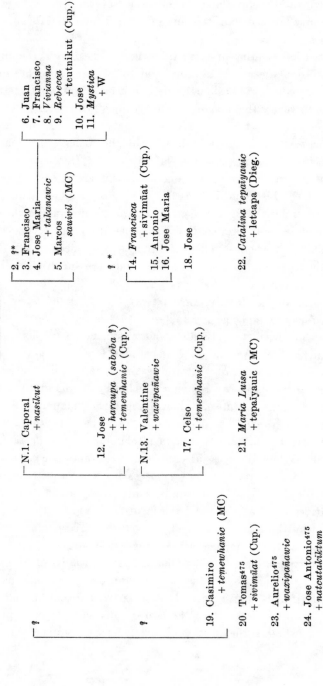

N.1. Caporal
+ *nasikut*

    2. ♀ *
    3. Francisco
    4. Jose Maria
       + *takanawic*
    5. Marcos
       sauivil (MC)

    6. Juan
    7. Francisco
    8. *Vivianna*
    9. *Rebecca*
       + *teutnikut* (Cup.)
    10. Jose
    11. *Mystica*
        + W

12. Jose
    + *haraupa (saboba ?)*
    + *temewhanic* (Cup.)

♀ *

    14. *Francisca*
        + *sivimũat* (Cup.)
    15. Antonio
    16. Jose Maria

N.13. Valentine
    + *waxipañawic*

17. Celso
    + *temewhanic* (Cup.)

    18. Jose

21. *Maria Luisa*
    + *tepaïyauie* (MC)

22. *Catalina tepaïyauic*
    + *letcapa* (Dieg.)

19. Casimiro
    + *temewhanic* (MC)

20. Tomas[475]
    + *sivimũat* (Cup.)

23. Aurelio[475]
    + *waxipañawic*

24. Jose Antonio[475]
    + *natcutakiktum*

[475] These were very old people when the Cupeño informant (Manuela sivimũat) was a girl. She did not know their exact
relationship to no. 19 but believes they were brothers or paternal first cousins.

At Puerta Cruz there were four clans living in the one village according to a census taken by Gifford in 1919. Three of these clans were independent and had their own nōta, while the fourth, a very small group, shared in the ceremonies of the largest clan of the aforementioned three. The genealogy (genealogy 24) of the mitcax clan is not altogether clear as to the relationship of all the male members. According to Cupeño informants they were all closely related, but the informants were unable to indicate the exact paternal linkage of the oldest members. This clan owned six houses. Nos. 1–12 and 19 lived in one house, nos. 13–16 in the second, nos. 17, 18 in the third, nos. 20–22 in the fourth, no. 23 in the fifth, and no. 24 in the sixth.

GENEALOGY 25

Mūta Family

♀	Jose Maria	
+ *Guillerma waxipañawic*	+ *Maria pumtum* (Cup.)	♀
	+ *Gertrudis temewhanic* (MC)	

GENEALOGY 26

Waxipañawic Clan

	2. Philomeno		4. Juan
N.1. ♀	+ *Dolores sivimŭat*		5. Antonio
+ *Juana pauatakik*			
(MC)	3. Jose Antonio		6. Benicio
	+ *Marianna* (Serr.)		
7. ♀	N.8. Bruno		
+ *Guillerma mitcax*			
9. Milton	10. *Cecelia*	11. ♀	
+ ♀ *iswitim* (MC)	+ Valentine mitcax		

The first nōta remembered was Caporal (no. 1), and on his death the office passed to his paternal first cousin Valentine (no. 13), who so far as the record goes was the last to hold office. Affiliated with this clan was the small mūta (horned owl) family whose only known genealogy is as follows (genealogy 25). They all lived in one house. Of these nos. 1–6 lived in one house, nos. 7 and 8 in another, and nos. 9–11 in a third. The oldest nōta remembered was no. 1 and on his death the office passed to his nephew Bruno (no. 8).

Thus at Puerta Cruz some fifty years ago, there were four clans living in ten houses, all but one of the clans being an independent ceremonial unit. Since a kinship bond between the members of these

clans is suggested it seems justifiable to call them by the latter name
rather than to designate them as parties. Puerta Cruz was an important village to the Cupeño because it was the first place at which
corpse-carriers from kūpa to the San Luis Rey mission stopped.
Cupeño informants say that the Cupeño only carried their dead on
the first and last stages of the journey, members of the other villages
carrying it in the intermediate stages. It is probable that these alien
carriers were paid for their services.

According to Francisco Ardea,[476] the oldest of the few surviving
Luiseño who lived at Pala before the Cupeño were transported there,
the original social and religious group was the clan and not the party.
In this he agreed with the La Jolla informants, but he added that
there had been parties at Pala as long as he could remember personally. This he said was due to the breaking down of the old clan system
after the mission period. The old site from which Pala (water) took
its name was a spring on the hill about two miles northeast of the
present town. This site belonged to the tcorī clan, which was the
earliest group to live there. Most of their members were taken from
there to the San Luis Rey mission to work, and only a few came back.
When Francisco was a boy many Luiseño lived at Pala, each group
with the same name living close together. It was considered wrong
for people with the same name to marry, but this rule is disobeyed at
present because of white influence. "Now it seems like we are marrying our sisters and brothers." When he was a young man, Sebastian
Tcorī, Ignacio wakpic, Manuel Beēbethe, and Geronimo Octonawa
were the nōtas of their respective clans. The luvakwis clan was under
the Aguanga aīyal nōta, and the tcehaīa clan was under the nasikut
clan also at Aguanga. Ventura Sōkisla was the oldest man of that
clan but whether he was regarded as a nōta is uncertain. The
pevēsesh clan was not mentioned by Francisco.

Francisco told the following story to account for the localization
of the clans. It seems to be a combination of migration legend and
general Luiseño creation myth.[477]

Long ago the country was divided among the Indians. The kēeñic people,
with all the others, first came traveling from the east. The kūpa people
(Cupeños) had been left there. When the kēeñic people came to the site of
Pauma another family, the kalaks, were living there, so the kēeñic people hid
and watched them. Finally the kalaks saw them and came up and talked to

476 The name Ardea is the Spanish translation of kēeñic or ground squirrel.

477 Du Bois, *op. cit.*, 110. Record 383 mentions a similar migration legend of
the Temecula Luiseño.

them. The kẽeñic people asked if they might stay there also for there were many acorns. They had to do this, for in the old days each family (clan) had a territory marked by rocks and they killed all trespassers. The kalaks agreed to let them stay and they became like brothers and sisters. Other families lived near by and each had its own territories. These had come ahead of the kalak people.

The people were scattered like that because of the death of their father. This was Wīyot, the son of e'kla (the earth) who was his mother, and tũpac (the heavens) who was his father. All people come from them as did all the animals. The frog (wahaukīla) was the last child of Wīyot. When he was born Wīyot said, ''My, what an ugly child!'' That was why the frog killed his father by bewitching him. All the sons of Wīyot took the body to burn it. All things were then alive, even the pine trees who were coming to the funeral. Those that stand along the ridges are the ones who didn't get there on time and they have stayed where they were ever since. His children burned Wīyot at wac, in the San Bernardino mountains, where there is a cross. Ant hills and nettles all arose at the place where he was doctored. All the places where they took the body of Wīyot were named, like malama (the Agua Tivia ranch), where they washed the body. From this place they took the body to wac and prepared to burn it.

The spirit of Wīyot was thinking what he could do for his children. At first he thought he would make them immortal, but he thought that the earth would then be overcrowded. Wīyot had a wicked son, Coyote (anō), and all the other children tried to send him away to the ocean for fire. Coyote would pretend to go but he always rubbed his face with evergreen branches and sneaked back. The black spider (kũwithiñic) that has a fiery red spot, set fire to the pyre. Coyote came running up and begged to see his father. When they would not let him he jumped over their heads and ate Wīyot's heart. That is why all people are after the coyote. The third day they heard Wīyot's voice but could not see him. He told them to watch for him in the west, and the moon came out as a sign that Wīyot would come back.

After this all the children of Wīyot scattered, and all found the places where they could live and have plenty of food. All the people in each place were related and all had the same name. They could not marry with others who had the same name, but the boys' parents always went away and picked out wives for them.

This is obviously a combination of myth fragments but it has value in demonstrating that the kinship group or clan and not the religious party is still regarded by the older Luiseño as the important unit of society. This persistence of the paternal lineage among the eastern Luiseño contrasts with the dominance of the party in the west where the original social conditions have disappeared. A consideration of religious party organization will demonstrate its superficial nature compared to the lineage or clan foundation from which it arose.

PARTY ORGANIZATION

According to Gifford, "a Luiseño party consists of a clan or family, with an hereditary chief, to which other numerically weak and chieftainless groups have attached themselves."[478]   This definition applies equally well to the western Mountain Cahuilla party, but as has been previously demonstrated it is not altogether adequate for the organization among the Cupeño which Gifford calls a party. Briefly to distinguish between a clan and a party, it can be said that the former may be made up of several branches of one lineage, whereas the latter is composed of branches of several lineages.

While La Jolla informants denied that parties were ever in vogue there, at Pauma, Rincon, Pala, San Luis Rey, Pichanga, and Saboba,[479] they flourished, and are today the last organized vestiges of native life.   But even where the party is dominant, native informants deny that it was the original social unit, and practically all claim that each clan formerly had a chief and performed its own ceremonies.   At Rincon today there are only two active parties, the anoyum, or coyote people (so called, informants say, because they were greedy and snatched at things), and the ivīum, meaning "to stand apart."   The first party is composed of three clans, kēeñic, ōmic, and sūkat.[480] According to Mrs. Maria Jesus Omish, her mother-in-law Pasquala, and her daughter-in-law Mrs. Gregorio Omish, each one of the clans in the first party formerly had a nōta, or chief, and performed its own ceremonies.   Jose Dolores Kēeñic, Cornelio Omic, and Jose Pedro Sūkat were the respective nōtas of the three clans, which today form one party.   The last named is the present leader of the united party. The second party, called ivīum, consisted of one clan, the kalaks (the term naxyum used by Gifford is that of the mythical ancestor of the clan).[481]   The use of the term party here is merely due to common native usage, for clan is obviously more correct as a descriptive designation.   Gifford stated that there were "other families" attached to this party,[481] but if so their names were not given by my informants. Of the three other parties listed by Gifford, each consisted of only one

---

[478] Present series, 14:206, 1918.

[479] Gifford, S. Cal., 206–214.

[480] Many people from Pauma, Potrero, and near-by places now live at the Rincon reservation. Gifford, S. Cal., 207, agrees to this clan alignment but adds the tovik (tōvac) La Jolla clan, which was not included by my informants.

[481] S. Cal., 207, also Du Bois, *op. cit.*, 161, tells how this transition occurred. The story was repeated to me by Juan Sotello Kalak, the acting nōta.

clan, but at the present time none is active. The name for Gifford's señyam party was given to me as pōnōum. It formerly consisted of the sōvenic clan. Bruno Sōvenic, who is nominally its head since the death of Geronimo Sōvenic some thirty years ago, did not know the meaning of the term pōnōum. The term señyam was not used by him, and he was strong in asserting that when he was a boy each clan had been an independent ceremonial unit. He had not assumed active leadership of his clan because giving ceremonies was too expensive, and since no one nowadays knew the old customs it was useless. Likewise the exvaiyum party was composed of the ñesikat (nasikut) clan which according to Gifford was located at Temecula;[482] and the navyam party was made up of the ciwaxum (sīwak) clan at Pauma.

From the foregoing it is obvious that at Rincon and its vicinity the party is a recent growth. It is possible to demonstrate that all five of the parties recorded by Gifford were made up of formerly independent clans, showing that one or at most two generations ago the Luiseño there were as free of parties as the La Jolla people claim always to have been.

At San Luis Rey, the site of the old mission, there is said to have been only one party. All the Luiseño families at this place were under one hereditary chief, and since twenty families or fragmentary clans are recorded from there, it seems probable that this centralization was due to Spanish influence.[483] At Pauma, in 1918, there were three parties each centered around one clan, and at Pichanga there was only one accepted party and one upstart affair less than a year old.[484] The name of this last, kiyuñahoic, which was translated by the male founder of the party as "my house and my property," suggests that it was founded because of his possession of a ceremonial house and equipment. Apparently the last requirement, i.e., the ceremonial equipment, in addition to a rudimentary knowledge of the externals of the old rituals, are the only requisites nowadays for founding a party. No very old party leaders are alive today, and their younger successors seem to have little detailed knowledge of their old religion. Certainly a comparison of the information received from them with that volunteered by the old clan leaders of the Desert Cahuilla, strongly indicates the lack of knowledge of the present Luiseño leaders.

---

482 S. Cal., 207.
483 Gifford, S. Cal., 207–208.
484 Gifford, S. Cal., 208.

At Saboba in 1918 there were three parties with hereditary leaders (both male and female) and ceremonial assistants.[485] As is true of all Luiseño parties (and clans), women became members both by birth and by marriage. It was possible to join the party and to leave it at will. Since the individual parties were not exogamous, owned no territories or special ceremonies, and were obviously composed of fragmentary clans, including Mountain Cahuilla as well as Luiseño families,[486] it seems safe to conclude that they were of relatively late origin.

Traces of Moiety Organization

In 1908, Miss Du Bois secured from Lucario Cuevish, an old Luiseño born at San Luis Rey, a legend concerning the origin of the Notish Mourning Ceremony.[487] Since it strongly suggests the dichotomy of the animate universe, common to the Miwok and to many other southern and south central Californian groups, it is here quoted in full:

The Sea-fog, Awawit, was the one who started the Notish ceremony. He was one of those who arranged all the ceremonies after the death of Ouiot (Wīyot). He was the one who used to provide the food and call all the people together.

Sea-fog set up the kutumit pole with baskets at the top, and arranged for a contest of skill between his people of the west and those of the mountains. The western people were sure that they could do better in everything than the people of the mountains.

So everyone tried to climb the pole to get the baskets, but no one could reach the top except the squirrel from the mountains, and he climbed the pole, cut the string, and the baskets fell down.

When the mountain people went to this gathering they took deer meat and much food; all they could carry; but Mechish from the ocean, a sea animal that crawls along and has little hollows or cups in his shell, got a bag and got all the food in that and carried it off. So the west won in that contest and got all the mountain people's food. In the first game the squirrel beat. In the second the west beat.

Then the western people gathered fish and other things to eat. There was a bird there from the mountains with a very big mouth [probably the night hawk or the poor will], and the mountain people said to him: "It is your turn now to eat." He said: "That is nothing for me to do." So he opened his mouth and they poured everything into it, and he ate it all up. So the mountain people beat.

Then they arranged a game between the fish and the owl. They were to look straight at each other and whoever closed his eyes first was to lose. The

---

485 Gifford, S. Cal., 212.

486 Gifford, S. Cal., 212–214.

487 *Op. cit.*, 148–150. Comments in brackets by present author.

owl and the fish sat and looked at each other, and finally the owl had to close his eyes, so he lost, and the western people won on that.

They were getting angry over all this contest and it seemed there would be a fight. When levalwish, the crow's skin, is hung on the pole, there is to be fighting.

Then Sea-fog made a house and told the mountain people to try to destroy it. So they got the Summer-cloud, Thunder-cloud, a very powerful man, to come and see if he could blow or break it down. He came, he roared and blew, but could do nothing to break the house down. So the west won. Then Thunder-cloud invited Sea-fog to come up to his house and see if he could destroy it. So Sea-fog came. A strong wind broke the trees and knocked down all the houses. So the west won again. Then they tried their skill in a long race. They went past Pala up through the mountains as far as La Jolla. Some of those that raced on the side of the mountain people were the hawk, frog, eagle, raven, and chicken hawk; and for the west Emamul (little birds on the seashore, very fast runners [Sandpipers?], the butterfly, grasshopper, and others. As they came by Pala to the foot of the mountain, at Rincon, Wasimul, a kind of a hawk, gave out in the race, and there he is now as a rock beside the road, right below the store. At the same time Chehuka, a person, coming along in the race, gave out, and his footprint can still be seen in the rock. When many of the racers had given out and died, or stayed behind, the eagle and the raven and the chicken hawk, mountain people, were ahead; and the grasshopper and the butterfly, western people, were close behind, so the mountain people won in this race.

The last race was between the deer, Sukut, and the antelope, Tonla. This race was from Temecula to San Bernardino mountain, and the antelope beat in this, for it was all on a level, where the antelope can go fastest. So they arranged to have another race between them, and this time it was over a mountain route, and here the deer won the race.

Summer-cloud [Thunder-cloud] was glad because the deer beat, and the mountain people had won in most of the contests. [Some trials were evidently left out by the narrator for in this list the mountain people are not ahead.] All these contests were made in the first Notish ceremony and ended it.

Since inter-moiety games are commonly associated with dichotomy in California, as is frequently the case elsewhere in North America where the moiety occurs, the present myth with its definite Luiseño provenience and geographic setting is important. The division of the animals and more or less animate forces of nature into two sides, resembles the Miwok, Yokuts, Mono, and Cahuilla custom. Among the Cahuilla, and probably others of the aforementioned groups,[488] the dual classification seems to have entered into the naming of children. Luiseño society is too disintegrated to determine whether this was formerly their custom in naming children. As will be demonstrated later, there is some reason to believe that this seemingly arbitrary division of animal forms into two groups was similar in detail

---

[488] Cf. Gifford, Miwok, 166.

over the entire Southwest wherever the moiety occurred. Another similarity of this sort, which seems to crop up too frequently for pure chance association, is the use of red and black paints to distinguish the moieties.[489] In this connection it is interesting to note that the Luiseño call the ceremonial assistant associated with the jimsonweed cult, paha. This term is translated as red racer (*Coluber flagellum*), a reptile common in the area.[490] They say that the coloration of the male snake is red and of the female black, and on this account the paha was painted red on one side of his body and black on the other thus representing both sexes. As there are strong traces of moiety reciprocity among the eastern neighbors of the Luiseño, and since the latter employed a paha from another clan to whom they were related by marriage, there is a strong suggestion that this sex symbolism is directly connected with moiety reciprocity.[491] The same symbolism applies to the Cahuilla and Cupeño paha, and among those groups the moiety was well recognized, and reciprocity practiced.

During their adolescence ceremonies, spotted and striped facial paints were employed to distinguish girls of the two moieties among the Miwok, Cupeño, and other dichotomous groups. The Luiseño seem to have used striped designs during the girls' puberty ceremonies, while dotted designs were used by adults at a special mourning ceremony called sūlahic. Stripes among the Cupeño signified the coyote moiety, the members of which constituted the main Shoshonean element of the Cupeño population. It may be significant in the case of the Luiseño that the two designs, stripes and dots, are used in separate ceremonies, with the striped design characteristic of the coyote moiety still associated with their girls' puberty ceremonies.

An actual record of the moiety among Luiseño at Saboba was secured by Gifford in 1918, from an old Luiseño woman named Canuta (in Luiseño salat or body louse).[492] Since this is the only definite record of the institution among the group, and rests on the statement of one informant, it must be received with caution. However in 1925, Mrs. Gregorio Omish, an old Luiseño woman at Rincon, in answer to my questions concerning a tuktum or wildcat people, said that at

[489] Strong, *op. cit.*, 46–48.

[490] The theory may be based on the fact that in Arizona and Lower California a red and a black phase of *Coluber flagellum piceus* occur. It is unknown for California north of Mexico. There is actually no sex distinction in color. Vandenburgh, Reptiles of North America, 669, 1922.

[491] The Diegueño custom of painting the faces of male images black and of female images red during the image-burning ceremony is very similar, but the colors are reversed. Waterman, present series, 8:313, 1910.

[492] Present series, 14:211–214, 1918.

Saboba there was such a group, but nowhere else in Luiseño territory.[493] She said it meant "many lions," and had always been at Saboba, but never at Rincon or any other Luiseño site. This is verification of Canuta's evidence, for Mrs. Omish stated that tuktum was more than a party; it meant a whole group of people or several parties. Canuta said that one moiety at Saboba was called anom (Luiseño for coyote), and the other tuktum or wildcat.[494] According to the same informant marriage between members of the same moiety was forbidden, the totem animals were not protected or sacred, and there were no associated totem animals other than coyote and wildcat. No political function or definite reciprocity seems to have been connected with the moiety at Saboba.[494] The present party alignment is apparently independent of moiety lines, hence the older customs of clan reciprocity if they formerly existed would have been lost.

Gifford is inclined to believe that Canuta assigned moiety names to Luiseño groups that were not so classified, but adds that the institution of the moiety may be spreading to the Luiseño at Saboba.[494] His first contention may be correct, but concerning the possibility of any recent spread of the moiety I disagree entirely. The moiety among these southern California Shoshonean groups is utterly dead as an institution, and its very name has almost disappeared. Even among the Cupeño and Desert Cahuilla who practiced the rule of moiety exogamy up to the last generation, the institution was subject to ridicule, and has every appearance of being an outworn custom. In the San Gorgonio pass the Pass Cahuilla knew the moiety classification of all clans but paid no attention to the rule of exogamy, and here the moiety division was viewed in a semihumorous fashion as an old, old custom whose origin was obscure and whose efficacy was *nil*. It seems much more probable that the Saboba Luiseño, being in close contact with the Mountain groups still retaining at least nominal dichotomy, did the same. The survival of other customs related to the moiety among the western Luiseño, where there was no very close contact with the dichotomous mountain people, seems to bear this out. From its distribution through many portions of the mountain region, from the Cupeño to the northern Miwok, it seems probable that the moiety was strong in the mountains, and in company with certain other customs survived there after it had been replaced by other institutions along the coast.

---

[493] Many of the Luiseño songs mention Tomaiyowit and Tukmit as personifications of land and sky respectively. The latter may well be a Luiseño version of Mūkat who was of the tuktum moiety. Du Bois, *op. cit.*, 122, Record 1098.

[494] Present series, 14:211–214, 1918.

The Clan Leader, Sacred Bundle, and Ceremonial Enclosure

As Sparkman says, "The religious chief of each clan seems to have possessed the most power, all matters pertaining to religion being under his control."[495] This official, called nōta by the Luiseño, was usually one of the older men in the clan, the office being inherited in the male line. The Luiseño say that women often held office and at the present time there are several living who claim this distinction. Ordinarily on the death of a nōta his eldest son was chosen to succeed him unless the latter lacked the necessary qualifications in the eyes of his clan members. In such a case a younger brother or collateral relative succeeded. Informants say that a nōta in the old days had to be generous and a good provider, know all the myths and rituals relating to clan ceremonies, and have in his possession by inheritance the maswut bundle containing the ceremonial impedimenta of the group.

According to Juan Antonio Wassuk, maswut was made of mashla,[496] a tall reed or fern, and was either sewn into a mat or woven into a big basket as described by Du Bois.[497] According to Sparkman's description this matting, in which was wrapped the ceremonial equipment of the clan, was about a yard long by two feet nine inches wide, sewed with four rows of twine. "In this mat were rolled up the articles used at religious ceremonies by the chief of festivals, not only his own, but also of the other members of his clan."[498] Thus both types of ceremonial matting mentioned by the above informant are corroborated by these earlier investigators. Du Bois also mentions Pauwhut Abahut, a hollow log used to keep sacred feathers in, and adds that a sacred canoe found on the beach was used as container for the sacred feathers at San Luis Rey.[499]

Juan Antonio Wassuk, as genealogy 23 (p. 280) shows, would be nōta of his clan if the old ceremonies were still continued, but when he was still a mere lad his father, then an old man, called all the Wassuk clan together. He told them that he would not appoint his son as his successor because the old days were over and they would

---

[495] *Op. cit.,* 215.

[496] *Woodwardia radicans* (probably). Sparkman however states that this ancient type of mat containing the clan ceremonial equipment was made of shoila (*Juncus* sp.), *ibid.,* 234. Both materials were probably used.

[497] *Op. cit.,* 94. Mention is also made of a rare and obsolete "basket" made of symmetrical splints sewed with twine, p. 172.

[498] *Op. cit.,* 210.

[499] *Op. cit.,* 118, n. 128.

have to give up their religion. This was done because the old people were dying and none of the younger people were learning the songs and rituals. Therefore he divided up the contents of the maswut bundle and buried the matting in a hidden place. This story was independently confirmed by Yēla Wassuk, the niece of Pedro Pasqual Wassuk, the last nōta. She described the maswut as a very old and black piece of tule matting, in which were wrapped tcēet (crow and owl feather headbands), pīwic (headband of eagle down and plant fiber) tōminut (feather bands about five inches wide), elatem (sharpened sticks tipped with owl plumes and snake rattles, that were worn on the head), and various kinds of ceremonial rattles. When this equipment was divided up its contents became scattered and most of it has been lost or destroyed.

When such a bundle was not in use it was put away in a dark corner of the nōta's house just under the rafters. No one save the nōta was allowed to touch it, and it was believed tculuhup, misfortune or evil, would afflict anyone who violated this rule. After the nōta had taken the bundle down and spread it out, it was then safe for other clan members to touch it. The maswut concept was very important among the eastern Luiseño, and it was the possession of such a sacred bundle, with its contents, that gave power to the nōta as a civil and religious leader. Among the parties still functioning at Rincon and other localities to the west it is such a bundle, though often without the matting, that seems to serve as an objectified nucleus for the organization, and the man who has the bundle is the religious leader.

While many of the involved mythological concepts connected with the ceremonial bundle complex have disappeared, we have highly significant references to it in the older literature. In referring to the song series designated as "our spirit," Kroeber quotes the following significant lines from Luiseño songs gathered by Du Bois.[500]

"North, east, south, west, the hair lives." Hair is symbolic for spirit; and there is allusion to hair ropes at the four ends of the sand painting representing the world.

"North, the hair, the *wanawut*, lives tied, fastened. My origin lives there." Presumably the other directions are also mentioned. The *wanawut* is the sacred rope in the initiation rite . . . . . Another song refers to the sky's heart as well as the *wanawut* and sand painting. . . . .

These quotations from the mourning ceremony songs take on new significance when the Pauma Luiseño story of Dakwish (the fire-ball

---

[500] Kroeber, Handbook, 658.

meteor that is said to live on top of San Jacinto peak) is considered. Here Tukupar, a mythical chief who has visited Dakwish at his home, says:

"I want my son's hair." Dakwish said: "Very well. Look there where the masawat is [for ornament made of or containing hair]." Tukupar could not find his son's hair. He said so. Dakwish said: "I cannot help it. There is another masawat. Perhaps it is in that." Tukupar could not find it there. Dakwish said: "That is all. I have no more." Tukupar said: "Yes, you have another." He went to another one, a new one. Dakwish was ashamed. He went away with it for a little while. Then he came back. He had hidden Tukupar's son's hair, and said: "There is nothing there, don't you see?" Tukupar said: "My cousin, you have it under your arm." Then Dakwish hit him in the face with the hair. He said: "You came here to cry." Tukupar said: "That is what I want, my cousin," and he put the hair around him. Then he cried . . . . .[501]

Thus maswut (or masawut), yula, and the wanawut are all three associated with human hair, which in turn is symbolic of the spirit and the abode of spirits in the milky way. Hair and Nahut, the mystic wanawut figure, were the firstborn of the earth mother, according to Luiseño creation myth.[502] In the above Dakwish legend it is significant that the masawut is referred to as a bundle or container. This also makes clear the Cupeño song, sung during the mourning ceremony, and previously quoted,[503] in which the image of the dead is said to have been made by wolf and coyote "of masvut and hair." Neither informants, nor the majority of authorities on the Luiseño, mention the use of maswut or ceremonial matting as a framework for the images of dead. Davis however says of the Luiseño: "Crude images of the dead were made of arrow weed woven together like a mat, with sticks inserted for shoulders and hips. . . . . When the images were completed they were supposed to be occupied by the souls of the dead."[504] It seems probable that this matting was the sacred maswut.

The Desert Cahuilla myth of the creation given by Hooper associates the maswut with seaweed and its location with the Pacific ocean;[505] the Palm Springs Cahuilla myth, previously given in full, does the same,[506] and Du Bois quotes the following from a Luiseño

[501] Kroeber, Two Myths of the Mission Indians of California, Jour. Am. Folklore, 19:320, 1906.

[502] Kroeber, Handbook, p. 678.

[503] Present paper, p. 268.

[504] E. H. Davis, Early Cremation Ceremonies of the Luiseño and Diegueño Indians of Southern California. Heye Foundation, Indian Notes and Monographs, 7:101, 1921.

[505] Present series, 16:326–327, 1920.

[506] Present paper, pp. 143.

myth: "He [Nahachanish, a mythical Temecula chief] came to the water. He had something with him in a basket, and this he threw out, and it still grows there in the water, a sort of greens, called Mawut."[507] Another Luiseño myth mentions "the seaweed on the seashore, one of the First People and sacred to Chungichnish."[508] In these fragmentary references from Luiseño myths we find that the maswut is associated with the chief, the water, and probably with the seaweed and the seashore. Its very sacred nature brought out by its association with hair or spirit and the wanawut is further emphasized by its sacred connection with Chungichnish. The invocation of this sacred bundle, which has been described as it occurred in Cahuilla, Cupeño, and Serrano ceremonies, finds a distinct reflection in Luiseño mythology, as the following testifies:

> This man [Hainit, Yuinit, double name, denoting headband and diver] when he made the sun, took the reddish milkweed plant that twine is made of, and twisted the fibers of it into twine, and out of that made a net, not an ordinary carrying net, but a long one. Then he called all the people and they got together in a place near Temecula. He took the net that was all rolled up, and with groaning invocation he laid it on the ground, and all the people standing in a circle bent over it and placed it before them on the ground. They sang about Temet, the sun, and putting him in the net, they raised their arms with the appropriate groans, cries, and gestures, and sent him up into the sky as the sun. [Then follows a description of the way the sun's daily course became set.][509]

A comparison of this mythical rite with the actual sacred bundle invocations among the groups just mentioned suggests a definite connection between the two.

The Luiseño only used the house of the clan leader for local clan affairs, and for any large ceremony a brush enclosure was built near the nōta's house. The outer wall of this structure was called hotahish and the enclosure itself wāmkic.[510] Juan Antonio Wassuk stated that there was often a sacred inner enclosure called eshūma nōyhūma.[511] The Luiseño wāmkic is very similar both in structure and etymology to Boscana's vanquech. The Spanish translation is *casa grande* or "big house," a term commonly employed by the natives. Its form was circular and the walls were of willow, arrow weed, and other brush woven between stakes. It was regarded as very sacred, and was

---

[507] *Op. cit.*, 152.

[508] *Ibid.*, 113.

[509] *Ibid.*, 144.

[510] Du Bois, *op. cit.*, 84.

[511] Meaning not known. Modern Luiseño informants often remember old terms whose meaning they cannot give.

burned at the close of a ceremony with appropriate songs. This occurred in the daytime after the toloache ceremony, although a small portion of it might be burned symbolically, rather than destroy the whole structure.[512]

From the foregoing data it can be seen that in spite of their more elaborate ceremonies the Luiseño recognized a strong relationship between the clan priest, the sacred bundle, and the circular ceremonial enclosure. This fundamental concept they shared with both their eastern and western neighbors, but through the latter peoples specialized cults had reached the Luiseño which made the basic pattern less pronounced. The sequence of these various cults will be dealt with later, but it is not amiss at this point to stress the importance of the house, priest, and fetish complex among both the Luiseño and their northwestern neighbors.[513]

OTHER CLAN AND CEREMONIAL OFFICIALS

The nōta was the primary official in the clan, but among the eastern Luiseño he seems to have had an assistant called the puhmutcvī, or "rear end." Just why this title was given him is not clear. The main duties of the puhmutcvī were similar to those of the Cahuilla takwa or kutvavanavac and the Cupeño kutvōvoc. He kept order at most of the ceremonies, did the announcing, and presided during a considerable part of the girls' initiation and of various mourning ceremonies. When the puhmutcvī presided at the image-burning ceremony he was called paīīakut, and he appointed a special fire-tender. At the time the jimsonweed was administered the puhmutcvī of the visiting clan prepared the decoction, and in this rôle he was called nōktōmic. These duties will be brought out in more detail subsequently when the ceremonies are described. An interesting person in Luiseño mourning ceremonies was the takō, or eater, who went through with the conventionalized ceremonial cannibalism.[514] This seems to have been a purely temporary office for which the person was paid. A similar temporary official was the morahash dancer, who was probably specially trained for his whirling dance. According to Sparkman this dancer was called totowish.[515]

---

[512] Du Bois, *op. cit.*, 84.

[513] Compare Boscana's account of the Juaneño or Gabrielino vanquech, *in* Alfred Robinson, Life in California (ed. 1; New York, 1846), 246.

[514] Neither Sparkman nor Du Bois mention the puhmutcvī or takō.

[515] See Du Bois, 102, n. 50, and 183.

The paha seems to have been connected almost entirely with the toloache rites, and was usually a shaman of repute. He kept order at all toloache ceremonies and had a great deal to do in all ritualistic activities. The symbolism connected with his name has been discussed in relation to the moiety, and will be referred to hereafter. On the whole his ritualistic activities seem to have been more highly specialized than were those of the puhmutcvī, who was really the ceremonial assistant to the nōta.

Girls' Adolescence Ceremony

Yēla Wassuk gave a brief description of this ceremony as she remembered it at La Jolla, where it was last performed some forty years ago. It was called we'enic[516] and was made for several girls, supposedly at the time of their first menses.[517] The girls' fathers told their nōta, and he in turn notified a related clan. Whether this "related" clan was always a branch clan related in the male line, or whether it was a clan with which intermarriage was common, is not clear.[518] This outside clan provided the presiding official called the puhmutcvī (rear end), the other members coming to the ceremony. The puhmutcvī prepared a hole in the wamkic which was lined with patc'hiyal, a reed which grew in the water. All the girls who had been hidden in their houses were brought out after they had been completely covered, and placed along the side of the pit. All the men sang (nūkwanic) and the older female relatives of the girls gave them advice, holding the initiates by the head as they did so. Yēla remembered being told, "Listen! Hear well! Hold back your head and look me in the face. Treat the old people well, feed them, care for them. If your face and eyes are dirty, wash them. If those of the old people are, wash them. Bring up your children well. Do not run around, but marry in the right way."[519] Then "to open their ears" the puhmutcvī and all the people grunt, "he-e-ri-th e," twice. Then they grunt a third time, and the puhmutcvī gives each girl a

---

[516] Given as wekenish by Kroeber and Sparkman, and wukunish by Du Bois.

[517] According to Kroeber, Handbook, 673, only one girl had to be at the actual physiological period indicated by the word *ash*.

[518] This clan was well paid for its services. Du Bois, *op. cit.*, 93.

[519] Sparkman, *op. cit.*, 225–226, gives a more detailed lecture of this sort. It brings in the Chungichnish warnings, and other features which are mentioned later in the above ceremony, and includes the customary triple blowing to waft away evil spirits.

drink of tobacco and water from a clay vessel, called peclīmul.[520] The girls then became dizzy and were laid in the pit which had been heated with hot rocks. They were covered with grass and sand and a loosely woven tule mat, called tcaīamul, was placed over their faces. Here they lay quietly, leaving the pit at intervals for it to be reheated; they were given warm water and tortillas made without salt. Each girl was attended by her mother. Wooden or shell implements were provided the girl to scratch herself with, for she must not use her finger nails lest pimples arise.

The girls stayed in the pit three days, and each day another clan (or village according to Du Bois) came to participate in the ceremony. These joined in the singing and the host clan provided ample food for feasting. Should another clan come on the fourth day, the girls would have to remain in the pit that day as well, but usually they leave the pit on the morning of the fourth day. They are hidden away, and according to Yēla she was given salt water to drink.[521] This temporarily ended the ceremony. The girls' faces were painted black for a month.[522] Then for a month vertical white lines were painted on each morning, and the third month wavy, red, horizontal lines were put on. This was called "the rattlesnake" design, and at the end of this month all the other clans were invited once more.

The invited puhmutcvī and his assistants had made a ground-painting some six feet in diameter,[523] and the girls were made to kneel in front of this. The puhmutcvī, facing the north after walking three times around the ground-painting,[524] placed a lump of sage-seed (pasal) ground and seasoned with salt (according to Yēla) and called pōīic, in the mouth of each girl. A long lecture was then given the girl,[525] at the close of which all present grunted or exhaled three times, and the girl attempted to spit the pōīic into the center of the ground-painting. If she succeeded it was very good and longevity was

---

[520] To vomit this ball of tobacco indicated that the girl had not been virtuous. Du Bois, *op. cit.*, 94. We agree with Kroeber, Handbook, 674, that this was a hard test.

[521] This is in disagreement with other accounts for southern California where salt is definitely taboo, but this rite marks the closing of a ceremonial period.

[522] The black paint was called na'lal; it was made from a light, soft black rock "like stove polish." No one knows exactly where it came from. The red paint was called paismul, and was of iron oxide collected in certain springs. White paint was tŏvic, made from a white clay obtained on the side of Palomar mountain. It was thinned down with water and became very white when dry.

[523] Kroeber describes the southern California ground-painting in detail, Handbook, 661–665, and illustrates the various types, fig. 56, opposite p. 662.

[524] Du Bois, *op. cit.*, 96.

[525] See Sparkman, *op. cit.*, 225–226.

assured; but if she failed it was very bad, and she was urgently advised "to get on the right road" as she had a very poor start in life. Then the painting was obliterated by the old men, who pushed it into the central hole with their hands.[526]

The ceremony closed with a race, called hayic (or hayish),[527] to a certain rock. Here a relative of each girl stood with red paint, and, as each girl arrived, she painted a design on the rock.[528] According to Yēla Wassuk any design was permissible, but other informants said such designs were always diamond-shaped and represented the rattlesnake. The known rock paintings of this type at Rincon and La Jolla are geometric with a preponderance of diamond-shaped designs.[529] The hair bracelets and anklets worn by the girls throughout this period were left at the rock after the race.[526] Kroeber mentions an initiation ceremony at Pauma where flat rocks were heated and placed on the abdomen of each girl while in the pit. This brings to mind the Mesa Grande (Diegueño) rite described by Rust, in which the girls were led up a hillside and shown a certain crescentic stone believed to symbolize or refer to the female genitalia. After the garlands worn by the girls had been deposited on the stone it was buried, and grain was scattered over the spot. Stones of this type have been found in various southern California sites and it is possible that this was once a common practice.[530]

CEREMONIES FOR THE DEAD

Tūvic, the Start

When a person died the body was prepared for cremation by clan members of the deceased. Just after, or when death was imminent, a pit about two feet deep was dug extending north and south. The earth was broken with digging-sticks and removed with flat stones or by hand. The pit was filled with brush and a log pyre erected over it on which the body of the deceased was placed, head to the

---

[526] Du Bois, *op. cit.*, 96.

[527] According to Sparkman, the race at the time of the new moon was called hayish. The term may simply refer to race. See Du Bois, *op. cit.*, 110, n. 93.

[528] Such paintings were called yunish. See Notes by A. L. Kroeber *in* H. N. Rust, A Puberty Ceremony of the Mission Indians, Am. Anthr., n.s., 8:32, 1906.

[529] Rust, *loc. cit.* Du Bois, *op. cit.*, 175. Sparkman, *op. cit.*, 225. Kroeber, Handbook, 675. The statements of my informants agreed with Du Bois that the painting occurred only once during the ceremony. Sparkman and Kroeber state that it occurred monthly three or four times at least.

[530] Rust, *op. cit.*, 28–32.

north and face upward. One man was appointed to superintend the burning of the body and the other relatives sat near weeping and wailing. It often took twelve hours to consume the entire body and usually the heart was the last portion to be burned, in which case it was punched full of holes to hasten its destruction.[531] When the body was all consumed the calcined bones and ashes were gathered up and placed in a basket (the Diegueño placed them in a pottery olla).[531] Davis does not mention the preservation of the bones in a basket, but from the fact that he described their ceremonial consumption later, it seems probable that the bones and ashes were not all buried in the fire pit as he states.[532] According to Kroeber a ritualistic washing of the dead person's clothes occurred at this time, but Pala informants claim this was part of the second ceremony. One selected garment was retained for the second ceremony, and all the other possessions of the dead were burned. At the close of the night's singing and dancing, intended to drive away the spirit of the dead, the nōta told his clan members to make preparations for the second ceremony.

Tcutcamic, the Burning

Among those Luiseño clans situated west of Rincon the clothes-burning ceremony occurred as soon as sufficient food had been gathered. The clan giving the ceremony built the wāmkic, but an outside clan was invited to preside at the ceremony. All food was in the hands of the nōta, and about four in the afternoon when all had assembled, he had his assistant the puhmutcvī divide the food among all the guests. A general feast followed, the members of the host clan serving the guests.

Then about dark the nōta giving the ceremony brought out the bundle of clothing and, while the practice of cremation still prevailed, the basket containing the ashes of the deceased. The nōta sat down near the leaders of the invited clans and formally went through the motions of washing the clothes. Formerly, the informant (Francisco Ardea of Pala) said, all the people present at such a ceremony paid a certain man to mix pinole flour and water with the ashes and drink them; after which the basket which had contained the calcined bones and ashes was burned. This man was called takō, a name said to

---

[531] E. H. Davis, *op. cit.*, 95–98. No supplementary data on these points were obtained by the present author.

[532] *Ibid.*, 97. It is interesting to note that the man who gathered up the bones purified himself by a sweat bath before the final rites.

mean "eater," indirectly referring to the coyote. Davis mentions this rite as follows:

While the assembled feasters sang and danced, some of the calcined bones of the dead were pounded to a fine powder in mortars, mixed with water and then drunk from small ollas by the relatives. This was believed to insure long life, without illness, and to endow those who drank with the virtues and qualities of the dead. At Pechanga a survival of this custom is found. The clothing of the dead is placed in water, and meal of chia seed is mixed instead of bone, and drunk. At Rincon only water is taken.[533]

This account, though circumstantial, and in part based on actual observation, does not seem to distinguish clearly between the various ceremonies. The account of Francisco Ardea accords so closely with that of the ceremonial flesh-eater at Juaneño ceremonies given by Boscana,[534] that there can be no doubt of the relationship of the two rites. The various substitutes for the rite have possibly arisen from the fact that burial was enforced by the mission fathers, who undoubtedly frowned on a ceremony suggesting cannibalism. Possibly the entire clothes-burning and washing rituals are similarly substitutes for forbidden ceremonies whose original significance has been forgotten by the modern natives. In the above case the resemblance is so close to the mythical account of coyote eating the creator's heart, that there seems little doubt as to its primary motivation.[535]

However, to return to the clothes-burning ceremony, when the ceremonial washing was completed, bolts of calico were draped over the heads of the invited clan leaders and gifts were distributed to the other guests. The takō seems also to have been the official fire-tender, and while these gifts were being distributed he prepared the fire for the last rite. The presiding nōta led his clan members three times around the fire, and stopped to blow up in the air three times. Then he shouted, "I am going to burn it," and thrust the bundle into the heart of the flames. This was a signal for all the host clan to throw away many presents for the guests to gather up. Songs of Pikmakvul, death, and Shangamish, finishing, are sung at this time.[536] Then the takō was paid for his services and though the old people might sing all night the main ceremony was finished.

---

[533] E. H. Davis, *op. cit.*, 102, 103. A version of the Wīyot myth told by a La Jolla Indian connects this rite with the cremation of the god, p. 109.

[534] See Kroeber, Handbook, 643.

[535] There is an allusion to the grinding of Wīyot's bones in a mortar and mixing them with water in the Luiseño Creation Myth, but no mention of drinking the mixture. Du Bois, *op. cit.*, 137.

[536] Du Bois, *op. cit.*, 101.

Sūlahic, the Nōta's Road

The more easterly Luiseño seem to have laid less stress on the clothes-burning ceremony, and I obtained no reference to it at La Jolla. It probably occurred there as Du Bois mentions it in passing,[537] but another somewhat similar rite seems to have loomed larger in their eyes. This ceremony is practically identical with sūlatcem, the "nuut's road" of the Cupeño; and like that ceremony it was last performed a great many years ago. As remembered by Yēla and Juan Antonio Wassuk, sūlahic occurred two or three days subsequent to a death in any clan, when the other clans from the neighborhood[538] came "to show their sympathy," and incidentally to have a feast at the expense of the bereaved clan. A related clan was invited to prepare the firewood and a wāmkic, and their nōta presided at the ceremony.[539] All the clan leaders who came to the ceremony brought presents, shell money, ceremonial equipment, or baskets to formally express their sympathy, and in return received larger presents from the presiding nōta. This last gift material was all provided by the clan members of the deceased, and they received no share of it. The members of the clan to which the presiding nōta belonged received an even share of the distribution. The presents consisted of baskets, shell money, acorn meal, wheat, and other foodstuffs. Obviously the clan which was thus consoled by its neighbors lost more than it gained by the formality. No definite system of exchange was remembered by informants questioned, but it seems highly probable that formerly there was a standard rule.

Both tcūtcamic and sūlahic seem to have much in common, and it is possible they were local variants of the same original ceremony. However, the main purpose of the former seems to have been the driving away of the spirit of the dead symbolized by the clothes which were burned, while the latter ceremony seems motivated mainly by ideas of ceremonial exchange. The accounts are fragmentary at best, but it is well to emphasize the prevalence of both these ideas in the ceremonies which occurred between the actual disposal of the dead and

---

[537] *Op. cit.* Sparkman, who was most familiar with the Luiseño at Rincon, comments on its importance there, *op. cit.*, 226.

[538] All the clans at and around Puerta Cruz, Yapitca, and La Jolla were included in this exchange. In turn it is probable that they were also connected with similar exchanges with clan groups bordering them in other directions.

[539] Whether this relationship was paternal (i.e., by blood) or by marriage is unfortunately obscure.

the final burning of the images a year later. Strangely enough neither Sparkman nor Du Bois mention the takō of the first, or the puhmutcvī of the second ceremony. They are important, first because the Luiseño takō is clearly a local manifestation of the Juaneño takwe or "eater,"[540] and secondly because these two officials preclude the employment of the paha who has been tacitly accepted by former writers as a general ceremonial assistant.[541] This latter office is definitely connected with the jimsonweed or toloache rite among the Luiseño, and has no connection with the more widespread and apparently older mourning ceremonies.

Toltcinic, the Image Ceremony[542]

The burning of the images was supposed to take place a year after the death of one or more clan members. Actually it occurred when there was a considerable number of dead persons to mourn for, and when sufficient material had been gathered to give such an expensive ceremony. A related clan was asked to supervise at this ceremony and their puhmutcvī seems to have been the presiding figure. He was called paīīakut, and he appointed a special fire-tender for the occasion. No clear statement concerning the exact nature of the relationship between the two clans involved was obtained. The actual case of this sort that was remembered included the wassuk and awaīū clans, which, as we have seen,[543] were related in the paternal line. The informants claimed however that clans related by marriage and not by blood often reciprocated in this manner, so the exact nature of the reciprocity involved remains a matter of surmise. The invited clan in turn summoned other clans with which they were ceremonially connected, and these clans arrived on certain nights appointed for their coming. Recent ceremonies seem to have lasted only one or two days, but formerly a week was the usual duration.

The images made by clan members of the deceased were concealed in the house of the nōta. They were dressed in native fashion, the

---

[540] See Kroeber's reference to this character mentioned by Boscana, *in* Handbook, 643.

[541] Kroeber, Handbook, 678. Sparkman in one place however states that the paha is "manager of morahash dance and of mani" (jimsonweed initiation for boys). See Du Bois, *op. cit.*, 78, n. 11.

[542] *Du Bois, op. cit.*, 101 and n. 43, gives Tochinish, and Sparkman, Tauchanish. The above account is based primarily upon information received from La Jolla informants, supplemented by the various published data.

[543] Present paper, genealogy 23.

frames being made of tule matting,[544] and were believed to resemble the persons they represented. When all the people had gathered, the various puhmutcvī took the images and assembled them in the center of the wāmkic.[545]   There the nōta gave each image to a relative of the deceased thus represented, and these people added finery to the costume of the image, weeping and wailing as they did so.   Then the images were again put in the center of the wāmkic with their faces hidden. When the images were turned facing the audience it was a signal for much lamentation. A woman, of uncertain clan affiliation, then led the singing accompanied by all the women.[546] This was called pēenic, and afterwards the men sang, which was called nūkwanic.[547] The images were then taken outside the wāmkic and piled up, while the various puhmutcvī took all the clothes from them to the guests. Then each puhmutcvī donated one garment and put it in a pile with the others. These were tied in a bundle with the denuded images and the paīiakut carried it on a trot to the wamkic. Followed by all his clan he circled the fire three times and then stopped, saying, "They are sending the soul up to the milky way (pīwiīc)."[548] Then he threw the bundle on the fire. Many gifts were distributed by the local clan at this time, while the paīiakut and fire-tender received special payment. Then a special dance called shuñuñic, accompanied by many songs, was performed until the last coal had burned out. The ceremoney ended with the local nōta thanking all present for their help and sympathy. He stated that he was glad it was all over and that he was now content.

The above description is almost verbatim that given the present author by La Jolla informants. The account of Du Bois differs in certain details and includes some rites not mentioned by my informants.[549]   An outline of her account is as follows: One night of singing precedes the making of the images, which takes place in seclusion. Then the main ceremony starts, the images are put in holes dug by the

[544] Not mentioned by my La Jolla informants, but Davis, *op. cit.*, 101, 102; and Kroeber, see Du Bois, *op. cit.*, 100, 180, refers to this custom. This matting was probably associated with the maswut concept.

[545] When there were more images than puhmutcvī any outsider, called taw, was asked to carry them.

[546] According to Du Bois, *op. cit.*, 101, and Sparkman, *op. cit.*, Tauchanish songs are sung. Tauchanish said to be derived from Towish, spirit, corpse, or devil.

[547] Du Bois states that the invited clan painted the faces of the images and conducted the entire ceremony, the clan of the deceased not even participating in the singing. *Op. cit.*, 101.

[548] This is a crude translation of the Kwinamish song series. See Du Bois, *op. cit.*, 109.

[549] *Op. cit.*, 101–103.

nōta, and gifts are piled around the base of each. There is a long
period of singing ended by the nōta whirling the bullroarer three
times, when the images are again removed to a distance. Then at a
signal from the bullroarer the dancers, painted and wearing head-
dresses, reappear and march around the wamkic accompanied by a
turtle-shell rattle. At this time a long series of songs is sung, and
the images are then burned. While these are burning the Sungamish
or finishing, and Topasish (meaning not given) songs are sung while
the men dance.

Morahash, the Whirling Dance

Then a special dancer performs the eagle or whirling dance, in
which he represents the circling and soaring of the eagle as it goes up
into the sky to the land of the dead. The dancer wears an eagle-
feather skirt, palat; head plumes of owl, crow, or raven feathers,
cheyat; ropes of owl feathers wound around head and neck, piwish;
and a headdress of long eagle feathers, apuma, worn upright on the
head. A rapid whirling motion causing the eagle-feather skirt to
stand out straight from the body seems to have been the most difficult
and climactic part of the dance. The dancer was called totawish, and
among the Diegueño the dance is commonly known as the ''tatahuila''
dance, a word which they say is not their own.[550] At La Jolla the
amagō clan owned this dance and all other clans had to ask permission
from the amagō nōta in order to perform it.

Further Details Concerning the Image Burning

While they burn the clothes (and the images), Pikmakvul or death
songs are sung describing the sickness, death, and burning of Wīyot.
The features of this song mentioned by Du Bois are very similar to the
Cahuilla image-burning songs describing the death and cremation of
Mūkat. At the end of this series all grunt three times and blow
toward the sky, while they throw many things on the fire. Then the
relatives of the dead distribute baskets and other presents to those
conducting the ceremony. After this interlude they sing, in order,
songs from ten song series, listed by Du Bois as:

1. Pikmakvul, the Wīyot songs of death.
2. Temengamesh, songs of seasons (concerning frog, earthworm, and water).
3. Chum towi, our spirit; the same as kwinamish (sending the spirit to the
    milky way).
4. Kamalum, the children of the earth mother.

---

[550] See Du Bois, *op. cit.*, 183.

5. Kish, the house (of the dead man?). Probably refers to the ceremonial house.
6. Anut, the ant; possibly referring to the ants who spread out the earth as in the Cahuilla creation myth (see p. 133, present paper) instead of the ant ordeal connected with the jimsonweed initiation for boys.[551]
7. Nokwanish, songs in memory of the dead. (According to Sparkman this word is nŭkwanic, or men's songs, mentioned above.)
8. Totowish, songs mentioning the Chungichnish avengers. Probably a later addition. According to Sparkman the term refers to the Morahash or eagle dancer.
9. Munival, songs of places and migration.
10. Nyachish, enemy songs. Such songs ended many of the Cahuilla ceremonies. In these they ridicule other clans.

Since Du Bois obtained her account from Lucario Cuevish, an old Luiseño born at San Luis Rey who remembered when the eastern Luiseño from La Jolla and Potrero were brought down to the Mission and initiated into the toloache rites,[552] it is probable that this account represents the ceremony of the west. The two accounts taken together give a comprehensive view of the entire rite and, allowing for slight local variations, in their totality suggest a ceremony very similar to that practiced by all three divisions of the Cahuilla, the Cupeño, and the Serrano. In other words, while the Luiseño had introduced a few western additions, the image-burning ceremony as carried out by them shared all its fundamentals with that of their eastern neighbors. Of the songs sung by the Luiseño at this time, only one (no. 8) and possibly another (no. 6), differ from songs of the creation sung by Cahuilla and Cupeño at their image-burning ceremony. It is certain that we have here an early and widespread ceremony, rooted in fear of the spirits of the dead and primarily seeking to drive them away, common to nearly all the Indians of southern California.

Notush Ceremony[553]

This ceremony, never performed by the eastern Luiseño groups, was an addition to the various mourning rites probably introduced by

---

[551] Du Bois, *op. cit.*, 112, Record 387, mentions the death of Wiyot in connection with this song, and the origin of death among the animals; also the chief hunting animals who took control after Wiyot's death. It is more probable that this song became attached to the ant ordeal at a later time, for it seems to contain no reference to such a rite. As the ant ordeal made boys hardy and strong for hunting, it is possible that this older hunting song came to be connected with it.

[552] *Op. cit.*, 74.

[553] No references to this ceremony were secured by the present author. The above account is drawn from that of Du Bois, *op. cit.*, 103, 104, and Kroeber, Handbook, 676.

the Juaneño or Gabrielino. It was apparently brought to San Luis Rey mission in the time of the padres. No images of the dead are mentioned, but the tall painted pole called kimul chehenish (little house, appearances or show; referring to objects hung on pole) was said to represent the spirit of the dead. The different colors on the various portions were supposed to represent the parts of the body. The top of the pole was always painted white and bore a raven skin called levalwash, "wide," below which were hung baskets and other valuables. The pole is said to have been "as high as a house" which must apply to a Caucasian house, the native habitation of southern California having a very low elevation.

There was singing and dancing when the pole was set up, and contests of skill were a prominent feature. A mythical contest of this kind at the first notush ceremony has been previously quoted (p. 288). The pole-climbing to reach the baskets and other valuables was undoubtedly a contest of this sort. Notush was a large ceremony involving several villages and was very costly. Lacking any detailed data concerning this rite among the coastal peoples, we can only point out its close resemblance to similar pole-climbing rites among the Pueblo peoples.[554] It was undoubtedly one of the many Pueblo traits received at an early time by the people of the California littoral, and diffused by them toward the east once more. Among the Luiseño it was clearly a late arrival.

Mōknic Ashwitī, Killing the Eagle[555]

As among the Mountain Cahuilla, eagles were killed ceremonially a year after the death of a chief or his close relatives.[556] As was true of all the southern California groups so far considered, eagles and their nests were owned by certain clans, or more exactly by the nōtas of the different clans.[557]

Mr. Frank Salmon, a white man of Pala, describes an eagle-killing ceremony he attended some thirty-five years ago, as follows. In this case the eagle's nest was on Palomar mountain,[558] and during the early

---

[554] See Goddard, illustration and text, 105, 106, Indians of the Southwest, Am. Mus. Nat. Hist., Handbook Series no. 2, 1921. Also Strong, *op. cit.*, 52.

[555] Kroeber, Handbook, 676, gives ashwut maknash or eagle-killing.

[556] The Diegueño dance leader for whom eagles were killed and the Luiseño "chief" or nōta are identical in position. See Kroeber, Handbook, 676.

[557] The California condor was ranked with the eagle in this regard. Sparkman, *op. cit.*, 227.

[558] The acketum clan at La Jolla owned an eagle's nest on Pine mountain.

spring it was watched by members of the Luiseño clan that owned it. When the watcher saw that game of rather large size was being taken to the nest he notified his nōta, and the village prepared for the cere- mony.   The next day a large number of people, nearly three hundred, went to the nest leaving sentries stationed within shouting distance of one another strung out all the way to the village.   When they came to the edge of the cliff, to Mr. Salmon's surprise, the heaviest Indian present, weighing some three hundred pounds, was selected to be lowered over the edge to the nest.   Just what the ceremonial position of this individual was, Mr. Salmon does not know, but he alone was allowed to handle the young birds.   When the young eagles were hauled up with their portly captor, a shout was raised which was immediately passed on by the sentries to the village.   There all the old people, especially, began to shout and sing with great rejoicings. The captor carried the two birds to the nōta's house where a special cage had been built for them.   While they were confined here all who wished to communicate with the spirits of the dead brought the eaglets food and then gave them their messages to the spirit world. After a week or so a ceremony was held at night, various men dancing and singing with one of the eagles; and after it had been given many messages it was killed by pressure over the lungs and the skin removed.

The above is a very brief description of such a ceremony which usually involved a contest between shamans to see who could kill the bird by means of his personal magic.   This connection of shamanism with the eagle-killing rite is most marked among the western peoples in southern California, and undoubtedly has some connection with the toloache cult.   According to Kroeber the actual lung-compression which killed the bird was a trick known only to toloache initiates,[559] but it was practiced among the Desert and Palm Springs Cahuilla where the toloache cult seems to have had but a slight hold.   As in the other mourning ceremonies an invited clan presided at this cere- mony, while the home clan provided the food and gifts.   After the skin of the eagle had been removed, the body was buried or burned with the proper ceremonies.

Two songs secured by Du Bois refer to the eagle-killing.   The first is a part of the Wīyot story and relates the attempt of the eagle to escape in each of the four directions, but everywhere death was waiting for him.   Thus in this song, which he sang when he became sick just before he died, he told the people of the spirit and of death

---

[559] Kroeber, Handbook, 676.

which must come to all. The second song refers to the dance with
the eagle, which took place one year after a death and ended the period
of mourning. The eagle connected with the spirits of the dead was
killed amid universal lamentations.[560]

La Jolla informants said that the first eagle was killed after the
death of Wīyot, therefore the ceremony was always performed after
a death, and the songs were all about Wīyot and the original eagle
killing. Local nōtas sometimes killed their own eagles and sometimes
sent them to other clans with whom they were ceremonially related.
Kroeber notes that the dead eagle was covered with gifts and presented to the chief of another village, who divided the presents among
his people and burned the body of the eagle. Such a ceremony was
given in honor of a dead chief by his successor. The same authority
notes that the condor was employed in the same way, while the people
of the coast used the bald eagle and chicken hawks.[561]

Manī Paic, the Jimsonweed Drinking

The following account of this ceremony, "the heart of the
Chungichnish religion" among the Luiseño, was obtained from Juan
Antonio Wassuk at La Jolla, and refers to a ceremony at Yapitca
(near La Jolla) some sixty-odd years ago. This was the last time the
ceremony was ever performed so far as Juan knows; he was a boy at
the time but does not seem to have been initiated.[562] Since the last
ceremony of this type was performed so long ago and the rite varied
in detail among different Luiseño groups, further details not mentioned by the informant but recorded by other authorities are included
and their sources indicated.

The ceremony occurred whenever several fathers told the nōta that
their sons were the right age to be initiated. The correct age for this
was believed to be between sixteen and twenty and before the youths
were married. It was strictly a clan affair and all food used during
the rites was gathered and prepared by clan members. When sufficient material was at hand the nōta sent word to the nōta of another
clan with which the first clan was closely related by marriage.[563] This

---

560 *Op. cit.*, 113–114, Records, 391, 392.

561 See Du Bois, *op. cit.*, 182.

562 According to Lucario Cuevish, a very old informant of Du Bois in 1906, the
toloache or jimsonweed ceremony was first performed by the Mountain or eastern
Luiseño in mission times when a group of them went down to San Luis Rey and
were initiated. Du Bois, *op. cit.*, 74.

563 This in general accords with Sparkman's statement, *op. cit.*, 221.

is the first definite statement received as to the exact relationship involved in these reciprocal functions among the Luiseño. The nōta thus notified presided at the ceremony and he in turn invited another clan with which his clan had intermarried. Several clans were notified in this manner and were given special nights on which they were to arrive. The boys were not informed of the impending event until the two clans had assembled and the paha of the invited clan gathered all the neophytes.

According to Juan Antonio the term paha meant "red racer" and this official was painted red and black, the two colors being divided vertically—the red half representing the male snake, the black half the female snake. This symbolism, considered in relation to the fact that two intermarrying clans were represented, suggests the moiety idea.[564] The Diegueño in their image-burning ceremony painted the faces of images representing males black and females red.[565] This inversion of the two colors representing sex dichotomy weakens the resemblance between Luiseño and Diegueño practice in this regard, but even so the parallel is striking. The paha was in actual charge of the ceremony and kept order among all the assembled guests. Du Bois adds the following:

One Paha is detailed to supervise the main place; the other, the place for drinking the toloache. By a well understood law no one is allowed to run around or make any noise. The Paha must be a hechicero, or shaman, of repute; and he could tell by looking at the mother of a boy whether she had been doing wrong in any way. No woman could be admitted to the ceremony who was unclean, unchaste, or menstruating.[566]

In addition to the paha, the puhmutcvī of the visiting clan was active in preparing the jimsonweed; in this rôle he was called nōktōmic. The decoction was prepared in a secluded spot away from the wāmkic where all the people were assembled, but close enough so that the pounding of mortar and pestle could be heard. The visiting paha and his clan members supervised the preparation of the drug. The paha would go to the wāmkic every now and then and trot around it three times, telling the assembled people that the jimsonweed was being prepared. While doing this he talked constantly in a low voice. Then he would return to the place where the decoction was being prepared. The paraphernalia used in this preparation were sacred.

564 At Zuñi the use of red and black paints seems to be a reflection of the moiety idea, as is the case at Isleta. For a discussion of these occurrences, see Strong, *op. cit.*, 13, 15, 47, 48.

565 Waterman, present series, 8:313, 1900.

566 *Op. cit.*, 78.

Du Bois gives more detail on these points:

In the main place the sacred enclosure of brush, the wamkish, is built in a circle to about the height of a man. On the ground inside are placed the sacred ceremonial objects: the tamyush or sacred stone toloache bowls, large and small—all but one which is to be used in the other place in drinking the toloache; feather head-dresses and eagle-feather skirts; and the paviut, the sacred sticks with flint in the end.

The tamyush, which since the last celebration of the ceremony have been buried in the ground, in a place known only to the chief, are taken out in good time and freshly painted so that they look nice. They are painted red, white, and black. Of the sacred ceremonial objects the tukmul is not in the main enclosure but at the other place. The tukmul is a flat winnowing basket sacred to the Chungichnish rites. It belongs to the men, that is, is possessed by every initiate, and during every ceremony it is placed on the ground containing grain, the sacred stone pipes, or other objects. . . . . It is dark in the place where they take toloache. The large tamyush selected for the purpose is placed on the ground before the chief. It contains the root, previously prepared and dried, perhaps a year before. The chief pounds the dry scraped bark with the stone mano (muller or pestle) to the accompaniment of a curious recitative, not a song: "Chanyoko, yoko," while the boys stand waiting in the darkness. The powder is then placed in a small twined sifting basket and sifted again into the tamyush, which is filled with water. The Paha goes about whispering: "Keep quiet all of you. Do not talk. Everyone keep quiet."

The chief superintends the drinking, and as the candidates kneel in turn before the big tamyush to drink out of it, he holds the head of each with the palm of his hand under the forehead, and raises it when they have drunk a sufficient quantity of the liquid, watching to see that they do not drink too much. They drink from the tamyush in which the toloache was mixed.

They give the toloache to the boys in the dark; and while it is being administered, the Paha goes over to the main place three times in succession, and the third time tells them to get ready for Mani is coming. He sings a curious recitative.[567]

According to Juan Antonio, at the La Jolla initiation he witnessed the presiding puhmutcvī gave each boy a small drink of the decoction out of a small basket, tcilkut, or a small pottery jar, peclic. After this the boys were given a lecture by the puhmutcvī and others, which warned them to be good, to marry, not to run loose, and especially not marry any relative. Then the paha returned to the wāmkic and told the people there to brighten up the fire, but before entering the enclosure he circled it three times chanting as he did so. In his hand he carried a stick painted red which was called wakut.[568] The naked bodies of the men and boys were painted and they wore feather headbands.[569] The paha dashed back and forth clearing the way to the

---

[567] Du Bois, *op. cit.*, 77, 78.

[568] Possibly one of the "Chungichnish" sticks mentioned by Du Bois, *op. cit.*, 82.

[569] White clay and charcoal on the backs of the dancers helped them withstand the heat, Du Bois, *op. cit.*, 81.

wāmkic, and all the dancers followed him, dancing and uttering a deep guttural ''heritha'' so constantly that it became like hiccoughing and they could not stop. It was believed that any spectator who might laugh at this time would be killed by the magic power of the paha.

The Fire Dance

On reaching the wāmkic the dancers circled the fire three times and the neophytes began to drop from the narcotic effect of the drug they had taken. The paha dragged these away from the fire and the various shamans, pūalem, sought to bring them back to consciousness. Outside the ring of male dancers all the onlookers danced clockwise around the fire, chanting the manī songs as they did so. Then the fire was stirred up, the dancers took off their headdresses and carried them in their hands, while the paha exhorted them to come up close to the fire. After circling the fire three times all the men sat down in a ring and, gradually approaching, feet first, put it out. Lead by the paha, they then rose and danced on the embers until all was dark.

According to Du Bois the fire was put out by witchcraft, and many feats of legerdemain were performed by the various shamans. The songs sung during these ceremonies referred to the sacred toloache mortar, which like the sacred winnowing basket walked of its own accord. Various Chungichnish songs were sung and new songs were sometimes composed. In the procession to the wamkish and in the dance which followed, certain of the dancers imitated the cries and actions of various animals.[570] Boscana makes a positive and clear statement concerning the acquisition of personal guardian spirits at this time,[571] and it is very probable that the above-mentioned antics are a reflection of this widespread belief. Unfortunately no very clear data on this point have yet been secured in southern California.[572]

---

[570] *Op. cit.*, 79–82. See pl. 1, figs. 1 and 2. This imitation of animals extended well to the north and west for, in an unpublished letter written by Señor Don José Bandini in December, 1828, is the following statement: ''I saw once at the Mission of San Luis Obispo a body of these gentiles who had arrived there to attend a fiesta, ... Their dances consisted of an attempt to imitate the coyotes, the deer, and other animals and are accompanied by a series of intolerable howls. The Catholic Indians in everything resemble the gentiles.''

[571] See Alfred Robinson, Life in California (ed. 1; New York, 1846), 270–271.

[572] The best reference on this question in southern California is Benedict's paper on the Serrano, *op. cit.*, 382–385. Sparkman, *op. cit.*, 215–221, and Du Bois, *op. cit.*, 80, 81, n. 17, touch on it.

Tanic Dance

To return to the La Jolla ceremony described by Juan Antonio, the fire dance was followed by the tanic ceremony as soon as the fire had been rekindled. This ceremony among the La Jolla clans was owned by the wassuk people, and any other clan wishing to give the ceremony had to ask the wassuk nōta to perform it. This special clan ownership probably was due to the wassuk nōta's having been the first to learn the ceremony from the western clans at San Luis Rey mission. In addition to being a regular part of the toloache initiation, tanic was also performed to avoid evil when any man dreamed of the various Chungichnish avengers.[573] If a man in an outside clan had such a dream he told his nōta, who in turn asked the wassuk nōta to come and hold tanic. Such a ceremony seems to have had no initiatory aspects.

However, as a part of the initiation rite, the tanic dance lasted for the remainder of the night with the half-conscious neophytes clinging to the older men who dragged them around the fire as they danced. When a boy became totally unconscious he was carried away to the place where the drink was administered and left to sleep off the effects of the drug. All the dancers, aside from the neophytes, were from the invited clan. In the morning all slept, the boys being kept together in seclusion by the paha. The neophytes received a small amount of food given them by the paha, but the entire period of their initiation ceremony was one of fasting and seclusion.[574] Each morning they bathed in cold water and their bodies were painted. The La Jolla ceremony lasted four days, and on each of the first three nights the above ceremony was repeated with a different clan and paha in charge of the boys. As soon as one invited clan had performed the night-long ceremony they departed and another took their place.[575] The paha and the older members of each clan seem to have given instructions, songs, and esoteric knowledge to the neophytes.

---

[573] This is similar to the Mountain Cahuilla custom of holding jimsonweed ceremonies to ward off disaster, pestilence, or drought. This belief among the Luiseño is mentioned by Kroeber, in Du Bois, *op. cit.*, 179.

[574] Salt and meat especially were taboo, Du Bois, *op. cit.*, 80–82.

[575] Du Bois, *op. cit.*, 82, states that four or five clans participated in such a rite. According to Sparkman, *op. cit.*, 221, the ceremony continued for a month, and for a year they were forbidden to eat meat or salt. Only at the end of this period were the final rites performed. As Kroeber suggests, Handbook, 670, the exact duration of the ceremony may not have been definitely fixed.

Final Initiation Rites

Juan's account of the toloache rites is unique in that he combines the ceremonial ground-painting and the wānawut pit into one figure. There seems to be no doubt that this was actually the case in the ceremony he describes, but it is probable that it was due to a local lapse in ritualistic accuracy rather than a general custom. The unification of the two figures was described to Kroeber in 1904, by Pauma and Rincon informants,[576] so there seems to be no doubt that this departure from general usage was a definite local trait.

On the morning of the fourth day of the La Jolla ceremony a rectangular pit was dug (4 by 3½ by 2 feet deep), in which were placed three small rocks. Around these evenly spaced central rocks were several figures designed with colored earths. The bear, rattlesnake, tree, house, devil (tōvic), "stick beetle" (nahatcic), and Tcungiknish (La Jolla pronunciation of Chungichnish) were represented, as well as other figures which the informant did not remember clearly. Juan was very vague concerning this symbolism; he believed the figures for the devil (tōwic) and Chungichnish were the same, and any figure might represent them for no one had ever seen either of them. The former was heard only in the squeak of the bat (tisuk), and the latter was an evil spirit whose crying was sometimes heard but whose person had never been seen. He was not the raven,[577] and any design called by his name might represent him. Among the eastern Luiseño, Chungichnish seems to have been a dangerous spirit rather than a great deity. The rattlesnake was symbolized by a series of diamonds meeting end to end, and the "stick beetle" by a small heap of gray ashes. (According to Juan this insect was about two inches long, gray in color, and was poisonous.) The other figures were not remembered by the informant. At this time the wānawut was not in the pit.[578]

The neophytes were grouped around this pit, with all the people forming a circle outside. The paha, or a near male relative of each

---

[576] See Du Bois, *op. cit.*, 177–179.

[577] Contrary to Sparkman's statement, *op. cit.*, 218, but in accord with other authorities. The raven was closely associated with Chungichnish, usually as his messenger, but the god does not seem to have been actually identified with the bird. The Cupeño however do call the raven tcingitnic.

[578] According to Juan Antonio Wassuk the figure, or ground-painting, without the wānawut, was called torōhaic, identical with eskanish tarohayish given by Du Bois, *op. cit.*, 89. The double term is characteristic, eskanish meaning any kind of images or figures, and tarohayish this particular kind of image. The term nahish or nawish (marking, writing, or painting) is also used.

boy, explained the meaning of the figures, telling the boys that the house would harm them, the rock fall on them, the tree break under them, and bear and rattlesnake kill them if they were evil; but if they were good, married in the right way (that is, outside their clan), and did the right things for the old people, none of these figures would harm them. Then all present grunted "heritha" three times and exhaled.

Then the nōta took a hair rope or string, the wānawut, out of his mouth. The wānawut had previously been carried all around the village to keep away evil spirits. This string the paha placed around the sand painting in the pit, shaping it into a human form with a head, two legs, and outstretched arms.[579] The three rocks were within this figure, one at about the waist, another in the middle, and the third near the head. One at a time the neophytes stepped into the pit with both feet on the first rock (near the waist of the figure), then jumped from that to the next two rocks and out of the pit. Should a boy slip off a rock all his relatives mourned loudly, for that was considered an evil sign, and he would die young. All cheered and rejoiced as every boy successfully passed over the stones. After this last ordeal the boys were entitled to dance at all ceremonies.

The above description of the final rites applies to the last ceremony of the sort at La Jolla, and is obviously much condensed. This may be due to the youth of the informant at the time, the fact that he was not fully initiated, or to an incomplete performance of the ceremony itself. Other informants, quoted by earlier investigators, go into more detail concerning the ground-painting and wānawut. Sparkman gives a full translation of the lecture and warnings received by an initiate,[580] and Kroeber gives a detailed and comparative discussion of the ethics involved.[581] There seems no need to repeat these statements here: sufficient is it to say that an exemplary conduct of life from the native viewpoint was demanded of the initiate, failing in which he would meet disaster at the hands of the Chungichnish avengers. According to Du Bois[582] the wānawut rite came before the explanation of the ground-painting. Her synoptic account of the lecture given over the latter figure is similar to but less detailed than that given by Sparkman. There is however no doubt that the wānawut and the ground-painting were separate figures in the usual Luiseño ceremony; as has

[579] See wānawut, figured in Du Bois, *op. cit.*, 85, fig. 1.

[580] *Op. cit.*, 223, 224.

[581] Handbook, 683–685.

[582] *Op. cit.*, 82–84.

been shown, this was true even among the Cupeño still farther east than La Jolla, so Juan's account of their combination may be regarded as a local anomaly.

According to Du Bois, the boys' initiation closed, as did that of the girls', with the mastication and expectoration of a lump of salt and sage seed into the center of the ground-painting.[583] Before the performance of this act the nōta touched the lump to the forehead, shoulders, breast, knees, and feet of the initiates, telling them to always make an invocation to the rising sun by grunting three times and exhaling. This seems to be a customary ceremonial act, and is said to waft away evil or dead spirits. When the lump of sage seed is put into the mouth of the candidate he kneels over the ground-painting and spits it into the central hole.[584] The lecturer examined this: if it was dry he said the youth had heeded his advice; if wet he had not. In the latter case the spectators showed their disapprobation by shouting.[585] Then the central portion of the painting was carefully covered up by the old men who thus obliterated the sand-painting.[584] Du Bois suggests the probability that the boys had a race and painted certain rocks as was done in the ant ordeal, but no mention of this has been recorded.[586] A feast, distribution of presents, and ceremonial burning of the wāmkic ended the ceremony.[587]

The foregoing account of the toloache initiation ceremony has only touched on the technical detail and symbolism involved in the wānawut figure and the sand-paintings. A consideration of these features, which have been dealt with at considerable length by other writers,[588] leads too far afield into the realm of native religion. Since the present study is primarily concerned with the organization of society, further consideration of these ceremonial details may well be left for a later study of religion and mythology in the area.

---

[583] *Op. cit.*, 83.

[584] *Op. cit.*, 83.

[585] *Op. cit.*, 222.

[586] *Op. cit.*, 84. Such a race closed the Serrano and Cupeño toloache ceremony.

[587] According to Kroeber, Handbook, 672, the wānawut is buried, a final tanic dance lasts through the night, ending with a fire dance.

[588] Du Bois, *op. cit.*, discusses the wānawut concept, 85–87; and the sand-painting, 87–91. Sparkman gives some detail on the ground-painting, *op. cit.*, 221, 222, and pl. 20. Kroeber discusses both concepts, the wānawut, Handbook, 671, 672, and the ground-painting, 661–665, and fig. 56.

ANTINIC,[589] THE ANT ORDEAL

This rite seems to have been a follow-up of the toloache drinking, aimed at demonstrating and increasing the hardihood and endurance of the older initiates. It was performed at varying intervals depending on the number of candidates for the ordeal. Prior to the actual ant ordeal there was a night of singing, or whistling,[590] and early in the morning the chosen candidates were taken into the house or sacred enclosure and given warm water to drink; then they were conducted to the place where the ants had been gathered. A pit had been dug and this was filled with hard-stinging ants gathered beforehand by the chief. The candidates, one at a time, lay down in the pit and their naked bodies were covered with ants, while a special song was sung. After a time the boys got up and the ants were whipped off their bodies with nettles.[591]

When all was over, the sand-painting was made as in the toloache rite and the lump of sage seed and salt used in the same way. A race was then run, similar to those at the time of a new moon, and the winner of the race painted the designated rock with red and black paint. After this the anut songs were sung to the accompaniment of ringing stones.

TATTOOING

It seems that there was once a similar ceremony for tattooing, when the subject lay down in a certain place, and was tattooed by persons who had previously fasted. The songs connected with this ceremony are not remembered.[592] Women were tattooed on the chin, with a vertical line down the forehead and a small circle on each cheek. On their wrists there were bands of tattooing and across the breast a curved band or line from which lines extended downward. Men tattooed less than women.[593] Since similar ceremonies occurred among all the southern California Shoshoneans as far east as the Desert Cahuilla there seems no reason for connecting these rites with the Chungichnish or toloache cults.

---

[589] Given as antish and tivihayish by Kroeber, Handbook, 672.

[590] Du Bois, *op. cit.*, 91.

[591] According to Juan Antonio Wassuk a sister of each boy was supposed to do this.

[592] This account, as well as that of the ant ordeal, is taken almost entirely from Du Bois, *op. cit.*, 91, 92. Modern informants remember that there was such a ceremony but can recount none of the details.

[593] Kroeber, see Du Bois, *op. cit.*, 184.

UNISH MATAKISH,[594] THE BURIAL OF A CHUNGICHNISH INITIATE'S PARAPHERNALIA

This occurred on the death of a man who had drunk the jimson-weed in his youth, and was held to bury the feather headdress, sacred stick, and other ceremonial objects he possessed. It was performed by the chief of his party or clan. As in the jimsonweed drinking two places are prepared, one in which the ceremonial objects such as the tamyush (sacred toloache mortars) are cleaned and painted, and another in which the sand-painting is made. The latter appears to be the same as that used in the boys' initiation rite. Tukmul, the sacred winnowing basket, is in the painting and represents Chungichnish. All march out from the place of preparation, led by the nōta, and singing Chungichnish songs proceed to the place where the sand-painting has been made. The ceremonial equipment of the deceased is placed in the central hole of this figure and is buried by pushing in the sand from the edges. All the songs sung at this time refer to Chungichnish and the sacred objects, always ending with the tamyush. These songs were given the people by Chungichnish and were not subject to clan ownership.

The sacred Chungichnish objects bear a close resemblance to those contained in the sacred maswut bundles of the various clans. Whether among the western Luiseño the Chungichnish cult had taken over the sacred-bundle concept from the local clans has not been determined. Among the eastern Luiseño the maswut bundles seem to have been definitely associated with the separate clans, and such paraphernalia as were connected with the Chungichnish or toloache rites were of a purely personal nature. This burial of the Chungichnish objects among the Luiseño suggests the burial of the maswut bundle recorded among the Mountain Cahuilla.[595]

OTHER CEREMONIES

The foregoing rites almost exhaust the list of known Luiseño ceremonies, but there are a few minor activities which deserve mention. There was a race at the time of a new moon described by Du Bois.[596]

---

[594] Sparkman translates yunish, as burying an initiate's ceremonial feathers; and matakish, as grinding stone. See Du Bois, *op. cit.*, 92, n. 34. This translation seems rather dubious, but no other has yet been obtained. The above account is taken from Du Bois.

[595] Present paper, p. 155.

[596] *Op. cit.*, 135. This seems to be a part of the creation myth. Also see Sparkman's note concerning hayish, the race at the time of the new moon, *ibid.*, 110, n. 93.

The chief men who had charge of these things would know when the new moon was expected and would watch for it. Then they would get ready, and just as the moon appeared one man would start a fire and shout, and all would come together. They would shout three times, and then all start together in a straight line, side by side, and run until the fastest runner got ahead of the others, when he cut across in front of them, and that was the end of it. There might be twenty to fifty who did the running. They made the indescribable guttural invocation to send their spirits to the moon, and they had to have a fire as they did in every religious ceremony. The head men always started the fire, and the long ceremonial pipes they smoked were lighted at it.

Certain songs were sung and rites performed to bring an abundance of rain, grass, and acorns. Namkush was such a ceremony to make acorns, rabbits, etc., plentiful. Tu'nish was a similar ceremony to make plants which were valued, such as chia, grow.[597] Some shamans claimed to have power to bring rain.[598]

Sometimes several shamans met together to kill some certain man. At such an occasion tukmul chayut (flat coiled basket and flat twined basket) were made ready, each man bringing his own basket. This was done at the command of Chungichnish.[599] Whether this meeting of shamans had any relation to the contests of shamans, previously mentioned as occurring among the Mountain Cahuilla, is uncertain. The above are the merest fragments of beliefs which may formerly have played a prominent part in Luiseño life.

THE RELATION OF SONG AND CEREMONY

Thanks to the efforts of Du Bois it is possible in part to correlate Luiseño songs with the various ceremonies. While the songs which she secured on phonographic records have not, so far as I know, been fully annotated or translated, in many cases they have been briefly summarized in her paper on the Luiseño.[600] In the following summary I have attempted to give under the heading of each ceremony the songs known to have been sung in connection with it, and to give a brief résumé of their content. Page and record numbers given below refer to Du Bois' paper.

---

[597] Du Bois, *op. cit.*, 111, n. 104, 105.

[598] Sparkman, *op. cit.*, 217, 218. Compare the Yokuts beliefs on this score, Kroeber, Handbook, 518.

[599] Du Bois, *op. cit.*, 111, 112. Kroeber, Am. Jour. Folklore, 21:41, 1908, mentions a Gabrielino (at San Fernando) rite wherein thirteen men caused sickness and earthquake by forming a ground-painting, with twelve strings which were shaken. This may refer to a shaman's meeting similar to the above, but it certainly refers to the use of the ground-painting among the Gabrielino.

[600] *Op. cit.*, 1908.

TABLE 20

ALIGNMENT OF SONGS AND CEREMONIES

1. *Mourning and Image-Burning Ceremonies: Song Series and Content*

Tauchinish (p. 101), the image ritual. Rec. 1098, p. 121, refers to making images in sacred enclosure.

Shangamish (p. 101), finishing songs.

Tapa'sash (p. 101), for men's dancing.

Pi'mukvul (pp. 101, 102), death and burning of Wīyot. Rec. 401, p. 117, Wīyot enumerates months in which he may die; p. 114 same; Rec. 412, p. 118, cremation of Wīyot; Rec. 379, p. 108, admonition concerning daily bath; Rec. 413, p. 119, Wīyot sick, enumerates months in which he may die; Rec. 1082, p. 121, woman's song of Wīyot, mentions months in which he may die; Rec. 1100, p. 121, Wīyot counts the months in which he may die.

Temenganesh (p. 102), song of seasons. Rec. 375, p. 107, mentions wānawut and humming sounds prior to the cremation; p. 108, mentions things in the ocean; Rec. 416, p. 121, mentions stars and Wīyot's talk concerning the east where he will rise; Rec. 1082, p. 121, woman's song of Wīyot, mentions months in which he may die.

Chumtowi and Kwinamish (p. 102), our spirit. Rec. 379, p. 109, mentions Wīyot, his death, council, and sand-painting. Rec. 408, p. 117, mentions First People, and hollow coffer in which sacred feathers are kept. Recs. 379, 380, 381, 382, pp. 109, 110, refer to sending the spirit to the milky way; Yula Wanawut, the spirit of the dead; the tying of the spirit in the sky; death.

Kamalum (p. 102), mentions "our sons or children." Children of the earth-mother, and the mountains that were the first people.

Kish (pp. 102, 105), of the house.

Anut (p. 102), the ant ordeal (?). Rec. 387, p. 112, mentions the arrangement of ceremonies and the first killing of various animals after the death of Wīyot.

Nokwanish (p. 102), songs in memory of the dead. Tovit, the little rabbit, first sang them when they burned Wīyot. General name for men's songs (Sparkman, n. 49).

Totowish (p. 102), refers to the avengers of Chungichnish. (Sparkman however translates totowish as the dancer of the morahash ceremony, n. 50.)

Monival (p. 103), songs of places and landmarks. Rec. 383, p. 110, an individual and inherited song.

Nyachish (p. 103), enemy songs.

2. *Songs Directly Connected with the Image-Burning Ceremony*

Rec. 406, p. 117, about Tomaiyowit the earth-mother and the noise when the first people were born.

Rec. 405, p. 117, Tomaiyowit making the earth larger for her children.

Rec. 1080, p. 121, song of Wīyot after he was burned.

Rec. 1102, p. 122, song of the dead, not used in dancing, sung in Image ceremony. When relatives come to console family they stay all night and sing this song. Mentions Antares and Altair rising in the early morning. When Antares rises winter is at an end, etc.

Rec. 393, p. 114, Wīyot names months in which he may die.

P. 95, Ashish (girls' puberty ceremony) songs used in Image ceremony.

3. *Eagle-Killing Ceremony*

Rec. 391, p. 113, song of eagle trying to escape death. Died at Temecula. Part of Wīyot story.

Rec. 392, p. 113, connection of eagle with spirits of dead. Song to which they dance with eagle.

4. *Morahash or Whirling Dance*

P. 183, songs descriptive of dancing. La Jolla informants say songs describe flight and death of the eagle. Said to refer to the Wīyot story.

P. 102, n. 50. Sparkman translates totowish as morahash dancer. Du Bois says totowish is a song referring to Chungichnish avengers. This point is obscure.

No songs recorded.

5. *Notish Ceremony*

6. *Girls' Adolescence Ceremony*

Rec. 410, p. 118, Ashish song, deer trying to escape death, killed by buzzard and blue fly.

P. 93, 95, mentions ashish songs.

Rec. 379, p. 109, Kwinamish songs (see above), come second in girls' ceremony.

Rec. 379, p. 115, first races, travels of first people.

Rec. 411, p. 118, Anut song, said to be a very ancient song, only sung at girls' initiation at a later time.

Rec. 414, p. 120, song of the rabbit hunt. An Ashish song which mentions the man who leads hunt.

Rec. 415, p. 121, mentions hill where painted rock is.

Rec. 1084, p. 121, sung to the accompaniment of ringing stones. Gives instruction to girls.

7. *Jimsonweed Drinking*

Rec. 394, p. 79, n. 14, refers to the tamyush (toloache mortar) walking and twisting of its own accord. (Also p. 114.)

P. 80, Chungichnish and newly composed songs sung.

P. 80, n. 18, song referring to placing bones of Wīyot in a receptacle and pouring them into a hole in the ground.

Rec. 1085, p. 121, toloache drinking song. Refers to the first feeling of intoxication.

8. *Ant Ordeal*

P. 91, toma no kwato (no meaning given).

P. 92, songs of Anut, four or five of which are remembered, sung to accompaniment of ringing stones.

(See also above under Mourning and Image-Burning Ceremonies.)

9. *Wānawut Rite*

No songs recorded. Considerable symbolism related to it, see pp. 85–87. Connected with death, which came from Wīyot, and the Milky Way where spirits of the dead go.

10. *Sand-Painting*

No songs recorded. Symbolism related to it, pp. 87–91. Connected with mountain lion, wolf, and sea-fog who first made it. They also were the first to institute mani or toloache drinking. Used in four initiatory (or allied) ceremonies: girls' puberty rite, boys' initiation, ant ordeal, and burial of dead initiate's feathers.

11. *Chungichnish Ceremony of Unish Matakish*

P. 93, Chungichnish songs sung at this time.

Rec. 1095, p. 123, Chungichnish dance song, tells about the feather head-dress and the owl whose feathers are used to make it.

12. *Chungichnish Songs*

P. 105. Chungichnish songs include Chatish, Numkish, and Tuknish. Chatish is a poisoning song. Numkish and Tuknish are songs to make acorns, rabbits, chia, etc., plentiful; p. 111, n. 104, 105.

• Rec. 390, p. 113, Chungichnish song, mentions horned owl whose feathers make sacred headdress. The seaweed on the seashore, one of the first people, sacred to Chungichnish.

Rec. 404, p. 117, Chungichnish song, in the extinct language of the coast.

Rec. 1085 (second song), p. 121, a Chungichnish song sung when they reach the dancing place.

Rec. 1078, p. 122, Chungichnish song, in the extinct language of the coast (Gabrielino). Brought from Los Flores, originally from Los Bolsas south of Santa Ana.

Rec. 1095, p. 123, Chungichnish dance song, sung when feathers of dead initiate are buried. Sung in the Unish Matakish ceremony (see above).

(Other songs which do not fit into this classification are shamanistic or individual clan songs, but the greater majorty of Luiseño songs recorded by Du Bois are included in the above list.)

The foregoing tabulation brings out several significant points. It shows that all songs connected with the mourning ceremonies[601] seem to refer to the creation story, especially that portion concerning the dying god Wīyot. Only one song has any reference to the Chungichnish cult, and that, the Totowish song, is said by Sparkman to refer to the morahash dancer. Until it is further verified as a definite part of the song series connected with the mourning ceremonies, it may be left out of consideration. This dependence on the creation myth extends to the allied eagle-killing ceremony, and probably to the morahash or whirling dance. These two rites seem to be especially connected with the dying-god portion of the myth.

The songs of the girls' adolescence ceremony seem to refer to the creation myth, but they have no direct reference to the death of Wīyot, nor have they any apparent connection with either the toloache or the Chungichnish series. The ant or anut song, said to be very old, is connected with the ant ordeal as well. It is not recorded for the boys' initiation. Apparently the mythical substratum from which the songs for the girls' puberty ceremonies are derived is not represented to any degree in other ritualistic activities.

---

[601] The Notish ceremony for which no songs are recorded is clearly a late addition to the ritualistic calendar of the eastern Luiseño. The above remarks do not refer to this ceremony.

Toloache songs refer mainly to the jimsonweed, the sacred mortars, and the intoxication. One song refers to Wīyot, and a reference is made to Chungichnish songs, though none are given in this connection. In general it seems that the rites connected with the jimsonweed drinking combine both the Wīyot and Chungichnish motifs with others revolving around the sanctity and narcotic effect of the drug itself. The same relationship seems to be involved in the symbolism of the ground-painting and the wānawut, but the mythical basis of these two concepts seems rather free from the various features that mark the Chungichnish cult. It would seem, therefore, that they represented older concepts readapted to the rites and ideas connected with the Chungichnish cult, but were more closely allied to the various initiatory aspects of the toloache complex.

The Chungichnish songs refer to shamanistic activities, to various objects connected with the coast, and are often in the language of that region, presumably Gabrielino. These songs are sung at the Unish Matakish ceremony when the feathers of the Chungichnish initiate are buried. On the basis of historical evidence alone they might be assigned to a relatively recent period for the Luiseño, and a consideration of the limited distribution of ceremonies with which they are connected bears this out.

To attempt to delineate too sharply the different cults or ceremonial complexes, and the songs with which they are associated, does some violence to the facts. In the nature of things there has been much intermingling of older and later ceremonies and song series, but, as the foregoing table demonstrates, lines of cleavage are still discernible. Purely on the basis of these associations we may set aside the girls' puberty ceremony as unique, while a glance at its distribution shows it to be ubiquitous in the area, and presumably of great antiquity.[602] In the same way we may set aside the mourning ceremonies, their mythical counterparts and their distribution, assigning them to an old and basic cultural level in southern California.[603] With the exception of the notish ceremony which is clearly a late addition from the west, and the morahash or whirling dance which is limited in distribution, the other mourning rites extend beyond the borders of all the groups we have thus far considered.

The jimsonweed drinking, its associated ground-painting and wānawut rite, and the initiatory and other concepts which the three

[602] See Kroeber, Handbook, 864, table 9, for a tabular treatment of this widespread rite in California. Also see Anthropology, 300, 301, 1923.

[603] Kroeber, Handbook, 859–861.

involve, may very well be summed up under the term toloache cult. Disregarding for the time being the larger problem involved in the basic diffusion of the use of this narcotic, we can safely say that in southern California it has spread from the shores of the Pacific east as far as the Santa Rosa and San Jacinto mountains and south well into Diegueño territory. With this secondary diffusion[604] it has carried the complex of ideas and ritualistic practices which may be termed the toloache cult.

The last cult to be distinguished in southern California had a late, almost historic start,[605] and a very limited range of diffusion. This is the Chungichnish cult, associated with the god of that name and the avengers or mythical monsters who enforced his dictates. As the foregoing study shows, this western cult reached the eastern Luiseño in some degree, but beyond them it does not seem to have penetrated.

The Chungichnish and toloache cults have often been grouped together as the Chungichnish toloache cult,[606] but the foregoing consideration of the Serrano, Cahuilla, and Cupeño demonstrates the need of splitting these terms. Beyond the boundaries of the Luiseño and Cupeño the term Chungichnish is unknown, but the toloache cult has in part penetrated to all these groups.[607] This is a matter for later consideration, but the point is here made that the content of Luiseño songs (in so far as they are known) associated with the different Luiseño ceremonies, clearly shows these ceremonies to be grouped. When the groups of ceremonies thus distinguished are studied in regard to distribution, they show that those connected with the creation story are the most widely spread, those connected with the toloache songs are intermediate in range, and those connected with the Chungichnish songs are limited almost entirely to the Luiseño and their western neighbors. Since the relationship of song to ceremony has such important correlates, it may be well to consider the even more fundamental relationship between Luiseño songs and myths.

---

[604] See Kroeber, Handbook, 793, and Anthropology, 810, 1923.

[605] Kroeber, Handbook, 622, 656.

[606] Kroeber, Handbook, 712, although they are clearly distinguished in Anthropology, 309–316, 1923.

[607] Waterman, *op. cit.*, 274–276, in his discussion of Diegueño religion brings out the above distinction. The importance attached by the Diegueño to adolescence and their fear of the spirits of the dead, beliefs which motivate their main ceremonial activities, likewise find expression among the Cahuilla, Cupeño, and Serrano. The later cult rituals have overlaid this more universal pattern in a degree which decreases markedly to the east and the south of Luiseño and Gabrielino territory.

Relation of Song and Myth

Cahuilla, Cupeño, and Serrano informants all state that the majority of their ceremonial songs are derived from their respective creation myths, with the occasional addition of certain alien song series acquired from near-by peoples. The Palm Springs Cahuilla story of the creation is actually a long song series translated into prose.[608] It was dictated, or rather sung by the clan leader, each verse being translated without the reiteration which made its recording last three days. At the ceremony which had just been concluded this song furnished the main theme for nearly a week's singing. My informants were definite in their statements concerning the agreement between song and myth. This applied to all mourning ceremonies, the only exception to the rule being the inclusion of the Mohave song series previously mentioned.[609] Whether this close accord applied to all other ceremonies is more doubtful. The song series connected with the toloache rites among the above mentioned groups contain many in alien western dialects, but those used at the girls' adolescence ceremony are said to be in the language of the respective groups and in accord with their individual mythologies.

Apparently the Luiseño songs are aligned with their various ceremonies in the same manner, and it seems equally probable that the song series used with the girls' adolescence and mourning rites is derived from their creation myth. That these creation myths and the songs derived therefrom vary locally accords with the universal scheme of small autonomous groups throughout southern California. Each group was a political and ceremonial unit, and while regional patterns are clearly discernible, the amount of minor differentiation in myth and ceremony is almost infinite. The fragmentary nature of recorded songs, and the seeming variety in myth tend to obscure the relationship between the two, but that there was a strong linkage between both manifestations seems certain. In this regard Kroeber makes the following statement concerning the Luiseño.

It appears that nearly all the songs except those of a specific shamanistic character consist of mythological allusions. They may be said to float in a web of tradition. Those that are not mythological are directly descriptive of the ritual to which they pertain. . . . . Precisely to what extent the Luiseño and Gabrielino songs of each kind constitute a series strung on a single plot can not yet be said. But it is clear that they approach closely to the song cycles of the Mohave and Yuma. On the coast, song and ceremony are two parallel developments, interconnected at innumerable points, yet essentially pursuing

---

608 Present paper, pp. 130–143.   609 Present paper, p. 127.

separate courses. In the Colorado valley ritual has been nearly effaced, or has come to consist essentially of singing, with the choice of the series dependent on the singer rather than the occasion.[610]

Since it appears that Luiseño song series and ceremonies are not as dissociated as seemed to be the case, while native testimony among the Cahuilla, Cupeño, and Serrano closely identify the two, the resemblance between Luiseño and Colorado river ceremonial practices becomes less striking. Among these latter groups song cycles vary widely with the individual performers, and on the whole they bear slight relationship to the actual creation myths.[611] Waterman has shown how similar are the Luiseño and Mohave versions of the creation,[612] but Kroeber's treatment of Mohave ritualistic singing tends to isolate their origin myth from their various song cycles. Since the latter strongly predominate in actual group religious activities, while the origin myth seems to be outside this pattern, it is possible that the origin stories of the Colorado river peoples were taken over from the Luiseño and their neighbors, or from the Pima and Papago,[613] whose creation myths in turn resemble those of southern California. There is the alternative possibility, as Kroeber suggests, that ritual has faded away in Colorado river society to be replaced by the singing of these dream songs, but the fact that these song cycles contain little that is fundamentally connected with the old ideas of the creation, militates against this view. The song series of southern California on the other hand are saturated with such ideas, and in all but the later cult activities are derived directly from the creation myths. This is a question whose final answer may only be given after a more intensive comparison of the religions of the groups involved, but it seems highly probable that there is more fundamental similarity in myth and ceremony between the Piman peoples and the southern California Shoshoneans than between the latter and the Yuman peoples of the Colorado river. The unique nature of Diegueño mythology is undoubtedly significant in this regard,[612] but until more is known of the Yuman peoples of the northern portion of Lower California many Diegueño concepts will remain obscure.

Concerning the basic similarity of Luiseño and Cahuilla mythology there can be no doubt.[614] Like those of the Cahuilla, the Luiseño

---

[610] Handbook, 656–685.   [611] Kroeber, Handbook, 770.

[612] Am. Anthr., n.s., 11:41–55, 1909.

[613] Frank Russell, The Pima Indians, 26th Ann. Rept. Bur. Am. Ethn., 3:389, 1908, and Carl Lumholtz, New Trails in Mexico (New York, 1912), 357, 358.

[614] In the following comparison the Palm Springs Cahuilla creation myth, present paper, pp. 130–143, is used as a basis of comparison with the various Luiseño myths on record.

myths state that in the beginning all was dark and quiet; there was a working together in the darkness, a cessation,[615] then the formation of two balls that became the two creators,[616] Tomaiyowit and Tukmit, the first of whom may be identified with the Cahuilla Temaĩyauit, and the second with Mūkat (who was of the tuktum or wildcat moiety).[617] The same conditions surround their birth,[618] and the quarrel concerning their respective ages which in each case is settled by the tobacco pipe incident, and their actions in making the earth larger for their children.[619]

At this point in the Luiseño myth the difference in sex between the two creators is mentioned, their cohabitation is suggested or inferred, and a subsequent series of births takes place. This series of events also characterized the Juaneño myth[620] and probably that of other westerly groups, but to the east of the Luiseño they seem to have been unknown. Commenting on Luiseño mythology, Kroeber refers to this matter as follows:

> The basis of the Luiseño origin tradition is a group of ideas that are widespread in southern California. But in the ritualistic cosmogony these appear in a very specialized shape. First, the concept of prime origins by birth, instead of a process of making, is more thoroughly worked out than by perhaps any other American tribe except possibly the Pueblos. Secondly, there is a remarkable attempt at abstract conceptualizing, which though it falls short of success, leaves an impression of boldness and of a rude but vast grandeur of thought. The result is that the beginning of the Luiseño genesis reads far more, in spirit at least, like the opening of a Polynesian cosmogonic chant than like an American Indian tradition of the world origin.[621]

While this portion of the Luiseño creation story is markedly different from that of the Cahuilla, there are in their respective

---

[615] Du Bois, Jour. Am. Folklore, 19:52, 1906.

[616] Du Bois, present series, 8:129, 1908.

[617] Sparkman translates tukmit as sky and tukomit as night. Du Bois uses these two terms rather indiscriminately, but nearly always in connection with the other creator, Tomaiyowit. The term mokat, which may have no etymological connection with mūkat, is used in connection with the seasons and the moon, meaning large or full. Du Bois, Jour. Am. Folklore, 19:56, 1906. The connection between Luiseño and Cahuilla creators seems highly probable, but the exact linguistic relationship of terms is obscure.

[618] Du Bois, *op. cit.*, 52, and present series, 8:129, 1908.

[619] *Ibid.*, 117, 129, 143.

[620] Kroeber, Handbook, 637.

[621] It may be significant that these rather alien concepts are found among the littoral peoples in southern California. The possibility of Polynesian or other Oceanic influences along the California coast should not be ignored in future archaeological and ethnological research in this area. Not only the slight similarities in myth and ceremonial exchange of shell money, but details of material culture such as shell fishhooks, plank boats, stone images of fish suggesting fetishes, use of lime and tobacco, etc., may be the result of casual contacts between the islanders of southern California and those much farther to the west.

versions of the dying god story many other similarities. Among these are the linguistic differences which developed when the sun arose,[622] the offense of the creator against a beautiful woman that led to his death, the connection of the frog with this event, the shaman doctoring of Wīyot, the long recital of the various periods of the month in which he may die, the death and cremation, the action of coyote in stealing and eating the heart,[623] and the somewhat extraneous addition of the first eagle killing to the creation myth.[624] Among both groups these songs are accompanied with the same triple invocation and blowing into the air to drive away dead or evil spirits, while both versions abound with the characteristic double esoteric names for all legendary phenomena. Such are the most outstanding similarities indicating the close relationship between Luiseño origin myths and those of their near eastern neighbors.

The foregoing discussion has shown the close accord between myth, song, and ceremony in the religious activities of the Luiseño. Thanks to the detailed and painstaking work of Du Bois it has been possible to demonstrate objectively how close this relationship actually was. Among the Cahuilla this accord is accepted on the basis of informants' statements, and a complete story of the creation and dying god myth said to be a condensed song series. Future work in studying the religion of the Cahuilla and their neighbors should follow further along the line adopted by Du Bois, for when the actual songs have been recorded and translated it will then be possible to absolutely check this hypothesis. Such a detailed study will throw much light on the exact nature of religion in the region and form a sound basis for wider comparisons.

---

[622] Du Bois, present series, 8:145, 1908.
[623] *Ibid.*, 132, 146.
[624] Du Bois, Jour. Am. Folklore, 19:56–60, 1906.

VII. SUMMARY AND COMPARISON

The social and ceremonial organization of the Serrano, Cahuilla, Cupeño, and Luiseño have been discussed in considerable detail. It may therefore be of value to sum up their outstanding characteristics so as to gain a coherent picture of each group, while indicating the many differences as well as the wider and more fundamental similarities between all of them. With these points clearly in mind it will be possible to visualize the relationships existing between the various groups, and to understand, in part at least, the reasons for the known distribution of social factors in southern California.

THE SERRANO

The early breakdown and almost complete disappearance of Serrano culture accounts in large part for the fragmentary and often contradictory state of our knowledge concerning their social organization and group activities. However it appears certain that the localized, autonomous male lineage was the political unit among the Serrano. These local units have been termed clans in the present paper, because in addition to the tie of kinship there was also present another bond formed by the possession of a group fetish bundle, priest, and ceremonial house. Among the Cahuilla, Cupeño, and Luiseño to the south of the Serrano, each clan was characterized by the possession of these three features, which formed one complex of associated traits. But the southeastern Serrano ceremonial organization seems to have been more complex and there were larger units each made up of two clans of opposite moiety who commonly intermarried. The Serrano therefore differed from their southern neighbors in that the very important fetish, priest, and house complex was often shared with another clan of the opposite moiety; and while each clan was largely autonomous it was dependent on this other clan for the performance of all ceremonies. Whether this unique organization applied to the extinct northern Serrano clans is unknown.

Every Serrano clan was designated as either coyote or wildcat, and according to native theory could not intermarry with any other clan bearing the same animal name. Aside from the animal names of the moiety divisions there was very little of totemic import connected with

them. Since clan names are for the most part place names the same
may be said of them. As two or more intermarrying clans of opposite
moieties formed one ceremonial unit, both moiety reciprocity and
exogamy were present. Obviously, dichotomy played a large part in
Serrano social organization, as was also the case among the various
south central Californian groups[625] to the north and west of Serrano
territory.

The details of many Serrano ceremonies are forgotten, but the
following appear to have been the most important. The girls' adolescence ceremony and the boys' initiation or toloache ceremony were
both practiced, but so far as existing data are concerned the Serrano
do not seem to have employed the ground-painting in either of them.
The biannual mourning or image-burning ceremony included the
naming of children, ceremonial eagle killing, and eagle or "whirling"
dance, in addition to the rites connected with the clan fetish bundle
and the making and burning of the death images. The clan leader
among the Serrano was known as the kīka, and the ceremonial assistant as the paha. The latter official had more important duties in connection with the fetish bundle than was the case among the southern
neighbors of the Serrano. Moreover, one clan of the Serrano char-
acteristically possessed the kīka and ceremonial house, while the ceremonially allied clan of the opposite moiety had the paha and the
ceremonial bundle. Whether this state of affairs applied to all Serrano
clans is uncertain, but it was so among the southeastern groups in
regard to whom information is available. A special clan singer
(tcaka) was formerly recognized among the Serrano, as well as a
certain man who danced the eagle or "whirling" dance. The shaman
(huremitc) was not a clan official, but was a man of individual power,
who through visions was able to cure sick persons. Such individuals
took part in many of the ceremonies but were not regarded as regular
group officials.

THE DESERT CAHUILLA

These people were likewise organized in male lineages, or paternal
clans of several collateral lineages, each characterized by the possession
of a clan fetish bundle, priest, and ceremonial house. Such clans were
occasionally grouped in villages at the infrequent sites where water
was available in sufficient quantity, but each clan was an autonomous

---

[625] Gifford, Dichotomous Social Organization in South Central California,
present series, 2:379–392, 1916; and, Miwok Moieties, present series, 12:105–164,
1916.

unit, and the grouping of independent clans into villages has the appearance of a rather late aboriginal custom. Such village territories were used communally by the clans that occupied them, but away from the village each clan had special food-gathering territories that were jealously guarded.

All the Desert Cahuilla clans were aligned with either the wildcat or the coyote moiety, and intermarriage between clans of the same moiety was strictly forbidden. Actual cases of marriage found among these people show that the rule was closely observed until recent times. Moiety reciprocity might occur between intermarrying clans of the opposite moiety, but it was not regarded as a definite rule. The main function of the moiety division among the Desert Cahuilla seems to have been the regulation of marriage.

The mourning ceremonies of the Desert Cahuilla included a night of singing after a death, and concluded in the morning by burning the body and possessions of the deceased. About a year later a week-long ceremony for the dead was held, concluding with the burning of the death images. The girls' adolescence ceremony was performed, but there was no initiation rite for boys. A small ceremony when specially selected boys had their nasal septa pierced and links of bone inserted was the nearest equivalent. At this ceremony all young girls had their chins tattooed. Later, a special ceremony was held in the dance house, and all boys and girls were given their clan names. At both these ceremonies "enemy songs" against other clans were sung. The only other Desert Cahuilla ceremony was the ritualistic killing of young eagles accompanied by a night of singing and dancing. While certain of the Desert Cahuilla clans had eagle-feather skirts wrapped in their fetish bundles they were not used in any eagle or "whirling" dance.

The clan leader (net) was the only important official among the Desert Cahuilla. His office was marked by the possession of the clan bundle or maswut, which was regarded as "the heart of the clan." He likewise resided in the kicumnawit or "big house," where he kept the clan bundle. The duties of the net were largely ceremonial, but he had considerable advisory and some judicial power. Since he knew all the ritual and mythology of the clan, presided at all ceremonial functions, and had in his possession the all important clan fetish bundle, his influence was great. The ceremonial assistant or paha was unknown to any but the extreme northwestern Desert clans; and the feast manager, or takwa, was unknown to all of them. Shamans (pūalem) were common to each group but were never regarded as clan officials although they had certain ceremonial duties. Singing at the larger ceremonies was lead by certain skilled men and women known as hauiniks. No other tribal or clan officials seem to have been recognized.

Simplicity of organization and ritual characterize the Desert Cahuilla, who manifested their native ability more in the ingenuity of their food gathering and water seeking than in the complexities of their material or social culture. A comparison with all the other groups considered in the present section shows that the Desert Cahuilla possessed fewer ceremonies and a more simple organization than any of their western neighbors. Since more of the old life exists today among the Desert Cahuilla than among any of the western groups, it is obvious that their lack of ceremonies is not due to the partial disappearance of their native culture.

The Pass Cahuilla

The Cahuilla-speaking people of the San Gorgonio pass and its vicinity were in basic social organization identical with those of the Desert. Unlike the latter, however, the Pass clans seem to have been isolated, and villages composed of several clans were unknown. The priest, fetish bundle, and ceremonial house complex possessed by each of these clans was of even greater importance here than among the Desert Cahuilla.

The Pass Cahuilla fall into two main groups, first the three clans near Palm Springs which might well be called the Palm Springs Cahuilla, and secondly the six Cahuilla clans that actually lived in the San Gorgonio pass and were therefore the true Pass Cahuilla. It may be well to repeat once more that this latter region was formerly occupied by Cahuilla-speaking groups, and not by the Serrano as has been recently claimed.[626] These western clans were much influenced by the Serrano, while the Palm Springs Cahuilla were formerly more closely in touch with their desert kinsmen.

While both the Palm Springs Cahuilla and the Pass Cahuilla proper recognized the coyote and wildcat moiety alignment of clans, only the former followed the rule of moiety exogamy. Among the Pass clans the rule was known to exist, but it seems to have been largely ignored, and treated as a mere tradition. Undoubtedly the

---

[626] See the discussion in the present paper, pp. 9, 10.

paucity of wildcat clans in this region had much influence in bringing about such a state of affairs.

The ceremonial life of the Pass Cahuilla was fundamentally the same as that of the Desert Cahuilla, but the calendar of the western groups was marked by more numerous and elaborate ceremonies. Traces of jimsonweed drinking or manet, the "whirling" or eagle dance, and analogies to the ground-painting are found. The Palm Springs story of the creation is one of the most coherent and schematically complete accounts yet recorded for southern California and appears to be almost entirely free of any late western or Chungichnish influences.

On the other hand the breakdown of moiety exogamy, the modern tendency to group clans into "parties," and the elaboration of ritualistic details among the Pass Cahuilla are all significant evidences of western influence. In this regard the intricate mortuary exchange of shell money seems to indicate a former ceremonial linkage that in aboriginal times may have indirectly connected these clans with the coastal peoples.[627]

The situation may be summed up by saying that in their ceremonial and social organization the Pass Cahuilla were intermediate between their southwestern neighbors, the Mountain Cahuilla, Cupeño, and Luiseño, and their eastern neighbors, the Desert Cahuilla; while in almost everything save clan organization and language they were identical with the Serrano.

The Mountain Cahuilla

The Mountain Cahuilla groups were under alien influences longer than were their Pass and Desert kinsmen. In aboriginal times they came under western cultural domination as the presence of many traits associated with the toloache cult demonstrates. Then the Spanish mission fathers and later the Mexican government dominated them, and for the sake of more unified control brought about the merging of the formerly independent clans into larger political units. This tendency was also aided by the United States government, and today, had not disease, sterility, and changed conditions almost wiped

---

[627] "Chumash money appears to have been the clam-shell disk bead currency that was the ordinary medium of all those parts of California that did not employ dentalia. In fact, it is likely that the Chumash furnished the bulk of the supply for the southern half of the state, as the Pomo did farther north." Kroeber, Handbook of the Indians of California, Am. Bur. Ethn., Bull. 78:564, 1925.

out the native population, there would probably have existed a unified tribal organization with appointed leaders, entirely resulting from alien pressure on once isolated groups.

Since the northern Mountain Cahuilla clans were for the most part influenced by the Luiseño groups at or near Saboba, and the southern Mountain Cahuilla influenced by the Cupeño and Diegueño to the south, there is a slight cultural split between them. However, it seems certain that under native conditions the autonomous, localized paternal clan was the Mountain Cahuilla social and political unit. In the north, owing to alien influences, these tended to unite in larger villages and fuse into religious parties; while in the extreme southern Cahuilla range one formerly vigorous clan had subdivided into various lineages still under central control, that externally had much the appearance of a typical party.

The characteristic moiety alignment of all clans into either a wild-cat or a coyote division was recognized by all the Mountain Cahuilla. Moreover, up to within the last generation the rule of moiety exogamy seems to have been closely followed. There are also distinct traces of former moiety reciprocity in the annual mourning and the eagle-killing ceremonies of the Mountain clans.

The Mountain Cahuilla clans had the full fetish bundle, priest, and ceremonial house complex, and it was this complex that later formed the center of the religious parties made up of broken-down clans. Besides the leader or net, the Mountain Cahuilla clan officials were the paha, and kutvavanavac among the southern groups, the takwa or feast manager, the eagle dancer, manet dancer, and singer or hauinik. Furthermore the Mountain Cahuilla clans made ceremonial use of long strings of eagle feathers similar to the Serrano "sacred feathers."[628] All the ceremonies known to the Desert and Pass Cahuilla were practiced by the Mountain Cahuilla, and in addition they made use of the ground-painting, the jimsonweed drinking or boys' initiation, the "whirling" or eagle dance, the stinging-ant ordeal for boys or young men, and the fire dance.

Thus, to the social and ceremonial framework possessed by the Cahuilla of the Desert, these western groups constituting the Mountain Cahuilla had added a great number of the elaborations characteristic of the Luiseño and other coastal peoples. These elaborations were all well integrated into the texture of Cahuilla ceremonialism,

---

[628] This is a very definite analogy to the sacred feathers of the Papago, described by Lumholtz, New Trails in Mexico, 49, 1912.

and appear to have been closely adapted to the local pattern in all cases. That these traits had spread eastward in a somewhat variable grouping is certain, but among the Cahuilla they do not seem to have brought with them any organized religious beliefs. The name Chungichnish seems to be unknown among all of the Cahuilla, the majority of their songs are in their own language, and their ceremonies accord with their own mythology. Hence the distinction may well be made between the widespread toloache cult, of which the above special features are an integral part, and the much more restricted Chungichnish cult, which had an almost entirely littoral distribution.

THE CUPEÑO

The complexity of Cupeño social organization is in part due to the fact that the favorable nature of the site allowed the localization of larger groups than elsewhere in the Santa Rosá mountains, and partly to the fact that they are a composite group, half the Cupeño lineages claiming Shoshonean and half Yuman ancestry.

There are six Cupeño clans on record, two living at Wilakal and four that formerly lived at Kūpa. Each of the Wilakal clans seem to have consisted of one lineage, but at Kūpa the wildcat clan was composed of three separately named lineages, and the three coyote clans of one lineage each. The wildcat clan possesses unusual interest for it was identical with the wildcat moiety, and was composed of two main lineages claiming Diegueño and one subordinate lineage claiming Luiseño ancestry. It was believed however that all three were kinsmen, and the three lineages actually formed one exogamous clan. Similarly, the three coyote clans at Kūpa claim to have been once related and to be of Cahuilla ancestry. Since each of these supposedly related coyote clans was an independent unit their political organization resembled that of the Los Coyotes Cahuilla, only in the latter case the five branch lineages were still ceremonially united. Each of the Cupeño clans possessed the full clan fetish bundle, priest, and ceremonial house complex.

Moiety exogamy was the rule, and actual cases demonstrate that it was closely followed at Kūpa, but not at Wilakal. Informants stated that this observance of moiety exogamy at Kūpa was entirely due to the assumed relationship of the two main clan groupings, and not at all to any rule of moiety exogamy as such, which they said was always unimportant. At Wilakal one clan claimed Cahuilla and the other

Diegueño ancestry; Kūpa informants stated that both belonged to the wildcat moiety but actual cases of marriage do not bear out this assertion. Since Wilakal has been more conservative than Kūpa, there seems no reason why such a rule, were it ever present, should not be demonstrated by the actual cases of marriage at hand. It is advisable therefore to place the inhabitants of Wilakal outside the area where moiety exogamy prevailed, at least until more data are at hand to settle this and other obscure points concerning their social and ceremonial organization.

It has been suggested that the animal names applied to the two moieties in southern California owe their origin to the mingling of Cahuilla and Diegueño lineages in the formation of the Cupeño population. Considering the strong Yuman attachment to the wildcat and the equally strong Los Coyotes canyon Cahuilla attachment to the coyote, in large part shared by the other Shoshoneans, the theory seems tenable. It is given much corroboration by the lineage and moiety alignment at Kūpa, where the clan mainly Diegueño in origin forms the wildcat moiety, and the three clans of the coyote moiety claim descent from the Los Coyotes canyon Cahuilla. It must be remembered, however, that while the idea of dichotomy and its associated features is widespread in southern and south central California, different names are applied to the dual division in the various regions. Thus while the Cupeño situation may account for the particular moiety names used by Cupeño, Cahuilla, Serrano, and Luiseño (Saboba), it does not pretend to account for the occurrence of dichotomy itself.

Cupeño ceremonialism was more elaborate than that of the Mountain Cahuilla, but slightly less complex than that of the Luiseño. In addition to all the ceremonies listed for the Cahuilla, the Cupeño used a more elaborate ground-painting, and the wānawut pit in connection with the boys' toloache initiation ceremonies. There was also a system of reciprocal gift presentation, including food, ceremonial impedimenta, and shell money, that was carried on between clan leaders. The exchange included the Cupeño and their neighbors irrespective of linguistic affiliation, and was called by the former people "the nuut's road." There is close similarity here to the system of shell money exchange that formerly occurred between the clans living in the vicinity of the San Gorgonio pass, both cases demonstrating an early ceremonial linkage between local groups that seems to have once connected nearly all the native peoples of southern California west of the desert.

The Cupeño clan leader was called nuut, and was associated with the clan fetish bundle and dance house (which was called wāmkic, as among the Luiseño). He was assisted by the kutvōvoc, who in his official capacity assumed the duties of the takwa and kutvavanavac among the Mountain Cahuilla. The paha was also employed in connection with the jimsonweed or manet dance. The hauinik or singer, eagle dancer, and probably the manet dancer completed the list. Shamans played a considerable part in all ceremonies, especially in the ceremonial killing of the young eagles, but here as elsewhere their activities were largely individualistic and not according to definite ritualistic pattern.

Thus the basis of Cupeño social and ceremonial organization was identical with that of the Cahuilla, but there were in addition certain ceremonial elaborations which they shared with the Luiseño. Likewise their clan organization and the relation of the clans to the moieties were unique in certain particulars. Undoubtedly many of the ritualistic practices of the southern Mountain Cahuilla and the Yuman Diegueño reached them through the Cupeño, who in turn received them from their northwestern neighbors. The trend of cultural influence in early historic times was clearly from west to east, and from north to south.

The Luiseño

It would be a safe assumption to say that almost all the social and ceremonial features described among the foregoing groups may be assigned to the Luiseño as well. But since the latter had also made or received several additions to this common stock, and had decidedly modified certain other features, the matter must be dealt with at somewhat greater length.

To briefly sum up the similarities it may be said that the basis of Luiseño clan and party organization was certainly the male lineage, and that to the fundamental kinship nature of this grouping was added the important house, priest, and fetish bundle concept. While the Luiseño as a whole did not recognize the moiety division, there were traces of this institution to be found among them, and they laid great stress on the feature of reciprocity between intermarrying clans. This latter custom is closely correlated with dichotomy throughout southern and south central California. Luiseño creation myths were fundamentally similar to those of their eastern neighbors, and not only were certain rites common to all reflected in these myths, but the songs sung at such rites were derived from a common mythic substratum. Such ceremonies included the mourning rites, girls' adolescence ceremony, and eagle killing. In all these features the Luiseño present no obvious departure from the general Cahuilla, Cupeño, and Serrano pattern.

With the jimsonweed drinking initiation of boys, the ground-painting, and wānawut rites, the morahash, eagle, or whirling dance, fire dance, and ant ordeal, we find a complex of traits which may be conveniently called the toloache cult that the Luiseño shared with the Cupeño, the western Mountain and Pass Cahuilla, and in large part with the Serrano clans.

Confined to the Luiseño, and it may safely be assumed to their extinct northern and western neighbors, were the rites centering around the god Chungichnish, including the symbolic avengers of that god and the teaching of certain moral precepts. Unish matakish, the burial of a Chungichnish initiate's feathers; the pole-climbing or notush ceremony, and a considerable number of minor ritualistic features are associated with these beliefs. This entire group of beliefs and ceremonial acts may best be designated as the Chungichnish cult.

The clan leader, or nōta, was the primary Luiseño official and his priestly duties were the same as those of the more eastern clan leaders. The paha was closely associated with the toloache ceremonies, and the general Luiseño ceremonial assistant was the puhmutcvī. Whether the Luiseño takō, who drank the ashes of the dead, had any connection with the Cahuilla feast assistant or takwa, is not clear. The maswut complex associated with the clan leader was identical for all the groups, but the union of dismembered Luiseño clans into religious parties tended to obscure this similarity.

To very briefly sum up the apparent integration of myth, ceremony, and social grouping among all these peoples, and to show the temporal relationships indicated, the following statement might be made. The ubiquitous girls' puberty ceremony based on a marked physiological and social change in status may well be older than any other ceremony in the region. Its antiquity and obvious physiological motivation preclude the presence or need of explanatory myths. Second, a creation story based on two creators, including mythological reference to the mourning rites, the idea of dichotomy and the priest, fetish, and ceremonial house complex, was once held in common by Luiseño, Cupeño, Serrano, and all three divisions of the Cahuilla. In the third place, additional ceremonies and myths featuring the use of the jimsonweed and apparently the ceremonial importance of the eagle reached all these groups save the most easterly Desert Cahuilla, who do not seem to have more than traces of the toloache cult. And last of all, a comparatively late series of ceremonies relating to the god Chungichnish originated in the west and reached the Luiseño in considerable strength, being diffused by them in only a slight degree to their eastern neighbors. This last florescence of native religion appears to have been largely contemporaneous with the mission period and was apparently only the last of a series of ritualistic and ceremonial concepts that had emanated from the now extinct coastal peoples and been passed on well to the east. The limits of this secondary diffusion seem to have been reached among the Desert Cahuilla, the arid reaches of the Colorado desert separating them from the Yuman peoples of the Colorado river, whose culture seems to have been markedly different. An intensive study of southern California society, west of the Colorado desert, indicates that the coastal region was the fountainhead of all the more complex social and philosophical systems herein considered, but a wider survey suggests still other sources of inspiration.[629]

TABLE 21

Distribution of Ceremonies

West ———————————→ to ————————————→ East

	Luiseño	Cupeño	Mountain Cahuilla	Serrano	Pass Cahuilla	Desert Cahuilla
1. Burial of initiates' feathers	×					
2. Ceremonial pole climbing	×					
3. Ceremonial cannibalism (Takō)	×					
4. Clothes-washing rite	×					
5. Tanic dance	×	?				
6. Wanawut rite	×	×				
7. Fire dance	×	×	×			
8. Ant ordeal	×	×	×			
9. Ground-painting	×	×	×			
10. Jimsonweed drinking	×	×	×	×	?	
11. Whirling or eagle dance	×	×	×	×	×	
12. Image-burning	×	×	×	×	×	×
13. Cremation ceremony	×	×	×	×	×	×
14. Girls' puberty rites	×	×	×	×	×	×

[629] Strong, An Analysis of Southwestern Society, Am. Anthr., n.s., 29:1–61, 1927.

TABLE 22

Distribution of Other Important Ceremonial Features

West ——→ to ——→ East

	Luiseño	Cupeño	Mountain Cahuilla	Serrano	Pass Cahuilla	Desert Cahuilla
Clan leader	nōta	nuut	net	kika	net	net
Ceremonial assistant	puhmutevi	kutvōvoc	takwa=N. kutvavanavac=S.	paha (no other recorded)	takwa	paha (NE)
Toloache leader	paha	paha	paha	paha	paha	
Other officials	eagle dancer takō, or "eater" manet dancer(?)	eagle dancer manet dancer(?)	eagle dancer manet dancer	eagle dancer		
Singer	?	hauinik	hauinik	tcaka	hauinik	hauinik
Shamans	pūlum	pūlum	pūalem	huremitcem	pūalem	pūalem
Ceremonial house	wamkie or big house	wamkie or big house	wamkie or big house	kitcateratc, wamkie or big house	ki'cammawut or big house	kicu'mnawit or big house
Sacred matting	ma'swut	ma'svut	mai'swut	muurtc	mai'swut	ma'swut
Invocation of sacred bundle	probable (recorded in myth)	recorded	recorded	recorded	recorded	probable

TABLE 23

Moiety Alignment of Natural Phenomena[630]

West ——————→ to ——————→ East

	Miwok	Yokuts Chuk-chansi	Gas-howu	Tachi	W. Mono	Salinan	S. Calif. General	Cahuilla Pass	Cahuilla Desert	Luiseño	Pima and Papago	Pueblo General
A =	Land	Down	Down	Down	Down	Bear	Wildcat	Wildcat	Wildcat	Up (Wildcat)	White	Winter
B =	Water	Up	Up	Up	Up	Deer	Coyote	Coyote	Coyote	Down (Coyote)	Red	Summer
Eagle	A	A	A	A	A			(B)		A	?	A
Crow, Raven	A	A	A	A	A			A		A	?	A (Zuñi)
Bear	A	A	A					A			?	
Wild Cat	A		A			A	A	A	A		?	
Fox	A		A				A	A	A		?	
Badger	A							A			?	
Lizard	A							A			?	A
Sun	A							A			?	
Coyote	B	B	B	B	B		B	B	B		?	A
Buzzard	B	B	B	B	B			B	B		?	
Deer	B		B	B	B	B				(A)	?	
Falcon	(A)	B									?	
Water, Fog (Corn)	B	B	B	B	B					B	?	B (Corn)

630 This list only includes phenomena whose recorded distribution makes them comparable. The general uniformity of the dichotomy is nevertheless too striking to be accidental for California, while the agreement with the scant eastern data is suggestive. For data concerning the Miwok, see present series, 12:106–161; for the Yokuts, present series, 11:294; for western Mono, Kroeber, Handbook, 588; for Salinans, present series, 10:189; and for southern California the present paper. The Pima-Papago data are too contradictory for inclusion, see Strong, *op. cit.*, 11. The suggested general Pueblo scheme is from Parsons, Am. Anthr., n.s., 22:60, 1920.

VIII. CONCLUSION

Since the primary purpose of the present study has been to set forth the available facts concerning the nature of aboriginal society in southern California we will first confine our attention to that region alone. For this area the term tribe with the political concepts thereto pertaining seems altogether inapplicable, for if the large number of local groups segregated under the linguistic appellations of Cahuilla, Serrano, Cupeño, and Luiseño ever had the slightest feeling of tribal unity it is not apparent today. Since practically all the alien influences of historic times have tended toward centralization the persistence of this entire lack of cohesion can only be a reflection of the true native pattern. The primary importance of the local group, in this case the male lineage, as the unit in native Californian society cannot be overestimated.[631] The relatively more advanced peoples of the southern California coast may have had something resembling tribal organization but in the light of the present study this seems exceedingly dubious. Eastward from the shores of the Pacific this condition of local autonomous groups extends until the warlike tribes of the Colorado river Yumans are reached. To the north and east the localized male lineage is found among Yokuts, Miwok, western Mono, and probably many of their neighbors, while to the south among northern and southern Diegueño the lineage is still ubiquitous. Since the adoption of a system of unilateral descent with matrilocal or patrilocal residence suffices to bring about the change from bilateral family to lineage, the phenomenon seems easily accounted for. Nevertheless among Great Basin and Plateau peoples to the east the bilateral or natural family alone appears as the social unit.

Cahuilla, Serrano, Cupeño, and Luiseño lineages, however, are distinguished by a new factor in the very important social and religious functions associated with the group priest, ceremonial house, and sacred bundle. The addition of this complex often welds several collateral lineages into one group and the latter organization may well be called a clan to distinguish it from the component lineages. Furthermore this complex forms an added bond to the primary one of kinship and transmutes the lineage into a religious body, or clan,

---

[631] First clearly stated by Gifford, Miwok Lineages and the Political Unit in Aboriginal California, Am. Anthr., n.s., 28:389–401, 1926.

capable of many modifications under various influences. The rather recent religious parties of the Luiseño are examples of such modification. Myths relating to the priest, house, and fetish complex point to the west as the source of the ideas thereto pertaining, and among the Gabrielino and probably their western neighbors the importance of the complex has been recorded.[632] From these littoral peoples the ideas were diffused eastward to all the groups herein especially considered, and in part at least reached the northern Diegueño.[633] The Yuman peoples of the Colorado river, however, are almost without traces of this complex and their clan organization is different. While the lineage may lie at the basis of these Yuman clans, whose names are borne by the women and are indirectly totemic, they do not closely resemble those of the western Shoshoneans.

A dichotomous organization of society is more widely spread in southern and south central California than is the clan (or lineage, plus the priest, house, and fetish complex), but is more restricted than the simple male lineage. In the various concepts associated with this dichotomy there is such uniformity over the entire area that its historical unity cannot be doubted. Exogamy, reciprocity, a dual conception of the universe especially as regards animals (see table 23), use of dotted and striped facial designs to distinguish the moieties, and a similar use of red and black paints are the most important of these concepts. While records concerning the coastal peoples are sadly incomplete, there is evidence that the Chumash and the Salinans once possessed a dichotomous organization.[634] The occurrence of a moiety classification at Saboba and the extreme importance of ceremonial reciprocity in addition to the symbolism relating to the paha, all point to a former recognition of the custom among the Luiseño.

While the recorded manifestations of dichotomy, especially exogamy, seem to have been stronger on the peripheries among Miwok, Yokuts, and Desert Cahuilla, there seems reason for believing that it was once an equally important concept on the coast. The situation among the Luiseño suggests that moiety names and their associated exogamy had largely gone out of vogue among the coastal peoples, while the relatively greater importance of dichotomy among Miwok, Tachi Yokuts, and Desert Cahuilla was probably due to its later diffusion from the west and the characteristic conservatism of peripheral peoples.

---

[632] Boscana, *op. cit.*, 246–261.

[633] Waterman, present series, 8:281, 1910.

[634] Strong, *op. cit.*, 9, and Mason, present series, 10:189, 1912.

In an earlier consideration of this problem Gifford came to the conclusion that from the distribution of clan and moiety in southern California two interpretations were possible: first, that both institutions had originated on the coast perhaps among the Gabrielino, from which center they spread north, south, and east, losing the clans in the north (Miwok, Yokuts, and Salinans) and the moieties in the south and east (Luiseño, Diegueño, and Colorado Yumans); second, the alternate hypothesis that the two were separate institutions originating in their respective areas and then diffused, giving the intermediate groups (Serrano, Cahuilla, and Cupeño) both institutions.[635] Of these two interpretations he favored the second as being most in accord with the then known facts. Since that time the recognition of the male lineage as the more important unit within the dichotomous organization of south central California has shown that between this lineage and the somewhat elaborated clan of southern California there exists only a difference of degree and not of kind. Moreover, the discovery of the uniformity of the concepts associated with dichotomy throughout all southern California, as well as the facts strongly suggesting its earlier western distribution, leads the present writer to accept the first of Gifford's alternate theories as by far the most probable. Certainly the distribution of the priest, house, and fetish complex, like the various rituals connected with the toloache and Chungichnish cults, must be explained in this way, and it seems reasonable to believe that the idea of dichotomy and reciprocity had the same history in native California.

The fact that the moiety divisions throughout this region, despite their general similarity in function, were often given different animal or directional names among the various linguistic groups, suggests that the idea of dichotomy was superimposed on the localized lineage organization. Cases cited among Serrano, Mountain Cahuilla, and Cupeño indicate that one moiety name was applied to lineages known or believed to be branches of a common ancestral stock, while the other moiety designation was applied to those clans with which marriage was permissible and with which it commonly occurred. The ceremonial pattern of reciprocity that inclined intermarrying clans to officiate in a reciprocal manner at one another's ritualistic activities seems to have brought about the clan groupings most clearly recorded among the Serrano and Cupeño. In many ways this reciprocity appears more important as a social force in the groups under

---

[635] Present series, 18:217–218, 1918.

consideration than does nominal dichotomy and exogamy. While regulation of exogamy was apparently the primary function of the moiety among the Desert Cahuilla, for example, there is no reason to assume that this was equally true of all dichotomous groupings in the region. The way in which dichotomy manifested itself may well have been a matter for local autonomy although this dualism in its inception seems to have had a common source.

In south central California the reasons for adopting the respective moiety designations are obscure, but in the case of the Cupeño there is good reason to believe that the specific moiety names originated with the intermarriage of Shoshonean and Yuman lineages, each clinging to the animal name of greatest importance in their respective mythologies. This use of coyote and wildcat moiety designations applied equally to Cahuilla, Serrano, and Luiseño, and since an examination of the maps (1, 2, 4, 5, 6), showing the respective distribution of the various clans, indicates that wildcat clans were most numerous in the south and east and coyote clans in the north and west, the origin of the moiety designations used in southern California seems rather clearly indicated. From the standpoint of kinship terminologies this secondary adoption of a dichotomous organization to a fundamental lineage organization explains the fact that designation of lineage and not moiety characterizes the classification of relatives among all these groups.[636]

From the fact that an idea of dichotomy was more widespread in south and south central California than was the priest, house, and fetish complex, it might be assumed that the moiety was of greater antiquity. However, the comparatively light impress of the moiety on the social structure in conjunction with the fact that it necessarily involves a number of groups, whereas the priest, house, and fetish complex is essentially local in nature, suggests that the idea of dichotomy was merely more volatile and diffused more rapidly. Apparently the original idea of dichotomy was only one of several important concepts introduced into southwestern California at a very early time.

This brings us to the second phase of our problem, that concerning the external agencies that have acted upon the older native patterns in southern California.[637] At present there is no direct archaeological evidence to indicate the exact time and manner in which these import-

---

[636] Kroeber, present series, 12:378–379, 1917; Gifford, present series, 22:7, 246, 1922; and Benedict, *op. cit.*, 373.

[637] Discussed at some length in an earlier publication, Strong, *op. cit.*, 45–57.

ant cultural traits reached the coastal peoples of southern California. It seems probable however, that the constantly extending frontier of early Pueblo cultures being revealed by the archaeologist's spade in western Arizona and Nevada, when combined with equally careful and extensive excavations in southern California and the Channel islands, will go far toward solving the problem. That there was once such a connection between the ancestral Pueblo peoples and their contemporaries of the Pacific coast, later severed by the movements of alien groups, seems certain from the many and complex identities existing in the two cultures. Ethnology clearly reveals this early cultural similarity, but the direct causes lost in the obscurity of the past may only be determined by archaeological investigation.

For the purposes of our present argument we may take this comparatively early intrusion of culture traits, tentatively assigned to the early Pueblo culture, into the coastal regions of southwestern California as demonstrated. In briefest form these traits include the priest, house, and fetish complex, the idea of dichotomy, and a large series of ceremonial concepts including the use of the ground-painting, placing of plume offerings in certain shrines,[638] asperging of water brought from certain springs,[639] ceremonial smoking of tobacco, consecration of fetishes with tobacco smoke, ceremonial pole climbing, sprinkling of meal at ceremonies,[640] ritualistic employment of ants, clan ownership of eagles and eagle dances. All these concepts are found among the coastal peoples of southern California while farther to the north, south, and east they gradually disappear. This marked areal concentration suggests a common origin and at least a general contemporaneity.

This is rather at variance with the generally accepted view that the infiltration of "southwestern" influences was a gradual process continuing until recent times.[641] Such a hypothesis neglects the fact that such diffusion would perforce proceed from east to west whereas the actual distribution of culture traits indicates clearly that in southern California the reverse has been true. Table 21 is a striking demonstration of this fact as concerns ceremonial activities. If on

---

[638] This is definitely recorded for the Santa Ynez mission in Chumash territory, Kroeber, present series, 8:16, 1908, which contradicts a later statement made by the same authority, California Handbook, 1925, 867–868, "that there is no reference to anything like the offering of feather wands in southern California."

[639] Boscana, *op. cit.*, 293–295.

[640] Kroeber, Handbook, 868.

[641] See Kroeber, The History of Native Culture in California, present series, 20:125–142, 1923. A gradual influx of Southwestern traits is indicated for the last three of the four periods.

the other hand we assume that early communication existed between the ancestral Pueblo culture and the contemporaneous culture of the south Californian coast, that this communication was interrupted by the incursion of alien groups, and that in both of the former regions somewhat parallel but independent institutions arose on this common ceremonial groundwork, the hypothesis is consonant with the actual distribution of social and ceremonial features.

Such an interpretation however seems to neglect other important factors less directly connected with social organization. Primary among these is the fact that agriculture does not seem to have been practiced on the California coast, and secondly that pottery while known in the area is crude, poorly decorated, and suggests no great antiquity so far as present archaeological records are concerned. Among the Yuman peoples of the Colorado river, however, agriculture was practiced and pottery attained a more important place and a better technique. Since both pottery and agriculture are known to have been of considerable antiquity among the Pueblo peoples, it seems strange that they were not introduced into southwestern California at the early period of contact we have assumed on other evidence.[642]

It has been shown that in southwestern California ceremonialism, female puberty rites, and ceremonies to drive away the spirits of the dead underlie all other ritualistic activities. On this widespread Californian substratum have arisen the elaborate cult activities containing the many Pueblo-like features. But the old basic religious ideas connected with crisis rites and fear of spirits persisted, and with all these other additions may still be observed today as the most important sources of ceremonial motivation in southern California. Similarly it would seem that the ingrained importance of the acorn complex as a source of food supply had never been supplanted by other methods. It is possible that the presence of the acorn as an abundant food staple largely precluded the need of agriculture, while the high development of basketry and the presence of steatite deposits on the Channel islands made the use of earthenware of equally little value. Whether there exists any causal relationship between the high development of Chumash steatite working and the introduction of earthenware vessels

---

[642] It is of course possible that this period of contact involves peoples of the Basket Maker culture whose agriculture was rudimentary. Certain isolated finds in south and south central California rather strongly suggest this culture. Compare present series, 23:49–51, 1926, Kroeber, Handbook, pls. 41, 54, and 63 with illustrations and text in Kidder and Guernsey, Basket Maker Caves of Northeastern Arizona, Papers Peabody Museum, 8:no. 2, 1921.

from the east is an interesting question for the archaeologist. Sufficient for our present purposes is it to say that underlying the influx of eastern ceremonial and industrial complexes were earlier native Californian concepts many of which have persisted until the present day.

For the sake of clarity it may be well to sketch the development of culture in southern California as indicated by the present study. The present analysis somewhat amplifies but in general agrees with Kroeber's previous conclusions concerning the problem.[643]   The earliest stage which can be predicted on ethnological grounds indicates that people of the Hokan linguistic stock were living along the southern California coast. The culture of the Hokan peoples then in southern California was in the main that Kroeber's first period, the acorn being the food staple and ceremonial life centering around the female adolescence ceremony and the propitiation of the dead.

The second stage seems to have involved a rather close contact with the ancestors of the sedentary or Pueblo peoples to the east. It was these contacts, perhaps due to trade relations,[644] that added the important clan priest, house, and fetish complex to the autochthonous lineage, along with the idea of dichotomy and the special ceremonial features listed above. At about this time the southwesterly drift of the Shoshoneans brought them into contact with the Hokan groups, and as the later and more easterly groups pressed in, tended to sever the relations between the relatively high cultures of the coast and the interior. The Yuman division of the Hokan, who seem to have been little affected by these early Pueblo influences, were thus cut off from their northern kinsmen. In time this period probably coincided with the early Pueblo period,[645] and the causes leading to the retraction of the latter culture likewise severed any western connection with the Pacific.

---

[643] Present series, 20:130–142, 1923.

[644] There are many records suggesting this early trade in shells between coastal and interior groups. The occurrence of shell ornaments, especially abalone, in Basket Maker caves in Arizona is perhaps the earliest. The ceremonial bundle also described from such a cave strongly suggests those of southern California. See Kidder and Guernsey, *op. cit.*, 49, 102, 103. In the Gila and Salt river regions shell ornaments are commonly found in early ruins, Hough, Antiquities of the Upper Gila and Salt River Valleys in Arizona and New Mexico, Bur. Am. Ethn., Bull. 35:23, 1907. For shell objects from early Hopi ruins see Fewkes, Pacific Coast Shells from Prehistoric Tusayan Pueblos, Am. Anthr., o.s., 9:359–367, 1896.

[645] Kidder, An Introduction to the Study of Southwestern Archaeology (New Haven, 1924), 124–128.

The third stage was marked by the cultural domination of the littoral Hokan groups and the assimilation of their culture, including the priest, house, and fetish complex, by the most westerly Shoshoneans who first reached the Pacific. In this period also arose the series of ritualistic activities, here designated as the toloache cult, which in slightly variable form spread east as far as the Desert Cahuilla. In a like manner many traits were passed on to the north, a fact which seems to account for the occurrence of isolated Pueblolike features among peoples as far away as the Pomo.[646] As Kroeber has pointed out this was a period in which the local cultures developed more or less uninterruptedly and the Chumash and Yuman centers became dominant in their respective areas. It was at this time that many of the generally distributed "Southwestern" traits seem to have been carried into southern California. These certainly included agriculture, decorated pottery, and perhaps the curved throwing stick and cactus-fiber sandals. All these features show a normal distribution from an eastern center to a gradual fading out western periphery.

The last stage brings us into historic times, being especially marked by the spread of the Chungichnish religion and the development of an elaborate system of shell money exchange. Since all the data in the present paper naturally pertain to this last period there is no need to recapitulate that which has gone before.

The study of native society in southern California lays emphasis on the fact that a clear understanding of such a culture seems only to be obtained by determining the temporal relationships as well as the functional importance of its component parts. Such a society can be conceived as a composite whole based on comparatively simple patterns that, stimulated by external influences, have developed into the historic institutions encountered by the ethnologist. Neither the intensive study of one culture from the functional standpoint, nor the cursory study of a great number of cultures solely to show diffusion, can make clear such universal cultural laws as may exist. Their determination would rather seem to rest on detailed linguistic, ethnological, and archaeological investigation of definite areas, whose cultures when fully understood and evaluated may then be fitted into the general pattern. In this way will the dynamics of social development gradually become clear.

Transmitted December 9, 1927.

---

[646] See Loeb, Pomo Folkways, present series, 19:399, 1926.

INDEX

Index

Index

Tukupar, 294.
Temaiyauit, 131, 235.
Tumaiyowit, 256, 268.
Tuva, 49, 86.
Tuvic, 299.
Twenty Nine Palms, 5, 11, 24, 99.
Twins, 127.

Ulukuh clan, 279, 281.
Unish Matakish, 318, 323, 338.

Vanquech, 295.
Vanyume, 5, 14.
Victorville, 11, 13.
Villages, 43, 49, 56, 185, 331, 332, 334.
Visions, 35, 64, 168, 175, 330.
Vumtc, 33.

Waatcem clan, 14.
Wahimaiam clan, 24.
Wahiyam, 23, 74.
Wakaikiktum clan, 41, 52, 59.
Wakwaikiktum clan, 181.
Wamkic, 45, 94, 164, 173, 174, 182, 249, 254, 255, 256, 258, 259, 262, 264, 295, 302, 304, 310, 312, 316, 337, 340.
Wamkitc, 94.
Wanawut, 293, 294.
Wand, 132, 136, 226.
Wanicōcem clan, 68.
Wanikiktum clan, 15, 68, 93, 103, 128, 129.
Wantcauem clan, 42, 44, 45, 47, 48, 57–59, 68.
Wantciñakik-tamīanawitcem clan, 41, 49.
Wantciñakiktum clan, 41, 44, 47, 58.
Warfare. *See* Battle.
Warner's Hot Springs, 183, 185, 187, 270.
Warner, J. J., 184.
Warner's Ranch, 73.
Washing, 300.
Washingtonia filifera, 60, 123.
Wassuk clan, 279, 281.

Watcicpakiktum clan, 13.
Water, 38, 43.
Waterman, T. T., cited, 171.
Wavaaīkiktum clan, 42, 56.
Wavitcem clan, 54.
Waxan, 30.
Wells, 38, 43, 52.
Wēwonicyauam clan, 42, 54.
Whipple, cited, 6.
Whirling dance, 31, 61, 84, 120, 167, 179, 257, 305, 321–323, 331, 333, 338.
Whirlwinds, 133, 134.
White Water, 68.
Whitewater, 91, 101.
Wiitem clan, 42, 51.
Wilakal, 146, 182, 185–187, 208, 220, 225, 243, 244, 249, 255.
Wildcat, 77, 341.
Wildcat moiety, 7, 12, 13, 14, 18, 23, 24, 25, 40, 41, 70, 91, 118, 136, 148, 157, 171, 181, 186, 221, 224, 227, 235, 238, 244, 249, 252, 255, 257, 258, 291, 327, 329, 331, 332, 334, 335, 336, 345.
Wiliya, 146, 148, 158, 169, 171, 237.
Wilson, J. R., Dr., 2.
Wineland, Reverend, 10.
Winter, 341.
Wīwaiistam clan, 146, 151, 158, 161, 165, 171, 237.
Wiyot, 112, 254, 285, 288, 301, 306, 308, 309, 320, 321, 322, 328.
Wolf, 25.
Woodwardia radicans, 292.

Yapitca, 279.
Yokuts, 36, 168, 289, 319, 342–344.
Yucaipaiem clan, 14.
Yucaipe valley, 8, 11, 14.
Yuhavetum clan, 12, 18, 19, 24.
Yuma, 15, 20, 38, 54, 68, 80, 126, 183, 275, 325, 335, 339, 342, 347, 349.
Yumisevul, 12.
Yuta, 150.

Zuñi, 310.